D1765150

WITHDRAWN FROM: UNIVERSITY OF PLYMOUTH LIBRARY SERVICES

University of Plymouth
Charles Seale Hayne Library
Subject to status this item may be renewed
via your Voyager account

http://voyager.plymouth.ac.uk
Tel: (01752) 232323

2 MAR 2005

- 3 MAR 2005

1 5 MAR 2005

UNIVERSITY OF PLYMOUTH

PLYMOUTH LIBRARY

CHARGES WILL BE MADE FOR OVERDUE BOOKS

Directions in Sign Language Acquisition

Edited by

Gary Morgan
Bencie Woll
City University London

John Benjamins Publishing Company
Amsterdam/Philadelphia

^{TM} The paper used in this publication meets the minimum requirements of American
National Standard for Information Sciences – Permanence of Paper for Printed
Library Materials, ANSI z39.48-1984.

UNIVERSITY OF PLYMOUTH

Item No. 9 005435627

Date 1 9 MAR 2003 2

Class No. 419 DIR

Cont. No.

PLYMOUTH LIBRARY

CIP-data for this book is available from the Library of Congress

ISBN 90 272 3472 8 (Eur.) / 1 58811 235 7 (US) (Hb; alk. paper)

© 2002 – John Benjamins B.V.
No part of this book may be reproduced in any form, by print, photoprint, microfilm, or any
other means, without written permission from the publisher.

John Benjamins Publishing Co. · P.O. Box 36224 · 1020 ME Amsterdam · The Netherlands
John Benjamins North America · P.O. Box 27519 · Philadelphia PA 19118-0519 · USA

Table of contents

Series editors' preface

We are very happy to present the second volume in the series *Trends in Language Acquisition Research*. As an official publication of the International Association for the Study of Child Language (IASCL), the TiLAR Series aims to publish two volumes per three year period inbetween IASCL congresses. All volumes in the IASCL-TiLAR Series will be invited (but externally reviewed) edited volumes by IASCL members that are strongly thematic in nature and that present cutting edge work which is likely to stimulate further research to the fullest extent.

Besides quality, diversity is also an important consideration in all the volumes: diversity of theoretical and methodological approaches, diversity in the languages studied, diversity in the geographical and academic backgrounds of the contributors. After all, like the IASCL itself, the IASCL-TiLAR Series is there for child language researchers from all over the world.

The present volume on sign language acquisition includes original contributions by leading researchers in the field. The unusual combination in one volume of reports on various different sign languages-in-acquisition makes the book quite unique. We are very grateful to the editors, Gary Morgan and Bencie Woll, for making it all happen.

We would also like to thank IASCL President Brian MacWhinney for his continued support, Seline Benjamins and Kees Vaes of John Benjamins Publishing Company for their enthusiasm, patience and trust, and the external reviewers for their role in quality control. We are very grateful to former IASCL Presidents Jean Berko Gleason, Ruth Berman, Philip Dale, Paul Fletcher and to present IASCL President Brian MacWhinney for accepting our invitation to become a member of the TiLAR Advisory Board.

Trends in Language Acquisition Research is made for and by IASCL members. We hope it can become a source of information and inspiration which the community of child language researchers can continually turn to in their professional endeavors.

Antwerp, January 2002
The General Editors

Preface

At the last IASCL meeting held in Donostia, the Basque Country, in July 1999, Bencie Woll and I took part in a workshop organised by Dan Slobin and Nini Hoiting on the cross-linguistic comparison of sign language development. When we were asked to compile a volume of current sign language acquisition research we first thought of the participants from Donostia. We were lucky to get several participants in the workshop as well as others who were not present to contribute to this volume. We would like to acknowledge the contribution of the workshop and its organisers to our compilation. In this volume we have attempted to demonstrate the diversity and richness of current sign language acquisition research as well as its importance for the general study of child language.

Gary Morgan

Introduction

Gary Morgan and Bencie Woll

Sign languages have most likely existed for as long as Deaf[1] people have come together to communicate; that is, we can assume that sign languages are as old as human communication. Over the millennia sign languages have changed and disappeared, while new ones have come into existence (Armstrong, Stokoe & Wilcox 1994, 1995; Lane, Pillard & French 2000). Sign languages are used in Deaf communities around the world. Each community uses its own unique sign language. There are links and similarities between sign languages in the same way that spoken languages fall into groups of language families. Certain communities have adopted naturally or through language planning, the sign language of another Deaf community.

Sign languages have been systematically studied as languages only since the 1950's and early 1960's (e.g. Tervoort 1959; Stokoe, Casterline & Croneberg 1965). While a formal linguistic description was being proposed for American Sign Language (ASL), Tervoort tackled the question of how these languages were acquired by young Deaf children (Tervoort 1953, 1959). Since these ground breaking efforts, studies have not only been carried out on Deaf children but also hearing children raised in signing environments and the acquisition by both groups of a sign language as a first language.

While sign languages are rule-governed in similar ways to spoken languages, the specific grammatical processes in each language are linked to the demands of the modality.

Sign languages have been described as having a phonological structure made up of 5 parameters: handshape, movement, location, hand orientation and facial expression (e.g. Siedlecki & Bonvillian 1993a). The term *phonology* is used in studying sign languages despite its sound-based etymology, in order to emphasise that the same level of structure exists as in spoken language.

Handshape refers to the configuration of the hand and fingers in a particular sign. Although there is no universally accepted transcription system for sign languages, handshapes are most often labelled with letters referring to hand-shapes in the ASL manual alphabet.[2] The assignment is conventional and there is no relation between handshape in the sign and written letters. In BSL the signs BOY, THINK and WHY use a G handshape. A selection of handshapes seen in British Sign Language (BSL) and in other sign languages are shown in Figure 1, together with the labels most frequently used.

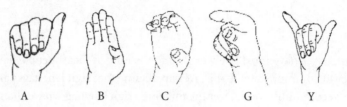

Figure 1. Handshapes

Movement of signs is also constrained by linguistic principles. For example, an aspectual iterative meaning is mapped onto verbs by articulating them with short and repeated movements. The location parameter refers to the place a sign in its citation form is produced. In BSL the signs SISTER, MOUSE and POSSIBILI-TY are located on the nose. The hand orientation parameter, as the name suggests, describes the particular orientation of the hand. The palm can face away or towards the signer, as well as upwards, downwards, right or left. The final parameter to consider is facial expression. In sign languages facial expression serves both affective and grammatical functions. Facial expression includes specific mouth, cheek and eyebrow patterns. There are other sets of grammatical devices carried on body parts of the signer other than the hands. These are termed accordingly *non-manual* features e.g. direction of eye-gaze. The lexicon of a sign language consists of sign forms, which differ across these five parameters. To illustrate this point, compare the two signs in BSL in Figure 2a and 2b, which are minimal phonological pairs, that is, they differ in only the location parameter; all other parameters are constant (Sutton-Spence & Woll 1999).

All signs are produced in an area in front of and on the body of the signer, termed the sign space. Signers place signs in areas of the sign space and subsequently point back to or look at these areas for anaphoric reference. Research on sign language refers to this process as indexing. Indexes established in sign space are sometimes referred to as loci. Verb signs can also be moved between these loci to express subject object agreement. More detail on terminology is provided in the glossary section.

a.   b.

Figure 2. a. AFTERNOON; b. NAME

There are two motivations for understanding language acquisition in signing children. The first as described above, stems from an inherent scientific interest in language and the brain. The second is a more practical reason. The majority of Deaf children do not acquire language in any straightforward sense. The typical experience for the Deaf child is late and impoverished exposure to a first language. The reasons for this are numerous but one major factor is that 90 to 95% of Deaf children are born to hearing parents with no knowledge of sign language (Spencer 1993b). Consequently, educationalists, therapists and parents need an understanding of what normal sign language acquisition looks like in order to intervene in contexts where language is not being acquired. This volume focuses mainly on sign language acquisition in the minority of Deaf and hearing children exposed to good sign language models from birth (i.e. they are atypical children developing language in a typical context).

To complicate matters further there also exist artificial gesture systems such as Makaton in Britain or Manually Coded English (MCE) in the USA, which have been created by hearing people for educational or intervention purposes (see Grove & Walker 1990). These systems are usually accompanied by spoken words and grammatical markers from a spoken rather than sign language. Often Deaf children are exposed to these systems rather than a natural sign language because they are better understood (as they are based on the spoken language grammar) by the hearing teacher or parent. The resistance of children to accept these systems as natural languages is good evidence for the resilience of the language acquisition device.

For much of recent history the use of sign languages by Deaf people has been actively discouraged by the wider hearing community (Facchini 1985). Consequently the Deaf children we study grow up using a minority language at home surrounded by more powerful majority spoken and written languages. This type of bilingual context undoubtedly affects language acquisition. This complex sociolinguistic situation makes the study of children's acquisition of sign languages more difficult than the study of spoken languages. There is a tension between presenting sign languages in isolation, as the subject of linguistic study, and presenting these difficult but ubiquitous factors alongside the data. The opening chapter by Marschark in this volume describes this tension in more detail.

Studies of sign language acquisition have produced unique research data. The study by Kegl and colleagues of children's contributions to the emergence of a language in Nicaragua has re-enforced the idea that part of language acquisition involves an innate component (Kegl, Senghas & Coppola 1999). Other work has allowed us to question previously well held assumptions. For example Petitto and colleagues have questioned the implicit relationship between language acquisition and the process of speech (Petitto 2000). General ideas have been changed because of these research projects. It is becoming increasingly clear that theories of language acquisition need to take into account emerging data on sign language research. As cross-linguistic comparison has enriched acquisition theory, so additional cross-modality work is providing useful insights. Developmental data from different sign languages are beginning to be included in conference sessions and publications on syntax, phonology and pragmatics, rather than just meetings and journals dedicated solely to sign languages. Sign language authors need to make the links to wider language acquisition theory explicit in their work, something that some researchers have achieved quite successfully (e.g. Lillo-Martin 2000). This will improve our understanding of sign languages and make the relevance of our work more explicit to the wider field. Part of this task is to make the terminology used in sign language research transparent to non-sign language specialists. With this aim we have provided a glossary section for this volume.

Previously two notable books have appeared on sign language acquisition: the volumes edited by McIntire (1994) and Chamberlain, Morford and Mayberry (2000). The McIntire collection is solely on ASL. The Chamberlain et al. volume presents several chapters on sign phonology acquisition and also on Deaf children's reading development. In the present volume we have included only one chapter on phonology and we do not discuss reading development directly. The Chamberlain et al. book is a good source of data on these two aspects of development.

The first studies on sign language acquisition began with Tervoort's work in the 1950's. During the major period after Bellugi & Klima set up the Salk ASL research programme in the 1970's there were several questions asked of sign language acquisition.[3] Are sign languages somehow less complex than spoken languages and thus learnable by non-human species? Are sign languages more easily acquired by children than spoken languages? The acquisition of ASL by primates was discounted early (e.g. Petitto & Seidenberg 1979) but the notion of the qualitative difference between sign and speech has persisted, despite the lack of evidence that primates can use signs with any more skill than they can use spoken language.

Some have suggested that because of the iconic features of sign languages, coupled with simpler articulation at the motor level, children could learn sign language easier and earlier than spoken languages. Some children have been documented to use single signs as early as 6 months of age (Meier & Newport 1990), suggesting that there may be some difference between first signs and spoken words to do with simpler articulation. However universal constraints operate on children's acquisition of syntax, morphology and semantics. There is no evidence so far, that children exposed to a sign language from infancy find the acquisition of these abstract principles any easier than children acquiring a spoken language. The recording of early signs in children may also be due to eager parents or researchers seeing sign-like behaviour as having linguistic status and thus interpreting a casual movement as being a 6 month old's first sign. In conclusion, sign languages present children with the same challenges as spoken language at the abstract representational level.

Another area of debate has centred on the transition between children's gestural communication and their use of a specific sign language. Deaf and hearing children exposed to sign language from infancy onwards progress through the normal stage of using proto-declarative gestures in their early development of communication to symbolic use of language. Is there a smooth transition from this gesture to linguistic use of sign or is development characteristic of an abrupt re-organisation as the child moves from gestural to linguistic communication? This issue is still being debated. The study of the development of early signs in the presence of earlier used gestures has been used as a test case for the debate between those who see language as being a separate autonomous cognitive module and those that see a more intimate relationship between language and other cognitive processes in development (e.g. Goswami 1998). The evidence has been strong on both sides. In a now famous study Petitto (1987) demonstrated that at a certain point in development of ASL, pointing gestures become re-organised as part of a linguistic system. Prior to this, gestural pointing at people for deixis is performed without difficulty. When re-organisation takes place children initially avoid the use of pointing followed by a period of errorful use, characteristic of the development of a pronominal system e.g. pronominal reversals. Reilly and colleagues have shown a similar abrupt re-organisation by children acquiring the non-manual aspects of ASL syntax (Reilly & Anderson, this volume). On the other hand Volterra and colleagues (Volterra & Iverson 1995) have demonstrated an intimate overlap and relationship between young children's earliest gestural communication and their emerging sign systems.

Up to this point in the study of children's development of sign language we have learned that in all important aspects the acquisition of sign and spoken languages are similar. Infants exposed to signing at home babble manually (Petitto & Marentette 1991). When children's first signs start to be combined the patterns resemble the morpho-syntactic characteristics of their parent's input (Chen 1999) as well as general principles of early syntax. Morphology develops gradually and during this development children over-generalise inflections. As opposed to adult learners children have an advantage in analysing signs at the morphemic level (Newport 1990). Specific features of sign languages appear to cause different acquisition problems for the child in the same way that typological factors affect development across different spoken languages (Slobin 1982).

This volume presents some of the most recent research on sign language acquisition and also presents work on different sign languages. The first chapter in this volume by Marschark sets up explicitly the set of complicated variables to consider in researching language development in signing children. In the tradition of Snow and Ferguson (1977), Marschark describes the interaction that takes place at the earliest stages of language acquisition, and in particular the skills of Deaf parents in detecting communicative behaviour in their infants and the adaptations they make in their use of child directed signing. There are modality differences in the dynamics of triadic attention, as signing adults must link a sign to its referent in the same visual field. The modality influences the extent to which adults can provide commentary on on-going activity. Marschark concludes that infants exposed to sign languages have an early ability for recognising the phonological contrasts in signing and when they begin to make movements of the hands these are interpreted as communicative by their deaf parents.

In the second chapter the phonological characteristics of early sign acquisition are described in detail. Karnop analyses early sign production within the framework of Dependency Phonology (Anderson & Ewen 1987) in a relatively under-researched language, Brazilian Sign Language (LIBRAS). In this framework signs have a basic representational structure. This is the earliest phonological representation for the child, composed of only the unmarked handshapes and locations in the language. Data come from one deaf child aged 8–30 months in a rich signing environment. Sign phonology is one of the most innovative areas of sign linguistics at the moment and is challenging speech based models of phonological theory. This approach allows Karnop to make predictions with regard to acquisition; she concludes with a developmental timetable for LIBRAS phonology.

At this point in time we are faced with the problem of how to analyse sign interaction in a comparable way to spoken language work carried out using the CHILDES set of tools (MacWhinney 2000). The chapter by Hoiting and Slobin presents the most advanced attempt to date at achieving this goal. The chapter presents both the Berkeley Transcription System (BTS) and data from both ASL and SLN child language acquisition. Data come from a large corpus of pre-school children's signing in the age period 18 to 36 months and revolve around issues in the development of morphology, semantics and pragmatic dimensions of ASL and SLN. Hoiting and Slobin's review of current sign transcription systems is followed by a description of the conventions used in the BTS and the motivations which underpin it. The authors' research to date concludes that sign languages are polysynthetic languages and that children develop linguistic strategies akin to those suggested for spoken language acquisition (e.g. Berko 1958). Children quickly grasp the polycomponential nature of sign languages and use meaning components productively in complex signs.

We then move onto research on the development of Italian Sign Language (LIS). The chapter by Pizzuto deals with the theoretical issues of optionally inflected signs, individual variation and the role of the input in Deaf preschool-ers' acquisition of LIS. Pizzuto describes the possible role of regular articulatory and morphological features in the language for extracting grammatical process-es by the child. The added complication of co-articulation at the word level is also discussed. Pizzuto links her findings to other cross-linguistic studies, such as the ones found in the Slobin (1985) volume and concludes that these typological features play an important role in shaping the learning process.

The chapter by Meier describes the acquisition of verb agreement in ASL. Agreement is expressed through the linking of a sign's movement with referential locations in sign space. Meier documents the acquisition data on this universal aspect of sign languages, and convincingly shows that errors made during acquisition and the emergence of agreement systems in a recently evolved sign language point to a process akin to the development of spoken language verb morphology systems. One piece of child sign data discussed is the use of a single indexed location in sign space to refer to more than one noun phrase. These errors are comparable with those observed in children acquiring spoken languages as they gradually master the binding of pronouns to antecedent noun phrases and verb morphology. Meier also analyses the role of iconicity in acquisition, concluding that there is no evidence that this feature guides children's mastery of verb agreement.

The acquisition of grammatical structures is explored in the next two chapters. Schick describes syntactic properties and grammatical relations expressed in the earliest sentences of 12 Deaf toddlers exposed to ASL at 24 months of age. There are a wide variety of word orders in ASL, some with accompanying complex morphology. Schick points out that this may pose special challenges for the child. Schick focuses on first verbs and the relative positioning of thematic roles. Individual verbs are examined in order to determine whether there are any verb-specific patterns as has been proposed by Tomasello (1992). Schick concludes that there is little evidence of regular word order patterns in the early combinations across the 12 children. This contrasts with earlier reports of children in this age range who are acquiring spoken languages. There were some examples of positional patterns associated with specific verbs however. Schick also points out that the possibility exists for these children to use knowledge of both their ASL and English-influenced signing (this last point is explored in detail in the chapter by van den Bogaerde & Baker — see also below).

In the next contribution, Reilly and Anderson describe seminal work on the use of non-manual (off the hands) aspects of ASL. They propose the *hands before faces* order of acquisition and describe the change from using facial expressions for affective non-linguistic communication to producing grammatical contrasts.

The study of bilingualism in sign language acquisition is the subject of the next chapters. Van den Bogaerde and Baker describe in detail how young children exposed to both SLN and spoken Dutch develop bilingual communication strategies. The study also reveals the complex communication strategies that Deaf mothers employ in their interaction with their hearing and Deaf children.

The chapter by Kegl describes the innovative language acquisition study carried out on data from the documented emergence of a new signed language in Nicaragua after 1979 and a comparative analysis of ASL. Kegl tackles the complex questions of critical periods for language acquisition, the differences between gesture and sign and also the difference between early and late learners of a first language. Kegl's approach puts great emphasis on the child's rule governed analysis of input. Young children's language-ready brains analyse gesture, non-native signing and fluent signing in different ways. Kegl proposes that children are initially attracted to the prosodic characteristics of sign languages. During the early years of life, this sensitivity allows them to discover the basic building blocks of the language. In the emergence of a sign language *de novo* there is the important factor of a critical number of signers to consider.

The theme of verb use in young signing children continues in the final chapter by Morgan and Woll. The emergence of verb argument structures in British Sign Language (BSL) is described in one child's first sign combinations between the ages of 1;10 and 3;0. This description of the foundation of early BSL grammar is related to theories of semantic representations (e.g. Pinker 1989). The intensive data set is related to previous BSL research on older children's production and comprehension of different verb phrases. The gradual mastery of several sub-components of BSL grammar is related to work on the overgeneralization of verb argument structure in spoken language.

Finally, Elena Lieven describes how current sign language research has provided interesting problems for the wider field to take into consideration. At the same time she points out the possible areas where sign language research will make most impact in the future.

We hope that this volume will provide much food for thought and stimulate a discussion of the relevance of sign language research to the general study of language acquisition. We believe there is much to learn from the study of sign languages and in carrying out this research we recognise we must make our developmental descriptions within the general theoretical approaches available, in order for our work to be understood but also in the hope that more collaboration with the wider field will take place. Of course an important motivation for this increased collaboration in the future relates to the practical motivation for understanding Deaf children's language development. If we can make the study of sign language acquisition more typical perhaps our research will have been useful for improving the lives of the many Deaf children who are growing up in exceptional situations. This volume is dedicated to all of those children.

Notes

1. The use of the upper case with Deaf is conventional for describing members of the linguistic community of sign language users. This is in order to contrast with the term 'deaf' which refers to the audiological state of deafness.

2. The manual alphabet is the set of hand configurations used to fingerspell words in a particular spoken language. The modern ASL manual alphabet is one handed while BSL signers use a two-handed system. When signers use the manual alphabet it is transcribed with hyphenated letters e.g. G-E-R-A-N-I-U-M.

3. A connection that is very pertinent for this book is that Bellugi was originally a student of Roger Brown. Her early work on the acquisition of ASL stemmed from her interest in the acquisition of English (see Emmorey & Lane 2000).

Foundations of communication and the emergence of language in deaf children

Marc Marschark

1. Introduction

Children do not come into the world pre-programmed to speak the language of their parents or the geographical entity within which they live. Nor do they come to language as *tabulae rasae*, blank slates passively waiting for language to be inscribed upon them. During the first weeks of life, if not before, a child's environment and place in the social mosaic begin to establish the context for language development. Various characteristics of that context — and of the child — will help to establish the course of what will be a lifelong process. This chapter focuses on what it is that children bring to language acquisition and the ways in which the contexts of language learning influence what the child learns and how. The foundations of communication and the emergence of language in deaf children will be seen to reside in and reflect the nexus of early social and cognitive development, with healthy doses of genetic and environmental influence (Akamatsu, Musselman & Zweibel 2000; Marschark & Everhart 1997).

Importantly in the case of deaf children, language development and language learning are not the same thing, even if we often use the terms interchangeably with regard to hearing children. *Language development* usually carries the sense of a natural or automatic unfolding of a plan along a regular course. *Language learning*, by comparison, refers to something that requires effort, perhaps a more artificial and certainly an intentional activity that involves both a learner and teacher(s). While this distinction may be superfluous in many situations, it clearly is not in the case of deaf children. Language appears to *develop* relatively naturally among deaf and hearing children of deaf parents and among hearing children of hearing parents. Deaf children of hearing parents, meanwhile, typically are *taught* language from the time they enter early intervention programming through their college careers. For this 90–95 percent of all deaf children, acquiring language is often a significant challenge and usually is seen to be delayed relative to both hearing children of hearing parents and deaf children of deaf parents (Erting, Prezioso & Hynes 1990; Spencer 1993a, 1993b).

The reasons for this difference between most deaf and hearing children are numerous, and it would be both oversimplistic and potentially damaging to assume that there is a single factor that can explain it. Such a view represents the wistful desire for a single solution for the observed language (and later literacy) challenges of deaf children and carries with it the risk of squandering both resources and opportunities. Recognition and understanding of this situation require continued efforts on both theoretical and practical fronts. But they also carry potential for considerable gains with regard to broad issues of language development as well as the education of deaf children.

2.   Articulating the issues

If we want a fuller understanding of the foundations of language development in deaf children, we first need to focus on research findings and reduce the rhetoric that often hinders rather than supports progress in this area and makes life difficult for many parents of deaf children. At the outset, therefore, it will be helpful to articulate some assumptions normally made with regard to the development of deaf children, but not all of which are true. Most generally, it is often assumed that except for differences in the auditory domain and related aspects of communication and language, deaf children are just like hearing children (e.g., Seal 1998). In many ways, of course, all children are similar. But for the purposes of understanding the development of deaf children in language, as well as in other domains, assuming that the two groups are essentially identical ignores the fact that they have rather different early childhoods. This is particularly true with regard to communication. Regardless of whether they have deaf or hearing parents and whether they are acquiring a signed or spoken language, deaf children have somewhat different language learning environments than hearing children. They also bring different social (Gregory 1995; MacTurk, Meadow-Orlans, Koester & Spencer 1993), perceptual (Spencer 2000; Swisher 1993), cognitive (Marschark & Lukomski 2001; Spencer & Hafer 1998), and even neuropsychological (Emmorey 2001; Neville, Kutas & Schmidt 1982) backgrounds to those contexts. While some of the differences are superficial and of little long-term importance, others are essential to our understanding of their development.

Similarly, or perhaps because of some of the differences between deaf and hearing children in early development, there is often confusion about a number of issues relating to communication and language development. For example, relations between spoken language and sign language, as well as any particular spoken language and its co-existing sign language, are often not fully understood or are misunderstood by parents and teachers of deaf children. Thus, it is sometimes assumed that the use of sign language eliminates any language-related lags in development, that cochlear implants allow children to develop normal speech and hearing skills, that learning to sign interferes with the acquisition of spoken language, and that spoken language and gesture are unrelated. But all of those claims are either unsubstantiated assumptions or overgeneralizations based on specific investigations rather than the overall patterns of results across studies. That is, none is generally true. Each of these issues will arise in the following discussion, as they relate to the foundations of communication and language in deaf children. None of them will be simple, however, so it is important to consider each of them with some care.

2.1 Language use by deaf children, where are we (they)?

Despite the long history of emphasizing spoken language in the education of deaf children (see Marschark, Albertini & Lang 2002: Chapter 2), research continues to show that, on average, deaf children with congenital or early-onset hearing losses consistently show significant delays relative to hearing age-mates, even when those hearing losses are in the mild to moderate range (Carney & Moeller 1988; Cole & Paterson 1984; Gregory & Hindley 1996). Recent studies involving children with cochlear implants have demonstrated significant improvements in that regard, with the acquisition of individual speech sounds generally proceeding in the same order as in hearing children and generally faster than in children with hearing aids (Paatsch, Blamey & Sarant 2001; Tobey, Geers & Brenner 1994; Tye-Murray & Kirk 1993). Nevertheless, the process generally is slower for the children with implants; and unintelligible speech remains the norm, particularly when those children have congenital hearing losses (Serry & Blamey 1999; Spencer 2002). As impressive as their gains might be, children with implants generally do not show language growth at levels comparable to hearing peers (see Spencer 2002, for a review).

As an alternative to spoken language, sign language clearly can serve as an effective mode of communication for young deaf children. Research during the 1980s demonstrated that deaf children of deaf parents, who were exposed to sign language as their first language, acquired that language at much the same rate and with the same milestones as hearing children acquired spoken language (see Morford s.d.; Siple 1997, for a review). Such results supported the linguistic and psychological similarity of signed and spoken languages while contributing significantly to our understanding of language and language development. Perhaps most importantly, such findings indicated that hearing loss *per se* could not explain the developmental and educational challenges observed among deaf children from hearing families. Other factors clearly have to be involved, and a significant body of research bears on differences between deaf children from deaf and hearing families as well as comparisons of both to hearing children from hearing families.

What is not clear to many observers is the extent to which the products and correlates of sign language acquisition are fully comparable to those of spoken language, particularly with regard to literacy and other academic skills (Marschark et al. 2002). Although there is strong sentiment to assume the functional equivalence of signed and spoken languages (i.e., beyond linguistic equivalence), the question remains an empirical one. Assessment of this possibility requires extensive investigation of both the contributors to deaf children's language and its outcome.

2.2 Challenges in understanding language development of deaf children

Beyond the heterogeneity of deaf children and the modes, styles, and completeness of the communication to which they are exposed, there are other challenges to our sorting out the real from the artifactual foundations of their communication and language. Take for example the contrast between exposing deaf children primarily to spoken language versus sign language. While a theoretically important distinction for many investigators and a matter of paramount social and educational importance for many parents and teachers, it is clearly an oversimplification. Regardless of the primary mode of their formal instruction, deaf children are rarely exposed only to spoken language or sign language, even if those are the intentions of their parents or their teachers. Children with residual hearing, for example, often benefit from the amplification of spoken language even if they use sign language in some or most contexts. At the same time, many hearing parents who seek to raise their young deaf children with a formal sign language such as British Sign Language (BSL) or American Sign Language (ASL) do not sign with any consistency, a situation also encountered when various forms of English-based signing or cued speech (a manual means of disambiguating spoken language on the lips) are used. Parents typically have had little formal training in these methods and may be uncomfortable using them in public. Further, they rarely recognize how much of language is learned indirectly from overhearing conversations of others rather than through direct communication, and they tend to use alternative modes of communication only when speaking directly to the child. Young deaf children of hearing parents thus frequently do not have any truly accessible and competent language models, either for sign language or for spoken language. Meanwhile, *early* language acquisition is generally *better* language acquisition, so it is important to get it right the first time (Calderon & Greenberg 1997; Calderon & Naidu 2000; Mayberry & Eichen 1991; Morford n.d.).

Even when deaf children are educated in spoken language environments, systems of gestural communication may develop between parents and children (e.g., Greenberg, Calderon & Kusché 1984). These systems play a greater or lesser role in communication in different contexts and may facilitate the acquisition of spoken and signed languages (Bates, Thal, Whitesell, Fenson & Oakes 1989; Volterra & Iverson 1995). According to most investigators (e.g., McNeill 1992; Stokoe & Marschark 1999; cf. Singleton, Goldin-Meadow & McNeill 1995), there is a communicative continuum from gesture to language. This continuum can be seen both ontogenetically in the development of language by both hearing and deaf children (Bates et al. 1989; Marschark 1994; Schley 1991) and phylogenetically in the development of human communication systems, including language (Armstrong, Stokoe & Wilcox 1995; Stokoe & Marschark 1999). Although the transition from gesture to sign often holds the greatest interest for those who study early language development in deaf children, the linguistic line between gesture and language may be blurred, even if both appear to have the same roots (McNeill 1992). Thus, we now see a movement to teach babies invented signs (i.e., not ASL, BSL, or another true sign language) in order to promote early language and symbolic development (e.g., Acredolo & Goodwyn 2000). For the present purposes, it will be more important that deaf children's spontaneous gestures — whatever their eventual relation to signs — elicit language and social responses from others in the environment.

Problems of interpretation also arise in attempts to compare the language abilities of deaf children who are enrolled in early intervention programs emphasizing sign language and those in programs emphasizing spoken language (see Calderon & Greenberg 1997). Such comparisons represent one of the most popular and potentially informative areas in research relating to language development and academic success among children with hearing loss, but also one of the most intractable. Beyond the issues raised above, programs focusing on spoken or signed language often have different educational philosophies and curricula as well as different approaches to communication. They may only admit particular children with particular histories, and different parents will be drawn to different programs for a variety of reasons. Thus, differences observed between children from any two programs might be the result of any of a number of related variables rather than, or in addition to, language orientation *per se.*

In short, conducting and interpreting research on the foundations of early language development in deaf children is a complex undertaking. If some of the above issues appear minor from the perspective of older, competent language users, they certainly are not trivial in the context of early language development. The challenge for researchers is to discover the *tricky mix* (Nelson, Loncke & Camarata 1993) of experiences that have significant impact on language development and to control or minimize those that are extraneous.

3.   Earliest communication

If we want to understand language development of deaf children, we must look at the earliest social interactions with their parents within the larger context of development. The competencies and strategies learned there will be intimately involved in the emergence of early communication and help to set the stage for language.

We know, for example, that sounds in a hearing child's environment even before birth have some role in development. During roughly the last trimester of pregnancy, the fetus rests with its head against the mother's pelvis. Her voice is transmitted (to hearing fetuses) through bone conduction, and it is a familiar stimulus at birth. Newborns recognize the intonation contours and particular frequencies of their mothers' speech (DeCasper & Spence 1986) and maternal vocalizations thus have a quieting effect on infants. For hearing mother-infant dyads, prenatal and early post-natal speech thus can play a role in initial mother-child bonding which, in turn, helps to *bootstrap* early communication and social processes.

As far as we can tell without any explicit research into the issue, deaf children are not at any particular disadvantage due to their failure to recognize their mothers' voices at birth, even though auditory cues are an almost universal feature in social development across mammals and birds. Deaf infants and their mothers appear simply to develop somewhat different interaction strategies. The interesting question is the extent to which these differences have different long-term consequences for language development. For example, we know that normally-hearing babies are able to link maternal mood with her facial expression and match different faces to their respective voices as early as 2 months of age; and they can decipher the affective tone of maternal speech by 9 months. Those linkages are based largely on the extensive, post-birth interactions of mother and infant rather than any *a priori* contributions from voices heard in the womb. With deaf infants, both deaf and hearing mothers spend considerable time interacting with them, and the importance of visual, tactile, and auditory cues is well documented (e.g., Harris, Clibbens, Chasin & Tibbets 1989; Koester 1994; MacTurk et al. 1993; Rea, Bonvillian & Richards 1988). In the absence of vocal-auditory cues, however, there is compensation from other sense modalities. We just do not yet fully understand what, if any, long-term effects they have on development.

Reilly and Bellugi (1996) examined the American Sign Language (ASL) productions of deaf mothers signing to their deaf preschoolers. They focused on *wh*-questions, which require lowering (*furrowing*) of the eyebrows similar to the expression of anger or puzzlement. Their analysis revealed that this characteristic underwent transformation from an indicator of affect to an indicator of an interrogative when the children were about two years of age. Prior to age 2, mothers tended to leave the *wh*- facial marker out of their questions, thus eliminating a potential conflict in meaning but resulting in the production of ungrammatical ASL. At the same time, Reilly and Bellugi found that facial marker deletion did not occur in *yes-no* questions addressed to the children, a situation in which the marker (raised eyebrows) does not carry negative affect. Mothers thus were implicitly sensitive to the need for clarity of communication, and were 'willing' to produce ungrammatical language in order to achieve it. Reilly, McIntire and Bellugi (1990b) reported that facial expressions associated with the basic emotions are produced consistently by both deaf and hearing children by 12 months of age. At 12 months, deaf children of hearing parents were found to have command of the basic affective displays and use a variety of nonvocal attention-getting devices, even when their parents were not ideal models. Taken together, these findings suggest that many of the earliest communicative interactions between mothers and their deaf infants can proceed quite naturally without audition, at least when the mothers are also deaf. Particular aspects of communication may be superficially different than they are for hearing mothers with hearing infants, but they serve the same communication and social functions.

In the case of hearing mothers, it is difficult to assess the full impact of the lack of vocal-auditory communication on early interactions with their deaf infants. Such effects would be less pronounced, of course, if parents are aware of their infant's hearing loss (e.g., when there is a history of deafness in the family) rather than unaware of the hearing loss. In the former case, parents could engage in a variety of strategies that enhance interactions in nonauditory domains (e.g., Erting, Prezioso & Hynes 1990; Koester, Brooks & Traci 2000). Although it is unclear to what extent such compensation is necessary, it likely contributes to the growth of parent-child relationships and fosters the development of effective language via social and communication.

3.1 Perception and reception of communication from prelinguistic deaf children

Consider the very beginnings of communication, early in the first year of life, when both deaf and hearing children are beginning to make regular vocal sounds and hand movements. At this point, a child's spoken, signed, or gestural productions first begin to have communicative consequences (Bjerkan, Martinsen, Schjølberg & von Tetzchner 1983; Marschark 1993: Chapter 3). Whether or not they are seen as true attempts to communicate, deaf and hearing parents frequently respond to infants' gestures and vocalizations, respectively, thus promoting both social communication and various language functions. Bjerkan et al. (1983) suggested that the probability of adult reactions in such situations varies according to the number of potential cues derived from the child and the particular context. These *cues* include such factors as the similarity between the child's production and parental language, parents' perceived understanding of related child gestures, and the presence of relevant referents. Prelinguistic, communicative interactions between parents and children thus "presuppose that the adult has found the child's activity meaningful" (Bjerkan et al. 1983:4), although what is perceived as meaningful for communicative purposes changes as the child becomes older. These early interactions establish the foundation for language development, making the accessibility of language an essential component of the first three years of life (Bjerkan et al. 1983; Luetke-Stahlman 1993; cf. Goldin-Meadow & Mylander 1984).

In general, deaf parents show greater awareness of the communication needs of deaf children than do hearing parents. This awareness likely results in part from their own communication experiences, but deaf parents also are more sensitive to visual signals from their children. Just as hearing parents of hearing infants 'look for' words in their early vocalizations, so deaf parents with either hearing or deaf children look for meaning in hand movements. Von Tetzchner (1984) thus suggested that deaf infants' motor control may be less important for early sign language acquisition than parents' receptive sign language skills. A parallel can be seen in it being unlikely that deaf parents would detect pre-linguistic vocal utterances by their hearing children (see Meadow-Orlans & Spencer 1996). But those children are more likely to encounter hearing adults (who can serve as language models/'tutors') than most deaf children of hearing parents are to encounter signing deaf adults.

Over time, a *synchrony* develops between (especially) mothers and infants, so that their nonlinguistic behaviors become intertwined. Given the greater sensitivity of deaf parents to prelinguistic nonvocal utterances that are similar to signs, it is not surprising that behavioral synchrony tends to be greater in dyads in which the mother is deaf (Gregory & Barlow 1989). Some hearing parents also may recognize cues from their young deaf children concerning the success or failure of communication, even before they are aware of their hearing losses. Although such sensitivity is predictive of later language development (Pressman, Pipp-Siegel, Yoshinaga-Itano & Deas 1999), most hearing parents lack competence and confidence in their ability to communicate with their deaf children. Interestingly, this may be particularly problematic for parents who are learning sign language. Those parents do recognize the importance of effective communication for young children with hearing loss — after all, they are learning sign language — including the quality of the visual signal and the appropriateness of the signing directed to the child (Ritter-Brinton & Stewart 1992). Nevertheless, Young (1997) found that hearing parents often try to balance their desire for sign language proficiency with the "emotional and practical considerations" of the family, and effective communication sometimes suffers. For their part, hearing fathers tend to have poorer sign skills than hearing mothers (Gregory & Hindley 1996), potentially both a cause and effect of mothers' apparently taking on a proportionally greater caregiving role than is the case with parents of hearing children.[1]

Several studies concerning the ways in which adults modify their language in communicating with young hearing children have found that both fathers and other adults who are not parents tend to adapt their language in ways similar to that of hearing mothers. Referred to as *motherese* or *child-directed language*, the ways in which language is modified depend on adults' beliefs about children's language capabilities and are seen regardless of whether a child is hearing or deaf and regardless of whether signed or spoken language is used (Gallaway & Woll 1994).[2] When directed to young hearing children by hearing mothers, for example, language tends to be slower, more prosodically varied or exaggerated, grammatically simpler, and more likely to include shortened versions of words than is the language directed to older children or adults.

Because language development in deaf children of deaf parents occurs in a natural manner, we would expect that deaf mothers' use of motherese in communicating with their young children would begin just as early as it does in hearing mothers of hearing children, and this turns out to be the case. When their infants are as young as 3 months of age, deaf mothers use primarily single signs in communicating with them, frequently involving repetition, exaggeration, and sign shortening parallel to that seen in hearing mothers' speech to their hearing babies (Holzrichter & Meier 2000; Masataka 2000). Deaf mothers' motherese tends to be accompanied by smiles, touching, and numerous mouth movements; and they use exaggerated facial expressions with their babies even more than hearing mothers (Harris et al. 1989; Koester 1994; Koester et al. 2000; Reilly & Bellugi 1996; Reilly et al. 1990b). *Baby talk* thus occurs in signing as well as in speech.

In the case of hearing parents and infants, speech makes language available to the child regardless of whether they are looking in the right direction, and motherese helps to attract and maintain a child's attention. This situation is rather different for deaf infants who may not be watching their mothers (and the visual motherese has to be seen before it is effective). Many hearing mothers have difficulty learning to time their communication to the attentional shifts of their children and often try to communicate with them or continue to communicate with them when their children look away. Deaf mothers, meanwhile, usually resist signing to their children until they have made eye contact or until they believe their children can see their signs. They may wait until the child 'checks back', or they will move their hands out in front of their child, so that the children will see their signs. Deaf parents do not turn the child's head or physically change their positions, as hearing mothers are seen to do, even if they often touch their child to gain attention (Harris et al. 1989; Mohay, Milton, Hindmarsh & Ganley 1998; Spencer, Bodner-Johnson & Gutfreund 1992).

Over repeated occurrences, deaf infants learn to attend visually to cues in the environment and become remarkably good at attending to mother across a much wider range of positions than one would expect from hearing infants (see Swisher 1993, for discussion). This ability does not result directly from their being deaf, but from the fact that for them, there are important things happening on the 'edges' of their visual range. Their perceptual strategies and skills adjust accordingly, with important implications for language, social, and cognitive development (Neville, Kutas & Schmidt 1982). The same phenomenon is seen in hearing children of deaf parents, because the same behavioral contingencies occur during their development (Neville & Lawson 1987).

The ways in which parents accommodate to the perceived communication needs of their deaf babies thus seem to play an important role in determining the actual effectiveness and interest in communicating on both sides of the 'conversation'. Accordingly, we might expect that a lack of language flexibility and fluency on the part of hearing parents would reduce the quality of their social and early 'educational' interactions with their deaf children (von Tetzchner 1984). When they are signing to their deaf children about a common object of attention, hearing mothers often tend to oversimplify their productions, producing language that carries far less information than the language they use with hearing children in similar situations. Such limitations are not unexpected given that most hearing mothers have little more than beginning competence in sign language. Their implications for subsequent development nevertheless may be considerable, and research concerning early language development needs to include consideration of social factors.

4. Parent-child social communication

The availability and accessibility of parent-child communication may be the single most important variable in development. By the 1980s it was widely recognized that hearing children's language acquisition was strongly influenced by their communicative interactions with their mothers (e.g., Fernald, Taeschner, Dunn, Papoušek, de Boysson-Bardies & Fukui 1989; Snow & Ferguson 1977). The search for solutions to observed lags in language acquisition by deaf children therefore focused on the ways that interactions of hearing mothers with hearing children differed from those of hearing mothers with deaf children. Such studies found that the strategies used by hearing mothers with their deaf children vary from those used with their hearing children both in terms of their own behavior and the functional significance of their behaviors from the child's perspective. These differences (usually seen as deficiencies) were broadly held to be responsible for the delays in deaf children's language as well as in social development (e.g., Schlesinger & Meadow 1972).

Shared communication greatly enhances language development and permits relaxed, parent-child social interactions (Harris & Mohay 1997). Effective early communication between infants and their parents (and especially their mothers) not only provides the foundations for language, but it may be the single best predictor of later academic success through its support for the acquisition of literacy and cognitive skills (Drasgow 1994; Hart & Risley 1995). Of primary importance here is the fact that most deaf children rely primarily on visual cues to make sense of their environment. For deaf children to acquire language, it needs to be unambiguous and visible to them on the lips and/or hands of their communication partners (Harris et al. 1989).

In interactions with their young children, parents comment on things of mutual interest. Hearing children can listen to what the parents say while visually exploring relevant objects or observing events. Information from the two sources is received simultaneously, and a link is implicitly or explicitly created between language and the objects or events to which it refers. Dependence on the visual modality, in contrast, requires deaf children to shift attention between their activities and their interlocutors in order to obtain information both about what is going on around them and about language itself (e.g., Harris 1992). Input from these two sources is received sequentially, potentially making the link between language and meaning less obvious. Frequent disconnections in this regard likely contribute to the observed lags in the expressive and receptive vocabularies of deaf children.

The introduction of sign language or a visually-supported spoken language, in itself, is not sufficient to resolve barriers to communication. Other aspects of the linguistic environment also have to be modified. Deaf children must not only be able to see language, but the links between language and meaning must be made explicit through repeated, sequential visual linkage (Erting 1988; Spencer et al. 1992) or *bracketing* a word or statement with pre- and post-indications of its referent (Mohay et al. 1998). Gregory and Barlow (1989), for example, studied a group of deaf and hearing mothers, all with deaf infants, from the time when the children's hearing losses were first diagnosed until they were 12 months of age. They found that deaf infants attended significantly more often to deaf mothers (94 percent) than hearing mothers (75 percent). Further, the actions of deaf mothers were more likely to be followed by contingent actions by their deaf children (59 percent) than were the actions of hearing mothers (23 percent). Beyond helping to ensure that communication is successful, the acquisition of visual attention skills also will contribute to development in a variety of other domains.

The importance to early language of *triadic attention* involving the infant, the mother or other caregiver, and the nonverbal context (e.g., object of attention) has been the focus of several studies. Harris et al. (1989) investigated the strategies used by deaf mothers to ensure that their deaf infants (aged 7–20 months) saw the signs intended for them. They found that by 20 months, most of the mothers' signs and their nonverbal contexts had become linked, providing redundant support for visual attention. Only slight delays in triadic attention were observed, relative to hearing peers.[3] Meadow-Orlans and Spencer (1996) examined triadic attention in deaf infants (aged 18 months) and found no delays in children having deaf mothers. Deaf infants with hearing parents and hearing infants with deaf parents, in contrast, showed less coordinated attentional skills. Such findings reinforce the importance of parental sensitivity to child communication for development in language and other domains.

Spencer (2000a) investigated the potential effects of visual and auditory communication experience in the development of visual attention in deaf and hearing children (aged 9–18 months). Deaf and hearing mothers were observed in play with their deaf and hearing children (i.e., a full 2×2 design), and the attentional states of the children were classified according to a six-category scoring system. For the present purposes, the most interesting finding was that there were no group differences that related to infant hearing status only. Both deaf and hearing children whose mothers used more visual communication were found to spend more time watching their mothers, as compared to mothers who used less visual communication. At the same time, hearing children who received auditory communication during play from their hearing mothers spent more time attending to objects than did either deaf or hearing children whose mothers used only visual communication. Spencer concluded that while auditory experience and coordination between auditory and visual modalities are not necessary for the development of visual attention during infancy, they do support it. Early visual attention was influenced by "a complex interaction of maturation, communicative experiences, and other developing skills" (Spencer 2000:291), however, and its role in early communication and language acquisition remains to be fully explored.

The development of children's attention skills and the use of effective attention-getting and communication strategies on the part of the mother are important for early language development. It thus should not be surprising that mother-child dyads in which such communication synchrony is greater generally show more advanced language development. The issue is not that hearing mothers of deaf children produce less speech than hearing mothers of hearing children. As Lederberg and Everhart (1998) noted, hearing mothers produce comparable amounts of speech to deaf and hearing children, regardless of whether they are also using sign language (i.e., simultaneous communication). The problem is that young deaf children are unable to benefit from spoken language and other auditory input in any way comparable to hearing children. In fact, deaf mothers typically direct less language, overall, to their children than do hearing mothers, but their communication is more accessible and meaningful (Harris 1992; Harris & Mohay 1997). Effective communication with deaf children — and its fostering of language development — clearly requires somewhat different strategies on the part of both parents and children than is the case for hearing mother-child dyads. Ultimately, however, observations of faster language development among deaf children of deaf parents, relative to deaf children of hearing parents, are the result of their having a greater *quantity* of effective communication facilitated by various *qualities* of their linguistic and nonlinguistic interactions, not the other way around.

When deaf children have to choose between watching their mothers or following their mother's pointing, they are likely to miss relevant information, despite having a wider range of visual perception for signs and gestures than their hearing peers (Swisher 1993). Even mothers enrolled with their deaf children in sign language programs are rarely able to manipulate situations in ways that optimize the linguistic information available to the child. Jamison (1994), Mohay et al. (1998), and Waxman and Spencer (1997), for example, have found that hearing mothers have a relatively limited repertoire of visually-oriented attention strategies, and tend to rely on object-related strategies, which have only limited communication success.

The situation is rather different when we look at the child-directed, social language of deaf parents. Koester (1994) and Swisher (1992) among others have gone further, describing the strategies used by deaf parents in interactions with their children to maintain attention and meet language-learning needs. Some of these strategies can be seen to parallel strategies used by hearing mothers in spoken language, but others directly concern the visual accessibility of communication to deaf children (see Harris & Mohay 1997; Mohay et al. 1998).

When communicative interactions between mothers and children are visually clear and accessible, they provide more opportunities for a child to control the interchange, thus making language more interesting and more motivating. Children of controlling mothers, regardless of whether they are deaf or hearing, therefore are more likely to be delayed in language development (Musselman & Churchill 1991). The establishment of effective mother-child communication strategies thus not only helps to promote better early interactions, but has long-term beneficial effects on language development and other domains.

5.   Babbling: Language and social consequences for deaf infants

Most babies come into the world with the potential for hearing a universal set of sounds and contrasts essential to spoken language. Not all languages, however, consist of the same basic elements. It is only over time and exposure to many examples that children learn the range of elements, either sounds or sign components, in their native language. Meanwhile, they gradually lose the ability to discriminate and produce language elements with which they have no experience.

There has long been disagreement about whether babbling is an epiphenomenon, unrelated to language development, or is the first step in the unfolding of language development, serving to *prepare* the articulatory apparatus for language (e.g., Bates 1979; Lenneberg 1967; Oller & Eilers 1988). Primarily for theoretical reasons relating to the possible role of vocal babbling in the development of spoken language, babbling in deaf infants has been of considerable interest for some time. In essence:

> If deaf infants babble in the same way and at the same age as their hearing counterparts, it would suggest that humans are born with a phonetic inheritance that unfolds without extensive auditory experience. On the other hand, if deaf infants' vocalizations differ from those of hearing infants, it would suggest that auditory experience plays an important role in the timely emergence of speech-like sound. (Oller & Eilers 1988:441)

Babbling follows a fairly regular course of development in hearing infants. During the first 3 months, they produce *quasi-vowels* and then *quasi-consonants*, usually made in the back of the mouth. In the *expansion stage*, from about 3 to 6 months, these sounds become progressively clearer and combined into consonant-vowel clusters. During the *canonical stage*, from about 7 to 11 months, well-formed syllables are produced, repeated, and re-combined to form the first vocalizations that parents might interpret as words: *mama*, *daga*, and so on (Oller & Eilers 1988).

Such repetitive and variegated babbling are important theoretically because they involve the syllables that will be the building blocks of words — the ontological-linguistic status of those repetitions aside. More broadly, however, repetitive babbling has clear communicative and social consequences, as parents respond to what they perceive as either attempts at communication or, at least, interesting communication-like behavior (i.e., such babbling has communicative consequences). We will come back to the issue of whether or not the elements of babbling play a linguistically-relevant role in language development, but the conclusion that it plays a socially- and language-relevant role seems beyond question, as long as parents are sensitive to the fact that it is occurring.[4]

5.1 Vocal babbling and speech production in deaf children

There is a popular notion that deaf infants' vocal babbling is generally comparable to that of hearing infants, with the groups diverging at around the point of the first words. Although the two groups do produce similar vocalizations during the first few months of life, the divergence happens long before words appear. Canonical babbling tends to be either delayed or absent in most deaf infants (Oller, Eilers, Bull & Carney 1985). When it does appear, deaf infants babble less frequently than their hearing age-mates. By 10 months, when babbling should be becoming more sophisticated, deaf infants show considerably less complexity in their babbling than hearing infants, most noticeably in the relative infrequency of producing consonants.

Stoel-Gammon and Otomo (1986), for example, observed a significant decline in the variety of consonantal sounds produced by moderately to profoundly deaf infants (aged 4–28 months), while that of the normally hearing infants (aged 4–18 months) increased. Differences were most obvious after 8 months, when only the hearing children showed age-appropriate canonical babbling. Oller and Eilers (1988) reported similar results with a group of severely to profoundly deaf infants. They found that whereas the hearing infants began canonical babbling at about 7 months, the deaf infants did not do so until 11 to 25 months, despite early amplification and intensive speech stimulation. The deaf infants did babble eventually, but did so at a rate that was only a fraction of the rate displayed by their hearing age-mates.

The finding that differences in the babbling of deaf and hearing infants are observed despite early use of amplification and concerted efforts to provide deaf children with exposure to spoken language is an important one. Residual hearing would be expected to ameliorate the babbling lag of deaf infants, but at least in those with moderate losses, significant differences are still observed despite early-identification of hearing losses (e.g., Spencer 1993a; Yoshinaga-Itano 2000;

Yoshinaga-Itano & Stredler-Brown 1992). Wallace, Menn and Yoshinaga-Itano (2000), for example, conducted a longitudinal study with a group of infants who initially were examined between 5 and 13 months of age and then re-examined, first between 2 and 5 years of age and then between 5 and 10 years of age. Despite intensive auditory and speech support, none of the children with profound hearing losses were judged to have intelligible speech between 5 and 10 years of age. This contrasted with 82 percent of children with mild to severe hearing losses who were judged to have intelligible speech at that point. Of the three children who showed normal babbling at the initial testing, two of them developed intelligible speech — one with a mild hearing loss and one with a moderate hearing loss (the third child had a profound loss). Overall, there was no consistent relation between babbling at the first testing and spoken language at the final testing.

The lack of complex early babbling by deaf children means that at the age when parents and siblings first start responding to their perceived attempts at communication, deaf infants already may be at a disadvantage relative to hearing children. Spencer (1993a), however, found that deaf infants (aged 12 months) with hearing parents produced vocalizations perceived as having communicative intent just as frequently as hearing infants. Because of the nature of their hearing losses, Spencer concluded that the use of hearing aids provided most of the infants with access to their own vocalizations as well as to those of others. Further, perhaps as a result of the families' participating in an early intervention program, she found that the hearing parents frequently responded to their deaf infants' prelinguistic vocalizations. In contrast to the findings of Wallace et al. (2000), Spencer found that deaf infants' canonical babbling at 12 months was positively correlated with their rate of spoken language production at 18 months, even if the relationship was not as strong as it was for hearing infants with hearing parents. It therefore appears that we need to look more closely at the link between early vocalizations by deaf infants and the communicative behaviors of their parents.

5.2 Manual babbling and language production in deaf children

At first blush, the availability of both manual and oral articulatory apparatuses at birth suggests the possibility that signed and spoken language might develop in similar ways (as indeed they do in many respects). Just as hearing infants are able to hear a variety of phonological contrasts beyond those that are important (i.e., phonemic) for the spoken language of their parents, they might also be born with the basic components necessary to learn any signed language. Schley (1991) used a habituation paradigm to examine the ability of hearing infants (aged 32 months) to discriminate classes of inflections used in ASL. She found that the infants were able to distinguish between different inflection types, even though they were learning spoken language, not sign language. The early ability to recognize basic perceptual contrasts necessary for the acquisition of sign language thus seems to be comparable to the ability to recognize the basic perceptual contrasts necessary for the acquisition of spoken language. The information is different and is received in different sense modalities, but the characteristics of the information processor (the child) seem to be much the same. Thus, manual babbling seems likely to occur and fulfill the same functions (at least in the presence of perceptive parents) as vocal babbling. In particular, manual babbling might selectively elicit socially- and language-relevant responses from deaf or sign-sensitive hearing parents, regardless of the actual linguistic status of babbling in language development.

Some young deaf children of deaf parents do appear to produce individual and repeated sign components without any apparent attempt at communication — the hallmark of babbling. Like vocal babbling, in which vowels, consonants, and their combinations may be more or less word-like, manual babbling could include individual components of signs (e.g., handshapes or movements), reduplication of a particular component (e.g., a handshape), or combination of components (e.g., repeated placement of a handshape at a particular place of articulation). Depending on the actual combinations produced, some such babbling will happen to coincide with actual signs, such as the opening and closing of the open hand in MILK or the repeated movement of an open hand toward the chin in MAMA or the forehead in DADA in the two previous examples, respectively (see Figure 1).[5] This kind of babbling has only been documented in a few children, but it seems likely to be a more general phenomenon.

Boyes Braem (1990) described the earliest handshapes used by deaf children, finding a relatively small set that appear to be uniform across deaf infants learning sign language as a first language (see Figure 2). She referred to these canonical handshapes as *unmarked* in the sense they are found across all documented sign languages and are both formationally and perceptually distinct. Even though other investigators have found different frequencies of use among these early handshapes (e.g., Siedlecki & Bonvillian 1997), they all comprise the primary stuff of later signs (see Martinsen, von Tetzchner & Nordeng 1983, described in Bjerken et al. 1989).

mother   father

Figure 1. American Sign Language signs for *mother* (*mama*) and *father* (*dada*), that might be produced spontaneously by deaf children. (Copyright, 1993, Oxford University Press, reprinted by permission).

Petitto and Marentette (1991) provided one of the more extensive examinations of manual babbling, although they only studied two deaf children (both acquiring ASL from their deaf parents). They found that the deaf children and a group of three hearing children produced similar hand movements, consisting of a subset of the potential phonetic inventory of sign language, demonstrating syllabic organization comparable to that in ASL, and seemingly devoid of reference. The deaf children's hand movements, but not the hearing children's productions, were reported to progress through the stages characteristic of vocal babbling, and they were both more complex and varied than the ones of the hearing children. Perhaps the most surprising finding was Petitto and Marentette's classification of over 60 percent of the deaf infants' manual activity at 14 months as syllabic babbling. By comparison, babbling in hearing infants at this stage typically comprises only about 20 percent of their vocal productions, and Petitto and Marentette observed 4 to 15 percent of the productions of the hearing children to be babbling. Sixty percent also seems remarkably high for native signing children of deaf parents who should be well on their way in

Figure 2. Common set of handshapes observed by Boyes-Braem (1990) to occur among infants acquiring sign language. (Copyright, 1993, Oxford University Press, reprinted by permission).

vocabulary development at this age (see Folven & Bonvillian 1987; Volterra & Iverson 1995).

Petitto and Marentette also found that 98 percent of the deaf children's manual babbling occurred within a restricted space in front of the body, appearing to be a precursor to the use of normal signing space. They concluded that young children discover the relations between the structure of language and the means for producing language, regardless of its modality. They argued that there must be an innate predisposition to discover the patterned input of language, although there is nothing in their data to indicate that manual babbling could not be learned through selective reinforcement by parents and others (Whitehurst & Valdez-Menchaca 1988). Meier and Willerman (1995) similarly analyzed the babbling of three deaf children of deaf parents and two hearing children of hearing parents, beginning as early as 7 months and continuing as late as 15 months. They reported no clear distinctions between the deaf and hearing children in their overall use of non-referential (meaning-less) gestures, the category in their scoring system that included manual babbling. Deaf children did exhibit more gesture repetitions than the hearing children, but the cause of that difference and its reliability were not clear. Overall, 60 to 95 percent of the deaf children's gestures were in the non-referential category during the first month and a half of observation, declining to between 40 and 65 percent of their gestures by about one year of age, when communicative gestures were on the rise. Meier and Willerman concluded that babble-like gestures might be relatively common in gesturing of all children, whether or not they have sign language input, and may offer no special advantage to deaf children. That conclusion clearly is consistent with the findings of Schley (1991) involving hearing children (cf. Volterra & Iverson 1995).

5.3 Social and language effects of babbling

Findings indicating reduced frequency and diversity of vocal babbling in deaf children of hearing parents over the first months of life indicate a potential social component to babbling. Hearing parents often respond as though they comprehend their infants' early vocalizations, engaging in *conversations* with them (more like *collective monologues*). Those early interactions contribute to the synchrony and reciprocity in parent-child interactions so important for normal social development as well as language development (Marschark 1993: Chapter 5). Deaf parents appear to respond similarly to the manual babbling of their deaf (and hearing) infants, although evidence is still scarce in that regard (but see Bjerken et al. 1989). Whatever the precise linguistic roles of vocal and manual babbling in language development, however, they clearly play a broader role in social and cognitive development — which will influence subsequent language development.

As babbles and other vocal or manual behaviors elicit responses from listeners, some remain in the infant's communication repertoire. Presumably, a subset of those productions gradually are shaped into real words (signed or spoken), others are replaced, and many drop out of the child's repertoire completely. At this point, however, it does not matter whether the productions are babbles, baby-talk, or *proto-words*, as long as there is some kind of social agreement between the child and her listeners that particular sounds have particular meanings. Indeed, some early, invented words remain with children for many years (if not into adulthood) as *home words* or *home signs*. We thus see a scenario unfolding in which deaf children who are ready to produce their first signs are being linguistically and socially encouraged by motivated parents who receive and respond to pre-linguistic utterances.

As the language-relevant parts of babbling become incorporated into communication, they are accompanied by meaningful gestures; and deaf children will be well on the way to acquiring language. Importantly, however, manual babbling appears to be different from gesturing insofar as gestures are meaningful while manual babbling, by definition, is not (Marschark 1993: Chapter 5; cf. Meier & Willerman 1995). We therefore now turn to the consideration of the social and linguistic roles of gestures in early language development.

6.   Gestures: Language, social, and cognitive consequences for deaf children

The relations between early gestures and the first words have been of interest for a long time. The theoretical issue is this: If particular gestures depict object-related behaviors as primitive forms of symbolic representation, one would expect that growth in speech or sign repertoires would be linked to a simultaneous reduction in gesture frequency, as symbols and referents become generalized beyond the contexts in which they were originally learned. In contrast, if gestures and words serve similar functions, one would expect a positive relationship between gestural and verbal production in frequency as they shift away from being contextually bound to particular referents. The focus language development, and they remain in the repertoire through adulthood (Marschark 1994; Stokoe & Marschark 1999). Comparisons of the gestural systems of deaf children with those of hearing children thus are likely to be informative, revealing the commonality of early communication behavior that is eventually replaced by more conventional signed or spoken systems. The nature of the link between gesture and sign therefore should be a central focus of investigation, along with the nature of their cognitive underpinnings.

The role of gesture as a precursor of sign language and the correlation of gesture use and later vocabulary are particularly interesting given the claims of several researchers that deaf and hearing children learning sign language typically produce first signs earlier than peers learning spoken language produce their first words (e.g., Maestas y Moores 1980). While it is unclear whether there is truly an advantage for sign language over spoken language in early childhood (see below), it is noteworthy that deaf children acquiring spoken language do not appear to use gestures with any greater frequency than hearing children. As the first words come to be used by children, near the end of the first year, they do not replace gestures, but first tend to fill other roles in the repertoire, regardless of whether the children are hearing or deaf (e.g., Caselli & Volterra 1990).

What is the link between early gestures and the transition to the first signs? Siedlecki and Bonvillian (1993a) examined the components of communicative gestures among deaf and hearing children of deaf parents (aged 6 to 14 months). Observations every 4–6 weeks revealed that the children were most accurate in the locations of their earliest signs, followed by related movement, and then use of handshapes. They argued that this sequence also represents the order of phonological development within ASL. Siedlecki and Bonvillian (1993b) further found that by 14 months, the deletion of one of the hands from two-handed signs already appeared comparable to that observed among deaf adults, although the likelihood of deletion varied across signs depending on whether or not the hands came in contact with the body. Similarly, reporting on the development of handshapes, Siedlecki and Bonvillian (1997) found that their acquisition was influenced by both the point at which handshapes normally contact the sign location and the physical position of the handshape within two-handed signs. Although we do not know about parents' role in shaping such behaviors, these findings suggest a relatively smooth transition from gesturing to signing and a link between expressive language and the complexity of the language produced.

their manual productions in a more direct manner than is normally the case for hearing dyads. Further, Meier and Newport and others have emphasized the fact that the component parts of signs — the distinctive features of the language — are completely visible to sign language learners. This 100 percent availability contrasts with speech, in which only about 40 percent of articulation is immediately available, and also may provide a significant advantage for language development.

More recently, Volterra and Iverson (1995:373) described the sign advantage as "an artifact of a pattern of development in prelinguistic communicative gesture that is also observed in children not exposed to signed input". They argued that it does not occur in vocabulary development any more than it does in morphological or syntactic domains. Instead, Volterra and Iverson suggested that because gestures of both deaf and hearing children share the same modality as sign language, they provide a smooth transition to language in the visual mode. Rather than signs being produced earlier than spoken words, observers simply might be more likely to bestow linguistic status on the prelinguistic gestures of children in sign language environments. Consistent with this argument, Gregory and Hindley (1996) reported that the early gestures used by hearing children are less likely than those used by deaf children to be seen as *real* examples of communication.

Volterra and Iverson argued that empirical support for the sign advantage in the acquisition of early vocabulary is more apparent than real, and ascribed positive conclusions in that regard to methodological differences across studies. For example, they noted that the studies by Folven and Bonvillian (1987) and Orlansky and Bonvillian (1995) most frequently cited as supporting claims of a sign advantage, used relatively liberal scoring criteria relative to studies with hearing children learning spoken language. Volterra and Iverson reported relevant data from a sample of one-year-old children, all of whom were hearing and exposed only to spoken language. On average, the children demonstrated competence with twice as many gestures as words, and gestures were found to appear at approximately the same age as children's first words, 10–13 months. These findings were taken as support for augmented gestural repertoires rather than a sign advantage and a refutation of findings from the Bonvillian studies. The hearing children studied by Bonvillian and his colleagues, however, had been exposed primarily to sign language by their deaf parents. Volterra and Iverson's findings therefore do not allow us to reach any firm conclusion concerning an early sign advantage even while they emphasize the important role of gesture in language development.

In short, there continues to be debate concerning both the extent of any sign language advantage and its functional significance. As in many other issues concerning the language development of deaf children, a variety of background, situational, and child variables (e.g., cognitive level) contribute to the heterogeneity observed among children and across studies (Spencer 2000). The existence of a sign language advantage may be of continuing theoretical interest, even if it is small. Most important, however, is the finding that early exposure to sign language leads to normal language development, thus providing the basis for subsequent growth in other domains.

8.   The broad perspective: A tentative summary

Language is an essential component of normal development. Because the vast majority of deaf children are born to non-signing hearing parents, however, many of them are denied full access to many parts of the world — and interpersonal communication about it — until they have passed the most critical ages for language acquisition, the first three to four years. All available research indicates that for children with greater hearing losses, exposure only to spoken language usually falls short of giving children the linguistic tools they need for academic and social purposes. While access to English (or any other spoken/written language) may be essential for literacy, it is most important that deaf children, like hearing children, be able to communicate with their parents from the beginning.

From vocal and manual babbling to the first spoken and signed words, abundant research demonstrates that normal language development depends on frequent and regular communication interactions between deaf children and those around them, regardless of its modality. In young deaf and hearing children, manual and vocal babbling, respectively, are received by parents either as 'cute' or as attempts to communicate (usually, a little of each). In either case, babbling elicits social and language behavior on the part of others that help to support language development. Similarly, the precise linguistic role of early gestures is still being debated, but they clearly serve both social and practical communicative functions.

As both deaf and hearing children develop, their communication repertoires become larger and more sensitive to their communication partners. Babbling overlaps with gestures, and gestures overlap with the first words. While gestures may have a special role in signed languages, they are natural and normal for both deaf and hearing children. With the support of these building blocks, communication and language skills are acquired and become increasingly complex. Signed and spoken language subsequently follow the same course in deaf and hearing children — indicating the functional equivalence of precursors in the two modalities — even if a lack of early language experience creates a lag in development for some deaf children.

Deaf children with early access to language through deaf or signing-hearing parents demonstrate patterns of early communication and language development that both follow the same sequence and occur at the same rate as that observed in hearing children of hearing parents. For deaf children of hearing parents, a variety of factors will influence language growth. In particular, communication for young deaf children depends on visual access. Although this chapter has not considered in any detail the parental side of the language development waltz, considerable research has demonstrated the variety of strategies used by deaf parents to ensure communication with their young children (see Marschark et al. 2002: Chapter 4, for discussion).

It also is important to note that observed differences between children acquiring a spoken language and those acquiring a signed language as their first language may or may not have long-term implications for other domains of development. Transitory differences between the two may result from either the nature of the specific dimension under consideration or from the context in which they occur. Similarly, we need to be aware of possible interactions of early language development with other aspects of development. Theoretical and empirical discussions of deaf children's language development frequently focus on the nature of observed or hypothesized relationships between language and social or cognitive development. Beyond any direct effects of hearing loss and the modality of communication, however, this chapter has described a variety of factors related to children's hearing losses that also are likely to affect language development (e.g., parental receptiveness to early productions, approximation of prelinguistic utterances to language). The consequences of early communication, especially with diverse adults, thus feed back into language acquisition and other aspects of development. Qualitative and quantitative differences will continue to be observed between hearing and deaf children and among deaf children raised in different language environments. Any attempt to identify *the* locus of such differences is destined to fail. Understanding the nature of development and its outcomes for deaf children nevertheless requires that we have a very clear picture of early language experience and its interaction with characteristics of children and contexts. Language may not be the most important variable in development, but it sure beats whatever is in second place.

Notes

1. Given this greater responsibility on hearing mothers of deaf children, it is not surprising that most research in this area has focused on mother-child communication. Calderon and Low (1998), however, found that among 22 deaf and hard-of-hearing children of hearing parents, aged 3 to 7 years, those children whose fathers were present in the home demonstrated significantly superior expressive and receptive language skills, as well as superior early reading ability, relative to those with absent fathers. Results of the Calderon and Low study emphasize the importance of including fathers in practical, theoretical, and research considerations of young children with hearing loss.

2. *Motherese* typically is used to refer to the whole range of modifications in language addressed to young children, from exaggerated facial expression to prosody to syntactic modifications or, sometimes, more specifically to refer only to the paralinguistic character of such language. *Child directed language*, in contrast, is most often used to refer to modifications of syntax and vocabulary. In this chapter, the former term is used, in its most general sense, to refer to all of these language characteristics.

3. Quittner, Smith, Osberger, Mitchell, and Katz (1994) have reported significant differences in visual attention in older children (6–13 years), but that age group is beyond the scope of the present chapter. See Marschark et al. 2002: Chapter 4, for discussion.

4. The distinction here between *linguistically-relevant* and *language-relevant* is intended to capture the difference between structural (morphological) and social-communicative (psychological) aspects of language development.

5. Words in capital letters indicate English 'glosses' of signs in ASL.

6. There is a body of research showing that gestures accompany the speech of older hearing children in much the same way as they accompany the signs of older deaf children. That literature has been summarized elsewhere (Marschark 1994).

Phonology acquisition
in Brazilian Sign Language[*]

Lodenir Becker Karnopp

1. Introduction

The objective of this article is to present a descriptive overview of the phonological acquisition of Brazilian Sign Language (LIBRAS). For this purpose, we
adopt here the framework of Dependence Phonology and focus on the acquisition of handshape, location and movement. Our primary concern will be to
answer the following two questions:

1. How can we characterize the acquisitional phase that precedes the production of signs?
2. What types of handshape (HS), location (L) and movement (M) appear
   before the age of 30 months?

Studies about the phonological acquisition of signs are scarce and recent. The
first studies on the topic appeared in the early 1970s. Boyes-Braem (1973–
1990), McIntire (1977), Siedlecki and Bonvillian (1993a), Bonvillian and
Siedlecki (1996, 1997), Marentette (1995), and Karnopp (1999b) are some of
the researchers who have studied the phonology of sign language.

It is presupposed here that in the acquisition of the phonology of signs, a
child starts out with a basic representational structure composed only of
unmarked features. The location and the hand configuration units of the sign
constitute the *head* in a dependency-style representation. In the model being
used, movement is not considered to be a primitive unit, but the result of a
change in handshape, orientation or location.[1]

In the early phase of acquisition, a child produces signs using only the
unmarked specification. Subsequent stages show the gradual addition of
marked features, that, in this model, form the dependent units in the structure
(complements and specifiers).

2. A dependence model of sign language phonology

The concept of dependency has been utilized in linguistic theory to characterize the claim that elements within a particular domain may be asymmetrically related. The introduction of dependency can be associated with the notion that the two constituents of a constitute display a head-modifier relation, rather than being simply sisters. The incorporation of the dependency relation into phonological representations, in particular those characterizing the internal structure of the segment, has been primarily associated with the theory of phonological structure referred to as Dependency Phonology (Ewen 1995:570; van der Hulst 1989).

The dependency relation is a binary asymmetric relation in which one element in a construction is the head, and the other the dependent. The head-dependent relation was initially more familiar in syntactic work, and its interpretation as dependency was indeed first found in syntax. The application of the relation to phonological sequences incorporates the claim that such sequences are headed (Ewen 1995:571).

Van der Hulst (1993, 1995) proposes a representational model of sign language phonology combining insights from Sandler (1989) and principles of Dependency Phonology (Anderson & Ewen 1987). This model exploits the dependency framework by establishing that each head has headlike properties, and each dependent node adds complexity to the representation, and thus expresses markedness.

The term markedness has more than one interpretation. Here, it is presupposed that markedness is a relative property that correlates with complexity. As Sandler (1996:127) claims, the types of evidence traditionally adduced for determining markedness in the handshapes are: articulatory complexity, frequency in the world's languages, order of acquisition by children, order of loss in aphasia, and substitution errors. Below, a simplified version of that proposal which will serve as a basis of description of the acquisitional process, will be introduced.

This model incorporates two units: Location (the central or head unit) and Handshape (the dependent). Location is taken to be the head because, as compared to the handshape, it represents stable, non-spreading information. Handshape, but not Location, can be involved in regressive or progressive processes (Sandler 1989). Both units are internally structured. We will first discuss Location and then Handshape. The unit Location comprises a Major Place (or Location), Settings (specifying points in the location) and Manner (specifying properties of path movements).

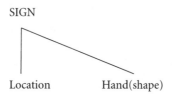

Figure 1. Dependence model of sign language phonology.

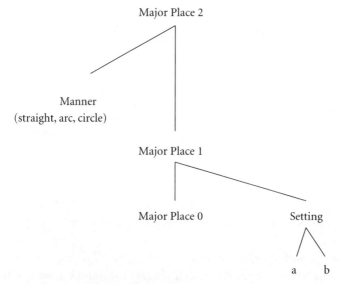

Figure 2. The internal structure of Major Place.

Path movement of the hand is analysed in terms of two Setting locations, specifying the beginning and the end of a (path) movement. Thus, in this model, there is no primitive unit Movement (as in Sandler 1989). To express different kinds of movement, van der Hulst (1995:26) uses three coordinates: high/low, ipsilateral/contralateral and near/far. In Figure 2 above, the letters *a* and *b* represent specifications for the initial and final settings within the major place or location. The Manner node allows features which specify properties of the path movement such as 'straight', 'circle', and 'arc'.

In Figure 3, we give the representation of the internal structure of Handshape. The handshape proper is embedded in a node called Hand, which dominates the unit Orientation as a specifier. The Orientation node can dominate features which represent the various orientations of the hand. If two such features are

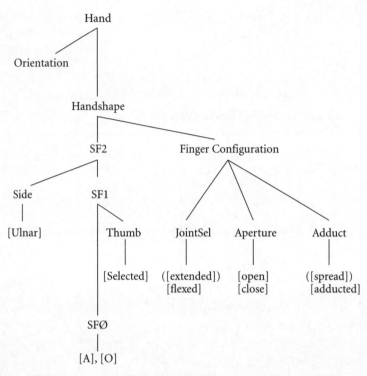

Figure 3. Model for the representation of handshapes (Brentari et al. n.d.).

specified this will represent an orientation change. The handshape node itself branches into two subunits: Selected Fingers (SF) and Finger Configuration (FC). SF itself is divided into a unit that specifies the fingers that will be selected in terms of two primitive features One [O] and All [A], and a unit which specifies the side of the hand (ulnar or radial) where a selected finger occurs. The selection of fingers tends to be constant throughout the sign (Mandel 1981). This is reflected by making Selected Fingers (SF)[2] the head of the representation of handshape. The elements [One] and [All] can enter in head-dependent relations and can be modified by a third element [Ulnar] specifying on which side of the hand fingers are selected. Radial side is the side of the index finger and Ulnar is located in the pinky side of the hand. The side of the hand is located in the specifier position of the Selected Finger node. The Finger Configuration node specifies bending of the finger joints, the aperture relationship between selected fingers and the thumb and also the spreading or non-spreading of selected fingers. The features [extended] and [spread] under Joint Selected and Adduct, respectively, have been put in parentheses. Brentari, van der Hulst, van der Kooij and Sandler (n.d.) assume that both dimensions are essentially unary, i.e. for both they have one feature which represents the marked state. Absence of a feature in both components implies extension and finger spread, respectively. The reason for including the parenthesized features is that they have been chosen in general to represent dynamic aspects of signs in terms of branching nodes.

We believe that a representational model of the sign that incorporates head-dependency relations provides a good starting point for the study of acquisitional stages because it introduces asymmetries that may be reflected in the order of incoming information. Other models which do not incorporate such asymmetries, while incorporating more or less the same units, simply make fewer predictions with regard to acquisitional stages. Acquisitional studies of syntax are routinely based on the idea that phrases are organized asymmetrically (i.e. have heads) and it seems unquestionable that such aspects of syntactic organization influence the progression of acquisition in syntax. In this article, I am accepting the basic premises of dependency phonology, viz. that phonological structure is asymmetrically organized, just like syntactic structure.

The dependence model also accounts nicely for acquisition facts as stated in Karnopp (1999). For instance, a child, Ana, essentially activated one node at the time, leading from the least complex structure to the most complex one. The model and the acquisition data that support this study also lend credence to the idea that features are unary, and oppositions consist of presence or absence of some element. Taken together, the arguments for the model of sign language proposed here are seen as leading novel support to dependency phonology as a universal theory. Considering these aspects, the dependence model was chosen as the framework to be adopted in this study.

3.   Studies on the phonological acquisition of sign language

Table 1 supplies some information about important studies of phonological acquisition in children acquiring signs.

In the first column, we observe that studies in the area of sign languages acquisition mostly deal with American Sign Language (ASL) data. My study complements this kind of research with data from a very different sign language, Brazilian Sign Language (LIBRAS). The number of informants in each study was between one and nine. The children's ages were between 1;0 and 5;9

Table 1. Studies developed in the sign phonological acquisition area

Author/Year/Language	Informant/Age/Sex	Children	Parents	Number of Signs	Session	Focus
Boyes-Braem (1973/1990) ASL	one child: Pola 2;7 F	Deaf	Deaf	–	1	Handshape
McIntire (1977) ASL	one child: FF (1;1–1;9) F	Deaf	Deaf	85–200	4	Handshape
Siedlecki & Bonvillian (1993) ASL	9 children (in months): (6–14), (6–15), (6–18), (7–18), (7–18), (8–17), (5–18), (11–16), (14–18)*	1 deaf 8 hearing	1 both deaf 1 deaf mother and hearing father; 1 deaf father and hearing mother	23, 31, 18, 31, 51, 46, 16, 139, 93	between 5 and 14, depends on the children	Location, Handshape, Movement
Bonvillian & Siedlecki (1996) ASL						Location
Bonvillian & Siedlecki (1997) ASL						Handshape
Marentette (1995) ASL	1 child: SJ (1;0–2;1)F (longitudinal)	Hearing		17, 34, 56, 151, 186, 176, 184	7	Location, Handshape, Movement
Karnopp (1994) LIBRAS	4 children: Lucas/2;8/M Carla/2;8/F Marina/4;9/F Marcelo/5;9/M	Deaf		67, 38, 80, 123	4	Handshape

* The corpus of the three articles in this block is the same. The difference is in the analysis focus.

years. In relation to sex, it is observed that the studies include more female informants than male ones, that is, the sum of all the studies results in eleven girls and five boys.[3] Columns 3 and 4 present some characteristics of the informants and their parents. In total, six children are deaf and nine are hearing, although all the parents are deaf and use sign languages.

The number of different signs produced by the children during the recording sessions is specified in column 5. The number of data collection sessions for each study was between 1 and 14, lasting around 30 minutes to one hour each. In total, there are five studies with longitudinal language sampling and two cross-sectional studies. Within the studies presented in Table 1, each one focused on some specific aspect of the phonological development. Handshape is the aspect that has received most attention.

4. Methodology

The results presented here are data from a deaf child, Ana, who is the daughter of deaf parents, and has two deaf sisters. Ana's entire family uses Brazilian Sign Language (LIBRAS). The filming sessions started when Ana was eight months old, and cover the period between 8 months and 30 months of age. This phase is very meaningful for sign acquisition and includes the emergence of the first productions. The sessions lasted around 30 minutes each and most of the time the filming was done in Ana's parents' house. The goal was to record different instances of spontaneous everyday communication in which Ana interacted with her parents and sisters. The data collection involved spontaneous communication situations in which Ana interacted with toys, drawings, house objects, food, children's books and copybooks, objects belonging to the informant or to the family. The filming sessions sought to record different children's routines in order to obtain a family lexicon, reflecting Ana's everyday life. All productions selected for the transcription, description and data analysis were produced in spontaneous situations. All signs produced immediately after the parents or interviewer were regarded as imitations and eliminated from the analysis.

All the video tapes (in total 29 video tapes lasting from 30 to 40 minutes each) were transcribed by the author of this study, who is also a LIBRAS interpreter. Doubtful cases were discussed with the informant's parents.

Ana's productions were included in two databases: one which contains only signs and one containing manual actions. The database containing manual actions was named PRO-GESTOS (gesture production) and was used for the transcription of productions referring to the pre-linguistic period. On the other hand, the database including signs — abbreviated here as AQUI-LIBRAS (LIBRAS acquisition) — used a scheme of phonetic transcription (SignPhon 1996)[4] with the objective of coding the linguistic production period in terms of the units that constitute the signs.

Manual actions included productions that can have a meaning, while their shape does not seem to derive from any adult lexical item in LIBRAS. Following Marentette's proposal (1995) *manual actions* were identified as belonging to one of three categories — pointing out, manual babbling, and social gestures. These can be described as follows:

1.   *Pointing:* This action involves finger extension directed to a person, object, or place. In sign languages, pointing also functions as a personal pronoun, when a child points at him/herself or at others (Petitto 1987; Pizzuto 1990). This deictic or anaphoric use could be considered as a lexical item. Pointing at body parts can also be a lexical item, as in the sign for EYE. Marentette (1995: 51–52) shows that it is not clear at which age pointing starts to perform such linguistic functions. Distinguishing pointing as a manual action from pointing that carries lexical information (pronominal, anaphoric or deictic) is difficult, and criteria for making a distinction seem arbitrary (Pizzuto 1990). While it is recognized that coding such productions appropriately is difficult, all pointing in the prelinguistic period was coded as a manual action. Accepting, then, the classification proposed by Marentette (1995), the following types of pointing action were noted: pointing at objects and places, pointing at herself and at other people, and pointing at body parts.

2.   *Manual babbling:* This action consists of a hand activity which, although it does not seem to carry any meaning, presents a specific phonetic shape. Manual babbling is distinct from signs because signs have both shape and meaning. Again, following Marentette (1995: 52–53), manual babbling is assumed to be a hand action if it shows phonetic structure but does not show a stable meaning, or at least its meaning is not perceived as stable by the parents.

3.   *Social gestures:* A social gesture is considered a manual action if it presents an interpretable meaning and a shape but does not correspond to a lexical item of the adult pattern in the LIBRAS. Social gestures are typically used both by deaf children and hearing ones, and include actions like waving and hand clapping. Such productions are normally excluded from a linguistic analysis because children are often trained to produce them (Acredolo & Goodwin

1988). Among the social gestures produced by Ana, the following are found: waving, hand clapping, kiss sending with the hand and some facial expressions.[5]

5. Development of manual actions

This section gives a brief overview of the findings based on the codes in the PRO-GESTOS (pro-gestures) database (Karnopp 1999a). That database supplies information about the interlocutor, the visual informer's attention (i.e., eye gaze, or the direction towards which the child looks while producing a certain sign) and the way the sign was produced.

Informal observation of the interaction between Ana and the adult revealed the emphasis given by the parents on visual contact between interlocutors. The parents use signs with special characteristics to attract Ana's attention; for example, they overact facial expressions, repeat signs and do slower and larger movements. Ana seems to appreciate this kind of communication and keeps looking at their faces.

A record of the productions considered to be pre-linguistic was kept during the whole period of investigation with the objective of identifying the kind and frequency of manual actions produced. The figures (4)–(7) below concern the percentages of manual babbling, social gestures and pointing.

Pre-linguistic production was recorded from the time the subject was 8 months old until she was 30 months old. Figure 4 shows the development of manual babbling, social gestures and pointing. As can be seen, most of the manual actions produced were instances of pointing (71%) during this period.

The development of manual babbling is shown in figure 5 below: it initially presents a high percentage of use (54%) but decreases with age until it disappears at age 2;1.

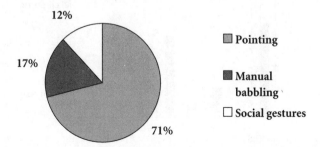

Figure 4. Production of manual actions.

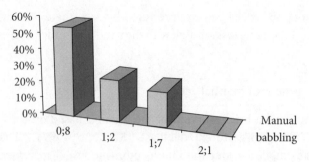

Figure 5. Manual babbling development.

Social gestures show a similar pattern, as shown in figure 6. They start with a relatively high frequency of hand clapping (28%) and farewell gestures (16%). At 1;2, kiss sending (5%) and facial expressions (2%) also appear; hand clapping and farewell continue to be produced, but drop in frequency (around 5% each). At 1;7, there is a slight increase in production for all social gestures (facial expressions increase to 10%, farewell to 9%, hand clapping to 14% and kiss sending 7%). At 2;1, however, no occurrence of any kind of social gesture is found at the filming sessions.[6]

In relation to the development of the pointing types, pointing to objects prevails as the most frequent, as seen in figure 7. One can observe that there was an increase in the variety and quantity of pointing types. Their production increases at 1;7 and becomes more varied at that time. At 2;1 there is a new increase, now for all types of pointing, and pointing to objects reaches 23%.

These data show that social gestures, manual babbling and pointing are the

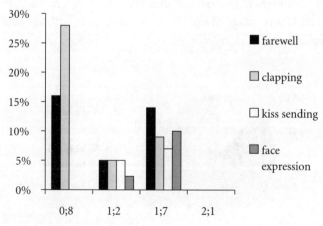

Figure 6. Social gestures development.

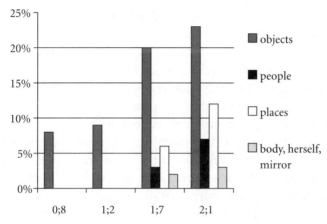

Figure 7. Pointing development.

first productions that precede sign articulation. Additionally, some pre-linguistic productions disappear with time, while others become more prominent. Manual babbling and social gestures start with a high percentage of use, and disappear at 2;1. Pointing takes place most often and, differently from the other productions, continues to take place, and increased with age.

6. Phonological description of signs

In this section, we describe Ana's first signs, and the pattern of increase in her early production, as well as the substitutions found in the phonological components of her first signs. The earliest signs recorded and the subsequent increase in Ana's vocabulary are presented in Table 2 below.

Table 2. Earliest signs and subsequent productions

Age	Nr. of sign types
0;11	2
1;1	4
1;5	12
1;9	28
2;1	49
2;5	81

Ana produced 176 sign types in 288 tokens. However, the analysis presented here is based on the 176 sign types. In the period between 8 to 30 months of age, Ana initially produced manual babbling, then started to produce utterances with one sign and later produced simple sentences. The signs were produced in contexts of one, two or more sign utterances. The findings indicate that of the 288 occurrences, 200 were obtained from the production of utterances of two or more signs and 88 occurrences from a one-sign utterance.

For the identification of sign meaning, two aspects were observed: the production of signs by the children and the target production. A list of signs produced by Ana was made and then compared with the production of the parents' signs (target). The interpretation of each sign in the corpus was discussed with the parents in order to check the meaning assigned to it. Ana made substitutions in at least one of the phonological units in a total of 57/288 signs. The kinds of substitutions as well as the percentage of productions of each phonological feature (handshapes, movements, hand orientations and locations) are shown in Figure 8 below.

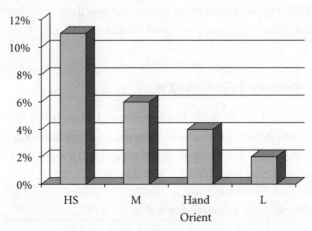

Figure 8. Substitution of the phonological units (in %).

It is relevant to highlight that the units *handshape, movement, hand orientation* and *location* produced by the child were considered correct if close to the target production, i.e., not phonologically distinct from the parents' production. If the child produced a sign differently from her parents, we analyzed which of the units were omitted or substituted, or, in other words, what differences there were between the child's production and parents' production.

Another instance of deviation from the target production observed was non-dominant hand deletion. Such deletion is characterized by the removal of the weak hand, which serves as place of articulation, resulting in a location change. The deletion of a hand, when both should be active, was not considered a substitution but an alternative option in the production. According to the findings, Ana's location productions are only 2% of substitutions; whereas 11% of handshapes are substitutions. These data are further evidence that locations have a central role in children's initial sign shaping.

In order to establish the stages of development of handshape, movement, and location, three kinds of criteria were used:

1. the order of appearance of handshapes, locations and movements in the signs of the child;
2. the frequency with which each unit appeared in the child's sign lexicon;
3. the accuracy of each of the units produced, and whether there were any changes in production accuracy and complexity with increasing age or vocabulary size.

7.   Handshape acquisition

The handshape (HS) acquisition phases were analysed using the model 'One over All and All over One' (Brentari et al. n.d.), previously referred to. The HS acquisition investigation considered the three criteria described above, i.e., the order of appearance, the frequency with which each HS appeared in the child's sign lexicon and the degree of accuracy of each of the HS's produced. Based on the findings, handshape production was grouped according to age as can be seen in Table 3.

Table 3 shows that HS's at the initial position of the sign were Ana's first productions and that final position (HS_FIN) and non-dominant handshape (HS_ND) were produced afterwards. Here I analyze only the HS's which occurred at the initial position of the sign. Table 4 shows a description of handshape features at the initial position (HS_ini) of the sign.

The features [One], [All], [adducted], [closed] and [Thumb: selected] which includes C1, C3, F2, B1, B2, F8, A1, A2, A3 handshapes were the most frequent HS in Ana's system. They were also the same as those which were produced earlier, around 11–13 months old. It is important to highlight that handshapes C1 and C3 are phonetic distinctions because they are produced

Table 3. Age at which the HS were produced at the initial (HS_INI) and the final position (HS_FIN) of the sign, and the non-dominant hand (HS_ND)

HS_ini	HS_fin	HS_nd
0;11	1;3	1;7
1;1	1;6	1;10
1;5	1;8	2;2
1;7		
2;0		

interchangeably in relation to a similar lexical item. Besides, there is an articulation similarity between H4, H5 and H6, because such HS contain the same fingers selected and the same finger configuration, which varies only at the degree of opening between the index finger and the thumb.

The emergence of the phonological system in Ana will be described in terms of characteristics of each phase by using the model of Brentari et al. (n.d.) and proposing a dependence relation between the components of the segments.[7]

Handshape

Selected Fingers

[One], [All]

Figure 9. Phase 1.

Phase 1 characteristics (C1, C3, F2):
Ana initially produced the selected finger opposition [One]–[All], in which only the nucleus of the node of the selected finger (SF) was activated. The phonological representation of these contrasting HS's involves the absence or presence of [One]. In a detailed study, Siedlecki and Bonvillian (1993a) establish an order of acquisition of ASL handshapes, and at stage I, the head Finger Selection node is activated. Thus, what is acquired is the basic ONE-ALL opposition, as the results of this study confirm.

Phase 2 characteristics (B1, B2, F8):
This phase involves the activation of the Finger Configuration node. A new feature — Adduction: [adducted] — is added to the basic shape [All]. Most

Table 4. Description of the features acquisition of HS_ini

Phase	Years; months	Handshape type	What is acquired?*
1	0;11	C1 F2	[SF: One/(All)]
2	1;1	B1 B2 F8	[Adduction: adducted] [Thumb: selected]
3	1;5	A1 A2 A3	[Aperture: closed] in [All]
4	1;7	J1 I1 K1 G1	[Aperture: open] in [All] [Aperture: closed] in [All]
5	2;0	H1 H4 G4 B5 F5 I4 C18	[Flexion: flex; base] in [One] [Flexion: flex; base] in [All] [SF: I^u] (side: ulnar)

* The criteria to analyse *What is acquired?* in Table 4 were accuracy of production, order of position and production frequency.

likely the feature [adducted] is the nucleus of Finger Configuration in Ana's phonological system because it appears earlier than other features. At this point in development, Ana starts to use the thumb by extending it. Thus, the node SF (Selected Fingers) branches out, as represented in Figure 10 below.

Phase 3 characteristics (A1, A2, A3):
The new development of this phase is the *opening* node under Finger Configuration Figure 11. The handshapes A1 and A2 can be seen as an elaboration of F2, resulting in the addition of an opening feature — [closed] — at the node finger configuration. If we consider the node [aperture] under Finger Configuration as a Complement, we may conclude that the acquisition of Complements follows the acquisition of Nucleus (as in phases 1 and 2 above). In the model proposed by Brentari et al. (n.d), the handshape A3 is considered a phonetic variation of A1 because there is no indication that these handshapes can be distinctive. Although A3 is produced later than A1 and A2, no new features are added; rather, A3 is formed by a new combination of the features already acquired.

Phase 4 characteristics: J1, I1, K1, G1, H1, G4, I4
Brentari et al. (n.d) propose that the I1 and J1 handshapes — curved shapes — result from the distinction applied to the node aperture. If this is the case, the J1 shape produced by Ana involves the open version applied to the form [All] and [adduction]. The I1 shape involves the closed version applied to [all] and [adduction].

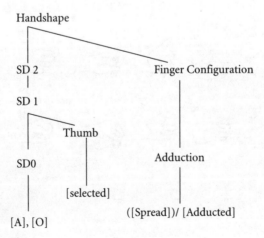

Figure 10. Phase 2.

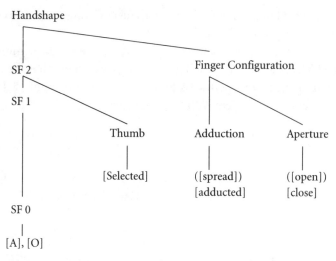

Figure 11. Phase 3.

Ana combines features already acquired and produces a handshape in which the aperture feature [closed] is applied to the selected finger feature [one]. That option already belongs to Ana's phonological system and is simply applied to a new handshape. The difference between G1 and K1 refers to the non-selected fingers, which does not carry any implications for the representations.

Phase 5 characteristic (H4, B5, C6, F5, C18):
Another characteristic of Ana's development refers to the node selection of the joints (SelJ). The model (Brentari et al. n.d.) makes the production of extension (non-flexion), flexion and a third option that restricts flexion to the base of the finger joints possible. Thus, the node SelJ presents the following development:

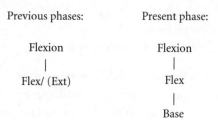

Figure 12. Phase 5.

A new feature in this phase introduces the use of the ulnar side to the node [Selected Finger]. In this phase, two new nodes are acquired: Hand Side under the node Selected Finger and Flexion under Finger Configuration. According to the Brentari et al. model, Hand Side is Spec of SF.

Therefore the handshapes produced by Ana are clearly the combination of features which are already part of her phonological system. They are combinations resulting from the nodes [Adduction], [Aperture] and [Selection of Joints], referent to the fingers [All] or [One] (Figure 13).

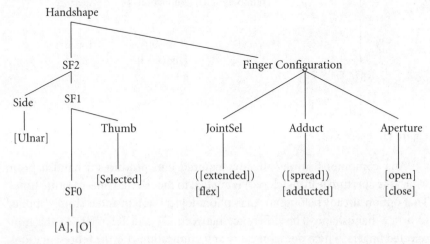

Figure 13. Phase 5.

We can conclude from the description presented that the Nucleus is acquired at the initial period, followed by the acquisition of Complements and Specifiers. Thus, Complements cannot be acquired before the Nucleus. Specifiers, in their turn, cannot be acquired before the Complement either. Thus, the component structure is built up as follows:

1. Nucleus
2. Nucleus + Complement
3. Specifier + [Nucleus + Complement].

Reviewing the most frequent handshape types at the initial position of the sign in Ana's repertoire, it is clear that the handshapes produced are non-marked. It is possible that some handshapes which were not produced during the data collection period might have been produced after the investigation period. Nevertheless, Ana's system presented all the features forecast by Brentari et al.'s model 'One over All and All over One'.

8.   Location acquisition

Our purpose in this section is to describe order of appearance, frequency and production accuracy of the location parameter in Ana's acquisition. In order to investigate such aspects, 176 signs were selected from the filming sessions. Locations are subdivided into locations on the body and locations in the space in front of the signer (neutral space). Locations in neutral space are subdivided into body-related locations and absolute locations. In body-related locations, a further distinction is made between locations on the non-dominant hand and locations on other parts of the body. Body-related locations are locations in neutral space that are close to a specific body location. Absolute locations in neutral space are defined in relation to the three Cartesian dimensions left-right, up-down, and front-back. These planes are called the horizontal plane, the vertical plane, and the parallel plane (Blees et al. 1996:49).

The procedure followed to determine location considered the major place as well as the subspace (setting) in which the sign was produced, for example, if the sign was produced at the nose, we regarded the body as the major area and the nose as the subspace of that sign. The production of locations in the initial position of the sign (LOC_INI) is grouped according to age and divided into the major area and subspaces. Within this grouping, the feature of location acquisition was described.

Table 5. Phases of acquisition of Location in the initial position of sign (LOC_INI)

Age	Major place	Subspace
0;11	Body	[nose], [mouth] [eye]
	Neutral space	[peripheral], [ipsilateral] , [high], [medium], [region of head], [above head region], [front side], [medium]
1;6	Body	[chin], [cheek] [face]
	Neutral space	[centre], [low], [back]
2;1	Body	[lip], [fronthead], [neck], [head side]
	Neutral Space	[contralateral]
	Related to the body	[head x] [trunk x]
	Non-dominant hand	[hand palm]

According to the analysis, Ana produced from 96% to 100% of locations correctly. The first locations were produced only in the body area and in neutral space. At 1;6 new features in the head area and in the neutral space started being produced. Locations related to the body or to the non-dominant hand were produced only at 2;1. The first sign related to the body was produced in a point near the head and also near the trunk. Besides locations in the head area, there were locations being produced near the neck. The production of locations at the contralateral side (i.e. the side opposite to the hand which is producing the sign) of the vertical plane took place in neutral space.

The results show that all three criteria for the identification of acquisition stages — the order of appearance, the frequency, and the accuracy of production — converge in the acquisition of locations in LIBRAS. The first locations produced were also those which had the largest number of occurrences. Regarding accuracy, the results show an invariable aspect: high precision of the correct production in all the environments (initial, final and in the non-dominant hand). Major area locations (LOC_INI) were produced (according to the frequency of occurrence) as follows: in the neutral space (63%), at the body and related to the body (35%) and on the non-dominant hand (2%).

9.   Movement acquisition

The approach used in this article follows the proposal of the No-Movement theory of van der Hulst (1993, 1995), van der Kooij (1997) and Blees, Crasborn, van der Hulst and van der Kooij (1996), which consider movement either as a location change, an orientation change, or a handshape change. The transcription system proposed by these authors regards movement as a result of the specification of two locations, i.e. two points in the body region or the neutral space. In a similar way, movement can be the result of specifications of two (or more) handshapes or orientations.

Changes in location are called movements of direction, and can be articulated in different ways: straight, circular, and arcing, among others. Changes in handshape or in hand orientations are called hand internal movements. Changes in handshape include opening, closing, clawing, hingeing, wiggling, waving, rubbing, scissoring. The movement resulting from the specification of hand orientation includes changes in palm orientation, and/or finger orientation. Thus first I have identified the movements produced at the initial phase of development; these are grouped into phases as shown in Table 6.

When she was eleven months old, Ana produced straight, wide movements. These movements are straight, contact takes place at the end of the movement

Table 6. Phases in the acquisition of movement (M)

Age	Changes	Path-move-ment	Contact	Repetition	Speed	Intensity	Size
0;11	Location	Straight	At the end	Multiple		Hold at the final M	
1;1	Hand orientation	Circular	At the beginning Continuous	A repetition of directional M Multiple repetition of hand internal M	Fast Slow	Strong	Small Big
1;3	Handshape	Arc	Double In the middle	A repetition of hand internal M		Tense	

(Loc_fin), and repetition of movement is characterized as multiple. The intensity shows that the hold is at the end of the movement. Hold here must be understood as a lengthening of the time during which the articulator is held at a specific location and gives an impression of increased strain.

From 1;1 onwards, the production of movements involving changes in the orientation of the hand begins. In addition to straight movements, circular movements are produced as well. If contact is produced, this occurs at the beginning, at the end or in a continuous way in relation to location. Movement can be fast or slow and can either be big or small.

From 1;3 years of age, changes internal to the sign appear. In addition to the straight and circular movements produced in previous phases, movement in an arc shape is first seen at this age. The repeated production of movement appears as well as double contact and contact which occurs in the middle of the movement. A repeated production of movement appears, more specifically, as an internal movement which is carried out by a change of hand orientation or handshape. More intensity of movements are observed in this stage.

Thus, based on an analysis of Ana's data we can see that movements are acquired in the order of their phonological complexity. Firstly she produces straight movements which is a result of location change, and then she produces hand internal movement, which is the result of specification of two different orientations or handshapes.

10. Conclusion

Following recent work in language acquisition, the approach used in this investigation has sought to describe some aspects of the phonological acquisition of LIBRAS. More specifically, two questions were discussed in this article:

1. How can we characterize the acquisitional phase that precedes the production of signs?
2. What types of handshape (HS), location (L) and movement (M) appear by the age of 30 months?

In this section, I will summarize the answers that have been provided in the previous sections. As far as the second question is concerned, we attempted to answer it by using empirical evidence based on the frequency of occurrence, production accuracy and order of appearance of handshapes, locations and movements in the initial vocabulary of a deaf child. We also attempted to systematize the LIBRAS phonological acquisition data in order to describe the phonological parameters of acquisition and the relation between the nuclear and dependent constituents. As to methodology, the programme used in the sign transcription process (SIGNPHON 1996) was used to code all the linguistic productions in this study, since it is a complete transcription system for the description and analysis of signs.

In the description of hand actions, we have sought to investigate productions which preceded signs: social gestures, manual babbling and pointing were identified as Ana's first hand productions. Ana's first signs were produced at 11 months of age. Her linguistic production during the period investigated included utterances consisting of a single sign, of two signs (often a combination of sign and pointing) and simple sentences. A comparison of LIBRAS and ASL shows precision in initial phonological production. Both in LIBRAS (Karnopp 1999) and in ASL (Siedlecki & Bonvillian 1993a; Marentette 1995), location was the first phonological unit produced correctly; movement was produced less precisely than location; and handshape was the last unit produced correctly. The observation of phonological development showed that, as time went by, there was an increase in the number of phonemes produced and in their variety. The articulation of phonemes (Handshape, Location, Movement) tended to be more precise as well.

Our research on handshape parameters yielded the following results:

1. Handshape was the parameter in which substitutions were most frequently found.
2. The handshapes used in substitutions were those considered unmarked cross-linguistically, i. e. those which were easily articulated.
3. Ana produced only a subgroup of handshapes, that is, a relatively small number of the group of 46 handshapes in LIBRAS (Ferreira Brito 1995).
4. Ana produced 20 different types of HS which involved the combination of features under the Finger Selected node and/or Finger Configuration node.
5. Ana acquired all the features forecast by Brentari et al.'s model 'One over All and All over One' at 30 months of age. This means that the head constituents of the handshape representation (Selected Fingers) are acquired in the initial period and that the dependent constituents [Finger Configuration] are acquired afterwards and based on the first.

The description of the acquisition of location showed that locations were produced in the body area (nose, mouth and eye) and in neutral space at the age of 0;11 to 2;0. From 2;1 years of age, locations started being produced in places related to the body and on the non-dominant hand. Locations which involved major place and salient contrasts (in the neutral space and in the head region) were acquired in the initial phases. Locations typically acquired in later phases involved the non-dominant hand or places which required more detailed distinctions in the articulation. Van der Hulst (1995b) suggests that locations are produced with high precision because they are head constituents in sign lexical organisation and, therefore, the information about location can play a central role in the child's initial phonology.

The description of movement acquisition by Ana shows moderate precision in the production of directional and internal movement of the hand, with the frequent use of a small range of possibilities. The data suggest that there is a gradation in relation to the complexity in the acquisition of movement, including the internal movement of the hand. The present study shows the development of accuracy over the course of the study. With few exceptions, Ana produced signs like the adult model (parental signers). She produced only permissible combinations of HS, L and M in her sign production. Her signs were well-formed in terms of the combination of phonological units. Ana showed a clear trend towards production of HS, L, and M as she got older. The HS, L and M produced by Ana provide the best evidence of phonological organization. This organization is not the same as that of the target language, LIBRAS, but it is Ana's first step toward that system.

Thus, in phonological acquisition, order, frequency and accuracy of formation and production show that:

1. For the handshape unit, the nucleus feature is Selected Fingers [one/all], and the dependent feature is Finger Configuration. The order of acquisition is Nucleus, Complements and Specifiers.
2. For the location parameter, the nucleus of representation is the major area and the subspaces in which the signs are articulated are dependent.
3. In the process of phonological acquisition, nuclear features were acquired in a precise and frequent way, and were the first to appear in the child's production. Dependent features are then substituted and acquired after the production of nuclear features.

Therefore, LIBRAS acquisition data show that in the initial phase of linguistic development the child operates with a basic representation of nuclear constituents, and maps all his/her productions within that representation. As acquisition continues, the child specifies other features which were not present in the initial representation. That specification takes place gradually and is represented as dependent constituents.

Notes

* I thank Harry van der Hulst and Denise Lacerda for comments on an earlier version of this text.

1. The basic argument is that movements are very often redundant in signs, if the beginning and endpoint of the signs are represented. In van der Hulst's theory (1993), movement is a result of two locations, orientations or handshapes which are specified in the phonological representation of the sign.

2. In the model (Figure 3), SF 0, SF 1, SF 2 represent the three different levels of the Selected Finger Node.

3. The subjects of Bonvillian's and Siedlecki's studies (1993a, 1996, 1997) were grouped together because the informants are the same in the three studies.

4. Sign Phonological Transcription System proposed by Blees, Crasborn, van der Hulst and van der Kooij (1996).

5. Examples of facial expressions categorised like gestures: head movement for affirmation (YES) and negation (NO).

6. Facial expressions have not disappeared from that moment on, but start being produced as one of the phonological components of signs. Since the study of facial expressions was not within the scope of this research, they are not mentioned again here (see chapter by Reilly and Anderson, this volume, for more details).

7. Discussion presented by Menuzzi (1999).

Transcription as a tool for understanding

The Berkeley Transcription System for sign language research (BTS)

Nini Hoiting and Dan I. Slobin

1. Introduction

Transcription is the very start of a linguistic analysis of a corpus. In this respect, the transcribing of sign language data is not different from transcribing data from any other language, although systematic linguistic research on sign language is less than half a century old. Stokoe's *cherology* (sign phonetic/ notational system) appeared in 1960. This means that there is hardly any notational tradition to build on. Although Miller (1994a) has provided the field with family trees of notational systems, including more recent technologically based ones, the basic problem is that there is hardly agreement on what constitutes a linguistic unit in sign languages.

Of course, transcription is not the first set of choices that a researcher is confronted with: one must begin with data. The conditions for data gathering in this young linguistic discipline have not been established, and there is a general need for a more ethnographic approach than appears to be the practice. In this paper we will restrict ourselves to issues of transcribing videotaped data of sign language interactions with preschool-age children. In addition, the fact that most sign languages are not standardized, and have not been adequately described, leads to reliance on the linguistic intuitions of a small number of native signers. Thus we are dealing with a language type that we still know very little about, whatever the linguistic level one wants to analyze. Our proposals for transcription are based on the need for developmental analysis of signing, with attention to units of meaning and conversational interaction.

The system presented here is the product of the Berkeley Sign Language Acquisition Project, developed in research meetings from 1998 to 2001.[1] Our raw data consist of about 400 hours of videotapes of signing deaf children and their Deaf and hearing interlocutors in home and preschool settings in the Netherlands and the United States. The research goal is to document quantitative and qualitative differences in adult input and children's uptake. The data include both Deaf parents and hearing parents who are acquiring a sign language. Thus the input is often imperfect, and the data represent both children acquiring a first language and adults acquiring a second language. Apart from selecting the relevant sequences of interactive signing from our naturalistic data, our more problematic concern was to capture the linguistic and communicative elements being used by these children and their parents. The basic research question is: How do children and parents construct shared meaning in their communicative patterns? Given these goals, a transcription at the level of basic elements of handshape, movement, and location would be too fine-grained. The widespread practice of glossing would also be inappropriate, since this would bias our analysis to issues of translation into a spoken language. (The inadequacy of glossing was made immediately obvious to us when we confronted English glosses of American Sign Language with Dutch glosses of the Sign Language of the Netherlands.) Our theoretical interest is at the level of meaning components — that is, the ways in which semantic elements are combined into lexical items and utterances. The fact that we have to deal with a language that uses simultaneous and successive manual and non-manual means to structure signed messages, set us the task of how to devise a transcription system that would capture the full array of meaning components in sign languages. We considered it essential to capture these components — manual and nonmanual, conventional and gestural — without prejudging their formal linguistic status. In our opinion, we must first have a full documentation of linguistic behavior before we can ascertain whether particular types of components are standardized signs or gestural accompaniments, and whether particular forms are productive in the use of an individual signer. This enterprise resulted in the design of the Berkeley Transcription System (BTS) for signed languages, presented in detail below.

2. Transcription as theory and as technology

Elinor Ochs (1979), in an important paper written a quarter-century ago, brought the issue of transcription to the attention of child language researchers. She underlined the facts that "the transcriptions are the researcher's data" and "transcription is a selective process reflecting theoretical goals and definitions"

(Ochs 1979: 44). These points are especially relevant to sign language research today. The sign languages used by Deaf people gained recognition as languages when a notation system was made available. Within the anthropological attempts to transcribe the sign languages used by Plains Indians of the United States, LaMont West (1960) laid the notational foundation that Stokoe (Stokoe, Casterline & Croneberg 1976) used and improved to represent the combinatorial structure of the signs used by the American Deaf population, thereby claiming the linguistic status of American Sign Language (ASL). Stokoe's notational efforts were supported by the use of film and photo, providing detailed depictions of the systematically structured sublexical components that seemed to be the building blocks of the lexical signs of ASL. This early stage of notation clearly shows the theoretical impact of transcription, in that it made a clear claim for a formational, *phonological* level in sign languages. That is, signs are systematically put together from component elements of handshape, location, and movement, in the same way that words are systematically composed of articulatory/acoustic elements. The support of the notations by still photographs of handshapes provided precise documentation of the proposed units of analysis. With the rapid developments in video technology — now digitized and accessible to computer processing — we have fully adequate documentation of the physical and temporal parameters of sign languages.

Nevertheless, although there are dozens of lexicons of various sign languages from around the world, and a few partial sign grammars, in the year 2002 there are still basic linguistic problems to solve in this field. One of the remaining puzzles that concerns us here is the determination of the components that construct form-meaning relationships in space and time. On the lexical level, comparable to the word level in spoken languages, we do know something about the units of many sign languages. However the morphemic level is still a hotly debated issue, and it is this level in particular — in acquisition — that we want to know about in more detail. We are concerned with the learner's mental processes of analyzing events and signed utterances into components, with the aim of producing and comprehending utterances in communicative contexts.

3.   Sharing the data

The goal of all transcription is to produce a permanent written record of communicative events, allowing for analysis and re-analysis. In the field of sign language research, many researchers have had to work in isolation from other projects, due to a lack of standard transcription formats and an internationally accessible database, such as has been available for many years in the field of acquisition of spoken languages (MacWhinney 2000). At the start of our project we made a clear decision: We wanted our data to be archived and publicly accessible for sharing, discussing, and other types of scientific analysis or re-analysis. That is, a major goal of BTS is to provide resources for other research-ers, now and in the future. Therefore, we aim at a standard means of represent-ing the data of sign language acquisition, across research projects and sign languages. Furthermore, given the expectation of new developments in the field, as well as varying research goals, we aim at a system that is open to revision and applicable to a range of analyses and theoretical approaches. It will come as no surprise, therefore, that the worldwide CHILDES system came to mind as our inspiration.

That system has provided child language researchers with a common format for transcription and analysis of data, along with a large and growing archive of materials from a large number of spoken languages.[2] The system describes itself in the following terms (http://childes.psy.cmu.edu):

> The CHILDES system provides tools for studying conversational interactions. These tools include a database of transcripts, programs for computer analysis of transcripts, methods for linguistic coding, and systems for linking tran-scripts to digitized audio and video.

BTS has joined CHILDES, where it is available as Chapter 11 of the online CHAT manual, as well as in the published version (MacWhinney 2000). Current versions and continuing discussion of BTS are available on a website organized by Brenda Schick (http://www.Colorado.EDU/slhs/btsweb/). The rationale for BTS can be found in Slobin, Hoiting, Anthony, Biederman, Kuntze, Lindert, Pyers, Thumann and Weinberg (2001). Our eventual goal is to contribute our sign language transcriptions, in BTS, to the CHILDES archive. For this reason, BTS adheres to CHAT format, allowing the international community to access and search sign language data using the CLAN software tools provided by CHILDES.

4. Challenges of transcription

Every publication on sign language has to decide on the appropriate level of analysis and means of representing handshapes, locations, movements, and information conveyed by face and posture. Representations of signs range from detailed notation of physical elements, through pictures and diagrams, to glosses in the written language of one country or another. In most instances, such representations cannot be reduced to the ASCII keyboard — a prerequisite to international data-sharing on the CHILDES model.

Stokoe began the modern era of sign language linguistics by developing a sort of *phonological* transcription[3], though his terminology is in some ways more appropriate: "Analogous with the *phoneme* is the sign language *chereme* (CARE-eem, the first syllable from a Homeric Greek word meaning 'handy')" (Stokoe et al. 1976:xxix). His system requires a large collection of idiosyncratic symbols, although Mandel has reduced them to an ASCII version (http://world.std.com/~mam/ASL.html).[4] Another phonological transcription system, using only ASCII characters, is SignPhon (http://www.leidenuniv.nl/hil/sign-lang/signphon2.html). There are several modern attempts to represent signed languages on the level of formational components such as those first isolated by Stokoe. These systems make use of sets of iconic symbols for handshapes, locations, movements, and nonmanual elements, and provide special keyboards and related computer facilities:

HamNoSys: http://www.sign-lang.uni-Hamburg.de/Projekte/HamNoSys/default.html
Sign Writing: www.SignWriting.org
SignFont: http://members.home.net/dnewkirk/signfont/

All of these are useful for various purposes, including detailed linguistic analysis as well as first-language literacy for Deaf children. However, none of them is at the level of analysis required by our sort of research, and most of them cannot function without special fonts. In any case, this level of transcription is too fine-grained for our purposes — that is, transcription and analysis of children's acquisition of lexicon, morphology, and syntax. Stokoe's system and its derivatives correspond most closely to the International Phonetic Alphabet (IPA), while child language transcriptions in the CHILDES database tend to be at the morphological level or in ASCII versions of the available orthographies used by the various spoken languages represented in the archive. Although study of the acquisition of sign language phonology is clearly of great importance, BTS is concerned with morphosyntactic, semantic, and pragmatic dimensions of language.

The first detailed sign language study by Klima and Bellugi (1979), and many others since, have used line drawings that are free drawings or modifications of tracings taken from videotapes. For the grammatical uses of the basic hand-shapes involved in a signed utterance, little diagrams of the signing space are frequently added. This is, however a quite inefficient technique, both in terms of time and expense. Also, different perspectives on the execution of ongoing signing hands requires techniques such as strobe-like drawings and arrows — again time consuming and expensive. Abstracted drawing, as shown in Zeshan's (2000) new concise study of Indo-Pakistan Sign Language, is a creative solution, solving the perspective issue by using a computer program for graphic presentations of signs. However, all such *picture* versions (including actual photographs and digitized video clips), are useless for computer-aided searching, sorting, and summarizing of data.

The most popular and traditional way of transcribing sign language is the use of glosses in capital letters, supplemented by various diacritics and discursive notes. This sort of transcription may seem to have the advantage of being a shared system, although every individual researcher seems to bring in new diacritics, given their research questions and the language they are dealing with. And, again, a mixed system of glosses and diacritics is inaccessible to computer programs of the sort used in child language research. More seriously, the glosses represent the nearest translation equivalent in the spoken language of the particular community, making it impossible to carry out serious linguistic analysis of the sign language itself. For example, in beginning our comparisons of acquisition of SLN and ASL, we were immediately struck by the fact that similar signs expressing desire in the two languages were glossed as an adverb in Dutch (GRAAG 'gladly, with pleasure') and as a verb in English (WANT). Clearly, neither of these words is a lexical element of SLN or ASL. Just as no linguistic analysis of a spoken language relies solely on glosses in the language of the investigator, linguistic analysis of a sign language requires representation at the level of the meaning components of that particular language.

5.   Transcription at the level of meaning components

Even a cursory examination of verbs in any sign language makes it evident that we are dealing with a sort of *polysynthetic* language that is quite different from the spoken languages of the surrounding communities. Those languages — be they as different from one another as English or Finnish or Chinese — do not demonstrate the morphological complexity of verbs that is found in such languages as SLN or ASL. To find somewhat comparable examples in spoken languages it is useful to turn to indigenous languages of North America. Consider, for example, Leonard Talmy's (1985) work on Atsugewi, a Hokan language of northern California. The verb roots in this type of language designate figures of particular shapes, postures, and consistencies, e.g.:

(1) *lup-*   'small shiny spherical object'

(2) *caq-*   'slimy lumpish object'

The roots take locative/directional suffixes, such as:

(3) *-ak*   'on the ground'

(4) *-mič*   'down onto the ground'

Polymorphemic combinations are similar to those of verbs of motion and object transfer in sign languages. Consider, for example, the Atsugewi construction: *s-´-w-it^u-mič*. The first three morphemes indicate a first-person subject in factual mood. The last two identify the postural figure and movement:

(5) it^u -mič
     'linear_object_in_lying_posture' '-move_down_onto_ground'

Glossing at this level of analysis is sufficient to indicate the morphological components of the verb. BTS, as demonstrated below, takes a similar approach to components of signs. In addition, following linguist practice, Talmy provides a discursive translation in English:

(6) s-w-´-it^u-mič
     'I lay down onto the ground'

BTS is not concerned with this sort of paraphrase, except as a possible additional comment for clarification. Nor does BTS present simple glosses in English (or Dutch, or whatever) for signs that are clearly polycomponential. Rather, the goal is to represent those *components of complex signs that can be productively used to create meaningful complex signs* in the particular sign language under investigation. That is, BTS is intended to be the equivalent of a morpheme-by-morpheme analysis, with a collection of abbreviations designed for signed languages. (Signs that cannot be analyzed into evident meaning components are transcribed in traditional upper-case format, such as book in ASL.)

6. Polycomponential verbs in BTS

We will present one extended example of the level of analysis that has been developed in BTS, and then will discuss applications to the study of first- and second-language development. Verbs of motion (self-movement, caused-movement, object transfer) are polycomponential, including handshapes or body parts that indicate the figure and/or ground involved in the motion event. These verbs have traditionally been designated as *classifier predicates* (e.g., papers in Emmorey in press; Valli & Lucas 1992). That is, the handshapes for figure and ground are components that specify, or *classify* a relevant semantic property of the corresponding referential entities. BTS treats *classifiers* as *property markers* — that is, handshapes that identify a referent by indicating a relevant property of that referent (for justification, see Slobin, Hoiting, Kuntze, Lindert, Weinberg, Pyers, Anthony, Biederman & Thumann in press).[5] For example, an *inverted V* handshape is transcribed as pm'TL (two-legged animate being), and never as *V-CL, inverted V*, or the like. If both figure and ground are part of a verb, the order of notation is always *ground* before *figure*, following the logic of manual representation of such events.

In essence, verbs of motion in signed languages (at least in ASL and SLN, the languages we have worked with in detail) consist of components of ground, figure, path, and various additional movement elements indicating features such as aspect and manner. Such verbs cannot be directly glossed in English or the other Indo-European languages that are characteristic of the surrounding speech communities that have been most extensively studied. Consider, for example, an ASL verb with the following components, with BTS conventions in parentheses: the non-dominant hand is held vertically, with flat palm, fingers extended forward (pm'PL_VL 'plane showing vertical length'); the dominant hand is in an inverted-V position (pm'TL 'two-legged animate being') and it moves to a goal at the top of the non-dominant hand (gol'PL_VL_TOP 'move to top of vertical plane') to straddle the hand (pst'STR 'posture straddle'). This verb could refer to a range of events, such as a cowboy mounting a horse or a boy sitting up on a fence. It can be represented as a verb with four meaning components (*morphemes*), as indicated by four hyphens.

(7)   -pm'PL_VL-pm'TL-gol'PL_VL_TOP-pst'STR

Note that the linguistic status of each meaning component is given in lower-case letters (pm, gol, pst), while upper-case letters indicate the semantic content of each component. (As mentioned above, upper-case letters are also used for unanalyzed signs, allowing for separate searches for morphological and lexical elements combined.)

This is, in fact, a sufficient transcription linguistically, but it lacks legibility — at least for hearing readers. We would like to be reminded of a comparable English verb, *but we do not want such a gloss to influence our transcription or analysis.* To solve this problem, BTS allows the transcriber to begin a verb with a parenthetical, lower-case possible equivalent. Thus one might type:

(8)   (mount)-pm'PL_VL-pm'TL-gol'PL_VL_TOP-pst'STR

The parenthetical gloss is not a conventional part of the system, and each transcriber can provide a suitable equivalent. For example, this verb could also be glossed as (get_up_on_horse) or (mount_straddling), or whatever seems useful to the transcriber. The parenthetical glosses stand outside of the analyses, and function only to facilitate reading.

If more contextual detail is needed it can be provided on a dependent tier, under the utterance line. For example, one could add a *gloss* tier (%gls). Following CHILDES format, the utterance line begins with an asterisk and an identifying code for the speaker in three upper-case letters, while dependent tiers begin with a percent sign and lower-case ID:

(9) *MOT: cowboy (mount)-pm'PL_VL-pm'TL-
            gol'PL_VL_TOP-pst'STR.
     %gls: the cowboy got up on the horse's back

The transcription is thus based on linguistic analysis, often resulting in initially non-obvious decomposition of complex signs. Note that this work cannot be done without the active participation of native signers. At almost every point in the development of BTS, the native signers in our group have helped us to discover contrasts, nuances, and possibilities that may not have been evident to second-language signers.[6]

Segmentation of a sign into meaning components depends on the availability of contrasts in the language. For example, our analysis of 'mount' is based on the possibilities of substituting the *ground* component (e.g., by use of a horizontal plane to indicate movement onto a different sort of ground), the *figure* component (e.g., by reference to an animal, such as a cat, mounting a horse), and the *posture* component (e.g., by contrast with a person standing on a horse's back). The search for contrasts is essential to the analysis, and contrasts are not always obvious without careful examination of a range of potential scenarios and their signed descriptions.

To continue the demonstration of this method, note that 'mount' is part of a collection of verbs that have a derivational relationship with one another, as revealed by the addition or removal of a meaning component:

1. If the path component (-gol-) is replaced by a static component (-loc-) the result is a verb describing a static configuration:

    (10)   (be_mounted)-pm'PL_VL-pm'TL-loc'PL_VL_TOP-pst'STR

Again, the parenthetical gloss is not part of the analysis. This verb could describe a man seated on a horse, a boy seated astraddle on a fence, etc.

2. If a movement pattern (-mvt-) is added to 'be_mounted' the resulting verb is dynamic: 'ride'. BTS is not concerned with a phonological description of this particular movement pattern, because it does not contrast with other movement patterns using this configuration of property markers: Its only function is to indicate that this configuration has the meaning of 'ride'. Therefore we simply designate the forward rotational movement of this verb as mvt'LEX, where LEX refers to the movement pattern that identifies this particular verb. That pattern is pointed to parenthetically: mvt'LEX(ride). (This is similar to spoken language transcriptions, such as transcriptions of English verbs as 'walk-PAST' or 'run-PAST', where the reader can provide *walked* or *ran* on the basis of knowledge of the language.) With regard to the parenthetical gloss, note that ASL has a different verb for riding in a vehicle, so we indicate the verb we are transcribing here as 'ride_mounted':

    (11)   (ride_mounted)-pm'PL_VL-pm'TL-loc'PL_VL_TOP-pst'STR-
           mvt'LEX(ride)

3. Once we have a dynamic verb of motion, we can then add further components of *manner* and *aspect*. For example, the following extended notation indicates that the referent event was rapid (-mod'RAP-) and that it came to a stop (-asp'CES 'cessive'):

    (12)   (ride_mounted)-pm'PL_VL-pm'TL-loc'PL_VL_TOP-pst'STR-
           mvt'LEX(ride)-mod'RAP-asp'CES

It is important to note that these relationships are not evident in the standard English glosses for each of the ASL verbs discussed above. That is, if one relied on glosses as the central element of transcription, there would be no reason to see the regular relationships that hold between three verbs that describe a human being mounting, straddling, and riding a horse: GET_ON, BE_LOCATED, and RIDE.

Sign language researchers with experience in typological linguistics should not be surprised by the elaborateness of BTS transcriptions of poly-componential verbs. Such relatively opaque morpheme-by-morpheme glosses are familiar in papers dealing with a wide range of agglutinative and poly-synthetic languages, as discussed with regard to Atsugewi, above. Poly-componential verbs are quite accessible to children learning spoken languages of this type. Consider the following example from Inuktitut, spoken by an Eskimo child of 2;6. Here we have an entire sentence in one polycomponential utterance (Allen 2000:495).

(13)   ma -una   -aq -si   -junga
       here -VIALIS -go -PROSPECTIVE.ASPECT -PARTICIPIAL.1SG
       'I'm going through here.'

Note that the morpheme-by-morpheme gloss is uninterpretable without knowledge of Inuktitut, just as BTS utterance-line transcriptions are uninterpretable without knowledge of the particular sign language. Because BTS is designed for investigators who know the sign language, however, the utterance line should generally be sufficient. The use of a %gls line, like the line in single quotes above, is always available for clarification.

7.   Nonmanual components of signs

A defining feature of signed languages is the use of the face and/or body to add meaning to signed utterances. BTS transcribes four distinct types of nonmanual components. These can occur simultaneously with a single sign, or can have duration (scope) over several signs. In many transcription systems, a horizontal line drawn above glosses of signs indicates the temporal scope of a nonmanual component. BTS restricts itself to a series of ASCII characters, using the carat (^) to indicate temporal onset and offset of a nonmanual component that has scope. The four types of nonmanual components are *operators, modification, affect,* and *discourse markers:*

1. A grammatical *operator* has scope over a phrase or clause (negation, interrogation, topic, relative clause, conditional, etc.). The notation is ^opr'X ... ^. For example, the following transcription format indicates negation of a proposition in BTS:

(14) *CHI: ^opr'NEG WANT BOOK ^.

2. *Modification* can add a dimension to the referential meaning of a lexical item or proposition by means of noncanonical articulation of the sign and/or accompanying facial expression, such as augmented or diminished size, rate, or intensity. The notation is ^mod'X … ^. For example, an SLN-signing 2-year-old wanted her mother to draw a big house. She greatly extended the sign HOUSE (AUG = augmented):

    (15) *CHI: HOUSE-^mod'AUG.

In this example, the nonmanual component is part of a single sign. There is no offset carat because such a nonmanual ends with the end of the sign. Of course, modification can also extend over sequences of signs.

3. *Affective* accompaniment to signing is provided by use of mouth, face, and body, indicating the signer's attitudinal stance towards the situation being communicated (e.g., disgust, surprise, excitement). The notation is ^aff'X … ^. For example, an SLN-signing teacher asks a child to do something and the child agrees, though with some worried concern (PNT_1 = point to self):

    (16) *CHI: ^aff'WORRIED CAN PNT_1 ^.

Note that affective information can be provided in spoken languages by prosody, as well as by affective particles and inflections. We think it appropriate to include all meaning components in our transcription, without prejudging their *linguistic* status.

4. *Discourse* markers regulate the flow of interpersonal exchange, such as checking if the addressee has comprehended, has agreed, and so forth. These sorts of nonmanual components correspond to discourse particles and intonation contours in spoken languages; again, BTS includes them in the complex of meaning components. The notation is ^dis'X … ^. In the following example, a Deaf SLN-signing mother responds to her 2-year-old's labeling of the lights on a picture of an ambulance. Note that there are two types of nonmanual elements in this utterance. The first is an operator, indicating confirmation (YES); the second is a discourse marker checking whether the child agrees (CONF = confirmation check). The operator (repeated head-nodding) extends throughout the utterance, including the discourse marker (a sort of questioning facial expression). The offset timing of the two non-manuals coincides (^ ^).

    (17) *MOT: ^opr'YES CAR ^dis'CONF LIGHTSIGNALS ^ ^.

8. Role shift

A pervasive aspect of sign language communication is the subtle shifts of gaze and posture that allow the signer to convey the utterances, thoughts, or actions of other people. This part of sign language needs much more careful study, and BTS does not present a fine-grained analysis of role shift at this time (see, e.g., Emmorey & Riley 1985; Engberg-Pedersen 1993; Liddell 1998; Taub 2001). However, we do consider it to be a meaningful dimension, and one that follows conventional, linguistic patterns. At this point, we simply indicate role shift by RS. Note that we use capital letters for this element, treating role shift as a meaning component in an utterance. We do not use the carat (^) to indicate onset and offset of role shift, because we want to search separately for non-manual features and role-shifting. Instead, we use the reverse apostrophe (left single quote, grave accent,) for this function: 'RS ...'. For example, in a book-reading activity, a Deaf ASL-signing mother points out a picture of a dog, and then role shifts into the dog to indicate that the dog is excited. She signs EXCITE with an accompanying non-manual indicating the dog's affect (INTENSE). The notation 'RS(dog) indicates that she has taken on the role of the dog. Note that ^aff can co-occur with role shift.

(18) *MOT: DOG 'RS(dog) EXCITE-^aff'INTENSE'.

9. Polycomponential analysis and the issue of morphological productivity

BTS relies heavily on criteria of *morphological productivity* for the analysis of a sign into components. That is, the level of transcription is based on a thorough-going analysis of signs into meaning components. To the extent that we have succeeded for a particular sign, this is a contribution to linguistic description. We are well aware, however, that children who are learning a language may not yet have carried out the adult analyses reflected in the transcription. This problem is a familiar one in child language research, where it is well known that children's early forms may be *amalgams* or unanalyzed gestalts that correspond to more complex and analytic adult forms. The only way to determine if a particular morphological analysis is productive for a given child is to try to find evidence of productivity. Such evidence is available in two forms: (1) One can search the corpus for uses of a given morpheme across lexical items and contexts, looking for diversity in use. Overgeneralizations are particularly informative; for example, when an English-speaking child says *breaked* we have evidence for the productivity of the past-tense inflection. (2) One can present the child with new lexical items (often nonsense, or *nonce* terms made up for experimental purposes), putting them in contexts that should elicit a particular morpheme if it is productive. For example, if an English-speaking child is presented with a nonce verb, *wug*, and says that someone *wugged* yesterday, we have evidence for productivity (e.g., Berko 1958).

The same issue of rote-learned versus productive forms applies to the acquisition of signed languages. The purpose of the detailed componential analysis embodied in BTS is to make it possible to discover, for a particular child, when there is sufficient evidence to credit the child with control of various components of signs. The advantage of detailed analysis is that it pushes us to describe the language carefully, and makes us sensitive to critical dimensions of acquisition.

10. Notations of communicative behavior, context, and additional coding

BTS is designed for studying the development of signing within the context of ongoing communication; therefore there are means of noting attention-getting devices and gestures and actions that are relevant to communicative events. Gestures (%ges) and actions (%act) can be entered as part of the utterance line, or on a dependent tier, at the discretion of the transcriber. In our preliminary transcriptions of parent-child interaction with 2-year-olds, we have often found it useful to include such information on the utterance line. For example, an SLN-signing 2-year-old is looking for a pen. The child gestures that she *doesn't know*; signs WHERE; and then looks around the room. The mother shows the pen to the child and signs FIND.

> (19) *CHI: [%ges: don't know] WHERE [%act: looks around room]?
>   *MOT: [%act: shows pen to chi] FIND.

BTS also provides means of indicating factors that are relevant to analysis of child signing, with notation conventions for gaze direction, errors, interruptions. For example, errors are noted by [*], with further information on a dependent tier (%err). In the following example, an ASL-signing child of 1;9 signs HORSE with a handshape error. For this analysis, the transcriber is not concerned with the phonology of the error and simply notes on the error tier that there was a handshape error ($hs); however, another transcriber might have added a dependent tier for phonological notation (%pho).

(20) *CHI: HORSE [*].
　　　%err: HORSE $hs;

In addition, following CHILDES format, dependent tiers can be created for additional information and coding (e.g., morphology, syntax, vocalization, situation, etc.). For example, a hearing ASL-signing mother is signing to a 3-year-old; the comment tier (%com) provides the transcriber's clarifications:

(21) *MOT: ^opr'Q SISTER ^ ?
　　　%com: asking if girl doll is sister
　　　*MOT: SISTER PNT_3 WHO PNT_3 ?
　　　*MOT: ^opr'NEG NOT SISTER ^ NO.
　　　%com: commenting on mislabeling of doll as SISTER

11. Using BTS to study sign language acquisition

We have been using BTS in the United States and the Netherlands to transcribe signed utterances produced by children between the ages of 18 and 38 months, Deaf and hearing parents, and Deaf and hearing preschool teachers.[7] In order to provide an idea of research applications of BTS, we present several examples from our recent paper, *A cognitive/functional perspective on the acquisition of "classifiers"* (Slobin et al. in press).

11.1 Early uses of handshapes in polycomponential verbs

As discussed above, BTS treats *classifiers* as *property markers* that reference entities on the basis of salient object properties, manner of manipulation, or by the use of fixed forms (*whole entity classifiers*). For purposes of demonstration, consider two types of handshapes that are based on properties involved in manipulation (*instrumental classifiers, handle classifiers, manipulators*):

1. *manipulative handle:* The handshape represents the hand that is manipulating an object (e.g., ASL property marker for 'screwdriver', using a rotating S-handshape for the grasping hand);

2. *depictive handle:* The handshape represents a physical feature of the object being manipulated (e.g., ASL property marker for 'screwdriver', using a rotating H-handshape for the tip of the screwdriver).

We expected that manipulative handles would be acquired earlier than depictive handles, both for our L1 (child) learners and our L2 (hearing parent) learners. BTS transcripts of both SLN and ASL, however, showed early use of both types, by L1 as well as L2 learners.

11.1.1   *Manipulative handles*

BTS transcribes property markers of this sort in a preliminary way, using an abbreviation for the physical form of the handshape involved. This is because we cannot yet determine the semantic categories underlying the use of such handshapes. By indicating the handshape in physical terms, we are able to search individual transcripts to determine the range of uses of a particular handshape. With sufficient data, these preliminary physical descriptions can be replaced by semantic definitions of manipulative property markers. Thus the transcription format allows for search of the contexts — linguistic and situational — in which individual meaning components are used. For example, a Dutch girl of 2;6 is seated on the floor with her hearing mother, looking through family photos. She describes a picture in which she is seated in a baby buggy being pushed by her father. The manipulative handle component of the verb 'push' is realized as two S-hands, palms down, arms straight, incorporated in a forward motion. The property marker is transcribed as a form of hold (pm'HO), with an indication of the handshape using designations derived from the ASL hand alphabet (pm'HO_S); a parenthetical 2h indicates that this is a two-handed form. The direction of the sign is represented by a *path* component (pth) that is realized as *forward* motion (pth'F):

(22) *CHI: FATHER PNT_1 (push)-pm'HO_S(2h)-pth'F.

Dependent tiers could provide further information, such as a description of the situation, a paraphrase (e.g., 'father push me'), and perhaps more detailed description of handshape form and orientation and the physical movement of the signer.

Our transcripts show that hearing parents also make early and appropriate use of manipulative handle property markers. The hearing mother of this Dutch girl had been using SLN for eight months when she produced the following utterance. The girl had put a doll to bed in a toy cradle. The mother tells her to close the curtains around the cradle, moving two S-hands in a closing arc towards her own chest. The *path* of movement is *backwards*, and the hands move toward *each other* (pth'B_EO):

(23) *MOT: (close)-pm'HO_S(2h)-pth'B_EO.

With a large corpus, it will be possible to search for all instances of property markers such as pm'HO, and all instances of pm'HO_S, in an attempt to determine the semantic dimensions and productivity of property markers, as well as their developmental changes. Note, too, that the use of hyphens between components allows for a calculation of sign complexity. In these two examples, both verb signs have two meaning components — a manipulative handle and a path. Parenthetical glosses ('push', 'close') are not included in quantitative analyses; they only serve to aid legibility.

11.1.2   *Depictive handles*

Property markers of this sort are transcribed in terms of the salient dimension of the referenced entity — e.g., whether it is a plane, a stick-like object, a cylindrical object, and so forth. For example, consider an utterance dealing with placement of a thin, flat object. The handshape is a horizontal flat 5-hand, palm down, which BTS treats as a *horizontal plane* (pm'PL_H). A Dutch girl of 2;11 comments to her mother about putting a flat rubber alphabet letter into the corresponding puzzle space. She points to the space, indicated by a *3rd-person point* (PNT_3) followed by a parenthetical indication of the aim of the point, and then moves her hand to that object as a *goal* (gol):

(24) *CHI: PNT_3(puzzle_space) (put)-pm'PL_H-gol'OBJ (puzzle_space)

BTS counts elements that are separated by spaces as lexical items; thus there are two lexical items in this utterance. The second item has two meaning components; thus there are three *morphemes* in this utterance. However, we prefer to withhold the linguistic label *morpheme* until we have done much deeper corpus analysis, along with more extensive linguistic work.

The transcription system also makes it easy to pick up nonconventional uses of meaning components (*errors*). For example, an American girl of 2;6, learning ASL from Deaf parents, is also signing about the insertion of a flat piece into a puzzle. In this case, the piece is a disc, which would be treated as two-dimensional in ASL. The child, however, uses a cylinder handshape (pm'CYL), moving it downwards, palm to the side, to make contact with the puzzle board. An asterisk in square brackets indicates that this is an error from the point of view of the adult language, and an asterisk within the poly-componential verb indicates the location of the error. A dependent tier (%err) identifies the nature of the error: that this is a property marker error, in which CYL should have been a *flat disc* (FD), indicated by a dollar sign ($pm = FD).

(25) *CHI: (put)-pm'CYL*-gol'OBJ(puzzle) [*].
    %err: CYL $pm = FD

A dependent tier for comments (%com) could add the transcriber's ideas about this utterance — for example, the task of inserting the piece into a puzzle may have highlighted its three-dimensional quality to the child; or perhaps this is a phono-logical error, reflecting lack of fine digit control. With a sufficiently large corpus, a search for errors can be useful in revealing acquisition strategies and problems.

11.2 Problems of mastering polycomponential signs beyond the early phases

Our data on the acquisition of both ASL and SLN show that by age 3, children are adept at integrating handshapes into polycomponential signs, along with other meaning components. Their hearing parents also have productive control of these basic morphological structures. However, there is much more to be learned, and even 12-year-olds do not use the entire set of options with the skill and flexibility of native-signing adults. Our preschool videotapes consist almost entirely of short utterances in dialog, with support from present context and adult scaffolding. In the school years, by contrast, children are faced with the demands of extended discourse, often monologic, and often without support in the physical context. This is especially clear in narrative productions, where the signer has to create a spatial and temporal scenario and maintain reference to individuals and events while shifting perspective. In our California research, the school-age narrative data of Michelle Anthony, Marlon Kuntze and Philip Prinz highlight these issues (Anthony 2002). BTS transcriptions have enabled us to identify several classes of linguistic and discourse problems faced by children beyond preschool:

1. *Establishing reference:* Who is acting? What other entities are involved?
2. *Specifying ground:* What are the reference points for location and movement? *Ground as anchor:* What part of the ground is a constant background? When and how does it change?

Scale of ground: What viewpoint is taken (close up zoom, distant view, lifesize, etc.)?
Flexibility of focus: Where is the signer's attention, and how does it move from utterance to utterance?

3. *Choosing from among multiple perspectives:*
   Shifts in narrator's perspective: From what angle is an event being signed?
   Shifts between perspectives of narrator and one or more protagonists: Whose perspective is being used from utterance to utterance?

BTS transcriptions of narrative discourse are complex, and we present only one example, to give a brief indication of the extension of the system beyond our preschool data. In Kuntze's recordings of a kindergarten story circle, a girl of 5;0, with Deaf parents, is telling the group about a vacation trip. In the following utterance, she is relating an attempt to crawl through a small opening, but she has trouble with the scale of the opening in relation to the figure (presumably her own body), and she has not specified what kind of opening this was. She uses a property marker indicating that the ground was a round opening, using an F-handshape (pm'CIR) on one hand, and indicates that the moving figure was human, using a V-handshape for *two legs* (pm'TL) on the other hand. Here she has run into a problem of relative scale of the two handshapes: the ground is represented as a view from the distance, while the figure represents a close-up view. This lack of correspondence between the scales of figure and ground property markers leads to an articulatory problem, because she cannot fully fit the figure through the space in the ground, as she presumably intended to do. Therefore pm'CIR is marked with an asterisk as an error; an adult signer would probably choose a C-handshape (pm'CYL) for the ground, allowing pm'TL to move through it. The BTS transcription also indicates that the posture of the figure was *reclining* (pst'RCL); that the handshape was oriented towards the signer's body (ori'B); that the motion was carried out with a *wiggling* movement (mvt'WIG); and that the goal of the motion was the interior of the circle (gol'INT_CIR). Thus this polycomponential verb has six components:

(26) *CHI: (crawl)-pm'CIR-pm'TL-pst'RCL-ori'B-mvt'WIG-gol'INT_CIR
              [*].
     %err: CIR $pm = CYL

12. Conclusion

The Berkeley Transcription System has given us a tool to look into the component structure of signs, with all of their simultaneous manual and nonmanual features. BTS is based on linguistic analysis of each sign language being studied, and is continually open to revisions as linguistic descriptions improve. It is also open to revision in response to insights about child language, as well as challenges of computer technology. We have succeeded in keying BTS transcripts to timecodes of analog videotapes, and are beginning to explore digital resources.

It is evident from analysis at the level of meaning components that child L1 learners, as well as adult L2 learners, quickly grasp the polycomponential nature of sign language and use meaning components productively in complex signs. This form of transcription also allows for detailed exploration and documentation of learners' mastery of the full morphosyntactic, semantic, and pragmatic structures of sign language. Although we are only at the beginning, it seems to be a highly promising first step. We welcome participation from the international community of sign language researchers, and look forward to criticisms, advice, and collaboration.[8]

Notes

1. The Berkeley Transcription System (BTS) represents the collective work of Michelle Anthony, Yael Biederman, Nini Hoiting, Marlon Kuntze, Reyna Lindert, Jennie Pyers, Dan I. Slobin, Helen Thumann, and Amy Weinberg. The work was carried out in the Child Language Research Laboratory, Institute of Human Development, University of California, Berkeley (UCB). Support has been provided by the Linguistics Program of the National Science Foundation under grant SBR-97-27050, "Can a Deaf Child Learn to Sign from Hearing Parents?" to Dan I. Slobin, PI, and Nini Hoiting, co-PI. Additional support has been provided by the Institute of Human Development and the Institute of Cognitive and Brain Sciences, UCB; by the University of California Linguistic Minority Research Institute (to Reyna Lindert); by the Vice Chancellor's Fund for Research (to Reyna Lindert); by a dissertation fellowship from the American Association of University Women (to Reyna Lindert); by Sigma Xi (to Reyna Lindert); by the Royal Institute for the Deaf *H. D. Guyot*, Haren, The Netherlands and by the Max Planck Institute for Psycholinguistics, Nijmegen, The Netherlands. The system has been developed on the basis of parent-child videotapes in Sign Language of the Netherlands (SLN), collected by Nini Hoiting, and American Sign Language (ASL), collected by Reyna Lindert. The current version reflects the consensus of a workshop held in Berkeley, April 12–13, 2000, based on examples from American Sign Language, Danish Sign Language, Sign Language of the Netherlands, and Nicaraguan Sign Language. In addition to the investigators listed above, the workshop included Paul Dudis,

Elisabeth Engberg-Pedersen, Philip Prinz, Brenda Schick, Ann Senghas, Richard Senghas, Eve Sweetser, David Wilkins, and Alyssa Wulf. We have been especially helped by the four native ASL-signers in our group, Marlon Kuntze and Paul Dudis (Deaf), and Jennie Pyers and Helen Thumann (hearing).

2. CHILDES is available on a North American website organized by Brian MacWhinney (http://childes.psy.cmu.edu/), on a European mirroring site organized by Steven Gillis (http://atila-www.uia.ac.be/childes/), and on a Japanese mirroring site organized by Hidetosi Sirai (http://jchat.sccs.chukyo-u.ac.jp/CHILDES/).

3. In the analysis of both spoken and signed languages, linguists distinguish a *phonetic* level, which is concerned with the basic articulatory units of production, and a *phonological* level, which is concerned with the combinatorial patterns of such basic units according to the rules of a given language.

4. To save space in this publication, we refer the reader to online facilities that represent each of the notation systems mentioned.

5. "While various categories of polycomponential signs can be proposed, our work has focused on alternative conceptualizations of *classifiers*. Rather than emphasize classification as the central feature of *classifier* handshapes in polycomponential signs, it seems more useful to treat them as marking a relevant property of a referent. The major function of such a handshape is to evoke a relevant referent in discourse, indexing a particular referent according to properties that are appropriate for the current discourse. That is, the *classifier* handshape designates, or specifies, or indicates a referent with a particular property (e.g., two-legged, horizontal plane, etc.). In the Berkeley Transcription System such handshapes are designated as *property markers (pm)*" (Slobin et al. in press).

6. In our Berkeley group there are three native ASL signers: Marlon Kuntze, who is Deaf, and Jennie Pyers and Helen Thumann, who are CODAs (hearing offspring of Deaf parents: *Child of Deaf Adult*). In the Netherlands, Nini Hoiting works with several native SLN-signing Deaf colleagues at the Royal Institute for the Deaf H.D. Guyot in Haren: Bottie Reitsma, Anne-marie Terpstra, and Diny Visch, who are Deaf, and Ari Terpstra, who is a CODA. We are grateful for the linguistic insights and expert advice of all of these collaborators.

7. See Lindert (2001) for a detailed report of the use of polycomponential predicates by ASL-using preschoolers and their Deaf or hearing parents.

8. We welcome discussion of BTS and applications to additional sign languages and datasets. We can be contacted at the following e-mail addresses: JFA.Hoiting@guyot.nl, slobin@socrates.berkeley.edu.

The development of Italian Sign Language (LIS) in deaf preschoolers[*]

Elena Pizzuto

1. Introduction

The aim of this chapter is to provide new information on the development of Italian Sign Language (LIS) in a sample of four profoundly deaf children of deaf parents of preschool age. I shall examine and discuss data on the children's expressive language abilities drawn from a picture description, language elicitation task. A central issue I shall address is whether and/or to what extent relevant features of adult LIS influence the learning process. These features include fairly general articulatory properties of LIS manual signs, as well as more specific aspects of LIS noun and verb morphology, where inflectional and uninflectional patterns coexist side by side (and inflections are often optional rather than obligatory), and the use of oral components in signed productions. The rationale for focusing the investigation on these features, and its relevance from a cross-linguistic perspective, are specified in Section 2.

It must be noted that most previous work on the acquisition of LIS by native signers has been limited to the early stages of signed language development, focusing primarily on lexical growth and on the patterns of production of the first two- and multi-sign utterances (Caselli 1983; Caselli & Volterra 1990; Caselli, Maragna, Pagliari Rampelli & Volterra 1994; Capirci, Montanari & Volterra 1998; Volterra & Iverson 1995). The major findings of this research are similar to those provided by most research on American Sign Language (ASL) and other signed languages (e.g. Newport & Meier 1985; van den Bogaerde 2000, for a recent review): the timing and pace of early development in LIS is substantially similar to that observed in hearing children acquiring spoken languages.

Research on signed language development in older Italian deaf children has been undertaken only in the last few years. The data provided by this research, including those described in the present chapter, were collected within a broad project conducted on a sample of eleven deaf preschoolers: five children of deaf parents and six children of hearing parents (Ossella, Ardito, Bianchi, Gentile, Luchenti, Tieri, Caselli, Pizzuto, Bosi & Cafasso 1994). The project aimed to explore several aspects of deaf children's cognitive, communicative and linguistic development. One of the major objectives of the project was to evaluate the children's receptive and expressive language abilities in both LIS and spoken Italian, trying as much as possible to use comparable assessment procedures for examining signed as compared to spoken language. The project also aimed to define an evaluation methodology that would allow us to compare the deaf children's developmental achievements with those of their hearing peers. The major results obtained by exploring the deaf children's cognitive and receptive language abilities are described elsewhere (Pizzuto, Caselli & Volterra 2000; Pizzuto, Caselli, Ardito, Ossella, Albertoni, Santarelli & Cafasso 1998; Pizzuto, Ardito, Caselli & Volterra 2001), and are only briefly summarized here.

Consistent with the findings of similar studies conducted in other national and linguistic communities, our results showed that the cognitive abilities of all the deaf children we examined were comparable to those of their hearing peers. The receptive lexical and grammatical abilities in LIS of deaf children of deaf parents were also found to be comparable to those exhibited by their hearing peers in the corresponding spoken language tasks. Interestingly, it was also found that even three of the six deaf children of hearing parents of our sample, who had limited exposure to LIS, performed fairly well in the LIS lexical comprehension task we used: their scores were comparable to those attained by the deaf children of deaf parents. These children, however, did not show the same good performance in the LIS grammatical comprehension task. In the lexical and grammatical comprehension tasks presented in spoken Italian all the eleven deaf children of our sample lagged considerably behind their hearing peers (see Pizzuto et al. 2001 for a more appropriate discussion of the significance of these findings).

The exploration of linguistic abilities in LIS presents a number of methodological problems that can be partially overlooked when dealing with early acquisition, but which cannot be ignored when exploring later stages of development. Research on LIS began in the late 1980s (Volterra 1987). Despite the advancement of our knowledge of the structure of adult LIS, the information we have on the lexicon and grammar of the language is still extremely limited. There is currently no reference grammar that can be used as guidance for relevant research questions that can be formulated with respect to the acquisition process. A wealth of videorecorded data on child and adult LIS is available, but these raw data cannot be seen as constituting appropriate corpora that are representative of the more salient regularities in child and adult LIS. Furthermore, although a relevant portion of these data has been transcribed by hand or in a computerized format, the system that is most widely used for transcribing signed utterances and texts is a gloss-based notation which severely limits our abilities to reconstruct and analyze the actual form of the signs under examination. These serious methodological problems are not unique to the study of LIS, but are encountered in research on all signed languages, due primarily to the fact that no signed language investigated to date has autonomously developed a written form (Pizzuto & Pietrandrea 2001; Pizzuto, Wilcox, Hanke, Janzen, Kegl & Shepard-Kegl 2000). At present no reference grammars are available for any signed language, not even for American Sign Language or ASL, the language that has been most thoroughly investigated, and this renders the study of developmental processes much more difficult, as also explicitly noted by van den Bogaerde (2000:254) in studies of the development of Sign Language of the Netherlands (SLN). Similarly, even with the advancement of computer and multimedia technologies, there are no computerized databases of transcribed or coded signed text corpora that are in any way comparable to those currently available for the study of spoken language and its acquisition (e.g. the CHILDES system as most recently outlined in MacWhinney 2000).

Although several major methodological problem still remain to be solved, in the study of some signed languages (most notably in ASL) sign language elicitation and evaluation tools that can facilitate the exploration of developmental patterns at early and at more advanced stages of development have been developed and are in the process of being standardized (Haug 1999; Supalla, Singleton, Wix & Maller 1998). In contrast, no such materials were available for LIS prior to the project developed by Ossella et al. (1994). The studies stemming from this project, including the one reported in this chapter, thus were aimed at the same time at exploring LIS development at later stages, and at designing new materials and methodologies for this exploration.

2.   Features of adult LIS and questions concerning the learning process

The present exploration of developmental patterns in the acquisition of LIS was guided by our current knowledge of the adult system (Pizzuto 1986, 1987; Pizzuto & Corazza 1996; Pizzuto, Giuranna & Gambino 1990; Pizzuto & Volterra in press). The study focuses on a set of features that I believe are relevant for a clearer understanding of signed language learning processes not only in LIS but also in other signed languages, where similar features have been noted but not thoroughly explored from the acquisition standpoint. These include some of the most general articulatory and/or morphophonological and morphological regularities that characterize LIS signs at the manual[1] level of linguistic expression, and the oral components (voiced or simply mouthed) that accompany sign production.

2.1   Regularities of LIS manual signs

In LIS, as in all signed languages that have been investigated, manual signs can be articulated with one hand or two hands. When two hands are used, they may be fully or partially symmetrical, or asymmetrical, i.e. they may or may not share the same formational parameters. For example, in LIS, the fully symmetrical sign DISH is articulated with two L handshapes, palm down, and a short downward movement, in a place of articulation that, after Stokoe, Casterline and Croneberg (1976), is commonly described as "neutral space": "a relatively large, not rigidly defined region in front of the signer's body where the hands move at ease and where a large number of signs are executed". In contrast, the asymmetrical two-handed sign HOME is articulated with a B handshape (palm, oriented sideways, fingertips up) which remains still, i.e. functions as the base or non dominant hand, while the other dominant or moving hand (a closed handshape, all fingers closed in a bunch, fingertips in contact) moves toward to the base hand and touches it once or twice in the middle of the palm.

These very general articulatory features are relevant to a clearer understanding of signed language learning processes, and the extent to which they are comparable to, or differ from spoken language learning processes. Since signs can be produced with one hand, there is the inherent possibility, in signed discourse, that two distinct signs can be coarticulated, either simultaneously, or in what can be partially described as a sequence: a one-handed sign may be produced and maintained in time and space while the signer articulates another one-handed sign with the other hand. The coarticulation of two distinct manual signs in the same time unit has been noted and partially described across several adult signed languages (see among others Miller 1994b; Padden 1983, 1990; Pizzuto & Corazza 1996; Russo 1999; Russo, Giuranna & Pizzuto 2001). The coarticulation phenomena observed in signed languages also appear to be significantly different from those observed in spoken languages, where coarticulation is realized for the most at the phonetic/phonological, and partially morphological levels (Crystal 1987) but not at the word-unit level, as in signed languages. Two related questions arise with respect to the acquisition processes. One regards the distribution of one-compared to two-handed signs in children's production and the extent to which it is comparable to the adult pattern. A second question regards the use of coarticulation in child as compared to adult signing. To our knowledge, these questions have not been systematically explored in research on the acquisition of signed languages. The present study aims to provide preliminary evidence on these topics with respect to the acquisition of LIS.

A second general articulatory feature of LIS manual signs that also recurs across signed languages is a distinction between two broad classes of signs which are easily identifiable at the *citation form* level as in actual discourse: one consists of signs that are articulated on the body, the other of signs that are articulated in neutral space (with one or more points of articulation). This very general articulatory or morphophonological feature has a direct impact on morphological structure. I shall illustrate this point in reference to relevant aspects of LIS noun and verb morphology. These aspects are:

1. the marking of numerosity in noun signs;
2. the possibility of dislocating noun signs in space for marking deictic/anaphoric reference and/or grammatical agreement;
3. the alteration of verbs' point(s) of articulation for specifying in space, discourse (e.g. person roles) and/or semantic-grammatical information (e.g. agent/experiencer/subject — patient/beneficiary/recipient/object roles, locative relations).

In our analysis of these aspects of LIS noun and verb morphology, we have found it useful to draw a major distinction between two broad classes of signs characterized as, respectively, *inflectional* and *uninflectional* signs (Pizzuto & Corazza 1996; Pizzuto & Pietrandrea 2001).[2] We characterize as *inflectional* all signs that can undergo regular alterations of their citation forms, notably of their point(s) of articulation and/or also movement pattern (direction, orientation) for specifying the discourse and/or grammatical information listed above. We characterize as *uninflectional* signs that cannot modify their citation form for specifying the same discourse or grammatical information.[3] Since in real discourse contexts the inflections we refer to are often optional in LIS (see below), a further distinction needs to be made within the class of inflectional signs, namely that between *inflected* and *uninflected* signs. *Inflected* signs are signs that belong to the inflectional class and that actually show, in discourse, regular morphological alterations of their citation form to convey discourse/grammatical information, i.e. they are in fact inflected. *Uninflected* signs are signs that also belong to the inflectional category, and hence could be inflected, but which in real discourse are produced in their citation, i.e., unmarked or uninflected form.

A comprehensive discussion of inflectional vs. uninflectional patterns in LIS would require a detailed examination of the controversial issues raised by the grammatical or non-grammatical status of the marked points of articulation, or loci, where signs can be produced, and of the questions concerning morphological vs. spatial agreement (Padden 1990; Liddell 1990, 1995; Pizzuto & Corazza 1996; Meir 1998). This discussion however is beyond the scope of the present work, and the reader is referred to Pizzuto (1986), Pizzuto et al. (1990) and Pizzuto and Corazza (1996) for more details on this topic. In this context I would like to draw the reader's attention to somewhat more basic issues: the need of fully recognizing the links between the signs' articulatory features and their morphological behavior, the presence of optional inflectional patterns, and the relevance this may have for an appropriate understanding of the most general typological features of LIS morphology, and hence also quite directly for explorations of the developmental patterns.

2.1.1   *Highlighting relevant articulatory, morphophonological and morphological features*

The articulatory, morphophonological and morphological features briefly outlined above can be better described by considering the gloss-based notation we use (given the lack of more appropriate notation devices) to code these features.

In the tradition of sign language research, we notate relevant articulatory and morphophonological features by means of letter/number subscripts on the signs' glosses. The notation developed for LIS differs from the one adopted by the largest majority of researchers in the field, however, in that it extends the use of subscript indices to notate not only signs articulated at marked positions in the signing space, but also signs that cannot or do not inflect in space. Notational conventions are as follows: a *0* subscript indicates signs characterized by a single point of articulation in neutral or unmarked space; an *x* subscript indicates signs characterized by a single point of articulation near or close to the signer's body. Subscripts *1, 2, 3a, 3b, 3c* (or other letters following the number *3*) indicate signs articulated at marked positions in the signing space. These correspond to, respectively: a position *1* at or close to the signer's body that marks first person; a position *2* close to the signer's addressee marking second person reference; different marked positions in the third person reference space, distinguished by different letters ($3a$, $3b$, $3c$, $3d$, etc.), where nouns, pronouns or verbs signs can be articulated. The use of two different subcripts on a sign gloss indicates that the sign has two points of articulation, where the first subscript indicates the beginning and the second subscript the ending point of articulation, e.g. $_{3a}$TEACH$_{3b}$ indicates a form of the LIS verb TEACH meaning 'she/he teaches her/him' where the beginning point of articulation $3a$ marks a 3rd person subject, and the ending point $3b$ a third person object. The subscript 0–0–0 indicates noun signs marked for numerosity as described below.

In LIS, nouns and verbs that are articulated in neutral space can alter their point(s) of articulation, and thus exhibit inflectional properties. In contrast, nouns and verbs that are articulated on (or very close to) the body cannot alter their point(s) of articulation and can be characterized as uninflectional (at least with respect to the discourse/grammatical functions specified above). For example, a noun sign articulated in neutral space, such as $_0$DISH, can undergo a morphological modification for *numerosity* that is found in all nouns with the same articulatory features: the place of articulation and also, partially at least, the movement pattern is modified, with a repeated displacement of the sign handshape(s) in at least three points (in the notation used here: DISH0-0-0). In contrast, a noun sign articulated on the body, such as $_x$DOG, cannot undergo the same morphological modification. To express the concept of 'many dogs' the sign $_x$DOG is followed by a quantifier LIS sign glossed as $_0$MANY. Similarly, a neutral-space noun can be dislocated at a marked position in space, while nouns articulated on the body cannot. For example, the LIS noun $_0$CHILD can be dislocated at a marked position in the third person reference space in the sentence context $_{3a}$CHILD $_{3a}$GROW (meaning 'the child is growing or has grown'). In this sentence, the noun and the co-occurring verb share the same morphologically marked position. In the same sentence context, the LIS noun $_x$SON cannot undergo the same displacement, and the sentence meaning 'the son grows/has grown' is produced as $_x$SON $_0$GROW, where the verb also appears in its unmarked, citation form (Pizzuto et al. 1990; see also below)

Within the class of verb signs, three major classes can be distinguished: one comprises uninflectional verbs articulated on the body like $_x$EAT or $_x$KNOW that retain their citation form regardless of the arguments they specify. Noted in many other signed languages, these verbs have been characterized by some authors as *plain verbs* (cfr. Padden 1983, 1990). The second and third class both comprise inflectional verbs that are (fully or in part) articulated in neutral space. However, the verbs of the second class are characterized by two points of articulation and usually exhibit a directional path movement between these two points. These verbs can alter their beginning and/or ending point(s) to mark one or two of their arguments. A prototypical example of this class of verbs is $_1$GIVE$_2$ which in LIS (as in ASL) can change its beginning and ending point to mark agreement with its subject and indirect object arguments. Note that the citation form of most verbs of this class coincides with the form marked for a first person subject and a second person (direct or indirect) object, and it is only in the actual context utterance, and often also by referring to the non-manual components that co-occur with the signs, that one can disambiguate whether the verb is produced in its citation form, or in a form effectively marked for first and second person reference (Pizzuto et al. 1990). The third large class consists of verbs characterized by a single point of articulation, like $_0$GROW or $_0$BREAK, which can alter their point of articulation to agree with only one of their potential argument, most commonly their semantic patient or experiencer. There are also different subclasses, surprisingly similar across signed languages, but these are ignored for the sake of the present discussion (see Pizzuto 1986). The key point I wish to make here is that in adult LIS uninflectional verbs appear to be represented in remarkably high proportions, and the same is true for uninflectional nouns (Pizzuto et al. 1990).

Another relevant feature of LIS morphology is the relative variability and optionality of inflectional patterns, especially within the class of verb signs — a feature that has also been noted for other signed languages such as ASL and Danish Sign Language (DSL) (see Pizzuto 1986, and Pizzuto et al. 1990 for relevant data and a more in depth discussion). For example, it has been found that verbs that potentially can be inflected for one or two arguments are produced in uninflected/unmarked forms when their arguments are specified by uninflectional nouns articulated on the body, as in the sentence $_x$SON $_0$GROW reported above (Pizzuto et al. 1990). In the marking of numerosity in noun signs, those nouns articulated in neutral space that, in principle, can take the numerosity inflection are not always or necessarily inflected. The concept of numerosity can also be specified when the noun citation form is kept and the lexical quantifier $_0$MANY is added to it, thus extending to these nouns the same pattern that is found in uninflectional nouns articulated on the body. Yet another option, for both inflectional and uninflectional nouns, is to produce the noun in its citation form and then add to it an appropriate 'classifier' sign[4] which can in its turn take on the numerosity inflection (Pizzuto & Corazza 1996).

2.2 Typological features and hypotheses concerning learning processes

It is well known from cross-linguistic research on the acquisition of spoken languages that the specific typological features of the language to be acquired play an important role in shaping the learning process (Slobin 1985). For example, the acquisition of some of the most frequent verb inflections for person in Italian, a language with a very rich and uniform inflectional morphology where nouns, verbs, adjectives, articles and pronouns are always obligatorily inflected, takes place at a relatively faster pace than the acquisition of the much more limited but fairly irregular system of verb inflections in English, a language with very little inflectional morphology (Pizzuto & Caselli 1992, 1994).

The evidence available on the acquisition of signed languages such as ASL, British Sign Language (BSL) and, more recently, Sign Language of the Netherlands (SLN) consistently indicates that verb inflections of different kinds (including those for person and grammatical role) are acquired fairly late: mastery of verb morphology is still on its way through age 6 (see among others Newport & Meier 1985; van den Bogaerde 2000, for data on SLN and a review; Baker & Woll 1999). Different explanations have been proposed for this delayed acquisition pattern. Van den Bogaerde (2000: 212) also reports data on the verb input native SLN children (age range: 1;0 to 3;0 years) receive from their deaf mothers which show that a very large proportion of verbs (as much as between 72% and 85%) are in their citation form, i.e., uninflected. Commenting on these data van den Bogaerde (2000: 249) notes that verb inflections, as well as some other structural regularities that were very poorly represented in the input data she analyzed (and as a result also in the deaf children's output language), do not appear to be so infrequent in adult SLN. The reason why these structural regularities are so infrequent in input to children thus remains obscure. Van den Bogaerde suggests that the cause may be related to the development of attention-giving behavior on the part of the children. Newport and Meier (1985: 920 ff.) also discuss a study by Kantor (1982a, 1982b) on ASL parental input showing that mothers often omit verb inflections in their input to children, and compare it with another study on the same topic by Meier (1983). Contrary to Kantor, Meier found that although parents used ASL verbs, which do not require agreement, and frequently omitted some optional verb inflections, they consistently used verb inflections in required contexts.

I would like to propose here that in order to gain further insights in the developmental process, more extensive information on the frequency and distribution of inflectional compared to uninflectional patterns and, more generally, on the broad typological features of the language to which the child is exposed, is highly desirable, both for LIS and for other signed languages. With respect to LIS, it is plausible that the sheer presence and diversity of the inflectional/uninflectional patterns and the optionality of inflectional patterns noted in several contexts influences the acquisition process. The appropriate use of inflected forms may be harder to master in a system in which inflectional patterns coexist along with uninflectional ones and are also optional in some contexts. The study described in this chapter aims to evaluate the plausibility of this hypothesis by providing new data on the frequency and distribution of inflectional as compared to uninflectional types of signs in the language produced by the children we examined and in a sample of adult LIS.

2.3 Oral components in signed production

Recent research on several European signed languages, including LIS, has uncovered the relevance of oral components in signed communication (Boyes Braem & Sutton Spence 2000, 2001). It has been shown that the production of manual signs is frequently accompanied by articulatory movements of the mouth, with or without voice, that represent in part words or word fragments of the contact-spoken language (used in a highly variable and on the whole idiosyncratic manner), and in part sign language-specific oral gestures that obligatorily accompany the production of particular signs, and that have no *word-equivalent* in the contact-spoken language. There is still much debate over the status that should be assigned to these oral components (especially to those representing spoken language words) in descriptions of signed language structure. However, it has become clear that oral components deserve to be fully recognized and investigated if we wish to achieve a more appropriate understanding of the structure of signed languages, the extent to which they incorporate elements of the (dominant) spoken languages with which they are in contact and, last but by no means least, the complex expressive possibilities that arise from the fact that words (or word fragments) can indeed be coarticulated with signs. As noted by several authors (see van den Bogaerde 2000 for a recent review) bimodal sign-word productions may reflect a signed or a spoken language structure, depending upon the context in which they are used and/or the competence of the signers who produce them and/or to whom they are addressed.

Evidence on the use of oral components in LIS comes from two recent, independent studies of adult LIS. Ajello, Mazzoni and Nicolai (1997, 2001) analyzed a large corpus of informal conversational exchanges among a total of twelve competent signers (age: 35–55 years). The sample of signers examined was well representative of the Italian deaf community: all signers had LIS as their first language, some came from deaf families, others from hearing families but had acquired LIS early in life in schools for the deaf. Fontana and Fabbretti (2000) analyzed elicited narratives produced in more formal contexts by four deaf native LIS signers (age: 20–37 years). All four signers were shown a short silent movie and then asked to describe its content. In order to examine the possible role that different interlocutors could play, two of the signers were asked to tell the story to a deaf, native LIS signer interlocutor, the other two to a hearing interlocutor who was familiar with LIS.

Despite differences in data sets and methodology, a common finding of these studies was that more than half of the signs produced (around 55–58%) were accompanied by oral components and that these were in the vast majority of cases (up to 97% in Fontana and Fabbretti's study of native signers) words or word fragments of spoken Italian (both voiced and unvoiced). A much smaller proportion of oral components (between 3% and 6%) consisted instead of sign language specific oral gestures that obligatorily accompany a specific set of LIS signs. Fontana and Fabbretti also report that the production of oral components did not appear to be influenced by the hearing or deaf status of the signer's interlocutor.

In her research on SLN, van den Bogaerde (2000:67) found that in the language deaf mothers addressed to their deaf children the proportion of utterances consisting only of SLN signs (which included sign language specific oral gestures, but not mouthed or voiced Dutch words) was on the average 34%, whereas the largest proportion of signed utterances (65%) which still followed a SLN structure consisted of simultaneous productions of signs and spoken words. Utterances made only of Dutch words were represented in a negligible proportion (2%). In the children's language, SLN utterances predominated, but simultaneous sign/word utterances tended to increase over time.

All of these observations suggest that, in adult as well as in child sign language, the use of oral components (including simultaneous and or sequential sign/word combinations) needs to be further investigated. The present study aims to contribute to this line of research providing new data on the use of oral components in children acquiring LIS.

3. Methodology

3.1 The sample of children examined and their language learning environments

Four profoundly deaf children of deaf parents (two girls, two boys) participated in this study. Hereafter they will be referred to by their initials: M, L, F and C. Their age at the time of the study was between 3;11 and 5;10. The children were all second-generation signers (all had hearing grandparents). Their families' socioeconomic-cultural background was in the middle (M and L) and lower-middle range (F and C). None of the children's parents had a university degree.

Although LIS was the primary input language for all of the children, their language environments at home, in school and/or within spoken language education programs varied. Three children (M, L and F) were exposed at home to spoken Italian, which they received primarily from their grandparents, while one child (C) was exposed exclusively to LIS. The parents of two children (M and L) also reportedly used at home what can be described as Sign Supported Italian (SSI), a form of bimodal communication which relies on spoken Italian words simultaneously accompanied by LIS signs of corresponding meaning. These same two children followed bimodal spoken language education programs where they were exposed to further SSI input, and to Exact Signed Italian (ESI). This is a more structured form of bimodal communication devised for educational purposes (Beronesi, Massoni & Ossella 1991). Unlike SSI, it includes artificially created manual signs for several grammatical morphemes of spoken Italian (e.g. for prepositions, nouns and verbs endings, and pronouns). All the children were enrolled in kindergarten, but they were differently distributed between a public school for hearing children (M), an integrated public school for deaf and hearing children which provided a program for bilingual education in sign and speech, and where communication in SSI was common (L), and a private, oralist school for deaf children only which did not provide any structured language intervention program, neither in speech nor in sign (F and C).

3.2 Materials and methodology used to elicit the children's production

A picture description task was used to elicit the children's production. Eighteen drawings of simple concrete objects and actions aimed at eliciting the production of LIS lexical and morphological elements and simple utterances of different complexity. In particular, four test items aimed at eliciting the production of plural forms of, respectively, two uninflectional nouns (e.g. $_x$CAT, $_x$BED) and two inflectional nouns (e.g. $_0$CHILD, $_0$DISH) (see Section 2.1.1. for an explanation of the subscripts). The remaining fourteen test items aimed at eliciting the production of utterances with morphologically different verbs that specified a range of semantic and grammatical relations. These included:

1. two simple uninflectional one-argument verbs (e.g. $_x$SLEEP, $_x$SMILE);
2. five inflectional verbs that are frequently described in the literature as *object incorporating* (e.g. verbs in which the handshape of the sign provides information on the object-argument of the verb, such as $_0$OPEN-BOX, $_0$OPEN-WINDOW, $_0$OPEN-DOOR, $_0$CUT-WITH-KNIFE, $_0$CUT-WITH-SCISSORS[5];
3. two inflectional verbs that may agree with their patient/experience and/or object argument (e.g. $_0$BURN, $_1$WATCH$_2$,);
4. four verbs that appear to possess both an uninflectional reflexive form (e.g. $_x$COMB-ONESELF, $_x$WASH-ONESELF), and an inflectional transitive form (e.g. $_0$COMB, $_0$WASH);
5. one verb expressing a complex locative relation ($_1$THROW-INSIDE$_0$).

The task was presented to each child individually by a deaf native LIS signer particularly skilled in interacting with deaf children (a sign language teacher in bilingual programs for deaf children). Prior to presenting the task, the examiner got to know the children a bit in a free play/interaction session. Each child was told she/he would be shown some drawings, and was asked to describe them as best as she/he could. Whenever necessary the deaf examiner encouraged the children to expand their descriptions with appropriate questions that were as natural as possible. All observations were conducted in our laboratory and fully videorecorded.

3.3 Data analysis, transcription and coding

All the children appeared to enjoy the task, and responded to it by producing not only utterances related to the illustrations they were presented with but also a variety of utterances linked to their own everyday experience. Since our primary interest was to obtain as much information as possible on major structural regularities in the children's production, and these unsolicited utterances provided valuable information on this issue, all the utterances produced by the children were included in the data to be analyzed, regardless of whether they were related to the target LIS utterances we aimed to elicit.

The children's productions were transcribed and coded by two independent coders: a sign language interpreter, and a speech therapist with a very good knowledge of LIS. A deaf colleague (native LIS signer) who is also an experienced sign language researcher then checked the accuracy of these transcriptions.

As mentioned earlier, there are currently no really appropriate notation/ transcription tools for analyzing and describing signed language texts and connected utterances (Pizzuto & Pietrandrea 2001). For the present study, we adapted to our needs the gloss-based notation described in Section 2.1.1. Transcriptions were initially made by hand. Since we aimed to obtain quantitative as well as qualitative information on some of the major structural regularities in the children's production, we implemented our notation in a computerized format, adapting to our purposes the CHAT transcription proposed within the CHILDES system for the analysis of spoken language data (MacWhinney 2000; see also Slobin, Hoiting, Anthony, Biederman, Kuntze, Lindert, Pyers, Thumann and Veinberg 2001, and the chapter by Hoiting & Slobin in this volume for different proposals on the use of the CHILDES system for signed language data). Most of the analyses were subsequently done with the FREQ program of the CLAN package (MacWhinney 2000). Examples 1 through 3 below illustrate our main transcription and coding tools.

(1) @s   Many dishes
     *CHI: EAT/FOOD-x-rh=ma DISH-0–2sh INDEX-0-rh MANY-0–2sh.
             EAT/FOOD-x-rh INDEX-0-rh SCHOOL-0–2ah.
             MANY-0–2sh=ta DISH-0–0–0–2sh. ORDER-1–0-rh FORCE-1–0-rh
             INDEX-0-rh EAT/FOOD-x-rh DISH-0–2sh.
     %eng: there are many dishes with food. in school there are dishes with
             food. many dishes.
             and you really must eat the food that is in your dish.

(2) @s   a girl watching TV
     *CHI: INDEX-obj-rh CL-RECTANGULAR-OBJECT-TV-0–3a-2sh
             INDEX-obj-rh CL-RECTANGULAR-OBJECT-TV-0–3a-2sh.
             SEE-x-3a-rh WATCH-x-0-rh.
     %eng: there is a TV here, a TV here. and a girl sees it, watches it.

(3) @s7   a dog asleep
     *CHI: DOG-x-rh=ca COST/MONEY-0–2sh=ompa INDEX-obj-rh
             COST/MONEY-0-rh.
             INDEX-0-rh ONE-0-rh INDEX-0-rh ONE-0-rh
             ONE-0-lh[coart+DOG] DOG-x-rh[coart+ONE].

SLEEP-x-2sh=do FALL-ASLEEP-x-2sh
SLEEP-x-rh LEAVE-0–2sh BY-HIMSELF-x-rh WAKE-UP-x-2sh
BY-HIMSELF-x-rh LEAVE-0-rh.
%eng: a dog is expensive, this (points to picture) is expensive. this is
one, this is one, one dog. it is sleeping, it has fallen asleep, sleeps,
let's leave it alone, it will wake up by itself, let's leave it alone.

Following the main conventions of the CHAT transcription system, lines
beginning with a @ symbol specify the stimulus presented to the child (e.g., in
(1), a drawing showing many dishes). The children's utterances are represented
in the main lines starting with a * symbol, followed by a three-letter code that
identifies the child (e.g. *CHI*). Although the CHAT format requires that there
be only one utterance on each main line, we did not follow this convention. All
the utterances that were interconnected, and produced after presentation of the
same stimulus were transcribed on the same main line. The appropriate CHAT
symbol (a period: ".") was used as an utterance delimitor (e.g. the stretch of text
transcribed in (1) contained four connected utterances). The manual signs
produced by the child are represented via annotated glosses in capitals. Hyphenated letter and number indexes attached to the glosses encode relevant
information on the signs' articulatory and morphological features, as described
in detail in the next paragraph.

The following general glossing conventions are used: a / symbol indicates
signs that correspond in meaning to spoken/written words that belong to
different morphological classes, such as that of nouns vs. verbs. For example, in
(1) above, the gloss EAT/FOOD indicates that the LIS sign represented by this
gloss corresponds in meaning to both the English verb *eat* and the noun *food*
(the distinction between noun and verb is not morphologically marked in this
case, see Pizzuto & Corazza 1996). Signs that require more than one spoken/
written word to be glossed are represented by more than one word, separated by
hyphens. The CL abbreviation indicates classifier signs. For example in (2)
above, the gloss CL-RECTANGULAR-OBJECT-TV indicates a descriptive sign the
child used to refer to the television set illustrated in the picture she was presented, and for which there is no single corresponding word in English or Italian.

The first index following the sign gloss signals the major morphological
distinction between uninflectional and inflectional signs as previously described. Signs that have a single point of articulation on the body, defined as
uninflectional in our framework, are signaled by a single x index (e.g.
EAT/FOOD-x). Signs that have one or more points of articulation in neutral
space, or that are articulated at morphologically marked positions in space, that

is those signs that are characterized as inflectional and/or actually inflected in our framework, are signaled as follows:

1. single 0 index on the gloss shows that the sign is articulated at a morphologically unmarked position in neutral space or, in other words, that the sign belongs to the inflectional type but was not actually inflected in context (e.g. DISH-0 in (1) above);

2. multiple and/or different indexes are used to signal signs that are articulated at morphologically marked positions in the signing space, i.e. that are inflected.

For example, in (2) above, the indexes 0–3a in the gloss CL-RECTANGULAR-OBJECT-TV-0–3a indicate that this sign belongs to the class of inflectional signs that have a single point of articulation in neutral space (0), but in this specific case the sign was articulated at a marked position 3a. In (1) above, the indexes 1 and 0 in the sign ORDER-1–0 and FORCE-1–0 indicate that these signs had two points of articulation: a beginning point near the signer, corresponding to the position for first person reference or 1, and an ending, unmarked point of articulation in neutral space, or 0 (see below for the appropriate interpretation assigned in context to these verb forms). The abbreviation obj (for object) is used to indicate pointing signs that the children in some cases produced and which were articulated directly on real world objects such as the drawings they were shown rather than in the signing space. These pointings were glossed as INDEX-obj (see example (2) above). Finally, the notation 0–0–0 is used to indicate signs that bear the morphological alteration for *numerosity* previously described in Section 2.1.1. as for example the noun sign DISH-0–0–0 in (1) above.

Glosses marked with the same indexes indicate signs articulated at the same marked position in the signing space. For example, in (2) above the same 3a index in the signs CL-RECTANGULAR-OBJECT-TV-0–3a and SEE-x-3a indicates that the final point of articulation of the sign SEE was the same as that previously used to locate in the signing space the sign CL-RECTANGULAR-OBJECT-TV (whereas the x index in the gloss SEE indicates that the beginning point of articulation of this sign is on the body, in this case close to the signer's eye).

The letters following the indexes described above indicate whether each given sign was articulated with the right hand (e.g., in (1), EAT/FOOD-x-rh), the left hand (e.g. in (3) ONE-0-lh), two symmetrical hands (e.g. in (1) DISH-0–2sh), or two asymmetrical hands (e.g. the sign for SCHOOL-0–2ah, not shown in the examples above).

Signs that are coarticulated with another sign are signaled by the notation [coart+SIGN] attached to the gloss of each of the coarticulated signs, as in ONE-0-lh[coart+DOG] DOG-x-rh[coart+ONE] in (3) above, where the child first produced with her left hand the sign ONE, and then maintained this sign in time and space while articulating with her right hand the sign DOG.

The oral components that in several cases were co-articulated with the signs were notated in the transcription, in standard Italian orthography, following a = symbol. When these components were voiced, the word or word fragment that was produced was transcribed, with no further notation. For example, in (1) above EAT/FOOD-x-rh=ma and MANY-0-2sh=ta show that the word fragments ma (for the Italian word *mangiare* meaning 'to eat') and *ta* (for the Italian word *tanto* or *tanti* meaning 'many') accompanied the signs EAT/FOOD and MANY. When these components were simply mouthed without producing sounds the Italian word recognizable from the child's mouth movements was transcribed and the notation [−voice] was added, as in INDEX-0-rh HOUSE-0-2ah=casa[−voice], where the Italian word *casa*, meaning 'house' was mouthed together with the sign HOUSE.

A broad English translation of the children's signed utterances in (1)–(3) is provided in the line starting with the %eng code. Note that the fragments of Italian words that accompanied some of the signs were not translated: it was very difficult, and indeed impossible to represent their fragment properties via an English translation. Note also that the translation we provided is necessarily broad, with no one-to-one correspondence with the basic meanings of the manual signs' glosses shown on the * line. The translation reflects the overall information conveyed by the children's utterances, part of which was either encoded at the non-manual level of expression (not explicitly explored in the present study — see note 1 at the end of this chapter), or inferable from the context. Without taking into account this information the translation would have been totally meaningless. For instance, the signs glossed as ORDER-1-0-rh and FORCE-1-0-rh in example (1) were ambiguous, and could not have been appropriately interpreted if we had considered only the information provided at the manual level: the signs could have corresponded to either the citation forms of these verbs, or forms marked for a first person subject argument and unmarked for their object argument (e.g. *I order/force someone*). But the non-manual components that accompanied these signs clarified that the child used the signs in their citation forms, while conveying at the same time an *impersonal you* meaning through the facial expression she used, as reflected in our English translation. Similarly, comparing the signs' glosses and their translation in example (2), the reader will notice that the translation includes reference to a girl watching TV despite the fact that no manual sign for *girl* is notated on the gloss line. Yet this information was at least partially provided by the child, and understandable in the specific context of the utterance at the non-manual level: the child used a marked facial expression and body posture for impersonating an animate referent — a device that is often used in LIS discourse, and which is also meaningfully related to the use of unmarked, citation forms of verb signs (Pizzuto et al. 1990). But this information could hardly have been rendered by such expressions as animate referent: the translation given above appeared to be more appropriate.

4. Results and discussion

The major results are summarized in Figures 1 through 7. Drawing primarily on quantitative analyses of the data conducted on sign types (as distinguished from tokens), we shall first examine some of the major articulatory and morphological features of the different signs used by the children, and compare them whenever possible with regularities noted in adult LIS. Second, we will consider the use of oral components in the children's production. Observations based on a more qualitative analysis of the data will then be reported and discussed.

4.1 Major articulatory features of the signs produced by the children

Figure 1 shows the number of different sign types identified in each child's production.

The data in Figure 1 evidence both developmental and individual differences. The repertoire of signs used in our language task by the youngest child (M, N = 35) was markedly smaller compared to that of the other three older children (N = from 70 to 119). Two of the three older children (L and C) used a larger repertoire of signs compared to that of the third child in the same age range (F).

Figure 2 shows the distribution of one- vs. two-handed sign types in the four children's productions.

It can be seen that one-handed signs were represented in larger proportions (from 51% to 66%) compared to two-handed signs (from 34% to 49%), especially in the productions of the two children M and L. The majority of two-handed signs belonged to the symmetrical type. Asymmetrical two-handed signs were represented in a very small number (from 2 to 5 sign types), and only

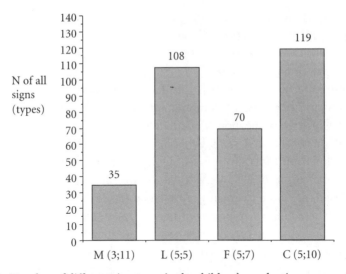

Figure 1. Number of different sign types in the children's productions.

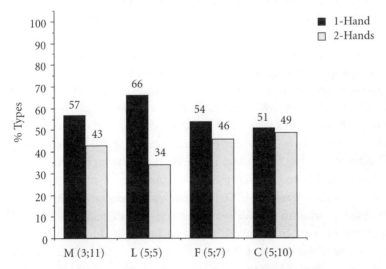

Figure 2. Proportion of 1-handed vs. 2-handed sign types in the children's productions.

in the productions of the three older children. It is of interest to note that in some cases two-handed symmetrical signs occurred both in their full form with two symmetrical hands, and in a reduced one-handed form. These one-handed variants of two-handed signs are not represented in Figure 2: in the computation of sign types, those that occurred in both a two- and a one-handed form were considered only once, and included in the two-handed group. These reduced forms constitute a quite unique feature of sign production as observed in analyses of LIS dictionaries (Pietrandrea 1995) and in actual adult discourse (Russo 1999). They are worth noting because they increase, at least in principle, the potential for coarticulation.

These patterns in the children's productions are fairly comparable to those recently identified in adult LIS monologues (formal lectures texts, see Russo 1999), in which the proportion of one-handed signs was between 40% and 52%, and that of two-handed signs between 30% and 48%. Interestingly, these patterns differ somewhat from those identified by Pietrandrea (1995, 1997) in analyses of a corpus of 2055 signs listed in three LIS dictionaries, where two-handed signs are more frequently represented (56,5%) than one-handed signs (43,5%). These differences point out that analyses of the frozen signs that are usually included in the dictionaries need to be validated and integrated with analyses conducted on signs taken from actual discourse, where remarkable differences may also emerge depending upon the specific texts that are analyzed (e.g. poetic vs. non poetic texts: see Russo 1999; Russo et al. 2001). The prevalence of symmetrical signs over asymmetrical ones also appears to be similar to that noted in adult LIS, as documented by both Pietrandrea's analyses of dictionary signs (1995) and Russo's (1999) study of texts produced in ordinary prose.

In principle, the remarkable proportion of one-handed signs in the children's productions provided a wide range of opportunities for simultaneous (or sequential) coarticulation of two different manual signs. However, the children exploited this possibility only to a very limited extent. Coarticulated signs occurred in the productions of only two children: F (1 occurrence), and C (6 occurrences), and were absent from the production of the remaining two children. This pattern differs from that noted in adult production. Analyses of adult texts in ordinary prose (Russo 1999; Russo et al. 2001) have revealed that the proportion of coarticulated signs and simultaneous syntax in such text is around 22–29%. The very limited use of coarticulation by the children examined in this study suggests that learning to use simultaneous morphosyntax is a slow process, as noted in studies of ASL focused on the acquisition of morphological facial expressions coarticulated with manual signs (Newport & Meier 1985; Reilly 2000).

4.2 Major morphophonological and morphological features of the children's signs

Figure 3 shows the distribution (percentages) of sign types articulated on the body compared to sign types articulated in neutral space.

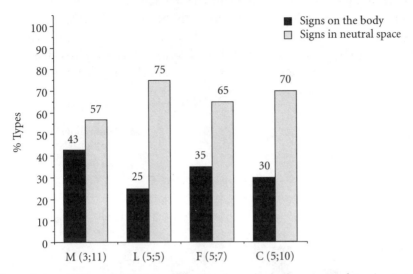

Figure 3. Proportion of sign types articulated on the body compared to sign types articulated in neutral space in the children's productions.

Looking at Figure 3 it can be seen that across all children signs articulated in neutral space were represented in larger proportions (57% to 75%) compared to signs articulated on the body (25% to 43%). This distribution is fairly comparable to that observed in adult LIS. Pietrandrea's (1995; 1997) analyses of a large corpus of dictionary signs (see above) show that 61% of these are articulated in neutral space and that 39% have points of articulation on the body. From a general standpoint (i.e., irrespective of the grammatical categories that can be attributed to different signs) signs articulated in neutral space are potentially signs of the inflectional type, whereas signs articulated on the body potentially belong to the uninflectional type as characterized above. From this perspective, it can be noted that although neutral space (potentially inflectional) signs are represented in larger proportions than body-articulated signs, the latter always constitute a relevant, and certainly not negligible proportion in adult LIS as in all four children's repertoire (from 25% to as much as 43% in the production of the younger child). These data provide a general indication of the relevance of potentially uninflectional features in LIS that cannot be underestimated when examining developmental processes. More specific information on this topic is provided by the data illustrated in Figures 4a–c. The figures show the distribution of uninflectional compared to inflectional noun and verb types in the overall production of the four children, and in the production of one adult native signer who was presented with the same picture description task that was administered to the children. The adult corpus consisted of 17 nouns and 18 verb types. The raw numbers of distinct nouns and verbs identified in the children's production varied between 12 and 28 (for nouns), and between 15 and 54 (for verbs).

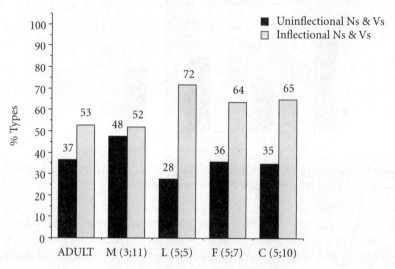

Figure 4a. Proportion of uninflectional compared to inflectional nouns (Ns) and verbs (Vs) types in the adult's and in the children's productions.

Looking at Figure 4a, where nouns and verbs are collapsed in a single class, it can be seen that both in the adult's and in the children's productions, inflectional noun and verb types were more prominent (from 52% to 72%) than uninflectional ones. However, the proportion of uninflectional noun and verb types was by no means negligible (from 28% to 48%). Figures 4b and 4c show the distribution of uninflectional and inflectional signs within the categories of, respectively, nouns and verbs. It can be seen from Figure 4b that in the productions of the adult and three of the children (M, L and C) inflectional nouns were more frequently represented than uninflectional ones. However, once again, across these subjects, uninflectional nouns constituted a noticeable proportion (from 32% to 42%) and also were more frequent than inflectional nouns in one child's production (F: 53% uninflectional vs. 47% inflectional nouns). Within the verb category, the proportion of inflectional

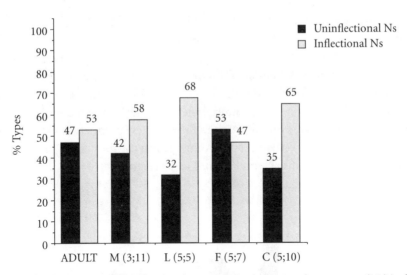

Figure 4b. Proportion of uninflectional compared to inflectional noun types (Ns) in the adult's and in the children's productions.

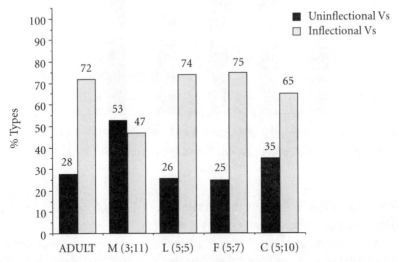

Figure 4c. Proportion of uninflectional compared to inflectional verb types (Vs) in the adult's and in the children's productions.

verbs was markedly greater than that of uninflectional verbs in the production of the adult and of the three older children (from 65% to 75%), whereas in the youngest child (M) uninflectional verbs were slightly more frequent (53%) than inflectional ones (47%).

It can be recalled from the previous description of adult LIS that noun and verb inflections are not always obligatory in LIS but are optional in several contexts. It is thus of interest to see how frequently inflectional nouns and verbs appeared in inflected as compared to unmarked or uninflected forms. Figures 5a–c show the relative distribution of inflectional noun and verb types that appeared at least once in one or more inflected form, compared to those that appeared always and only in uninflected forms. These production patterns are shown for nouns and verbs collapsed into a single category in Figure 5a, and within the class of nouns (Figure 5b) and verbs (Figure 5c).

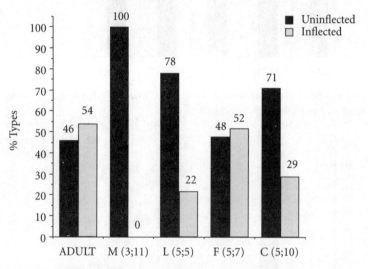

Figure 5a. Proportion of inflectional nouns and verbs in uninflected vs. inflected forms in the adult's and in the children's productions.

The data in Figure 5a show that in two cases (the adult's and F's production) inflectional verb and noun types that appeared in inflected forms (hereafter termed *inflected* for brevity) were represented in slightly larger proportions than inflectional nouns and verbs that appeared in uninflected forms (hereafter called *uninflected*). However, on the whole a large proportion of inflectional nouns and verbs followed the uninflected pattern (from 46% in the adult's production to as much as 100% in the youngest child). The uninflected pattern was thus very productive, and it was the dominant pattern in the youngest child's production. Since inflectional nouns and verbs were present in the production of this child as well as in that of the older children (albeit in a

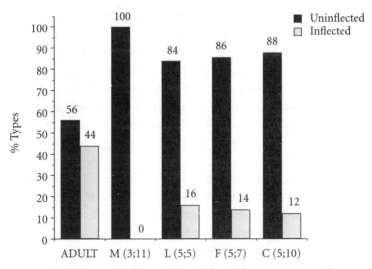

Figure 5b. Proportion of inflectional nouns in uninflected vs. inflected forms in the adult's and in the children's productions.

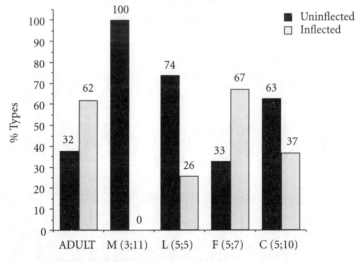

Figure 5c. Proportion of inflectional verbs appearing in uninflected vs. inflected forms in the adult's and in the children's productions.

smaller proportion: see Figures 4a–c), the absence of inflections in this child indicates a clear developmental difference between this child and the older ones. Inflections appear to be a late development in LIS as in other signed languages.

Figures 5a and 5b reveal that inflected forms were produced more frequently within the verb category than within the noun category. Leaving aside the youngest child, it can be seen that the proportion of inflected nouns ranged from 12% to 16% in the remaining children, and was 44% in the adult production. Thus, across all subjects the majority of inflectional nouns appeared in uninflected forms. The proportion of inflected verbs was larger across all subjects (from 26% to 67%), and in the adult and in one child (F) inflected verbs were markedly more frequent (62% and 67%) than uninflected ones (38% and 33%, respectively). However, the proportion of uninflected inflectional verbs was still remarkable, even when we disregard the youngest child's production (from 33% to 74%).

These data provide information on the incidence of the inflected pattern within the category of inflectional nouns and verbs. However, as noted, a remarkable proportion of nouns and verbs belong to the uninflectional type. An accurate evaluation of the overall incidence of inflected patterns requires that we consider the production of inflected forms with respect to the categories of both inflectional and uninflectional noun and verb types. Figures 6a–c show the overall proportion of inflectional noun and/or verb types that appeared in at least one inflected form in the adult's and the children's total production of inflectional and uninflectional nouns and/or verbs.

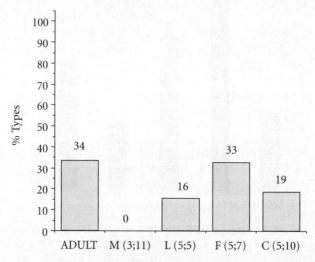

Figure 6a. Overall proportion of inflectional nouns and verbs appearing in at least one inflected form in the adult's and in the children's total production of nouns and verbs.

In Figure 6a inflected nouns and verbs (as defined above) are collapsed together. Their overall proportion was calculated counting the number of

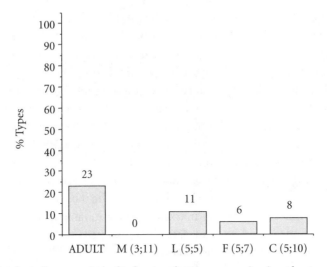

Figure 6b. Overall proportion of inflectional nouns appearing in at least one inflected form in the adult's and in the children's total production of nouns.

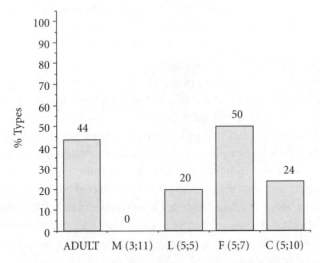

Figure 6c. Overall proportion of inflectional verbs appearing in at least one inflected form in the adult's and in the children's total production of verbs.

inflectional noun and verb types that appeared in at least one (or more) inflected form, and dividing this number by the total number of inflectional and uninflectional noun and verb types. It can be seen that on the average actually inflected verbs and nouns constituted a relatively small proportion in the production of the adult (34%) and that of the three older children (from 16%

to 33%), and were completely absent in the production of the youngest child.

Figures 6b and 6c show the overall proportion of inflected noun and verb types computed *within* these categories: the number of noun and verb types that appeared in at least one inflected form was divided by the total number of, respectively, inflectional and uninflectional nouns (Figure 6b), and inflectional and uninflectional verbs (Figure 6c). Leaving aside once again the production of the youngest child, who did not produce any inflected forms, it can be seen that the inflected pattern was particularly poorly represented within the noun class: the proportion of inflected nouns was 23% in the adult, and in the 6% to 11% range in the remaining three children. The inflected pattern was most frequent for the class of verbs: in the adult and in the three older children, the proportion of inflected verbs was markedly higher, ranging from 20% to 50%. These data confirm and expand those summarized in Figures 5a–c, and highlight relevant differences between nouns and verbs with respect to the frequency with which the inflected pattern occurs. At the same time, it is worth underscoring that the proportion of verb types that occurred in actually inflected forms remained within the limits of at most 50% (as in the most productive case, viz. F's verb production). This implies that at least one half, and often much more (from 56% to 100%) of the verb and noun types followed the uninflectional/uninflected pattern.

Taken together, these data support and expand previous observations made on adult LIS: in child as in adult LIS, the inflected pattern does not appear to constitute the more frequent pattern used in producing verbs and nouns, despite and beyond the fact that inflectional noun and verb types appear to be more represented than uninflectional ones. This is because inflectional nouns and verbs are not always and obligatorily inflected. Inflectional patterns are thus less productive than one might expect. If uninflected forms of inflectional nouns and verbs are considered together with noun and verb forms that belong to the uninflectional type, it becomes clear that the uninflectional and/or uninflected pattern is at least as frequent, and often more frequent than the inflectional/inflected one.

4.3 The use of oral components

We turn now to consider the role of oral components in signed production. Figure 7, outlining the adult's and the children's productions, shows the proportion of sign types that always occurred without any accompanying word or word fragment, compared to that of signs coarticulated at least once together with an Italian word (or word fragment), and of spoken words produced without any accompanying sign. The adult data were drawn from the adult's rendition of our target utterances, as previously described, and consisted of a sample of 41 distinct signs. These included the adult noun and verb signs described in Figures 4a–6c, and a few other quantifier and classifier signs. Note that the oral components identified in the children's and in the adult's production were all Italian words or, most frequently, word fragments corresponding in meaning to the signs with which they were coarticulated (e.g. *ta* recognizable as a fragment of the Italian word *tanti* = 'many' accompanying the sign $_0$MANY). There were no sign-language-specific oral gestures such as those described by Ajello et al. (1997, 2001) and Fontana and Fabbretti (2000). The absence of this second type of oral components in the corpus analyzed here is probably due to the relatively restricted context of language use from which the data were drawn.

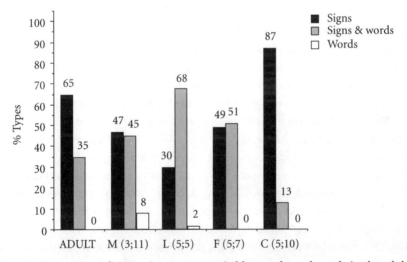

Figure 7. Proportion of signs, signs accompanied by words, and words in the adult's and in the children's productions.

When we first look at the children's productions, the data in Figure 7 highlight strong individual differences but also similarities among the children. There was only child (C) who relied almost exclusively on the visual-gestural modality for her production of signs, and who produced a very small number (13%) of signs accompanied by words. In two of the remaining children (e.g. M and F) signs produced alone and signs coarticulated with words were almost equally distributed, while in the fourth child examined, bimodal productions of signs and words prevailed over sign-only ones (e.g. L: 68% vs. 30%). Two children (M and L) also produced, albeit in a very small number (2% to 8%) spoken language words with no accompanying signs. These were totally absent from the production of the other two children and the adult.

These individual differences may in part be explained by the different global language input the children received. The child who used a very small number of sign-word combinations, C, was the only child who had LIS as single language input at home. M and L, the two children who produced some spoken words without accompanying signs, were those who received a considerable amount of spoken/visual Italian via the bimodal spoken language education programs they followed, and SSI at home from their parents. However, the children's production patterns also appear to reflect idiosyncratic individual variation that cannot be easily explained by referring to their language environments. For example, M's and L's exposure to SSI (and hence to a larger use of bimodal sign-word combinations) was roughly comparable. Yet there were marked differences in the number of sign-word combinations these two children produced. M's use of these combinations was more comparable, at least from a quantitative standpoint, to that observed in F, a child who, to the extent that we could ascertain, did not receive much SSI input. This idiosyncratic individual variation is similar to that noted in adult LIS signers (Ajello et al. 1997).

While children differed with respect to the amount of signed-only or sign-and-word productions they used, their sign-word productions were remarkably similar in one respect: in all cases but one the words or word fragments that accompanied the signs were voiced, not just silently articulated. In contrast, in the adult production the words that accompanied the signs were always articulated silently, with no emission of sounds. Looking at the adult production patterns in Figure 7 it can be noted that although the majority of sign types (65%) were produced without words, the proportion of sign-word combinations was by no means negligible (35%).

It is of interest to relate the children's use of oral components with their use of noun and verb inflections as described in the previous section. One could hypothesize that a greater use of sign-word combinations, such as that noted for example in L, is an indication of a greater influence of the dominant spoken language of the surrounding hearing community which, in turn, may negatively interfere with a child's control of his/her signed language. Assuming that the use of LIS noun and verb inflections is one of the indexes that reveals children's control over the morphological system, and that this is an area where negative interference from spoken language could reveal itself, one could expect marked differences in the use of LIS noun and verb inflections, between a child who used a large number of sign-word combinations, such as L, and a child who used a much smaller number of sign-word combinations, such as C. But the differences in the use of inflections between L and C were not so marked (see Figures 5a–c and 6a–c). It must also be noted that the child who had the larger repertoire of inflections, F, was the same child who produced an almost equal number of signs and sign-word combinations. These data indicate that such bimodal productions do not negatively interfere with children's mastery of their signed language, at least with respect to morphology.

Although differences in data sets and methodologies do not allow precise comparisons between the present study and those conducted on the same topic by other researchers, the data described here are fully in agreement with those reported on adult LIS by Ajello et al. (1997, 2001) and Fontana and Fabbretti (2000), and on child and adult SLN by van den Bogaerde (2000). These data indicate that both in child and in adult signed communication oral components, most notably spoken words and word fragments simultaneously coarticulated with signs of corresponding meaning, constitute a relevant, by no means negligible phenomenon which can and/or must be analyzed as an integral part of signed communication. It was of interest to find that the oral components described here were voiced by the children, but mouthed without sound by the adult. However, the evidence currently available is not sufficient to assess whether this finding reflects a general feature of child as compared to adult LIS, or rather idiosyncratic individual variation. Appropriate information on the frequency with which oral components are voiced or simply mouthed without sound in adult LIS is currently missing.

4.4 A more qualitative view of the children's productions

A qualitative analysis of the data uncovered other relevant aspects of the children's production that help clarify some of the factors that may shape the learning process in a signed language such as LIS.

One of the semantic/morphological distinctions our test aimed to elicit was that of numerosity as it can be expressed with inflectional and uninflectional nouns. Recall that the adult system offers three options. Two of these can be used with both inflectional and uninflectional nouns, namely: adding to the noun's citation form either the quantifier $_0$MANY, or a classifier sign which itself takes the numerosity inflection. A third option can be used only with inflectional nouns, which can be inflected for numerosity via changes of their location and movement pattern. All the children chose the first option: they added the quantifier $_0$MANY to the citation forms of inflectional and uninflectional nouns. The children thus appeared to prefer one option that applies to both noun classes, and which uses a lexical rather than a morphological/inflectional device for specifying numerosity. It would be interesting to know to what extent this preference manifested by the children is related to, and/or is an indication of the relative unmarkedness or higher frequency of this lexical specification of numerosity in LIS. However, the data currently available are not sufficient for evaluating what patterns can be considered more or less marked in child and/or adult LIS.

Individual differences were noted in the sign-order patterns children used in their noun-quantifier utterances, and these appeared to be related to the children's lesser or greater exposure to forms of spoken Italian. The two children who received more SSI input, M and L, used a quantifier+noun order, thus producing a structure that, albeit still acceptable, is considered by native signers closer to Italian than to LIS. The other two children who were less exposed to Italian, F and C, used the more standard LIS order noun+quantifier. More generally, F's and C's overall utterance patterns followed the style that is considered more appropriate in adult LIS more closely. In particular, in utterances requiring that the patient/object of an action be specified, both F and C followed the typical LIS sign order pattern, and first produced the sign for the object, then the verb specifying the action, and last the sign for the patient/subject. In contrast, L followed an agent/subject-verb-patient/object sign order pattern that was closer to the structure of Italian. This point is illustrated by the two utterances in (4) and (5) below, produced by F and L in describing a picture showing a girl watching television. The utterances are represented in a simplified gloss rendition that does not include oral components, with a broad English translation placed between single quotes. Note that F and L used two different signs for 'child': F used an uninflectional sign articulated on the body which also means 'small', L the more standard, neutral space inflectional sign which means only 'child'.

(4) F: $_0$TV $_x$CHILD $_{3a}$TV $_x$SEE$_{3a}$.
    'There is a TV and a child watches it'

(5) L: $_0$CHILD $_x$SEE$_{3a}$ $_{3a}$TV.
    'A child watches TV'

The utterances reported above exemplify two other relevant features of the children's productions. Note in the first place that both children used some inflections, despite and beyond the stylistic differences that characterized their utterances with respect to sign order. Second, note the variability of the inflectional pattern, even within a single utterance. This is particularly evident in F's utterance: the first occurrence of the sign $_0$TV was uninflected, while the second one was inflected, and the marked location used to articulate this sign was subsequently used to mark agreement between the object $_{3a}$TV and the ending point of the verb $_x$SEE$_{3a}$. In L's utterance, the inflectional sign $_0$CHILD appeared in an uninflected form. As it was also evident from the quantitative analyses reported in the previous sections, this variability or optionality in the use of inflections was a salient and recurrent feature in the production of the three older children, amplified to its extreme in the youngest child, who produced no inflections at all. As noted earlier, a similar variability has been reported for adult LIS, where inflections are often optional rather than obligatory.

In child and in adult LIS much remains to be discovered on the grammatical and/or discourse conditions that regulate the use of inflected or uninflected forms. For example, in line with observations made in Pizzuto et al. (1990) on the morphophonological contexts that limit the production of inflections in adult LIS, it is possible that the use of the uninflected form $_0$CHILD in L's utterance above is influenced or determined by the morphophonological features of the verb $_x$SEE$_{3a}$. This verb has as its beginning point a locus on the body which cannot be displaced to mark agreement with its experiencer/subject argument $_0$CHILD. Since agreement with this argument cannot be marked, the sign representing this argument is likewise unmarked. It is also possible that agreement with the experiencer/subject argument is in general less likely to occur compared with agreement with the object argument — a tendency that has been noted in LIS as in other signed languages, including ASL (e.g. Coulter & Anderson 1993:3).

To summarize, the observations reported here confirm and support the results provided by the quantitative analyses on the use of LIS noun and verb inflections discussed above. Perhaps not surprisingly so, regardless of individual and/or stylistic differences, the children's performance in our language task appeared to be guided by regularities proper of the adult language, in which the use of noun and verb inflections is often optional.

5. Summary and concluding remarks

The study described in this chapter is certainly limited, and the generalizability of its results needs to be assessed and validated by more extensive studies on a larger number of subjects and on larger corpora of both child and adult LIS. With this caveat, I would like to conclude by highlighting its major findings and relevant indications for further, more comprehensive investigations of signed language learning in LIS, but also in other signed languages.

Several studies of the acquisition of signed languages, especially ASL, have provided a wealth of information on the internal, phonological and morphological structure of signs and related it to the developmental patterns that are observed (see the reviews by Newport & Meier 1985; van den Bogaerde 2000). However, information on the broad articulatory, morphophonological and morphological features of signs that were considered in this chapter (i.e. frequency and distribution of one- vs. two-handed signs, of inflectional vs. uninflectional and/or uninflected signs) is surprisingly limited in studies of both child and adult signed language.

The data reported above on the distribution of one- vs. two-handed signs are useful, and indeed necessary, for evaluating the very limited use of coarticulation by the children with respect to the possibilities of coarticulation they had due to the high proportion of one-handed signs they used. In this context the non-use of coarticulation by the children as compared with its use in the adult language assumes a developmental relevance, though obviously this finding must be validated in more extensive studies.

I tried to argue here that, because of the inherent links between some of the most general articulatory features of the signs (most notably those related to place of articulation) and morphological regularities, information on the interrelation between articulatory features and morphological regularities is much needed and may help in understanding at least some of the features that shape the developmental process. As noted, these aspects of signed language structure exhibit remarkable similarities across signed languages, and this appears to have quite direct effects on morphological structure, leading for example to very similar verb classes across different signed languages (see Pizzuto 1986; Supalla & Webb 1995, among others). It is thus plausible to think that the structural features we focused upon are relevant not only with respect to the exploration of LIS and its acquisition, but also from a cross-linguistic perspective.

In studies of the acquisition of ASL and, subsequently, of other signed languages, much attention has been focused on inflectional properties, especially on verb inflections (while much less attention has been devoted to noun inflection). A recurrent finding of most studies is that verb inflections are acquired late. There have been recent (e.g. van den Bogaerde 2000) and less recent (e.g. Kantor 1982a, 1982b; and also Meier 1983) reports on parental signed input suggesting that verb inflections may be more sparse in the input to the child than is generally assumed. However, to the knowledge of this writer there have been no attempts to assess the overall incidence of inflectional regularities within the context of the broader morphological patterns of different adult signed languages. The fact that inflections are in some cases optional rather than obligatory has also been underestimated.

The study reported on in this chapter extends to the exploration of developmental patterns the approach we have pursued in the study of adult LIS, where we have tried to pay equal attention to inflectional and uninflectional morphological patterns. What the present study suggests is that, at least in LIS and with respect to the noun and verb inflections examined, the inflectional pattern is not the dominant pattern. Insofar as regularities in the adult language are one (albeit certainly not the only one) of the key factors that may influence developmental processes, the present study provides one possible explanation for the delayed acquisition pattern recurrently observed in the development of signed languages verb inflections. These inflections are acquired late, and with apparent difficulties, because they are less frequent in the input than is commonly assumed. Perhaps even more importantly, acquisition may be delayed by both the diversity of morphological patterns (i.e. inflectional and uninflectional), and the optionality of the inflections to be used. Similar observations can be made with respect to the development of noun inflection. The present study also provides new information on LIS noun morphology, and points out that in both adult and child language the inflectional pattern is less productive within the category of nouns compared to that of verbs.

The results of the present study corroborate and extend the recent findings of studies on several European signed languages demonstrating the widespread use of oral components, most notably bimodal sign-word combinations, in both adult and child signed communication. Relevant individual differences among the children were noted with respect to the number of sign-word combinations used, and it was of interest to find that while such combinations were unvoiced in the adult, they were voiced in the children's productions. Although much remains to be understood with regard to the role and functions of oral components of different kinds, it is becoming increasingly clear that these cannot be disregarded as a marginal phenomenon, but rather must be more thoroughly explored and understood at several levels of analysis. Oral components are certainly of interest for more appropriate, primarily sociolinguistic investigations of the complex contact-language situation that characterizes signed languages in their interaction with the dominant spoken languages. However, it may also be of interest to pursue a more appropriate understanding of signed languages' oral components in the framework of research on coverbal gesturing (e.g. McNeill 1992, 2000), which highlights the inherently multimodal features of spoken language communication. In principle, it cannot be excluded that signed languages' oral components are revealing of deeper psychological and neurological links between the vocal and the gestural modality. Appropriate comparisons between vocal behaviors in signing, and gestural behaviors in speaking may lead to a more comprehensive understanding of the features of multimodal communication in both signed and spoken languages, and of the extent to which they are similar and/or different.

The analyses reported above revealed some developmental differences: the youngest child used a smaller repertoire of signs, and had a much more limited control of LIS morphology compared to the three older children, as evidenced by the absence of inflected nouns and verbs in her production. The patterns noted in the three older children's production appeared to be relatively similar in several respects (e.g. the overall distribution of inflectional compared to uninflectional verbs, the overall frequency of inflected vs. uninflected nouns used, the fact that all used voiced sign-word combinations).

Remarkable individual variability was also found. Individual differences in the group as a whole were most evident in the number of sign-word combinations the children used, and these could in part be explained by the different total language input (in LIS, SSI, spoken Italian) the children received. Within the group of the three older children, interesting quantitative and qualitative differences were noted. These concerned for example a more or less productive use of verb inflections, but also stylistic variations of sign-order patterns in the children's utterances that were at least in part related to the children's lesser or greater exposure to forms of spoken Italian. It was of interest to find that even when the children's utterances showed sign-order patterns that were closer to the structure of spoken Italian than to the structure proper of LIS, this did not appear to interfere with their use of LIS inflections. At the same time the individual variability in expressive styles cannot be underestimated. It reflects and underlines the complex and heterogeneous language environment proper of each deaf child, characterized by variable contact (at home, in school, in language education programs) with the dominant vocal language of the surrounding hearing community.

Notes

* The study described here stems from a broader research project conducted in collaboration by the Division of Neuropsychology of Language and Deafness of the Institute of Psychology now Institute for Cognitive Sciences and Technologies, CNR, and the Vatican Pediatric Hospital *Bambino Gesù* in Rome. Part of the data and observations reported in this chapter have been described, in different form and/or from different perspectives, in Ossella et al. (1994), and Pizzuto, Ardito, Caselli, and Corazza (1999, 2000a). Minor discrepancies between the results reported here and those described in previous publications or presentations are due to new analyses of the data conducted for the present chapter. The research reported here would not have been possible without the generous contribution provided by many people. I am particularly grateful to my Deaf, native LIS signers colleagues Serena Corazza, Paolo Rossini, Benedetto Santarelli and Vannina Vitale for substantial help in data collection and/or analysis, to Barbara Ardito and Maria Luisa Franchi for assistance with data coding and transcription, and to Silvia Del Vecchio for her help in clarifying some of the children's utterances. Partial financial support from National Research Council (CNR) Targeted Projects *FATMA* (1991–1996), *Safeguard of Cultural Heritage* (1996–2001), the European Commission Project *Intersign* (1993–1995) (Network, Contract N. ERBCHRXCT 920023), and the European Science Foundation Project *Intersign: Sign Linguistics and Data Exchange* (1997–2000), is also acknowledged. Finally, I would like to thank Gary Morgan, Bencie Woll, and one anonymous reviewer for helpful comments and suggestions on the first draft of this chapter.

1. The non-manual components that occur with manual signs (e.g. facial expressions, body postures, eye gaze) were not examined for the purposes of the present study, despite the fact that in LIS as in other signed languages, non manual components play a crucial role in LIS structure, and specifically in LIS morphology and morphosyntax (Franchi 1987; Pizzuto et al. 1990; Rossini, Reilly, Fabbretti & Volterra 2000). However, our current knowledge of the role and functions of non-manual components in LIS utterances and texts, at several level of analysis, is still too limited, and not sufficiently detailed to make reasonable generalizations on the regularities that govern the use of non-manual components in adult LIS. Without the appropriate reference data on the adult language it is very difficult to examine and specify whatever developmental patterns there may be in the process of acquisition of the target non-manual components. This investigation was thus limited to the morphology of manual signs, for which more reference data are available.

2. This terminology differs from the one we used in earlier work, where we used the term *inflective* for what we now call *inflectional* signs (Pizzuto 1986; Pizzuto et al. 1990), and the terms *uninflective* (Pizzuto 1986) and *invariable* (Pizzuto & Corazza 1996) for what we now call *uninflectional* signs.

3. Note that the inflectional/uninflectional distinction made here is not to be interpreted in absolute terms. Signs that are characterized as uninflectional with respect to some morphological marking may be inflected for marking other morphological information. For example verbs that exhibit an uninflectional pattern in marking person role, may be inflected for durative aspect. The morphophonological regularities observed are different, as inflections for person

involve alterations of the point of articulation, whereas aspectual inflections involve primarily alterations of the movement pattern (Pizzuto 1987; Pizzuto & Corazza 1996).

4. Classifiers are roughly defined here, after Brennan (1992: 46 ff), as "linguistic units which indicate what kind of grouping or category a particular referent belongs to (…) and which mark out what is referred to as belonging, for example, to the class of animate entities, (…) or humans (…) or round things (…), or flat things (…) or vehicles, and so on". This type of signs has been noted and researched in LIS (Pizzuto & Corazza, 1996) as in most other signed languages. However, recent research in several signed languages, including LIS, has cast serious doubts on the uselfuness of the notion of classifier for characterizing this kind of signs (see among others Brennan in press; Emmorey 2000; Schembri 1999; Pizzuto & Corazza 2000). The double quotes delimiting the term in the text and this note are intended to draw the reader's attention to these issues. At present however the term continues to be used as more appropriate characterizations of the signs referred to as classifiers remain to be found.

5. The description of these semantically complex verbs as object incorporating stems primarily from early research on ASL, where different authors described a morphological process of verb formation whereby the handshape of a base verb is modified to incorporate the verb object. For example the base verb GIVE may change its handshape, and assume the same handshape proper of the sign BOOK, in the ASL sign BOOK-GIVE, which expresses the meaning of 'giving a book' (see Wilbur, 1979: 112–113, for a review of relevant literature). In research on LIS we have proposed an alternative description which does not posit the existence of base verbs and object-incorporating morphological processes (Pizzuto 1987; Pizzuto & Corazza 1996). We explains the relationships between these semantically complex verbs and their related nouns in terms of processes of lexical-derivational morphology which simply relate specific nouns to specific verbs, similarly to what is observed in many morphologically complex languages such as Italian. For example, within the description proposed for LIS, a verb like CUT-WITH-SCISSORS is morphologically related to the noun SCISSORS (the two signs share the same handshape and the distinction betwen the noun and the verb is marked by specific features of the movement of the signs), and it is only semantically (but not morphologically) related to other verbs that map the domain of 'cutting'. The morphological and semantic relations we posit are comparable to those that hold, for example, between the Italian verb *sforbiciare* ('cutting something in several places with scissors', a verb that is semantically but not morphologically related to other verbs encoding 'cutting actions') and the noun *forbici* ('scissors'), although of course the meanings encoded in Italian and LIS are not exactly alike.

The acquisition of verb agreement

Pointing out arguments for the linguistic status of agreement in signed languages*

Richard P. Meier

1. Introduction

Verb agreement is one of the most studied phenomena in linguistic research on the signed languages of the Deaf. Yet despite the close attention it has received, agreement remains one of the most controversial topics in the study of sign languages. Indeed the issue of whether agreement in signed languages is properly viewed as a linguistic rule is now a topic of lively debate. In this chapter, I first describe some properties of agreement in signed languages; in doing this, I sketch several arguments that suggest to me that agreement is indeed a part of the morphosyntax of signed languages. Then I turn to a review of the acquisition literature. The literature on the acquisition of agreement in mature signed languages and in emerging ones yields several arguments to suggest that agreement is part of the morphology of signed languages and is acquired as such by young signing children.

2. Linguistic overview

Natural languages have three primary means to indicate who does what to whom: word order, morphological case, and verb agreement. As it happens, English makes use of all three, but case and agreement are vestigial. Except for the possessive marker, case appears only in the pronominal system, as in the sentence *She kissed him*. But, however distinctive, English pronouns for nominative and accusative case do not license freedom in word order, as is true of languages with rich case systems (e.g., Latin). Similarly, verb agreement is, for regular verbs, limited to a single distinctive marker, the third person singular suffix -s. And once again, this limited verb agreement system does not grant the speaker any flexibility in the use of English's strict SVO word order, no matter that the third person singular marker sometimes provides sufficient information to distinguish subject and object, as in the sentence *Mary kisses you*.

Signed languages have recourse to these same ways and means for marking the argument structure of verbs, but primarily they depend on word order and verb agreement. Case appears to be absent entirely or to be very limited (except in possessive pronouns, although see Meir 2000, for arguments for accusative case in Israeli Sign Language). The sign language that I am most familiar with, American Sign Language (ASL), has a much richer system of verb agreement than does English. But, as appears to be true in other signed languages, that system is restricted to certain verbs (Padden 1983). When a verb permits agreement, null subjects and objects are also possible, just as null subjects are possible in Spanish, Italian, and other Romance languages with rich verb agreement (Lillo-Martin 1991). When agreement is impossible, as with verbs that Padden called *plain*, relatively strict SVO sign order distinguishes subject and object.

So, what do I mean by agreement? Simply that if we take a verb from the language in question we find changes in the form of that verb that signal one or more of its arguments.[1] In Spanish, suffixes mark the person and number of the subject, as shown in the present indicative paradigm for the verb *hablar* 'to speak' in Peninsular Spanish:

(1)   1SG *hablo*   1PL *hablamos*
      2SG *hablas*   2PL *habláis*
      3SG *habla*   3PL *hablan*

In Spanish, agreement does not demand the presence of an overt NP with which the verb agrees, although our theory may posit covert, unpronounceable elements (*pro*) that carry the same person and number features (*phi-features*) as are marked on the verb. Thus, colloquial sentences in Spanish frequently have no subject NP that is pronounced:

(2)   *Hablo   español.*
      speak.1SG Spanish
      'I speak Spanish.'

Other Spanish sentences — those with full NPs or with contrastive or otherwise emphasized pronouns — do have overt subjects that carry the same person and number features as the verb:

(3) *Yo hablo   español.*
     I   speak-1sg Spanish
     'I speak Spanish.'

In signed languages, agreement takes the form of changes in the verb's direction of movement, palm orientation, and/or location such that — when an argument's referent is present in the visible environment of the conversation — the verb *agrees with,* or *indexes,* or *points to* that referent. When a referent is absent, the signer may associate an empty location in the signing space with that referent; verbs may *agree with* or *point to* such locations as well. So that we don't prejudge the issue of how similar this process is to agreement in spoken languages, let's call this property of sign verbs *directionality.* Figure 1 is an example of directionality in what has long been considered to be an agreeing verb in ASL, the verb GIVE. Verbs that are much less iconic than GIVE are also directional; Figure 2 shows different forms of the verb ASK.

For Scott Liddell (2000), a verb such as GIVE is best treated as pointing to the referent (or referents) of either one or two of its arguments, because — among other considerations — there is no phonologically listable set of locations with which verbs may agree. Instead, any spatial location that a referent happens to occupy is available for a verb to point to; verbs are directed to those locations by "the human, cognitive ability to point at things" (Liddell & Metzger 1998:690). Although we may accept his characterization of the locations that verbs indicate — a characterization that has intellectual forerunners in the literature (Meier 1982, 1990; Lillo-Martin & Klima 1990) — we should, I think, hesitate before accepting Liddell's further conclusion that directionality is essentially the same as the ostensive indication that must often accompany demonstratives in English, or that may accompany agreeing verbs in Spanish. Very briefly, here are some arguments that suggest that directionality is linguistic and thus that more is involved than the ability to point at things:

1. Verbs are constrained with respect to which entities they may point to. Aronoff, Meir and Sandler (2000) argue that, if agreement were purely gestural, we would expect directional verbs to show considerable variation with respect to where they point. For example, there are three entities associated with an act of giving: the donor, the donated object, and the recipient. One might anticipate that a gestured description of giving could include points to any or all of these entities (and also perhaps to the location where the act of giving transpired). But an agreeing verb in ASL does not have this freedom: the ASL verb GIVE must point to the location associated with its indirect object (the recipient),

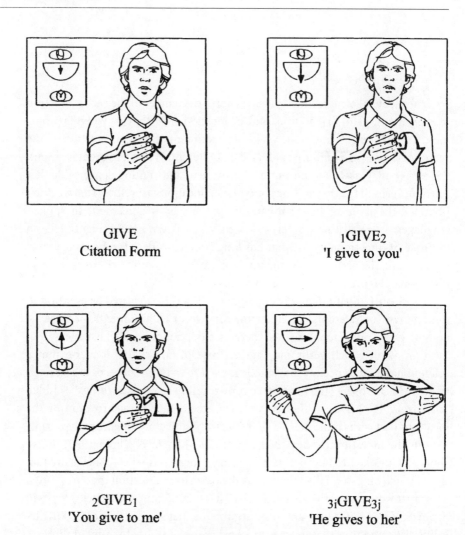

GIVE
Citation Form

₁GIVE₂
'I give to you'

₂GIVE₁
'You give to me'

₃ᵢGIVE₃ⱼ
'He gives to her'

Figure 1. Four forms of the ASL verb GIVE.

may optionally point to the location associated with its subject (the donor), but may not point to the location of the direct object (the gift).

Across signed languages, verbs that differ minimally in form and meaning may nonetheless differ in whether or not they are directional. T. Supalla (n.d.) noted that the verb TELEPHONE has virtually the same form in a variety of signed languages; yet in the six languages he examined, the verb varied in whether or not it permitted agreement and in the extent to which it participated in the agreement system. In Japanese Sign Language, the verb LIKE is, in

ASK
Citation Form

₁ASK₂
'I ask you'

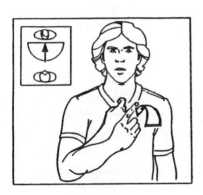

₂ASK₁
'You ask me'

₂ASK₃ⱼ
'You ask him'

Figure 2. Four forms of the ASL verb ASK.

Western Japan, an agreement verb, but is not in Eastern Japan (Fischer 1996).

Verbs may also be constrained in how they may point to particular arguments. Specifically, the form of directionality in some verbs appears to be
constrained by the kinds of semantic factors that constrain morphological
systems in spoken languages; for example, Janis (1995) argues that the form of
the ASL verb ANALYZE (particularly, its palm orientation) is conditioned by
whether its object is animate or inanimate. Liddell (2000) presents evidence that
directionality in verbs is lexically constrained, such that the verb SAY-NO points

high (e.g., toward the addressee's nose when he or she is the referent of the direct object), INVITE points low toward the abdomen, and GIVE points at chest-level. Such idiosyncratic properties of verbs mean that they don't point freely.[2]

2. Signed languages differ in how much they use directional signs and, thus, some signed languages would seem to point more than others. Specifically, Taiwanese, Japanese, German, and Brazilian Sign Languages resolve the problem of how to mark argument structure when the main verb is a plain verb — that is, a non-directional verb — by introducing auxiliary-like elements that are directional and that carry agreement (Smith 1990; Fischer 1996; Rathmann 2000; de Quadros, Lillo-Martin & Chen 2000). Individual languages may have more than one such element, and as Rathmann (2000) shows, there are interesting linguistic restrictions on the use of these auxiliaries. In contrast, ASL and other signed languages that lack these auxiliary-like signs fall back on relatively strict sign order to mark argument structure in sentences with a plain main verb. In Brazilian Sign Language, preverbal objects are possible in sentences with agreeing verbs, but SVO order is mandated in sentences with plain verbs (de Quadros 1999, reviewed in Lillo-Martin in press). Thus, within and across languages, directionality in verbs predicts relatively flexible word order and the occurrence of null arguments. This pattern is strikingly similar to what is encountered in spoken languages with rich agreement systems (Lillo-Martin 1991).

Agreement may have other syntactic consequences. In Brazilian Sign Language, the presence of agreement conditions the placement of the negative sign NO (de Quadros 1999, reviewed in Lillo-Martin in press). Specifically, the negative sign may intervene between a subject and agreeing verb, but not between a subject and a non-agreeing verb. With non-agreeing verbs, the negative element must appear sentence-finally.

3. Signed languages have idiosyncratic verb forms that are unsurprising if we assume that directionality is a linguistic process. For example, ASL and Danish Sign Language (DSL) each have at least one verb that has an irregular first-person object form (Meier 1990; Engberg-Pedersen 1993).[3] In ASL, that verb is CONVINCE; this verb has a first-person object form that contacts the signer's neck. In contrast, the citation form and the non-first person agreeing forms contact the upright, extended index finger of the nondominant hand. In DSL, the citation form of the verb COMFORT is articulated in neutral space, but the first-person object form has contact on the signer's cheeks. The occurrence of such signs underpins one argument for the claim that ASL and DSL have a grammatical category of first person (Meier 1990).

4. The verbal systems of signed languages become more directional as those languages develop. Engberg-Pedersen (1993) notes systematic differences across generations of signers in the use of directional verbs in DSL. Specifically, older signers generally lack first-person object forms and produce no verbs that mark both subject and object; for these older signers verbs can mark only non-first person objects.[4] Younger Danish signers regularly produce directional verbs that mark first-person objects. Another argument suggesting that signed languages gain directional verbs over time is founded on the lexicalization of fingerspelled forms. Fingerspelling loan signs in ASL sometimes become directional verbs (Battison 1978; Padden 1998): for example, the fingerspelling form N-O has been lexicalized as a sign NO that has a related verb SAY-NO. SAY-NO is a directional verb that can mark both its subject and object. These two sources of evidence suggest the following: If we were to say that agreement is merely ostension, we would need to say that the gesturing that accompanies signed verbs become more elaborate as signed languages mature. On this view, younger signed languages would be seen as having verbal systems that are constrained to point to fewer referents.

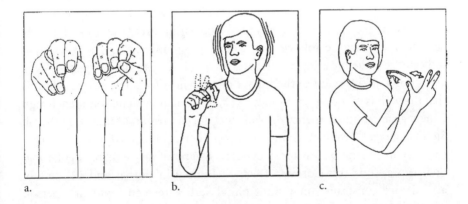

a.   b.   c.

Figure 3. Examples of the nativization of fingerspelled forms in ASL: (a) The English word *no* can be represented by a sequence of fingerspelling handshapes, here N-O. (b) In the ASL sign NO, handshape changes have obscured its source in fingerspelling. Note, in particular, that the ring and little fingers are closed throughout the production of this sign, unlike in the fingerspelled form for the letter O. (c) The verb SAY-NO is a directional verb that appears to be derived from the ASL sign NO. The pictured form is SAY-NO$_1$ 'say no to me'.

5. Not all pointing expressions point clearly; this may be particularly true of plurals. One argument that ASL has a system of person contrasts is founded on its relatively non-indexic first-person plural pronoun WE. This index-hand sign contacts the ipsilateral and contralateral sides of the signer's chest; only the signer — and not any of the other referents of this sign — is indicated (Meier 1990). In expressions of numerosity in the verbal and pronominal systems of ASL and other languages, sign sequences occur in which a non-indexic or partially indexic form — sometimes even a verb or a pronoun that would appear to be a singular — is juxtaposed to an independent pronominal sign that more precisely specifies the locations of a set of referents. In the pronominal system of ASL, Cormier (1998) observed the pronoun OUR produced in sequence with the fully indexic dual pronoun TWO-OF-US. In the sign OUR, the B-hand describes an arc from the ipsilateral to contralateral sides of the torso; its referents are not indicated. In contrast, the pronoun TWO-OF-US has a back-and-forth movement between the separate locations associated with its two referents. The sequence OUR TWO-OF-US was used to indicate that it was the referents of the dual sign who were the possessors.

In the verbal system of ASL, Mathur and Rathmann (2001) have observed that number marking is sometimes neutralized when the verb agrees with a first-person object; instead a verb that is singular in form (e.g. $GIVE_1$, typically 'give to me') may be followed by a dual pronoun (e.g., TWO-OF-US) that indicates that the meaning of the construction is 'give to the two of us.' Thus, verbs don't always point to the full set of referents of whatever argument it is that the verb is marking (cf. Moody 1983, for similar evidence on French Sign Language and Sutton-Spence & Woll 1999, for discussion of plurals in British Sign Language). Two factors may be at work here: (1) Expressions of numerosity may in general be less indexic — less like pointing — than singular and dual expressions (cf. Cormier 1998; McBurney in press); and (2) certain articulatory constraints may limit plural verb agreement with first person objects; Mathur and Rathmann (2001) state these constraints in terms of restrictions on movement at joints of the arm. Further exploration of non-singular pronouns and verbs is needed in order to determine just how similar the pronouns and directional verbs of signed languages are to pointing.

Even when verbs do seem to mark the locations of their referents, we have little idea of how accurately they do so; that is, we have little idea of how precise this pointing behavior is. This is a particular limitation on our knowledge of how verbs agree with non-present referents. In her dissertation, Cormier (2002) is uses exacting instrumental techniques to examine the fit between the sign that establishes some location in space for a referent (or set of referents) and a subsequent verb that agrees with this previously established location. Her results show that the fit is significantly less good for plurals than for singulars.

These arguments suggest to me that directionality in signed languages is properly viewed as a linguistic rule, notwithstanding the fact that the locations to which — and from which — verbs are directed are not phonologically listable. Thus, although the form of agreement may be gestural (in the sense that the particular locations with which verbs agree are not phonologically constrained), the integration of these gestural elements into verbs is linguistically determined. Whether a verb can point, how it points, and how reference to the arguments of plain verbs is indicated are all linguistically determined. I conclude that directionality is the overt manifestation of an agreement system.[5]

Nonetheless, there are typological differences between agreement systems in signed languages and those in spoken languages. Signed languages evince a strong preference for object agreement over subject agreement. Agreement is largely limited to transitive verbs and/or to "spatial" verbs that take locative arguments.[6] Although there may be a few spoken languages that have only object agreement (Keenan 1976, as noted in Engberg-Pedersen 1993), spoken languages strongly favor subject agreement. The high degree of similarity among signed languages with respect to the linguistics of their agreeing systems is a surprising difference between signed and spoken languages (Newport & Supalla 2000; T. Supalla, n.d.; Supalla & Webb 1995; Aronoff et al. 2000; Rathmann & Mathur in press). In contrast to signed languages, some spoken languages have little or no agreement, some have only subject agreement, and some have subject and object agreement.

The fact that every signed language examined to date has an agreement system is consistent with the presumptive gestural origins of agreement (if we assume that there is little relevant cross-cultural variation in the form of nonlinguistic gesture), but is not a strong argument that agreement remains a strictly gestural system within mature sign languages. Instead, this apparent uniformity in the structure of signed languages may be consistent with the fact that signed languages are young languages. Young spoken languages — in particular, the creole languages — have also been argued to be relatively uniform in their structure (Bickerton 1984, and for discussion, Arends, Muyksen & Smith 1995; Mühlhäusler 1986; and Romaine 1988), although the creoles differ in important ways from signed languages. Moreover, signed languages — like creole languages — may owe much of their structure to children (see, for example, Fischer 1978; Meier 1984; Singleton & Newport in press). Presumably, the biases that children bring to the task of language acquisition vary little from one part of the globe to another. Given similar input environments, the uniform biases of deaf children may yield grammatical outcomes that are also relatively uniform.

Why may children be such important contributors to the structure of signed languages? Unlike hearing children born into speaking communities, most deaf children do not have access to native-signing models. In the United States and Europe, only 5 to 10% of deaf children have deaf parents. A still tinier minority of deaf children also have a deaf grandparent. Only such third-generation deaf children are likely to have a native-signing parent. Without native-signing models, the language of deaf children may more closely reflect the biases of those children, as opposed to the conventions of an established linguistic community.

In the remainder of this chapter, I will examine the development of verb agreement in two quite different circumstances.[7] First, I look at the acquisition of verb agreement by children who are immersed in well-established signed languages, such as ASL. These children are the offspring of deaf parents and are exposed to a conventional sign language in the home. The second set of circumstances are quite different: there is evidence that children who have no exposure to a mature signed language sometimes innovate the use of directional verbs. As I have already discussed, directionality is a crucial component of the agreement systems of mature signed languages.

3.   The acquisition of agreement in a mature signed language

In the early stages of the acquisition of signed languages, the iconicity of many signs could not be accessible to the young infant. For example, the ASL sign MILK presumably has its origins in a gestural representation of the action of milking a cow. But most 10- or 12-month olds know little about the dairy industry. Thus, it seems unlikely that the iconicity of this sign in any way facilitates its acquisition by the infant. In fact, the literature on the early vocabularies of young signing infants suggests that iconic signs are not over-represented in their vocabularies (Orlansky & Bonvillian 1984).

In contrast to signs such as MILK, agreement verbs in ASL and other signed languages are often remarkable for their transparency; more than many signs in these languages they look like what they mean. So a verb such as $_1$GIVE$_2$ 'I give to you' looks much like the action I would perform were I giving a small object to another person.[8] At least in ASL, iconic mapping between form and meaning is much more systematic in the verb agreement system than it is in the language generally. In Meier (1981, 1982, 1987), I sought to develop specific predictions as to how the iconicity of agreeing verbs might facilitate the acquisition of verb agreement. In doing this I noticed that there are systematic differences among agreeing verb forms in the nature of the iconic form-meaning mapping; these differences appear even among the different agreeing forms of a single verb, such as GIVE.

Let's consider various verb forms in the GIVE paradigm; again see Figure 1 for examples. The double-agreeing verb $_1$GIVE$_2$ 'I give to you', as well as the singly-agreeing forms GIVE$_2$ 'give to you' and GIVE$_3$ 'give to him/her' (not illustrated), can be understood as having their iconic basis in mime. Specifically, all three forms look roughly as if the signer is performing the act of giving to some other person; the signer seems to play the part of the agent.[9] In contrast, $_2$GIVE$_1$ 'you give to me' cannot be construed as a mime of the agent's action. Another intersecting set of verb forms can be construed as diagrams showing the participants in an event and the direction of the action that relates them. I considered all doubly-agreeing forms of verbs of motion and transference to be *spatial analogues* of the events they represented. Thus, $_{3i}$GIVE$_{3j}$ 'he gives to her' can be seen as a map of the transference of some object from a location associated with one individual to a location associated with another non-addressed participant. The earlier discussed form $_2$GIVE$_1$ 'you give to me' can also be considered to be a map of this same sort.

Now let's assume that children acquiring verb agreement are sensitive to the iconicity of agreeing verb forms. But to what type of iconicity? From the two contrasting forms of iconicity that I observed, I developed two models of how children would acquire verb agreement in ASL. The *mimetic model* suggested that: (1) Children will make earlier use of verb agreement with verbs such as GIVE than with verbs such as ASK that cannot be construed as mimes. (2) For verbs such as GIVE children will make early use of those agreeing verb forms that are mimetic. So for GIVE (and other verb stems that have mimetic properties) we would expect to observe early acquisition of singly-agreeing verb forms that have second- or third-person objects. (3) Doubly-agreeing verb forms will be restricted to those with a first-person subject, and (4) children will erroneously substitute an uninflected citation form verb only when the verb has a first person object. In contrast, the *spatial analogy* model suggested that: (1) Children will make early use of agreement with verbs of motion and transference, in which motion in the world is represented by motion in the sign space. (2) Children will favor double-agreeing forms, inasmuch as such forms are better diagrams than singly-agreeing verb forms. And (3), children will not show ungrammatical use of the uninflected citation forms of agreement verbs.

Having developed these two models of how iconicity might influence the young child's acquisition of agreement, I then pitted them against a third morphological model. On the basis of the grammatical characteristics of agreement, I predicted that: (1) The acquisition of verb agreement will be relatively late, consistent with typological characteristics of agreement (e.g. the markers of agreement are not suffixal, not syllabic, and not stressed; cf. Slobin 1982). (2) Children will favor single agreement, because singly-agreeing forms are simpler morphologically than doubly-agreeing forms. And (3), consistent with this bias toward morphologically simplex forms, children will frequently omit agreement, thereby producing citation forms in contexts that demand the use of agreement. I tested these three models against longitudinally-collected data on the acquisition of agreement by three Deaf children reared by Deaf, signing parents. The samples from these children, which were generally collected on a monthly basis, spanned the age range from 1;6 to 3;9.

3.1 The developmental timecourse

Let's first consider the developmental timecourse for the acquisition of agreement.[10] Figure 4 shows children's percent correct usage of verb agreement in contexts that require agreement between a verb and the real-world location of the verb's arguments. Note that inasmuch as these data pertain only to agreement with real-world locations, the analysis is not confounded by the linguistic and memorial demands required to establish — and refer back to — empty loci in the sign space that the signer or addressee associates with non-present referents. As Figure 4 reveals, mastery of verb agreement appears to occur at approximately 3;0, a result that is consistent with the results of earlier studies (Fischer 1973; Hoffmeister 1978b; Kantor 1982b).[11] The age at which children acquire verb agreement is not especially young given findings of the precocious acquisition of arbitrary, but agglutinative, case morphology in languages such as Turkish (Slobin 1982). Children acquiring Turkish seem to acquire much of the case morphology of that language before age 2, while still in the two-word stage.

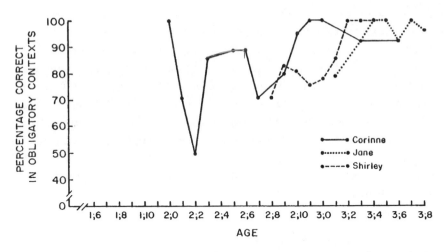

Figure 4. Three children's production of verb agreeement in contexts that require its use.

3.2 Error types

Prior to their acquisition of verb agreement, all three children reported in Meier (1982) made errors of omission (although note that the data are sparse on Jane, given the short span over which she was videotaped). For example, Shirley at 2;11 had just handed a sandwich to the experimenter; she then directed her to give it to the cameraman: POINT_{cameraman} GIVE POINT₂, GIVE. Both tokens of GIVE were uninflected citation forms; neither indicated the identity of any potential recipient of the sandwich. However, context indicated that the correct interpretation of the utterance was 'You give to him'. Across all samples, Shirley omitted obligatory verb agreement in 30 instances. As it happened, all these instances involved verbs such as GIVE that might be seen as having some mimetic properties (i.e., none involved verbs such as ASK or LOOK-AT in which the citation form has no mimetic properties). Moreover all these errors of omission involved the failure to agree with a second- or third-person referent.

Occasional errors of commission have been reported in the literature on the acquisition of verb agreement in ASL. Fischer (1973) and Casey (2000) report a few tokens in which a child overgeneralized agreement to verbs that do not govern agreement (specifically, the verbs EAT, DRINK, and SLEEP). In a few other instances, children produced agreeing verb forms that agreed with the wrong argument: both examples listed in Meier (1982) show agreement with the direct object, rather than with the indirect object (as would have been grammatical in the case of an erroneous token of GIVE produced by Shirley at 3;0) or with the goal (as would have been grammatical in the case of an erroneous form of PUT produced by Jane at 3;6). Fischer had previously observed an error of this sort from Shirley (2;8) in which, once again, GIVE agreed with the location of the direct object rather than the indirect object. More recently, Casey has also identified errors of misagreement, including instances in which children (aged 2;7 and 2;11) ungrammatically moved verbs (PUT and THROW, respectively) toward the real-world locations of their subjects. Note that all the errors of misagreement noted here are coun+ericonic on both the mimetic and spatial analogy models; these errors are also less iconic than the grammatically-required forms.

3.3 Doubly-agreeing verb forms

Many verbs in ASL, such as TELL, can agree with only a single argument; agreement with that argument (for TELL, the direct object) is obligatory. Other verbs may agree with two arguments. For the verb GIVE, agreement with the notional indirect object is obligatory, whereas agreement with the subject is optional. Thus, for verbs such as GIVE, a singly-agreeing verb form agrees with its notional indirect object; doubly-agreeing forms agree with subject and indirect object.

Figure 4 displayed only results for obligatory agreement. Averaging across the three subjects from Meier (1982), agreement was produced in 88% ($SD=4.5\%$) of the contexts that required its use, whereas double agreement was produced in only 32% ($SD=20.5\%$) of the contexts that allowed its use.[12] An elicited imitation study yielded further evidence that children are sensitive to the optionality of doubly-agreeing forms (Meier 1987). Ten deaf children (ages 3;1 to 7;0), all of whom had deaf parents, were asked to imitate simple sign sentences consisting of a topicalized noun (which encoded the direct object) followed by a doubly-agreeing verb (which encoded the subject and indirect object). Verbs always agreed with the location of a referent present in the room (a doll, the child, or the experimenter). The modeled verb was either a GIVE-type verb which moves from subject to object, or a TAKE-type verb (a so-called *backwards* verb; cf. Padden 1983) that moves from object to subject. In designing this study, I reasoned that, if children prefer that sign predicates be spatial analogues of the events those verbs describe, then they should reliably imitate double agreement. But if children are sensitive to the morphological complexity of verbs and to the grammatical options that the language gives them, then they may sometimes strip the optional subject agreement from the modeled sign. If so, their imitations would be morphologically simpler than the modeled forms.

The results showed that, for both verb types, the children were less likely to imitate subject agreement than object agreement. Children sometimes produced a verb which agreed with a referent that was not modeled by the experimenter; the frequency of this intrusion error did not differ between subjects and objects. But omissions were much more frequent for subject agreement (n = 33) than object agreement (n = 4). Nine of 10 subjects showed more frequent omission of subject agreement than object agreement. The tenth subject showed no omissions whatsoever. Clearly children are sensitive to the optionality of subject agreement in ASL and will omit subject agreement even when the result is a less iconic form, at least less iconic on the spatial analogy model proposed in Meier (1982).

3.4 Directional signs and directional gestures

In light of evidence that children and adults — whether deaf or hearing — use gestures in which the direction of movement identifies the participants in actions signified by those gestures, Casey (2000, in press) argues that the origin of directional, agreeing verbs is to be found in gesture, but that its use in sign has become grammaticized. She tracked the development of five deaf children of deaf parents; those children ranged in age from 0;8 to 2;11 over the course of her study. From the earliest samples, the vast preponderance of children's action gestures (95% on average) were directional. In contrast, children omitted agreement from most of the directional verbs that they attempted. With present referents (real-world locations), children produced agreeing forms in, on average, 35% of the pertinent instances, with little improvement from 1;6 to 2;11. This result suggests that the acquisition of directional, agreeing verbs lags the acquisition of directional gestures, notwithstanding the fact that directionality apparently takes a very similar form in gesture and in sign. Interestingly, Casey (in press) has also found that deaf children's 'give' gestures generally mark the location of the patient, not the location of the recipient, as would be expected for the ASL sign GIVE.

Petitto (1987, 1988) has similarly argued that pronominal pointing signs in ASL have a very different developmental course from nonlinguistic pointing gestures. She reports that two deaf children first used communicative points at 9 months, but did not use them to mean 'you' or 'me' until 17–20 months.

Moreover, her subjects used names or kinship terms rather than pointing signs, just as young hearing children often favor names over deictic pronouns. Lastly, Petitto reports examples of pronoun reversals, in which the child referred to him- or herself using a pointing sign that, given its form, would be expected to mean 'you.' Similar pronoun reversals are produced by some children acquiring the deictic pronouns *you* and *me* of English (e.g., Chiat 1981, 1982).

3.5 Agreement with non-present referents

In order to discuss non-present referents, signers may associate referents with empty locations in the signing space (see, for example, Klima & Bellugi 1979). For purposes of subsequent anaphoric reference, the signer can point to previously established loci. Moreover, directional verbs may agree with these loci. In their use of agreement with respect to abstract spatial loci, children show a prolonged period of acquisition that continues through 4;9 (Loew 1984). In Loew's study, children made a variety of errors: for example, they produced apparently agreeing verbs, but failed to identify the argument with which the verb agrees. Within a single discourse, children sometimes seemed to pile many referents onto a single locus; that is, verbs referring to different events with different characters all agreed with the same location in space. And even after age 4;0–after they had started to establish loci — children often neglected to maintain those loci across the discourse. In their review, Newport and Meier (1985:905) concluded that "we see no reason to implicate the morphology of verb agreement per se as the source of these errors. Rather, the data seem to us to suggest that the errors arise from difficulties in establishing and maintaining spatial loci."

3.6 Critical period effects on the acquisition of verb agreement

Studies of the acquisition of signed languages have yielded an unparalleled opportunity to test Lenneberg's (1967) hypothesis that there is a maturationally determined period in our lifetimes — a so-called *critical period* — during which we are uniquely able to acquire native-like knowledge and abilities in language.[13] This research opportunity is rooted in a sad fact: it is only in the deaf population that there are large numbers of intellectually-normal individuals who are not exposed to a conventional language (whether signed or spoken) during infancy and early childhood.

Ted Supalla and Elissa Newport (reported in Newport 1990b) used a battery of tests of the production and comprehension of ASL to compare three groups of signers who differed systematically in the age at which they were first exposed to ASL. These subjects were native learners who were the children of deaf, signing parents, early learners who were first exposed to ASL between the ages of 4 and 6, and late learners who were first exposed to ASL after age 12. All signers had attended the same residential school for the deaf, all were members of the deaf community, and all had had long years of exposure to ASL (30 or more). The test of verb agreement production probed subjects' use of three classes of agreement verbs: (1) Verbs such as GIVE that permit double agreement, (2) Body-anchored verbs, such as TELL, that allow agreement with only a single argument, and (3) Verbs such as BITE and BLOW whose citation forms have initial contact on the body (just like TELL), but that nonetheless allow double agreement. The stimuli were videotaped events which, as per the instructions, subjects described using one of the 9 verbs of interest. The events involved two videotaped characters and/or the subject him- or herself, the subject having been instructed to think of him-/herself as being behind the camera. So that the subjects' responses were not dependent on their ability to control abstract spatial loci, subjects were told to articulate verbs with respect to still photographs of the characters portrayed in the videotaped stimuli. Thus, the test sought to examine the subjects' use of agreement with real-world loci: either to the two still photos or to the subject him- or herself.

The results showed a clear effect of age of exposure to ASL, such that native learners showed superior performance to early learners who in turn showed superior performance to late learners. In this respect, the test of verb agreement yielded results that were very similar to those obtained for subjects' production and comprehension of other aspects of ASL morphology (including, for example, the comprehension and production of verbs of motion). Across the board, tests probing subjects' knowledge of ASL morphology showed very different results than did a test of word order. Subjects' knowledge of basic ASL word order was unaffected by their age at first exposure to ASL. In sum, subjects' acquisition of verb agreement, like other aspects of ASL morphology but unlike word order, was subject to a critical period.

Converging evidence for a critical period effect in the acquisition of verb agreement comes from a study of sign monitoring (Emmorey, Bellugi, Friederici & Horn 1995). Subjects were instructed to press a key as soon as they noticed a target sign. In the stimuli of interest, that target sign invariably followed an agreeing verb. Half the time the agreeing verb was ungrammatical in the stimulus sentence. For native signers, but not for later learners (age at initial exposure ranging from 4 to 20), detection of the target sign was significantly slowed by the presence of an ungrammatical agreeing verb immediately prior to it. Emmorey et al. interpret this result as suggesting that the language processor of native learners is efficient in recognizing grammaticality violations and that this recognition slows subjects' responses to the subsequent target sign. A follow-up study examined aspectual morphology as well as verb agreement and employed three groups of subjects (native learners, early learners who were first exposed to ASL between ages 2 and 7, and late learners whose first contact with ASL came between ages 10 and 20). Native learners were slower to detect the target sign when it was preceded by an error, whether in agreement or in aspect. But early and late learners were only slowed by errors in aspectual morphology, even though all groups of subjects were equally good in detecting errors in agreement and aspect in an untimed, *off-line* judgment task.

3.7 Summing up the acquisition picture from ASL

We now have a fairly clear picture of how agreement is acquired in ASL, based on converging results from different investigators. The acquisition of agreement is not precocious, but instead is complete around age 3. This result holds for agreement with real-world locations; mastery of agreement with abstract spatial loci is later still. As suggested by Casey's (in press) work, signing children use directionality less frequently with verbs than with verb-like gestures. Children show much more reliable use of single agreement (generally, object agreement) consistent with the fact that it is obligatory; they make less use of subject agreement, as is consistent with its optionality. The error data suggest that children must learn which verbs agree (hence their errors of omission). More limited error data suggest that children must learn how verbs agree (hence, their errors in which verbs agree with the wrong argument). There is no evidence to date that would show that iconicity (whether mime or spatial analogy) guides children's acquisition of verb agreement; instead it seems to be acquired as a morphological system (Meier 1982, 1987). Lastly, age of exposure matters: native learners show superior performance to early and late learners in their knowledge and use of agreement (Newport 1990b; Emmorey et al. 1995).

4. The acquisition of agreement in emerging sign systems

Directional verbs appear not only in conventional sign languages such as ASL but also in the sign systems innovated by deaf children of hearing parents and in the sign language now developing in Nicaragua, a country where deaf individuals — virtually all born to hearing families — had long been so dispersed that a sign language had not developed (Kegl, Senghas & Coppola 1999; Polich 2000). The fact that directional verbs seem to emerge even in children who receive little or no linguistic input might be seen as support for the suggestion that agreement in conventional signed languages remains fundamentally gestural. However, I will argue that this is the wrong conclusion to draw.

4.1 Home signs

Susan Goldin-Meadow and her colleagues have documented that isolated deaf children who are born to hearing parents with no knowledge of signed language innovate language-like gestural systems (Goldin-Meadow & Feldman 1977; Goldin-Meadow & Mylander 1990). This is true even when such children have no exposure to a standard sign language. These innovated gestural systems have been called *home sign*. Among the linguistic properties that characterize home sign systems are a small lexicon, statistically-reliable gesture order rules, recursion, and gesture-internal morphology. The most typical gesture order rule noted in the deaf children examined by Goldin-Meadow is a tendency to place patients before verbs.[14]

In an analysis of the analogues of nouns and verbs in the home sign system of one deaf child (David), Goldin-Meadow, Butcher, Mylander and Dodge (1994) identified directional verbs that bear some resemblance to the directional verbs of ASL and other signed languages. They first showed that directionality — that is, producing a gesture near its referent or producing a gesture so that its movement brings it toward its referent — was reliably more frequent on verb-like gestures than on noun-like gestures. More importantly, directionality in David's verbs was conditioned by the argument structure of those verbs. Intransitive verbs, such as 'go', typically marked the goal, whereas transitives and ditransitives typically marked the patient. So, for example, David modified a transfer predicate such that the endpoint of the gesture's movement was near a cookie, that is, near the object that he sought to be transferred.[15] This tendency to mark patients is consistent with the *patient bias* that seemingly governs many of the structural regularities in these home sign systems. Interestingly, three-place predicates were significantly more likely to be directional than were either one- or two-place predicates; 83% of David's ditransitive gestures were directional. In three-place predicates, directional marking of the location of the patient was often accompanied by a separate deictic point to that same location;

the frequency of patient marking by the verb itself was unaffected by the presence or absence of a redundant point.

As Goldin-Meadow et al. (1994) observe, two properties distinguish directional verbs in David's home sign system from their counterparts in ASL. Many verbs in ASL are double-agreement verbs: that is, they can be inflected for both object agreement and, optionally, for subject agreement. Goldin-Meadow et al. found no instances of double agreement in David's gesturing. Second, ditransitive agreeing verbs in ASL and in other signed languages — e.g., the sign GIVE — invariably show agreement (specifically, agreement at the endpoint of the verb) with the recipient (the indirect object) not with the object to be transferred (the patient/direct object). This last point is crucial: in developing his home sign system, David has settled upon a grammar that is not just a simplified version of ASL. Instead, David's nascent agreement system shows distinct properties from its counterpart in ASL. For three-place predicates, different arguments control agreement in David's system than in ASL.

4.2 Agreement in children exposed to Manually-Coded English

Many deaf children in the United States are exposed to some form of Manually-Coded English (MCE) as part of their school curriculum. Sam Supalla (1991) examined the signing of a group of children who had been exposed to Signing Exact English 2 (SEE2), which is one of the MCE systems now in use. These artificial sign systems follow the grammar of English, not of ASL. Accordingly, SEE2 uses none of the spatial devices that are characteristic of ASL and other conventional signed languages; to the extent that it has verb agreement, it is signaled by a semi-independent sign that employs the S-handshape (i.e., a fist) and that has the distribution of the third-person singular marker of spoken English.

Using the same experimental procedures as in Newport's (1990b) study of critical period effects, Supalla (1991) asked deaf fourth- and fifth-graders (aged 9–11), all of whom came from hearing families and none of whom had any ASL exposure, to describe a set of videotaped events. Strikingly, the SEE2-exposed children, like David (Goldin-Meadow et al. 1994), innovated the use of directional modifications of verbs, despite the fact that their input contained little such modification, as suggested by Supalla's analysis of a teacher's responses to the same stimuli that the children viewed.[16] Although many of the children's responses were quite similar to what would have been an appropriate response from a native ASL user, not all were. For example, the ASL verb YELL admits only object agreement; subject agreement is disallowed, consistent with the sign's initial place of articulation at the mouth. Supalla describes two distinct error types in children's descriptions of an event in which one videotaped character yelled at another. One child produced a doubly-agreeing form that moved, as would be expected in ASL, from subject to object. Remember, however, that on Supalla's analysis YELL does not permit double agreement. Another child produced a response that lies completely outside the ASL agreement system: in the child's response, the verb YELL agreed — at the endpoint (not the onset) of its movement — with the location of the grammatical subject. Subsequently, the child produced an auxiliary-like sign that moved from the subject's location to that of the direct object. Such auxiliary-like signs do not occur in ASL, although they do in other signed languages. The presence of auxiliary-like elements in the signing of some MCE-exposed children suggests that such auxiliaries could be rapidly innovated in signed languages (cf. Fischer 1996, for pertinent discussion).

In sum, children acquiring a non-spatial sign system such as SEE2 nonetheless adapt it so that it uses spatial devices much like those of ASL. They do so by converting the English-like verbs of SEE2 into verbs that index distinct spatial locations. However, the fact that these verbs now point to locations associated with the referents of their arguments does not constrain them to function in just the way agreeing verbs work in ASL. As we saw with David, there are different ways in which verbs can point. Only some of those ways are permissible in ASL.

4.3 The creation of an agreement system in Nicaraguan Sign Language

The results from Goldin-Meadow's work on home sign systems and from S. Supalla's studies of the innovative use of space in children exposed to MCE are crucial evidence that, in systematic ways, children can go beyond the linguistic input that is presented to them. Deaf children do this in situations in which there is no conventional language — signed or spoken — available to them. This was the situation for the deaf children of hearing parents whom Goldin-Meadow has studied. And, as Supalla (1991; Supalla & McKee in press) has shown, deaf children exposed to MCE restructure their input to bring it into greater conformity with the processing demands of the visual-gestural modality and to avail themselves of its unique resources. It is likely that the innovative strategies demonstrated by these groups of children have contributed to the development of ASL and other signed languages, but we have not witnessed this. Home signers, such as David, do not have the opportunity to form a community in which a new language could evolve; ultimately these children are schooled in established sign systems, whether true languages such as ASL or signed encodings of English such as MCE.

We can now trace the evolution of a new language — and, in particular, its system of verb agreement — by looking at the recent development of Nicaraguan Sign Language (NSL). NSL is a language that seems to have emerged only since the late 1970s when, for the first time, a Deaf community formed in Nicaragua (Kegl this volume; Kegl et al. 1999; Polich, 1998, 2000). Ann Senghas has examined the use of verb agreement in that language (Senghas 1995; Kegl et al. 1999; Senghas & Coppola 2001). Although we do not yet have a full description of verb agreement in NSL, it seems that the system works much like that of ASL and other mature signed languages (Senghas 1995).

In order to examine the use of verb agreement by Nicaraguan signers, Senghas and Coppola (2001) enlisted 24 deaf individuals, who were assigned to three groups based on when they were first exposed to NSL, specifically early-exposed learners (exposed before age 6;6), middle-exposed learners (first exposed between 6;6 and 10;0), and late-exposed learners (exposed after 10;0). These same subjects also differed with respect to the year when they were exposed to Nicaragua's emerging sign language: 13 *first cohort* signers were exposed to NSL in 1983 or earlier, whereas 11 *second cohort* signers were first exposed after 1983. Senghas and Coppola showed each subject a short cartoon; the subject's task was to retell the story to a peer. The resultant narratives were then coded; each instance of a sign being produced in a non-neutral location (as well as each instance in which a non-neutral location was incorporated into the sign's movement) was coded as a token of *spatial modulation.*[17] One caution here: unlike the studies of home signers and of MCE-exposed children that I previously discussed, the Senghas and Coppola data do not bear on subjects' use of agreement with real-world locations, but instead pertain to their ability to refer to referents not present in the immediate environment.

Senghas and Coppola's results revealed that individuals who entered the Nicaraguan signing community before age 10 produced more spatial modulations per verb than did those individuals who entered after age 10. Also, early-exposed (<6;6) and middle-exposed (6;6–10) individuals produced more spatial modulations if they entered the community after 1983 in the second cohort of Nicaraguan signers, rather than before. Late-exposed learners did not benefit by being in the second cohort. These results provide further support for the notion that the acquisition of verb agreement in sign — perhaps even its innovation — is subject to a critical period.

How do second cohort signers differ from those in the first cohort? Early- and middle-exposed members of the second cohort are more fluent than first cohort signers: they produced more morphemes per minute in their signing (Senghas & Coppola 2001). Second cohort signers — especially those exposed to NSL by age 10 — also made greater use of what Senghas and Coppola term shared reference: "If a previously-produced sign shared both the location and the referent of the current sign, it was coded as a shared-reference use." On this notion, both the current sign and its antecedent agree in being produced with respect to the same location in the signing space. Based on the results of other tasks, Senghas (Senghas, Coppola, Newport & Supalla 1997; Senghas 2000) has shown that second cohort signers are more consistent than first cohort signers in their use of directionality in verbs. Moreover, their interpretation of directional verbs is much more constrained than is that of first cohort signers. These results are consistent with the hypothesis that verb agreement is more grammaticized for second cohort signers.

The linguistic situation in Nicaragua is in flux and, as the results reviewed here have already suggested, there are different varieties of NSL in use in different cohorts of signers. First cohort signers use what Kegl et al. (1999: 181) call *Lenguaje de Señas Nicaragüenses*, "a peer-group pidgin or jargon between signers." In contrast, the early learners of the second cohort are users of *Idioma de Señas Nicaragüenses* (ISN), which Kegl et al. consider to be a fullblown language. These authors also indicate that directional marking of persons (as opposed to directional marking of locations) is much more common in ISN than in LSN. Moreover, to the extent that there is any person marking on verbs in LSN, it is by means of what they consider to be an encliticized pointing gesture that retains its index handshape. In contrast, it appears that in ISN the verb SPEAK has become a fully directional verb, such that the movement path of the verb itself spans locations associated with the subject and object. No separate pointing sign with an index handshape is necessary.

5.   Conclusions

The form of directional verbs in ASL and other signed languages is akin to pointing, but the function of such verbs is akin to an agreement system in spoken languages. As sign languages mature, so does agreement. Across generations of Danish signers, first-person object agreement and also double agreement with both subject and object have been established. In ASL, directionality has sometimes spread to verbs that have their origins in fingerspelling. In Nicaragua, second cohort signers use verbs more directionally than do the members of the first cohort. Directionality is not just a gestural resource on which signed languages are built. Instead, the directional use of verbs is elaborated as sign languages evolve and mature. And, in Nicaragua, the interpretation of those verbs has become more constrained. These facts are consistent with the claim that directionality is the form that agreement takes in signed languages.

In their agreement systems, signed languages present certain complexities not expected in spoken languages: for example, agreement as marked on the hands is limited in its applicability in ASL.[18] Only certain verbs in ASL take agreement; the same is true in German Sign Language and other signed languages that have auxiliary-like elements, except that in such languages these auxiliaries carry agreement when plain verbs cannot. Despite the iconicity of many agreeing verbs, even the form of agreement may present problems to the child: the markers of agreement in signed languages are not discrete, affixal linguistic units.

The results reviewed above show that children are inattentive to the iconic properties of agreeing verbs. If we accept the suggestion that the markers of agreement within directional verbs are a kind of pointing gesture, the findings reviewed here nonetheless make it clear that the integration of these pointing gestures into verbs takes time for children. In contrast to simple pointing, which appears in most children (whether exposed to sign or not) by age 9 or 10 months and which is used communicatively at that early age, the acquisition of pointing in combination with directional verbs takes much longer. When pointing and language are assigned to separate articulators, as in the gesturing that accompanies spoken languages, children can coordinate the simultaneous production of points and words by 13–15 months (Butcher & Goldin-Meadow 2000). Yet, verb agreement is not fully acquired until age 3, well after deaf children reliably use directional gestures. Children opt for morphologically simplex forms over morphologically complex forms, a preference that is reflected in their omissions of verb agreement and in their apparent bias toward single agreement over double agreement. These results suggest that children are acquiring agreement as a morphological system.

Like many aspects of first language acquisition, the acquisition of verb agreement is limited by a critical period within which children must be exposed to a language model if they are to become native signers of a mature sign language such as ASL. In Nicaragua, it is just children who have benefited by being in the second cohort of signers. The critical period effects identified in signers' use and knowledge of agreement indicate that the native acquisition of agreement may involve cognitive or linguistic capacities that are fully available to very young children but that may be less available (or unavailable) to later learners.

It is not just in its development that verb agreement patterns like other linguistic abilities. On a variety of linguistic measures, left-hemisphere damaged subjects perform more poorly than right-hemisphere damaged subjects (Hickok, Bellugi & Klima 1996; and, for reviews, Hickok, Bellugi & Klima 1998 and Corina 1999). This finding extends to the grammatical use of space in verb agreement: case studies have found that damage to the left hemisphere can lead to impaired production and comprehension of agreeing verbs, although the right hemisphere appears to have a role in their comprehension (Poizner, Klima & Bellugi 1987). Damage to the left hemisphere can impair signing, but spare gesturing (Corina, Poizner, Bellugi, Feinberg, Dowd & O'Grady 1992; and, for a study of an epileptic child exposed to French Sign Language, Metz-Lutz, Saint Martin, Monpiou, Massa, Hirsch & Marescaux 1999). Finally, a double disassociation has been identified in two subjects between the use of space to signal grammatical relations, as in verb agreement, and the use of the sign space to describe spatial relations (Hickok, Say, Bellugi & Klima 1996). Left-hemisphere damage impaired the use of agreement, while having no effect on the use of space to describe a room layout; right-hemisphere damage yielded the opposite.

Lastly, and very importantly, this review has revealed that, at least in child development, there is no one way to point with directional verbs. The diversity of directional forms in native-signing children's errors of misagreement, in David's home signing, and in the innovated use of directional verbs in MCE-exposed children comes as a surprise. Native-signing children occasionally err by producing agreement with an argument (sometimes a direct object, less often — it seems — with a subject) not sanctioned by the parental language. It appears that David regularly used directional verbs to mark patients in contexts in which ASL sanctions agreement with the recipient. And the MCE-exposed children sometimes showed agreement with the subject instead of the object, double agreement when the ASL verb only allows single agreement, and auxiliary-like elements in lieu of agreement on the main verb. These results on the diversity of directional verb forms in children's early signing suggest a new mystery as to why agreement seems to be so uniform in conventional signed languages. Are these languages indeed as uniform as we think, or is this uniformity an artifact of the limited sample of signed languages examined to date? If signed languages are indeed as uniform in their agreement systems as we now suspect, then why? Why are they uniform if children's innovations have been an important contributor to the creation of signed languages? This is a reminder that we need to examine the structure and acquisition of more signed languages and we must undertake this work in an era in which many signed languages are endangered (Meier 2000).

Notes

* I thank Shannon Casey, Ann Senghas, Diane Lillo-Martin, Kearsy Cormier, Sadia Rahman, and Christian Rathmann for reading a draft of this chapter. I also thank Elissa Newport and Susan Goldin-Meadow for discussion of the issues raised here. Figures 1, 2, and 4 were drawn by Frank A. Paul; Figure 3 was drawn by Tony McGregor; all figures copyright Richard P. Meier. Lastly I thank Sam Supalla for serving — some years ago — as the model for Figures 1 and 2.

1. See Engberg-Pedersen (1993: 173–183) for an extensive discussion of agreement in Danish Sign Language and its functional and formal similarity to agreement systems in spoken languages.

2. For Liddell, this phenomenon allows him to probe the way in which space is structured in ASL conversations. This is an issue that I cannot address here.

3. In referring to object agreement forms, I use the term *object* loosely. For a verb such as CONVINCE, this is the form that agrees with the direct object. For a three-place predicate such as GIVE, this form agrees with the notional indirect object.

4. Engberg-Pedersen notes that older signers may have a few verbs that permit first-person object agreement.

5. For a formal analysis of ASL's system of verb agreement within the theory of head-driven phrase structure grammar, see Cormier, Wechsler & Meier (1998).

6. Both Padden (1983) and T. Supalla (n.d.) argue that certain intransitive verbs may show agreement. However, this possibility has received little attention in the literature.

7. For an earlier review of the literature that touches on some issues not raised here, see Newport & Meier (1985). Included there is a discussion of the limited available evidence on maternal input with respect to verb agreement (Kantor 1982b).

8. The subscripts indicate whether the verb agrees in its initial and final locations with first, second, or third-person arguments. The use of the subscripts 2 and 3 is for convenience only, inasmuch as I have previously argued that ASL does not have a grammatical distinction between second and third person, but only between first and non-first person (Meier 1990). This same analysis has also been adopted for Danish and Taiwanese Sign Languages (Engberg-Pedersen 1993; Smith 1990), among others. The subscripts 3i and 3j indicate spatially distinct third-person locations. In subsequent examples, I will use the notation POINT to refer to pronominal pointing signs that use an extended index finger. This sign also carries subscripts that mark the location indexed by the sign. Neither gender or tense is

marked on the verb in ASL; thus the use of present tense or of *him* vs. *her* in the translation of ASL verbs is purely a matter of convenience.

9. In forms that I considered to be mimes, the articulator of the sign (i.e., the hand) and the prototypical articulator of the action being referred to were the same.

10. In this review, I will have little to say about the distinction that Padden (1983) makes between *inflecting* verbs, such as GIVE, and *spatial* verbs, such as PUT. Inflecting verbs agree with subject and object, whereas spatial verbs agree with locative arguments, such as source and goal. The status of these two hypothesized verb classes is unresolved in the linguistic literature. Unfortunately, the developmental literature has little to say about these two classes of verbs. When I refer to verb agreement, I will be referring to both classes. Acquisition analyses that distinguish between these two classes of verbs will be helpful.

11. In Meier (1982), I discussed the U-shaped curve that appears in Figure 4 in Corinne's data. I attributed her surprisingly accurate use of verb agreement at 2;0 to her 17, possibly rote, uses of a single agreeing verb form, specifically SAY-NO$_2$ *(I) say no to you.* My data on Corinne's language development began at 1;6. I could not identify any obligatory contexts for agreement until the sample at 2;0.

12. For each subject, samples were first pooled over age. The data here include samples through 3;9. Given that each of the children had shown mastery of agreement around 3;0, the inclusion of later samples in these figures accounts for the high overall accuracy on object agreement.

13. See Meier (2001) for a recent review on this topic.

14. Consistent with the terminology that Goldin-Meadow and her colleagues have used in describing home sign systems, I will refer not to signs, but to gestures. Likewise I will use semantic terms such as patient and recipient to refer to the arguments of verb-like gestures.

15. Note that David's gesture is not maximally iconic. A more iconic gesture would have as its endpoint the recipient and its beginning point the cookie.

16. See Stack (1999) for further evidence of innovated use of verb agreement in a child exposed to SEE2.

17. Senghas and Coppola (2001) do not use the term *verb agreement*, but instead use the term *spatial modulations*. This term has a ready operational definition. Elsewhere (e.g., Kegl et al. 1999) they have used the term *person agreement* to describe the verbal modulations under discussion here.

18. In this chapter, I have not discussed proposals that there are non-manual markers of agreement in ASL (Bahan 1996). I know of no developmental evidence that is relevant to these proposals.

The expression of grammatical relations by deaf toddlers learning ASL*

Brenda Schick

1. Introduction

In the acquisition of language, a key element of grammatical structure is how the verb relates to its arguments representing conceptual roles. Basically, languages can use two different syntactic devices, word order or case markings, to communicate the argument structure of the verb. The acquisition of these devices is one of the earliest aspects of grammatical development (Bloom 1991; Tomasello 1992). By investigating the verb, and its surrounding arguments, we can gain insights into what a child knows about grammatical structure. Research shows that children begin learning argument structure early, using either word order or case marking by the time they are producing multiword utterances.

For example, in a language such as English, which uses word order to indicate grammatical role, children appear to acquire word order with ease. As summarized by O'Grady (1997:56), English-speaking children appear "to master the verb's combinatorial and positional properties more or less simultaneously" resulting in the correct use of word order in the "vast majority of their utterances from the earliest stages of multiword speech." Tomasello (1992), in a detailed diary study, found that by her second birthday, his daughter was using word order as a productive syntactic device. In languages that use morphological markings to indicate the conceptual role of a noun phrase, researchers have also found relatively early acquisition of affixes, even in languages where the systems are quite complex (Bloom 1970; Hirsh-Pasek & Golinkoff 1996; MacWhinney 1985; Slobin 1982).

However, there are indications that grammatical structure is not present in the earliest of combinations, and that children learn grammatical rules on a verb by verb basis. Tomasello argues that the earliest combinations his daughter used did not show evidence of any grammatical devices for indicating argument relations and he describes the combinations that as "concatenating words"

(Tomasello 1992:226). Between ages 16 to 18 months, he observed that she did show some consistent ordering patterns during this period similar to those found by Braine (1976), who termed them "positionally productive patterns". But none were productive in the sense that she used contrastive orderings. His hypothesis was that these ordering consistencies reflected "nothing more or less than the ordering preferences following adults' models" (Tomasello 1992:226) without an underlying grammar. In other words, sometimes her concatenations would replicate the orders that she heard in the adult grammar, and sometimes they did not, with the result that her word order was non-adult-like and inconsistent. He proposed a Verb Island hypothesis in which verbs are individual islands of organization in an otherwise unorganized grammatical system. The child may be demonstrating ordering preferences, but unless the child actively controls the pattern, he does not consider it a functionally significant symbolic device.

This paper will examine the early development of grammatical structure in American Sign Language, or ASL, used throughout the United States and parts of Canada. While ASL is an SVO language, similar to English, there are aspects of the language that are quite different from English. The goal of this chapter is to investigate how children who are learning ASL as a native language express grammatical relations in their earliest word combinations. In addition, it will provide an overview of the development of early syntactic structure. The paper will first provide an overview of grammatical structure in ASL. Following this, it will present previous studies on the acquisition of grammatical structure in ASL, followed by data from deaf toddlers who are learning ASL as a first language.

2.   Grammatical structure in ASL

The general consensus is that ASL is a subject-verb-object (SVO) language, similar to English (Fischer & Gough 1978; Liddell 1980; Padden 1981). This is the basic or underlying word order that occurs in unmarked sentences. However, there are many morphological and syntactic processes in ASL that alter the basic SVO structure, such as topicalization, null arguments, and verb sandwiches (the repetition of a verb in a sentence, as explained later). For the most part, when sentence order is altered from SVO in ASL, there is an increase in the morphological complexity in the utterance, most often in the form of non-manual markers (e.g., grammatical facial expression) and forms of verb agreement. Others have argued that while ASL is an SVO language, its surface word order is best explained by discourse or pragmatic functions (Fischer 1975; Liddell 1978; Wilbur 1994, 1997).

For example, in topicalization, a syntactic object can be moved to a sentence initial position, resulting in a surface OSV order, as in (1). This dislocation serves to foreground information (Wilbur 1994). However, the topic must be accompanied by a grammatical nonmanual marker in the form of an eyebrow raise that spreads over the topic (Aarons 1994; Neidle, Kegl, MacLaughlin, Bahan & Lee 2000). This nonmanual marker is represented in the gloss as a line above the topic that extends over the domain of the nonmanual marker, with *t* representing *topic*. Without the nonmanual marker, topicalization is ungrammatical.

```
        ____ t
```
(1)   BOOK, BROTHER BUY.
      'My brother bought a book'

Another syntactic structure that may alter the surface word order is the fact that ASL permits null arguments in that subjects and objects may not be expressed phonologically, with an overt nominal or pronominal (Lillo-Martin 1991). For example, a signer may not include an overt subject or object in a sentence even though it has syntactic reality. In order for an utterance to have a null argument, the NP must be recoverable from context, prior knowledge, or previous mention. This can mean that what is actually produced could be only a verb, or an SV, or VO order. In the examples shown in (2), the verb 'inform' occurs without an explicit subject or object and 'ski' occurs without a subject.

(2)   LAST-WEEK, BROTHER SEE FRIEND. INFORM SATURDAY SKI
      'Last week my brother saw a friend. He informed him that we would ski on Saturday'

A third syntactic operation that alters the underlying SVO order is sentence-final tags (Liddell 1980; Neidle et al. 2000), in which material from the main clause is repeated in a reduced version. Neidle et al. claim that a pronoun coreferential with the main-clause subject is commonly found in the tag. These tags may co-occur with a null pronominal subject in the main clause, and with right-dislocated pronominal in sentence-final position. This may result in a surface form of VO, S as shown in example (3).

(3)   HUSBAND ENJOY BOOK. READ THREE-TIMES, PRO-HE
      'My husband enjoyed the book. He read it three times.'

Finally, there is a structure in ASL called verb sandwiches by Fischer and Janis (1990) in which a verb is repeated at the end of a sentence but in the repetition the second verb is highly inflected. Similar verbs have been identified by Supalla (1990) and Kegl (1985). Fischer and Janis identify the structure in these verbs as shown in (4) with an example shown in (5), in which the final verb is inflected with an aspectual marker. So what might be produced is an SVOV.

(4)   SUBJECT VERB+SOME-INFLECTION (OBJECT) (ADJUNCTS) VERB +DIFFERENT-INFLECTIONS...

(5)   SALLY TYPE PAPER TYPE [aspect: unrealized inceptive]
      'Sally began to type her term paper, but didn't really start'

It is likely that there are other means of altering fundamental word order in ASL so that even though the language might be an SVO language, a wide variety of orders actually appear on the surface. In fact, the use of structures that alter the underlying SVO order are used quite frequently in ASL. Wilbur (1994) states that analysis of conversations in ASL shows extensive use of syntactic structures that result in word order that is not SVO. Baker-Shenk and Cokely (1980) observe that the process of topicalization occurs frequently in ASL.

3.   Acquisition of ASL

For children who are acquiring ASL, it is clear that they must learn the underlying SVO word order and the variety of operations that alter that order. It is probable that they see a wide variety of surface word orders, some with accompanying complex morphology and some without. It is not clear how a young child, who is just beginning to control grammatical relations in two and three word utterances, handles this acquisitional task..

In ASL, while word orders other than SVO are often accompanied by morphological markers, there is evidence that this morphology may not be accessible to very young children. There is ample research that shows that young children do not have control of inflectional morphology in ASL until after they are producing early sentences. Newport and Meier (1985) conclude that native signing deaf children begin acquiring the morphology of ASL at about 2 1/2 to 3 years of age and acquisition continues for the more complex morphological systems beyond age 5. Particularly relevant to the issue of word order is the acquisition of pronominal agreement morphology, which associates spatial loci with nominal. Meier (1982) found that children only begin to use agreement morphology at about age 2;0 to 2;6 but still produce many verbs without inflection. Acquisition continues until about age 3;6. However, acquisition is even later for pronominal agreement forms that are abstract, referring to nominals that are not actually present during signing (Loew 1984).

In addition, the morphology in ASL that appears in the form of nonmanual facial expressions appears to be particularly difficult for young children. While a great deal of ASL involves using the hands for signs, there is also linguistic information communicated using facial expression. This facial expression isn't just communicating affective emotions, but is often required for specific grammatical structures. For example, conditionals in ASL have an obligatory nonmanual marker consisting of a constellation of behaviors, including eye brow raises and head tilts (Baker & Padden 1978; Liddell 1986). It appears that children find these nonmanual grammatical markers somewhat difficult to comprehend and use in early acquisition. Reilly, McIntire and Bellugi (1990a) showed that deaf children who are learning ASL as a native language still struggle with the complex nonmanual markers that accompany conditionals in ASL until at least five years of age. They found that children produced some conditionals at age three, the age where they began testing, but did not use any facial morphology, relying only on the manual sign to convey the conditional. Not until age five were their subjects able to coordinate the facial morphology with the lexical sign. They also found evidence that young children, ages 3 and 4 years, do not comprehend sentences as conditionals if they occur with only the nonmanual marker and the lexical sign for the conditional is omitted. Reilly and her colleagues have found similar results for other types of nonmanual facial morphology (Anderson & Reilly 1998; Reilly & Bellugi 1996).

It is clear that children do not have mastery of the complex morphological system that accompanies alterations from SVO order yet they see numerous surface orders. It is not clear how this affects acquisition. Previous researchers have claimed that children learning ASL use consistent word order to mark grammatical roles during the earliest stages of development (Hoffmeister 1978a; Lillo-Martin 1991; Newport & Meier 1985). Newport and Meier report an investigation completed by Hoffmeister on the development of syntax in three children, from 2 to 5 years of age. He found that children showed a strong tendency to use SV, VO, SVO orders both before they used inflections for thematic role as well as after they were consistently using inflections for role. The use of inflection on the verbs didn't appear to affect the use of order. As Newport and Meier (1985: 893) state, "it is clear that young signing children are biased to acquire order prior to inflections, despite the fact that their input language uses inflections more consistently than word order." Similarly, Lillo-Martin (1991) reports that some of her subjects, beginning around three and a half years of age, produced very few null arguments and that word order was used to signal grammatical relations for all verbs.

While word order appears in hearing children learning English as early as 18 to 24 months of age (Tomasello 1992), it is not clear whether it will appear as early in children learning ASL. It is possible that the variety of surface orders and the complexity of the markings for dislocated arguments may result in differences in acquisition in ASL. This paper will present data from deaf children who are learning ASL as a first language from their deaf families to investigate their earliest uses of verbs and their arguments. The analysis focuses on verbs and the relative positioning of thematic roles to see whether the children are using a general SVO word order with the verbs. Following previous research on the acquisition of early sentences (Braine 1976; Tomasello 1992), individual verbs are examined in order to determine whether there are verb-specific patterns or verb islands, to use Tomasello's term.

While there are many thematic roles that map onto the grammatical categories of subject and object, this investigation focuses on the use of two main semantic roles, *agents* and *themes*. Agents are prototypical subjects although they are not the only semantic roles that appear as subjects. Similarly, themes are typically objects of the verb. If children show a preference for ordering of subjects and objects, one would expect to see these preferences with agents and themes.

4. Method

Subjects were 12 profoundly deaf toddlers, at 24 months of age. All were learning ASL as their only language from their deaf parents. All of the families reported that they used ASL exclusively at home. All but two of the children were at least third generation deaf, meaning that the maternal or paternal grandparents were deaf also. All families lived in large metropolitan communities that had large deaf communities. The majority of the children were the second child (8), 3 were first-born, and one child had two older siblings. All siblings were deaf and no families had any hearing individuals living with them.

Subjects were videotaped within two weeks of their two-year birthdate in their home with a parent present, typically the mother. Children were video-taped a total of five hours, with each session lasting about one hour. Most of the time, there were two sessions per day, requiring videotaping on three consecutive days. All mothers were informed that the goal of the videotaping was to capture, as much as possible, their child's language. Sessions consisted of the parent interacting with the child using their own toys and books. The researcher conducting the videotaping talked with the families before and after the sessions. She joined the families for meals and events outside the homes. Because of this, all of the children and families were familiar and comfortable with the researcher.

Sessions were scheduled for a variety of times of the day in order to capture the child in a variety of settings. Prior to videotaping, mothers were informed that if the researcher did not understand what the child signed, she would signal the parent, who would clarify. Because these data were part of a larger project and the researcher had been visiting the family since the child was 12 months old, there were not a significant number of interruptions. All taping was conducted by the investigator, a native hearing signer, or in a few cases, a deaf research assistant. All sessions were recorded using a handheld Super VHS camcorder to allow free movement throughout the home and outside.

Videotapes were transcribed at a later date into a computer database that allows for data coding. The transcription system used English glosses to represent all signs, with transcription codes to indicate verb agreement. All points were included as well as references to what the child was pointing to. However, the data were coded by watching the videotape for each sentence, coding directly into the computer database. Data were not coded from the transcription alone because of the difficulty in representing sign language in a written system. All data were transcribed by hearing graduate students who had conversational fluency in ASL and subsequently checked by a native deaf signer and the researcher. In order to investigate the extent to which the children used word order to communicate grammatical role, all multiword utterances that contained a verb were coded for the semantic categories of theme and agent, rather than subject and object, in order to avoid an assumption of a grammatical role. These roles were selected because they were the most common in the children's productions. Agents and themes could also be in the form of a manual point, which may be pronominal in ASL. Examples of the coding are shown in Table 1. In addition, the use of nonmanual morphology to mark topicalization was coded. All frequency analyses were conducted on the transcripts using a CHILDES CLAN (MacWhinney 2000) program that calculates the frequency of use of all words in a sample.

Table 1. Examples of semantic categories used in coding the data

Semantic Category	Examples
Agent + Verb	BIRD EAT, THROW BALL
Verb + Theme	WANT FOOTBALL, BLANKET LOOK-FOR

5. Results

Shown in Table 2 are the results from general measures of language productivity in order to provide an overview of the children's expressive language. Table 2 includes the total duration of the sample, the total number of utterances produced by the child, and the number of multiword utterances. In order to show the length of the utterances that the children produced, the Mean Length in Words (MLW) was calculated which counted points as a word. This was done because points may be pronominal in ASL, although not always. In addition, the MLW was calculated excluding points (MLW–POINT) in order to show utterance length when only lexical elements were produced. Finally, because many of the children's utterances were a noun phrase plus a point (NP+POINT), the percentage of total multiword utterances that were this specific structure was calculated. As expected, the children varied in how much language they produced and in the number of multiword utterances they produced. On the average, 28% of their utterances consisted solely of a simple NP+POINT, which was most often used as a naming function, similar to a child saying *That's a dog* in English.

In general, the children produced explicit theme arguments far more often than they produced agent arguments, as shown in Table 3. Many of the subjects expressed almost no agent arguments. The mean number of multiword utterances that had agent arguments was 7 percent while the mean for theme arguments was 55 percent. The order of the verb and theme, and verb and agent was determined for all multiword utterances that contained a verb as shown in Table 4 and 5. If the children were using an underlying SVO word order to represent grammatical role the majority of their utterances should be in the order of AGENT VERB and VERB THEME. However, as the data show, most of the children produced utterances in which the agent and the theme were in both preverbal and postverbal position. For the agent ordering, only three children produced AGENT VERB ordering more than 75% of the time. For the theme ordering, no child produced a VERB THEME ordering consistently

Table 2. Summary of language measures for each child and the duration of the complete sample

Child	Duration	Number of Utterances	Number of Multiword Utterances	MLW	MLW – POINT	Percent NP + POINT
1	5 h	562	387	2.1	1.6	22
2	4 h 41 m	758	183	1.3	1.1	39
3	4 h 37 m	734	216	1.5	1.3	25
4	4 h 11 m	765	180	1.4	1.2	38
5	4 h 20 m	850	204	1.3	1.2	25
6	3 h 42 m	473	90	1.3	1.2	44
7	5 h 5 m	693	155	1.3	1.2	22
8	4 h 33 m	804	216	1.5	1.4	18
9	4 h 31 m	653	118	1.3	1.2	40
10	4 h 45 m	1306	408	2.1	1.9	14
11	4 h 45 m	761	205	2.1	1.3	25
12	4 h 28 m	963	323	1.5	1.3	25
Mean	4 h 33 m	776	223	1.5	1.3	28
sd		209	100	.03	.02	9.7

although three children produced a THEME VERB ordering at least 75% of the time, opposite of what would be expected given the underlying word ordering in ASL. In order to show which children may have more productive patterns, the total number of utterances is shown. As can been seen, children who produced more than 20 utterances with an agent and a verb or a theme and a verb were not more likely to use an SVO word order. Of the two children who produced a specific order more than 80% of the time, none had more than five exemplars of the relationship. The children did not use nonmanual morphology to mark topicalization.

The transcripts were examined to determine whether the children showed positional tendencies for specific verbs. That is, were there verbs that tended to appear with a set positional pattern even though there were no clear patterns when all verbs were combined? To accomplish this, a frequency analysis was conducted on the transcripts using a CHILDES CLAN program that calculates the frequency of use of all words in a sample. Three children were selected for 1further analysis, those who had a high number of utterances and a high MLW. For each child, all verbs that were used with nominal or pronominal point arguments at least four times were examined. Results are shown in Table 6,

Table 3. Agent and theme arguments produced by each child in terms of number of instances and percent of all utterances with more than one word (multiword utterances)

Child	Number of Agent Arguments	Percent of Multiword Utterances that contain an Agent	Number of Theme Arguments	Percent of Multiword Utterances that contain a Theme
1	42	11	206	53
2	6	3	97	56
3	21	10	141	66
4	5	3	103	61
5	1	0	76	37
6	4	4	68	73
7	10	7	76	53
8	25	12	124	59
9	5	4	75	64
10	105	19	245	45
11	22	11	91	44
12	13	4	154	48
Mean	21.6	7	121.3	55
sd	27.6	5	53.9	10

Table 4. Percent and number of utterances with an agent and verb produced using an Agent Verb ordering, with the percent of utterances with a lexical agent.

Child	Percent of utterances with AGENT VERB ordering	Number of utterances in AGENT VERB ordering	Percent of utterances with a lexical agent
1	69	27	67
2	50	4	50
3	57	12	71
4	57	4	29
5	100	1	100
6	100	4	50
7	63	10	44
8	78	21	74
9	43	3	57
10	49	34	85
11	71	15	86
12	53	10	53
Mean	66	8	64
sd	19	9.3	21

Table 5. Percent and number of utterances with a theme and verb produced using a Verb Theme ordering; percent of utterances with a lexical theme

Child	Percent of utterances with a VERB THEME ordering	Number of utterances in VERB THEME order	Percent of utterances with a lexical theme
1	67	28	55
2	65	20	7
3	62	28	60
4	63	10	17
5	58	23	5
6	46	6	14
7	43	9	19
8	43	15	55
9	62	8	5
10	47	27	62
11	51	19	33
12	68	34	26
Mean	56	19	30
sd	10	9.3	22

which shows the VERB+THEME combinations for high frequency verbs. There is some indication that the children had some positional tendencies for specific verbs but clearly, for the most part, they were preferences and not strict positional patterns. For example, for subject 1, five verbs had strong positional tendencies (EAT, SEE, DRINK, PUT-IN, LOOK-FOR) but two did not (WANT, LIKE). However, notice that the positional tendencies were not the same for all verbs. Three verbs had VERB THEME ordering and two verbs had THEME VERB ordering. But for subjects 10 and 12, although there were positional tendencies, they were not as clear. Similar to subject 1, their positional patterns differed for different verbs. For subject 10, LOOK-FOR and WANT tend to appear with VERB THEME ordering but EAT tends to appear with THEME VERB ordering. A similar contrast can be found in subject 12, with the verbs WANT and FIND.

Because there were so few agent arguments expressed, there were very few repetitions of a verb with an agent, which made it difficult to determine whether there were positional patterns associated with specific verbs. As shown in Table 7, subject 1 exhibited a tendency for preverbal agents (69%) but she did produce specific verbs with alternate orders. Both WANT and EAT occurred with preverbal and postverbal agents. Subject 10 was more evenly split in her preference for a position for agent (49% preverbal) and there is not much data

Table 6. Positional patterns with individual verbs for specific children. Numbers represent instances of occurrence

Child	Verb	Verb Theme	Theme Verb
1	WANT	5	9
	EAT	8	1
	SEE	5	1
	DRINK	4	0
	LIKE	2	2
	PUT-IN	1	5
	LOOK-FOR	0	4
10	LOOK-FOR	15	6
	WANT	10	2
	EAT	4	9
	LIKE	4	2
12	WANT	27	14
	FIND	4	9
	THROW	3	2
	EAT	4	1

to investigate positional preferences. She only used two verbs repeatedly that had agents. One showed some positional preferences (LOOK-FOR) in that 3 of the 4 occurrences were with postverbal agents. For the verb VIDEOTAPE there was no preference in that 6 of the 10 occurrences were with postverbal agents. Subject 12 had no repeated verbs with agents so Subject 8 was selected for analysis. Of the three verbs she used repeatedly, one occurred only with preverbal agents (SEE, 3 uses). The verb WANT occurred in both positions (4 of 6 were preverbal) and CRY occurred once in each position.

There were no clausal nonmanual markers produced by any of the children. Although some of the children used some facial expression, its function appeared to be for yes-no questions and emphasis, rather than for syntactic purposes.

6. Discussion

The data provide little evidence that children use a word order strategy to communicate grammatical role for common semantic functions in early multiword utterances in ASL. While there was a slightly greater tendency for some children to produce AGENT VERB orderings than VERB AGENT

Table 7. Positional patterns with individual verbs for specific children

Child	Example with agents
1	WANT ME
	ME WANT POINT-object
	ME WANT GRAPES
	EAT ME
	DADDY EAT
10	LOOK-FOR REBECCA
	REBECCA LOOK-FOR
	VIDEOTAPE BRENDA
	BRENDA VIDEOTAPE
	POINT-BRENDA ME VIDEOTAPE
	'Brenda is videotaping me'
	VIDEOTAPE REBECCA VIDEOTAPE BRENDA
	'Brenda is videotaping Rebecca'

orderings, it was not strong. There did not appear to be any tendency to produce VERB THEME orderings among the children. Children were far more likely to represent a theme in their utterances than an agent, even when pronominal points were included.

However, there is some indication that for some children, there might be positional patterns associated with specific verbs. When the data for VERB+THEME combinations from the most productive children were investigated, one child seemed to have positional patterns for 4 of the 7 verbs she used repeatedly. A second child had a positional pattern for 1 of her four verbs and a third child might have had a pattern for 1 of her 4 verbs. This might mean that while there doesn't seem to be any strong word order rule evident in the children's productions, they may still use word order in specific verbs. There were not sufficient exemplars to determine whether a similar trend existed for VERB+AGENT combinations, but the limited data did not indicate the use of positional patterns. These data are similar to those found by Tomasello for his daughter in her earliest multiword combinations, from 16 to 18 months. However, by the time his daughter was the age of these children, she was using correct word order the majority of the time. It is apparent that something different is happening with these children, who are learning a language with the same underlying word order as English, but with considerable other differences as well as exposure to orderings other than the underlying form in the adult model.

There might be two sources of conflicting information available to deaf children regarding the role of word order in ASL. First, there is the frequent use of topicalization in adult ASL in which a topic of a sentence appears first in an utterance, marked with the appropriate non-manual markers. When the topic is the theme of the verb, a child would see many utterances where the theme occurs before the verb. When a theme occurs preverbally it would occur with nonmanual markers; however research shows that grammatical nonmanual markers are acquired relatively late, both in terms of comprehension and production (Reilly et al. 1990a). Given the current findings, it may mean that children learning ASL are aware of the positional patterns associated with topicalization in that they are sensitive to the fact that nominals are not required to appear in only an SVO ordering. But for the current subjects, they may simply not be aware of the nonmanual markers needed to indicate a dislocation. One would need careful testing of comprehension in order to determine whether children could interpret a dislocated nominal as an object of the verb, using a preferential-looking paradigm, such as that used by Hirsh-Pasek and Golinkoff (1996).

Second, it is also possible that the children do not treat word order as a means to represent grammatical role in ASL. The variety of word orders may indicate that, in general, the children are working with the assumption that word order is relatively free in ASL. Similarly, it may reflect an emerging understanding that word order reflects pragmatic and discourse notions, which have priority in determining ordering. There is some evidence that this may be true of other languages that are spoken. Aksu-Koç and Slobin (1985) report that neutral word order in Turkish is SOV but that there is a high degree of variation for pragmatic purposes. They observed that while children use a variety of word orders at a young age (1;7–2;4), contextually inappropriate word orders are extremely rare. They conclude that pragmatic variation in word order is a precocious acquisition. Aksu-Koç and Slobin also report that the language produced by adults and directed to children reflect a high variation in word order in that the SOV order only occurred in 48% of a broad sample of input to preschoolers. They noted that the input provides little basis for a child to induce word order rules but does provide a great deal of information regarding pragmatic influences on word order. Other evidence for a developmental relationship between syntax and pragmatics can be found in Bates & MacWhinney (1982).

While this study did not investigate the input that deaf parents provide their children, researchers have noted how common dislocation is in adult ASL.

Although observational, in watching mothers and fathers interacting with their deaf children for nearly 400 hours while videotaping, it seems that parents are producing a great number of word orders that are not SVO. It is plausible that deaf children learning ASL see the same type of input that a child learning Turkish hears; input that reflects pragmatic influences rather than the strict underlying order.

It was also the case in these data that the children produced far more theme arguments than agents. This result may be related to the context of the data collection, which was in the child's home with familiar people and objects. Much of the time, the topic of conversation was what was happening during play and daily routines. Because the agents were typically present, they may have been more semantically redundant than themes. These data are consistent with data from hearing children who are learning spoken English. Bloom (1991) in an investigation of verb subcategorization in children during the early stages of multiword expression, found that children were more likely to produce action words with objects than with agents. For her four subjects, for the time periods where their MLU is roughly comparable with the MLW in the current subjects, about 60 to 96 percent of their utterance were verb and object combinations without the agent specified. Valian (1991) found that children learning Italian, a null subject language, produced lexical and pronominal subjects at half the rate of their English-speaking peers. Given these data, we should expect to see agent arguments expressed less often than theme arguments. And because ASL is a null subject language we can expect to see agents expressed at a lower rate that we might see in children learning English.

In conclusion, deaf children learning ASL appear to be sensitive to the variations in word order that occur in their language in the sense that their productions reflect the diversity of word orders that they see in their input. This means that they are actually sensitive to word order, thus following an operating principle proposed by Slobin (1985), termed Variable Word Order. Following this principle, when a child finds more than one word order, he will "attempt to find a distinct function for each order" (Slobin 1985:1233). As Slobin states, pragmatic notions are a highly possible function for variable word order. MacWhinney (1985) also recognizes that children may use pragmatic notions when ordering elements in terms of a predisposition to order the newest or most informative element first.

How do we reconcile the findings of the current study with previous reports that children learning ASL use a more rigid word order (Hoffmeister 1978a and Lillo-Martin 1991)? The previous studies included children who were older than the current subjects and it might be the case that at a later stage in development, children rely on word order to communicate grammatical role. This may reflect an interaction among agreement, syntax, null arguments, and other grammatical aspects. It might also reflect the fact that deaf children are in a diglossic language community, seeing ASL and English-like signing especially within the educational community. Lillo-Martin (1991) reported that the use of fixed word order occurred in only some of her subjects. It would be interesting to investigate these issues using a longitudinal methodology that included aspects of the child's input in order to determine whether the later use of word order reflected language acquisition factors or reflected the complex linguistic community that deaf children are in.

Notes

* The author gratefully acknowledges the participation of the families who volunteered to be in this research project, which required a considerable amount of time and commitment. Franky Ramont and Elaine Gale helped with data collection and analysis; their skills and expertise were invaluable. The project was funded with a grant from NIH-NIDCD (DC00952).

FACES

The acquisition of non-manual morphology in ASL

Judy Reilly and Diane Anderson

1. Introduction

While earlier research in signed languages focused primarily on the hands (Bellugi & Klima 1982; Klima & Bellugi 1979; Launer 1982; Meier 1991; Newport & Meier 1985; Prinz & Prinz 1981; Meier & Newport 1990), a growing body of literature has demonstrated that in American Sign Language (and other signed languages, as well) specific facial behaviors serve not only the affective functions they do when accompanying spoken discourse, but they also constitute a part of the grammar of the language (Baker 1977; Coulter 1979; Baker-Shenk 1983; Baker & Cokely 1980; Baker & Padden 1978; Liddell 1978; Engberg-Pedersen 1995, in Danish Sign Language; Poulin & Miller 1995, in Quebec Sign Language; and Rossini, Reilly, Fabretti & Volterra 2000, in Italian Sign Language). Particular constellations of facial behaviors signal structures such as conditional clauses, topics, negation and relative clauses. In fact, facial signals are frequently the only morphological marker for certain grammatical structures (Baker-Shenk 1983). In this chapter we chart the acquisition of non-manual behaviors, especially facial morphology in ASL in Deaf children of Deaf parents who are acquiring ASL as their native language.

Similar to infants growing up in other communities, Deaf babies are competent affective communicators by their first birthday; that is, they use a repertoire of emotional facial expressions both productively and receptively for social communicative purposes. That facial behaviors are used for both emotional and linguistic purposes in ASL presents a challenge to the child acquiring a signed language: just at the moment when productive language emerges, at about one year of age, Deaf infants must learn to use faces linguistically as well as affectively. Charting the emergence and development of such grammatical behaviors will permits us to address some basic questions in language and development: What are the relationships of these two communicative systems, language and affect, as they emerge and co-develop? Do we see particular associations and dissociations within and across these communicative systems? And finally, because sign language, unlike spoken languages, exploits multiple channels simultaneously, how do children acquire linguistic structures that are signaled simultaneously in two channels: hands and faces?

2.   Non-manual morphology in ASL

Before we begin to discuss the development of non-manual morphology in ASL, and to set the stage for our acquisition studies, we present below a brief overview of non-manual morphology in the adult model.[1] In ASL, non-manual morphology includes grammatical facial behaviors which occur on the upper face, the lower face, or both, and can also include head and shoulder movements as well as eye blinks as part of the grammatical signal. Non-manual morphology occurs with single manual lexical items, with multi-signed predicates, or they can have phrasal or clausal scope, as exemplified below.

2.1 Lexical behaviors

In some instances, single lexical signs are accompanied by non-manual behaviors:

(1)   a.   _____gaze +head (head and eyes move as if searching)
             SEARCH
             ___puff (cheeks filled with air)
             FAT
       b.   LATE,
             _____th (tongue slightly protruding between teeth)
             NOT-YET

The two manual signs (LATE and NOT-YET) share the same manual form; however, they are distinguished by the occurrence of the non-manual *th*. (Transcription conventions follow Baker and Cokely (1980) in which manual signs are written in capital letters, and non-manual signals are denoted above the manual signs with which they co-occur. The line denotes the scope and timing of the non-manual behavior relative to the manual signs. A full list of transcription conventions used in this paper can be found in Appendix A. The numbers accompanying the non-manual behaviors are AUs (Action Units, see

Appendix B) reflecting contractions of individual muscles according to the coding system devised by Ekman and Friesen (1978).

2.2 Adverbial facial behaviors

ASL also uses a group of non-manual adverbials which tend to involve the lower face; they co-occur with a variety of predicates to semantically modify the meaning of the manual predicate. (See Appendix C for a more comprehensive description of different adverbial behaviors and their corresponding meanings.) For example, the adverbial *mm* can be glossed as 'regularly, easily, or pleasurably' whereas the adverbial *th* is often glossed as 'awkwardly or carelessly' as in the following trilogy of examples:

(2) a.   BOY WRITE LETTER
'The boy is writing/wrote a letter'
b.   _____mm (AU 15+22)
BOY WRITE LETTER
'The boy writes/wrote letters regularly or easily'
c.   _____th (AU19+26)
BOY WRITE LETTER
'The boy writes/wrote letters carelessly'

In the above examples, the string of manual signs (glossed by capital letters) are identical for all three sentences. However, the facial adverbs (signaled by the letters *mm* or *th* above the signed string) co-occur with, and modify the meaning of, the manual predicate WRITE LETTER.

2.3 Syntactic facial behaviors

The repertoire of non-manual morphology in ASL also includes syntactic structures that are clausal or phrasal in scope, as in the following examples:

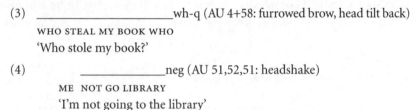

(3) _____wh-q (AU 4+58: furrowed brow, head tilt back)
WHO STEAL MY BOOK WHO
'Who stole my book?'
(4) _____neg (AU 51,52,51: headshake)
ME NOT GO LIBRARY
'I'm not going to the library'

In examples (3) and (4), the grammatical facial behavior signaling the *wh*-question and negation is required in each case, even though the manual signs also convey such information. That is, the *wh*-question is signalled with an initial and reduplicated manual sign who; however the structure additionally requires the non-manual grammatical question behaviors as well (furrowed brow and slightly raised head, Baker and Cokely 1980; Baker-Shenk 1983). Similarly, the example (4) includes a negative manual sign NOT, yet, like all negative sturctures, it also requires the negative non-manual grammatical behavior that spans the predicate. In each case, the non-manual morphology is obligatory and appears to be partially redundant with manually signed components. In contrast, in example (5) (a)–(b), the non-manual behavior is the only indication that the utterance is a conditional sentence. Without the non-manual signal, the utterance is interpreted as a sequence of two declarative statements (b).

(5)   a.   (AU 1+2: raised brows, AU 57: nod closing ante-
        _____cond   cedent clause, AU 45: a blink between the clauses)
        EAT BUG   SICK YOU
        'If you eat a bug, you'll get sick'
      b. EAT BUG   SICK YOU
        'You ate a bug'   'You got sick'

Similarly in example (6a) and (b), negation is uniquely conveyed by the non-manual signal. Without the non-manual signal, the sentence is affirmative, as in (b).

(6)   a.   _____neg (AU 51,52,51)
        ME LIKE CANDY
        'I don't like candy'
      b. ME LIKE CANDY
        'I like candy'

In sum, non-manual grammatical behaviors co-occur with manual strings of differing length and complexity; in some cases, they appear to be redundant with the manual signs and in other cases, they are the sole grammatical marker.

3.   Grammatical versus affective faces

From the descriptions accompanying the non-manual signals, it is clear that the grammatical facial behaviors often resemble emotional facial expressions and recruit many of the same muscles as do affective expressions. How do signers distinguish the two sets of behaviors? One significant difference between affective and linguistic facial behaviors is that emotional facial expression is not tied to any linguistic production. For example, without talking or signing at all, we can smile in response to a child toddling across the lawn; grammatical facial behaviors, however, always co-occur with a manually signed string. Second, the scope and timing of the non-manual behavior is linguistically constrained relative to the manual signs with which it is produced (Baker-Shenk 1983). Specifically, a grammatical facial behavior begins milliseconds before the manual sign and terminates milliseconds before the end of the manually signed string over which it has scope (ibid.). Emotional expressions, in contrast, are not so constrained and may begin and end at any time regardless of the manual signs that may be produced. A third distinctive aspect is in the intensity and continuity of the expression. Grammatical facial signals reach apex intensity immediately and remain at apex for the duration of the signed string; in contrast, emotional expressions vary in their intensity and continuity and can wax and wane during the production of an utterance. In sum, there are specific linguistic rules governing the production of grammatical signals, but the production of emotional expression is considerably more variable and is not linguistically dependent. The following examples illustrate the different profiles of emotional versus grammatical facial signals.

3.1 Grammatical facial expression: Scope and intensity

(5) a. ⌐‾‾‾‾‾¬cond
         EAT BUG   SICK YOU
         'If you eat a bug, you'll get sick'

3.2 Affective facial expression: Scope and intensity

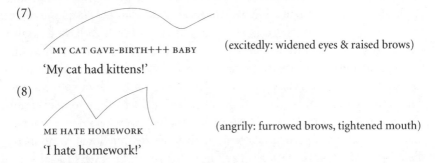

(7)

MY CAT GAVE-BIRTH+++ BABY   (excitedly: widened eyes & raised brows)
'My cat had kittens!'

(8)

ME HATE HOMEWORK   (angrily: furrowed brows, tightened mouth)
'I hate homework!'

Each of these emotional profiles represent just one of many possible shapes.

As we mentioned above, by the end of their first year, both deaf and hearing infants consistently use the basic affective facial expressions both to express and to interpret emotional states (Campos, Barrett, Lamb, Goldsmith & Stenberg 1983; Hiatt, Campos & Emde 1979; Klinnert, Campos, Sorce, Emde & Svejda 1983; Nelson 1987; Reilly, McIntire & Bellugi 1991; Stenberg & Campos 1990; Marschark 1993). However, around age one, as language emerges, infants acquiring ASL must learn to use faces linguistically as well. How do toddlers make this transition to using faces linguistically as well as affectively? One obvious route to the acquisition of grammatical facial signals would be for the child to extend and generalize pre-linguistic affective communicative abilities to appropriate linguistic contexts. This would imply one global system of facial expression that serves both linguistic and affective functions. Alternatively, children might ignore the similarities in the signals and treat the grammatical facial signals as a separate system, i.e., as information to be analyzed independently, within the context of acquiring a linguistic system.

In sum, because facial expression in ASL is multifunctional, serving both affective and linguistic purposes, its development serves as a unique context to address issues bearing on the relationship of language to other symbolic and cognitive systems, in this case, affect. In brief, charting the emergence of grammatical facial expression permits us to trace the re-organization of innate behaviors (that is, affective facial expression) for linguistic purposes.

To investigate this area of development and to address these issues, we have examined the development of a variety of non-manual behaviors (facial expression, eye gaze, head movements and body shifts) used for grammatical purposes in over 50 Deaf children of Deaf parents acquiring American Sign Language as their first language. The children range in age from infancy (12 months) through school age (10 years). Our acquisition studies include a range of linguistic structures from non-manual facial adverbs with scope over single predicates to the non-manual signals for conditional clauses, *wh*-questions and direct quotes in discourse contexts, that is, structures which have clausal or sentential scope. Data were collected through a variety of measures including both home and school visits;[2] situations included both naturalistic contexts, e.g., conversations, storytelling, and probes to elicit particular target structures. Each session was videotaped and then transcribed according to conventions devised by Baker and Cokely (1980), and all utterances were coded for non-manual signals with particular attention given to the individual components, their onset, offset and duration. In addition, Ekman and Friesen's Facial Action

Coding System (FACS 1978) was used for coding facial behaviors.[3] In the sections below, we draw from our studies over the past 15 years to present a chronicle of the acquisition of non-manual morphology in ASL by Deaf children acquiring American Sign Language as their first language.

4. From affect to language: What is the nature of development?

4.1 Single-sign utterances

We began our studies by searching for the first indications of facial behaviors to be used in conjunction with manual signs. The earliest examples of co-occuring facial behaviors we observed occurred in children around 18 months of age (Reilly, McIntire & Bellugi 1990b). In these cases, children accompanied single sign utterances of emotion signs with the appropriate emotional facial expression. (In the adult model, appropriate emotional facial expressions regularly co-occur with signs for emotion; without the appropriate emotional facial expression, sentences are anomalous.) At this stage, the children's utterances were generally single sign productions, for example:

(9)   _____smile
       HAPPY

(10)   ___furrow brow
       MAD

(11)   ___lip pout
       CRY

These emotional signs first appear with the appropriate facial expression, as they do in the adult model. Because of the semantic overlap between the manual sign and the facial expression, it is possible that the emotional facial information has simply transferred to the linguistic context, or it may be that the child is expressing her own emotions as she is signing. However, other single sign utterances that were not emotion signs, but were accompanied by facial behaviors, were also produced at this single sign stage:

(12)   (age 2;3)   _____mm (AU 15+22)
                      VACATION

(13)   (age 2;0)   _____furrowed brow (AU 4)
                      WHAT

(14)   (age 2;3)   _____sh (AU 18+22)
                         SHARE

In this last example, the child pursed her lips to mimic the *sh* shape of the initial sound of the word *share* even though she does not know or use the English word for *share*. However, adults may co-articulate the initial sound of the word as they produce a sign. In all three of these cases (examples (12)–(14)), it appeared that the child had analyzed the manual and non-manual signals together as whole packages. We suggest that this may also be the case with emotion signs (see examples (9)–(11)) and that these single sign utterances co-occurring with facial behaviors represent unanalyzed *amalgams* or *gestalts* similar to those noted in the spoken language acquisition literature (MacWhinney 1975; Peters 1983) in which children regularly produce multi-morphemic utterances without having mastered the individual components.

The next pertinent step was observed when children produced emotional signs with blank faces, as if they had separated the two channels, hands and faces, with the manual channel designated for the service of language and the face serving emotional functions. Further evidence for the separation and analysis of the two channels stems from examples of utterances such as the following where the child first pouted, then with a neutral face, signed CRY, and then re-assumed a pouting face.

(15)   (age 2;3)   _____lip pout   _____lip pout
                                   CRY

In this case, it is clear that the child has separated the two systems, and that the non-manual emotional expression and manual linguistic signals are distinct.

4.2   Multi-sign utterances

4.2.1   *Negation and facial adverbs*

As we move away from the one-sign stage to multi-sign utterances, we began to focus on the development of non-manual morphology with broader scope, in this case, phrasal scope. Two candidate structures were those signaling negation and non-manual adverbials. These forms are of interest because they are functionally similar in that they both modify predicates. However, these forms differ in that negation in ASL is signaled non-manually by a headshake which is strikingly similar to the communicative headshake used by both American deaf and hearing people to signal negation whereas the non-manual adverbials have no communicative correlate and are unique to ASL. Thus, the acquisition of negation provides a test to our earlier findings on the acquisition of emotional signs as both emotion and negation have non-linguistic communicative correlates which are formally and semantically similar to their linguistic counterparts. By tracking the development of negation and comparing its profile to that of the non-manual adverbials, we can clarify the role of pre-linguistic communication and its relation to grammatical acquisition. Drawing from our earlier studies (Anderson & Reilly 1998a), below we give a sketch of negation in ASL and then chronicle its acquisition; following negation, we turn to the facial adverbials and their development.

4.2.2 *Negation in ASL*

In ASL, negation is signaled by a headshake that is semantically and formally similar to the early communicative headshake used by hearing and deaf toddlers, as well as adults. This communicative negative headshake can occur alone, for example, as a response, that is, without any words or signs; it is not dependent on any linguistic utterance. However, the grammatical headshake for negation co-occurs with a manually signed utterance, and its scope is precisely timed with the predicate of that utterance. In addition, ASL also has a number of manual signs that signal negation (e.g., NOT, NONE, NO, DON'T-KNOW); utterances with these signs also require the co-occurring negative headshake. Additionally, as previously discussed, a negative headshake can serve to negate an otherwise neutral or affirmative sentence. Some typical examples of negation are:

(16) a.   _____neg
      ME   NOT HUNGRY
      'I'm not hungry'
      b.   _____neg
      ME   CAN'T FIND SHOE
      'I can't find my shoes'
(17)   _____neg
      ME   LIKE CHOCOLATE
      'I don't like chocolate'

4.2.3 *The acquisition of negation*

From our studies of gesture and early vocabulary development (Anderson & Reilly 2002; Provine, Reilly & Anderson 1993), we know that, similar to hearing children, the communicative headshake to signal negation appears about 12 months of age in Deaf children. The first negative manual signs then appear at about 18–20 months, with NO and DON'T-WANT being among the earliest produced. From our study looking at the development of negation in more than 50 Deaf children from 1;0 to 4;11 (Anderson & Reilly 1998a), we found that these negative signs are initially produced without the required co-occurring headshake. Then, sometime between one and eight months after the emergence of the negative manual sign, these same negative lexical signs are accompanied by the required headshake for negation as shown in Figure 1 below.

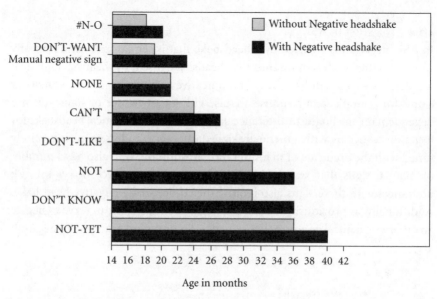

Figure 1. Acquisition timeline of manual and non-manual negation; column endpoint indicates the age of emergence of the given sign either with or without the corresponding non-manual headshake.

This pattern of acquisition is striking: The child fluently uses a headshake to signal negation, yet when negative manual signs first emerge, she does not recruit this behavior to the required linguistic context. Rather, it appears that the children first must analyze the forms independently before they can integrate the manual and non-manual channels. Interestingly, it is the manual channel that takes developmental precedence. Similar to the acquisition sequence for the signs for emotions, once the children have separated the manual and facial behaviors, manual negative signs were produced with blank faces. It was not until later that the children were able to integrate the manual and non-manual channels.

4.2.4   The acquisition of adverbials

As we have mentioned, similar to the negative headshake, facial adverbs modify predicates, yet they are neither semantically or formally similar to any non-linguistic communicative behaviors; they thus provide a context to investigate the acquisition of grammatical facial morphology without the potential competition from a prelinguistic communicative counterpart. In ASL, facial adverbs represent a restricted set of facial behaviors that are produced on the lower face. They always occur with a manually signed predicate: adjectives or verbs (individual, serial or classifier verbs); they can scope multi-signed predicates; however, they generally co-occur with only a single sign manual predicate, especially in young children's discourse. Their onset and offset are co-terminous with the manual predicate; and they may be required with certain lexical items (e.g., FAT, NOT-YET) or when manual predicates are modulated for aspect (e.g., SICK 'repeatedly'). (For a more extensive discussion of the non-manual adverbs and their development, see Anderson & Reilly 1998b).

By looking at both naturalistic data from toddlers and data from a repetition task (Reilly et al. 1990b; Anderson & Reilly 1998b) we found some early amalgams or gestalts at the one-sign stage, and then as noted above (example (12)), the first instance of productive non-manual adverbial use in our data occurred at age 2;0, and it was used in the presence of a single manual sign. The first occurrence of an adverbial used in conjunction with a multi-sign predicate was at age 2;3, and by the age of 3;6, children were using a range of adverbials as is shown in Figure 2 below; these forms occurred frequently in their discourse (see Appendix C for a complete description of the adverbials and their meanings).

4.2.5   Acquisition across channels

Children appear to acquire manual signs and non-manual adverbials as separate morphemes. That is, within the same testing session, a child was frequently observed producing a manual sign both with and without a facial adverbial. Similarly, a child often produced the same manual sign with different facial adverbials (see examples (2b–c)). Moreover, individual verb signs emerged first and then, later in the data, those same signs were produced with co-occurring facial adverbs. Taken together, these findings suggest that manual signs are acquired independently and grammatical facial behaviors appear subsequently as bound morphology. It is worth noting that for the earliest of these facial

Facial Adverbs

Figure 2. Acquisition of non-manual adverbs (from Anderson & Reilly 1998b).

behaviors, i.e. *mm, th,* the children had mastered a manually signed lexical correlate well before the emergence of the bound form. This sequence of acquisition, hands before faces, that characterizes both negatives and adverbials, suggests that for linguistic purposes, once children are producing sentences, the manual channel appears to take developmental precedence.

Errors. Errors produced by children have long been a source to discover the underlying nature of language acquisition. Although relatively infrequent, we observed several types of errors in the production of adverbials. Timing errors were the most common, and these occurred in the repetition data and also in the naturalistic data. In these instances, the timing of the non-manual adverbial did not correspond to the production of the manual predicate (e.g., the onset and offset of the non-manual behavior were not integrated with the manual sign) as in the following example where the child added the adverb *puff* after she had produced the manual sign soft:

(18)   (age 2;7)   _____puff
                            SOFT

In the examples below, Jason produced three utterances in sequence and it is only on the third attempt that he succeeds in co-articulating the non-manual adverbial with the modulated manual sign WORK.

(19) (age 3;10)   _____mm
                         WORK [+ + + +]
                              _____mm
                              WORK [+ + + +]
                              _____mm
                         WORK [+ + + +]

Such errors in timing are additional evidence that non-manual morphology is acquired independently of the manual signs.

Another type of error concerned lexical category errors. In these cases, children produced adverbials with manual signs which do not co-occur with facial adverbs:

(20) (age 2;0)   _____puff
                       GRANDMOTHER

These lexical errors also suggest that non-manual morphology is acquired independently of the manual signs as they are clearly novel productions created by the child and not repetitions of utterances observed in their environment.

Finally, the repetition task offered the possibility to observe children's responses to anomalous adverbial productions. In these cases, children frequently appeared to be puzzled by requests to produce ungrammatical utterances. In their responses, many of the children changed the anomalous adverbial to a possible adverbial or, more interestingly, changed the manual sign to correspond to the modeled facial adverbial, as in the following example from a child age 3;11

(21) a. Target Sentence:
                  __pursed lips
          ELEPHANT BIG
          'The elephant is big (but the non-manual pursed lips indicates quite small or thin)'
      b. Child's response:
                  _____pursed lips
          ELEPHANT SMALL
          'The elephant is very small'

Such a modification demonstrates that at this stage, the child is attending to the non-manual signal and its relation to the manual string, that the non-manual signal conveys meaning to her, and that the manual and non-manual behaviors are separate linguistic components.

In brief then, in the acquisition of adverbials in American Sign Language, Deaf children recognize and produce adverbials from as young as two years old. By the age of 3;6, children have acquired a diverse repertoire of adverbials and use them frequently. From analyses of both their productions and errors of adverbial markers, there is considerable evidence that after the one-sign stage, in which we saw some unanalyzed productions of single signs and non-manual adverbials, children acquire adverbials as independent morphemes rather than as an aspect of a specific manually signed predicate. Confirming this finding was the fact that within the same testing session, a child was frequently observed producing a manual sign both with and without a facial adverbial. Similarly, a child often produced the same manual sign with different facial adverbials. Moreover, individual verb signs emerged first and then, at a later date, those same signs were produced with co-occurring facial adverbs. Together, these findings provide strong evidence that manual signs and grammatical facial adverbials are acquired independently.

From these studies of negation and non-manual adverbials, we can draw the following conclusions:

1. After the early one sign stage, manual signs have developmental priority over facial morphology. This developmental pattern, hands before faces, is true for negation where the communicative and linguistic structures share both formal and semantic similarities, and for structures like facial adverbials which have no communicative correlate;

2. After the one-sign stage, at about 20–24 months of age, pre-linguistic communicative abilities are not directly utilized by the language system. Even though the communicative headshake for negation constitutes part of the child's repertoire, she does not immediately recruit it to the appropriate linguistic contexts; rather, she enters the system of linguistic negation through the manual channel. In both cases, non-manual grammatical behaviors are acquired as bound morphology, after the manual signs are productive. At the transition point when children are favoring the manual channel, it is not that children do not use facial expression. Rather the face appears to be restricted to affective purposes, consonant with the principle suggested by Slobin (1970) of one form – one function.

We are now ready to tackle non-manual structures with clausal scope; our studies in this area have concentrated on *wh*-questions and conditional sentences as they offer an interesting analogue to the adverbials and negation. In each case, as we present these structures below, we begin with a brief description of the structures in the adult model and then review our studies on their acquisition.

4.3 Clausal level structures: *Wh*-questions and conditionals

Wh-questions and conditional clauses are both signaled by non-manual morphological constellations which, as noted previously, are clausal in scope. The signal for *wh*-questions includes a furrowed brow which is formally and semantically similar to the communicative facial gesture conveying 'puzzlement'. Thus, similar to negation, the non-manual signal for *wh*-questions has a non-linguistic communicative correlate that is similar in both form and semantic function. However, the non-manual morphology for conditionals (which includes raised brows, a nod over the last sign of the antecedent clause, and a blink between the clauses) is unique to ASL, and has no clear communicative correlate. In addition, for *wh*-questions and for conditionals, in the vast majority of cases, these structures are signaled both manually and non-manually. That is, both structures have manual signs that signal or introduce the structure, e.g. WHAT, WHERE, or, IF, SUPPOSE, as well as the required non-manual morphology. As we have seen in the studies of negation, children first used the manual sign to signal the structure, and only after they were fluently using the negative manual signs did they then also include the non-manual components of negation. *Wh*-questions and conditionals thus provide another syntactic context to look at the acquisition of structures that are signaled in two channels and to test our hypothesis regarding *hands before faces*.

4.3.1 *The acquisition of* wh-*questions in ASL*

The careful analyses by Baker-Shenk (1983) demonstrated that the grammatical signal for *wh*-questions is a furrowed brow with a slight head tilt which co-occurs with the manually signed question. As in other cases, the non-manual behaviors commence just prior to the first manual sign of the question, rise quickly to apex intensity which is maintained throughout the question. The head and face return to neutral just prior to the termination of the last sign of the question (Baker-Shenk 1983). In addition, there are a number of manual signs that introduce *wh*-questions (e.g., WHO, WHAT, FOR-FOR ['what for?', 'what is it for?'], DO-DO ['what do you do with it?', 'what does it do?']) and they are often repeated at the end of the string. Some examples of *wh*-questions are:

(22) a. _____*wh*-q (AU 4+58)
      WHERE CAT WHERE
      'Where's the cat?'

b.   _____*wh*-q
WHO COME VISIT WHO
'Who's coming to visit?'

When we survey the acquisition data, we find that, similar to the use of facial behaviors in other single-sign utterances, a few early gestalts in the acquisition of facial expression with *wh*-signs occurred (Reilly et al. 1990b; Reilly & McIntire 1991). Specifically the manual signs WHAT or WHERE were frequently produced as single sign utterances and they were accompanied by furrowed brows. However, as children began producing sign combinations, *wh*-questions tended to be produced uniquely with manual signs, as in the following examples:

(23)   a.   (age 1;6)   WHERE DOLL
'Where's (my) dolly?'

b.   (age 2;3)   WOLF WHERE
'Where's the wolf?'

Overall, children under three use few, if any, non-manual behaviors with their manually signed questions. In fact, only five percent of the questions produced by children under three included a furrowed brow, and only 16 percent were accompanied by some other non-manual behavior, in this case head movement, as shown in Figure 3 below.

If we continue to the slightly older children and look at the questions produced by the three-year-old group (Figure 4 below), in 80 percent of the cases, children use some head movement, but only 10 percent of the time do they use the appropriate adult form. In fact there is little evidence of the required non-manual morphology until children are entering school age (Reilly & McIntire 1991) although they produce and respond to a range of manually signed *wh*-questions (e.g., WHAT, WHERE, WHO, WHEN, DO-DO, FOR-FOR). These surprising findings were confirmed in a complementary study by Lillo-Martin (1996).

In spite of these results, we did find a few rare examples of preschoolers producing appropriate *wh*-question non-manual morphology:

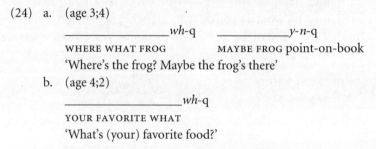

(24)   a.   (age 3;4)
_____*wh*-q   _____*y-n*-q
WHERE WHAT FROG   MAYBE FROG point-on-book
'Where's the frog? Maybe the frog's there'

b.   (age 4;2)
_____*wh*-q
YOUR FAVORITE WHAT
'What's (your) favorite food?'

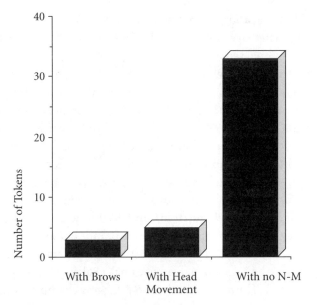

Figure 3. Non-manual morphology in *wh*-questions from children under three.

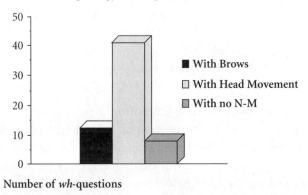

Figure 4. Non-manual morphology in *wh*-questions from three-year-olds.

Overall, however, the acquisition data for *wh*-questions are consistent with the acquisition sequences we reviewed above for negation and facial adverbs. They provide converging evidence that Deaf children consistently acquire the manual signals for a given linguistic structure before they acquire the required facial morphology. That is, children use free lexical morphemes, the manual signs, before they acquire the bound non-manual morphology.

4.3.2   The acquisition of conditional clauses in ASL

As in other languages of the world (Traugott, ter Welen, Reilly & Ferguson 1986), conditional sentences in ASL are complex syntactic structures including an antecedent and a consequent clause. In ASL, the antecedent is accompanied by a collection of non-manual behaviors, and the consequent clause is usually signed with a neutral face. First discussed by Baker and Padden (1978), as well as Baker and Cokely (1980) and Liddell (1978), the consensus is that the non-manual morphology for conditionals includes raised brows and a head tilt that span the antecedent clause; just before the end of this clause, there is a nod. A blink separates the clauses, and the consequent clause is generally signed with a neutral face (except if it individually requires non-manual morphology, for example, if it were a wh-question). In addition to the required non-manual morphology, the antecedent clause may also be introduced by a manual conditional sign, (e.g., IF, SUPPOSE). However, at least for simple predictive conditionals (see example 5a), the manual sign is optional (Baker & Cokely 1980; Reilly & McIntire 1991). Thus, either of the two following examples is acceptable:

(25) a. _____cond
          SUPPOSE MILK SPILL,   MOTHER ANGRY
          'If the milk spills, Mother'll be angry'

      b. _____cond
          MILK SPILL,   MOTHER ANGRY
          'If the milk spills, Mother'll be angry'

Given this situation (which clearly differs from negation where a comparable pre-linguistic form exists), the acquisition of conditionals represents an interesting puzzle. If, as we have seen, manual signs take precedence over the non-manual morphology, how do the children respond when the conditionals are only signaled on the face? Below we will see that this situation indeed presents a challenge.

To explore the acquisition of these structures, we devised some tasks for preschoolers (Reilly, McIntire & Bellugi 1990a) and from these data, four steps emerged in the acquisition of conditionals. At the very earliest ages, Deaf children, like their hearing counterparts (Reilly 1982, 1983, 1986), are juxtaposing two simple clauses. The second clause is contingent on the first, a possible event, and the two are separated by a blink:

(26) (age 2;6)

        (blink)   _____*y-n*-q (AU1+2: raised brows)

BITE YOU,   SPANK ME

'(If I) bite you, (will you) spank me?'

In the second stage, when the children first begin to mark conditionals, only manual signs are used to signal the conditional antecedent; the children's faces are blank although the clauses are separated by a non-manual signal (final nod, blink) as in the following sentences from an experimental task to elicit predictive conditionals:

(27) a. (age 3;10)

      SUPPOSE IF PUT-DOWN WHISKERS (nod, blink) ME GIVE-YOU STICKER

      'If you put on whiskers, I'll give you a sticker'

  b. (age 4;4)

      SUPPOSE WHISKERS STICK-DOWN, (blink) WILL GIVE-YOU STICKER

      'If you put on whiskers, I'll give you a sticker'

Even when given a model to imitate, children at this point ignored the facial morphology, but substituted a different lexical conditional marker (IF) indicating that they understood the sentence to be a conditional.

(28) a. Experimenter:

      _____cond

      SUPPOSE MILK SPILL,   MOTHER ANGRY

      'If the milk spills, mother will be angry'

  b. The child, age 3;3, responded:

      MOTHER ANGRY IF MILK SPILL, MOTHER ANGRY

      'Mom will be angry if the milk spills'

Interestingly, when the stimulus sentences were marked solely by non-manual morphology, as in the following example, these same preschool age children failed to respond appropriately:

(29) Experimenter:

      _____cond

      PUT-DOWN EYE,   GIVE-YOU STICKER

      '(If) you put on an eye, I'll give you a sticker'

The children's lack of appropriate responses to such structures confirmed their reliance on the manual signal at this age for both comprehension as well as production of conditional clauses.

After this stage, where conditionals are produced and comprehended solely via the manual channel, the third step involves the first and partial use of the non-manual signal. Interestingly, the non-manual signal is present, but its scope is abbreviated; in these cases, it only co-occurs with the conditional manual sign (IF, SUPPOSE), rather than the entire antecedent clause, as in the following utterances, first from a child talking about a Ferris wheel, and then from the task data:

(30) (age 3;11)

       _____neg   __cond

TERRIBLE, NOT SAFE,   IF   SLEEP, FALL-OUT

'It's terrible and not safe. If you fall asleep, you'll fall out'

(31) (age 6;10)

      _____cond

SUPPOSE   THERE NOSE, ME GIVE-you STICKER

'If you put a nose there, I'll give you a sticker'

Finally, in the last stage, the scope of the non-manual behavior extends to include the entire antecedent clause as it does in the adult model.

(32) (age 7;7)

      _____cond

SUPPOSE YOU PUT EYE, TWO EYE, (blink) ME GIVE-you STICKER

'If you put an eye or two eyes, I'll give you a sticker'

In sum, from the data on *wh*-questions as well as conditionals, we again see that manual signs take priority over the non-manual signal whether or not the form is unique to ASL, as in the conditionals, or is isomorphic with a non-linguistic gesture, as in *wh*-questions. That is, in this more complex syntactic context, children approach linguistic structures that are signaled across channels, hands and faces, in the same manner as other multi-channel structures. In addition, the conditional data reveals an interesting type of bootstrapping in which initially, the non-manual signal is associated only with the conditional manual sign, e.g., IF or SUPPOSE. This phenomenon further exemplifies the child's reliance on the manual signs as a pathway into the non-manual morphology.

5. Conclusion

In this chapter, we have reviewed some of our studies on the acquisition of grammatical facial expression in Deaf children learning ASL as their first language. We have charted the development of a number of linguistic structures in ASL that are signaled non-manually, including negation and facial adverbials, and *wh*-questions and conditional clauses. In all these cases, once children are producing multi-signed utterances, we see a consistent developmental pattern in which manual signs take developmental precedence over non-manual behaviors. This pattern holds true irrespective of whether the grammatical signal has a non-linguistic communicative correlate, as in the case of, for example, negative headshakes, or is unique to ASL. In the acquisition of each of the structures reviewed, Deaf children use a linear, lexical strategy before they tackle the complex simultaneous facial morphology. A variation of this acquisition strategy was first noted by Roger Brown (1973) in his studies of Adam, Eve and Sarah who were learning English. Before acquiring the bound past tense marker-*ed*, the children used free lexical items, such as *yesterday* or *last night* to signal the notion of past time. As such, this pattern appears to be a general strategy of language acquisition, not bound to any particular language modality, that is, signed or spoken.

Moreover, for those linguistic structures which have non-linguistic cousins, e.g., negation, emotional facial expression and *wh*-questions, we have seen repeatedly that pre-linguistic behaviors do not automatically generalize to the appropriate linguistic context. This neglect of apparently relevant knowledge, i.e., affective and communicative behaviors, in the acquisition of non-manual morphological structures indicates that facial expression and other non-manual communicative behaviors are not treated as a single unified system. Rather, grammatical facial behaviors and other concomitant non-manual grammatical behaviors are acquired as part of the linguistic system, in a gradual, analytic manner. Thus, these data suggest an early bifurcation of systems and a re-organization in which facial expression becomes differentially mediated by affect and language in the developing Deaf child.

Appendix A: Transcription conventions

SIGN   Words in capital letters represent English glosses for ASL signs. A gloss is chosen on the basis of common usage among Deaf researchers and consultants. It represents the meaning of the unmarked basic form of a sign.

SIGN-SIGN   Multiword glosses connected by hyphens are used where more than one English word is required to translate a single sign.

W-O-R-D   Fingerspelled words are prepresented in capital letters with hyphens between the letters.

SIGN^SIGN   Sign glosses conjoined by a circumflex denote a compound sign.

SIGN [+++]   Sign glosses accompanied by a plus indicate that the citation form of the sign
has been modified and the meaning modulated.

_____x

SIGN   A line over a sign or string of signs, indicates a particular non-manual signal
occurring simultaneously with the sign, adding some grammatical meaning.

Appendix B: Some pertinent Facial Action Units

(from Ekman & Friesen 1978 Facial Action Coding System)

AU 1	Inner Brow Raise
AU 2	Outer Brow Raise
AU 4	Furrowed Brows
AU 5	Widened Eyes
AU 6	Cheek Raise
AU 7	Lids Tight
AU 9	Note Wrinkle
AU 13	Cheek Puff
AU 15	Lip Corner Depress
AU 18	Lip Pucker
AU 19	Tongue Show
AU 20	Lip Stretch
AU 22	Lip Funnel
AU 23	Lip Tight
AU 24	Lip Press
AU 25	Lips parted
AU 26	Jaw Drop
AU 31	Jaw Clench
AU 45	Blink
AU 51	Head Turn Left
AU 52	Head Turn Right
AU 55	Head Tilt Left
AU 56	Head Tilt Right
AU 57	Head Forward
AU 58	Head Back

Appendix C: Adverbials

mm: lips pressed together; the bottom lip may protrude in a slight pout; indicates performing an activity with regularity or normally. (FACS AU 15 + 22)

cheek puff: formed by puffing both cheeks with air; it indicates a rounded or swollen quality. (FACS AU 13)

th: produced by relaxing the jaw, parting the lips slightly and showing the tongue; it conveys something done carelessly. (FACS AU 19 + 26)

nose wrinkle: produced by wrinkling the nose; it acts to intensify the meaning of accompanying signs. (FACS AU 9)

ee: tightened lips are drawn back and teeth are clenched together; it describes an unusually large amount or degree (FACS AU 20 + 25 + 31)

pow: begins with tightly pressed lips that open suddenly to form the (unspoken) word *pow*. Depending on its context, it has a variety of meanings; it can indicate that an awaited event finally occurs or something happening quickly and unexpectedly. (FACS AU 27)

pursed lips: This adverbial has two forms: In one, the lips are pressed together and drawn slightly back with a small opening in the center. The second type is formed by closing the jaw and tightly puckering the lips. Among the several meanings of this adverbial is an indication that an object is very small or tiny, skinny, or that a close call occurred (FACS AU 23 + 25, and FACS AU 18, respectively)

Notes

1. For more thorough descriptions of non-manual morphology in ASL, please see Baker & Cokely (1980), Emmorey & Lane (2000), and Emmorey (2001).

2. Our thanks go to the children, teachers and parents of the California School for the Deaf at Fremont for their help with these studies.

3. FACS is a micro analytic system that distinguishes the movements of the more than 40 individual muscles of the face thus providing an objective means to code facial behaviors. For a list of pertinent Action Units (AUs), see Appendix B.

Are young deaf children bilingual?

Beppie van den Bogaerde and Anne E. Baker

1. Introduction

A deaf child growing up in a deaf signing family will learn the sign language offered in the language input just as a hearing child in a hearing family learns the spoken language offered in the input. It is also the case that that deaf child will be exposed to and learn, to some extent, the spoken language of the hearing community around her, albeit with considerably more difficulty as a result of the hearing impairment. One might expect in families where all the members are deaf that exposure to the spoken language first occurs in contact with hearing people outside the family at a later age. However, earlier research on other sign languages has shown that deaf parents use a spoken language as well as a sign language, with their children from the beginning (for example Mallory, Zingle & Schein 1993 for American Sign Language and English). There is, therefore, at least in terms of the input offered, the possibility for deaf children to learn two languages in the family from an early age. But does this language learning occur? The aim of this paper is firstly to describe in linguistic detail the type of bilingual input offered by deaf parents to their young deaf children and then to analyse the production of these children in terms of their acquisition of the sign language and the spoken language offered.

1.1 Bilingualism in adult deaf signers

There are many definitions of bilingualism. The broadest definition refers to the use of more than one language on a daily basis (Appel & Muysken 1987) without any specification of the level of language skill that needs to be reached in any of the languages used. According to this definition most pre-lingually deaf[1] adults must be considered bilingual (Grosjean 1992). Deaf adults as a group have been shown to be very heterogeneous in regard to the linguistic level they reach in both their sign and spoken languages (Lucas & Valli 1992;

Mayberry 1993). This variability in language level achieved is related to a number of different factors. The most important ones are degree of deafness, age of onset of deafness, language input, and schooling.

The use of residual hearing can greatly influence the ultimate success in acquiring a spoken language. Any hearing loss has an effect on the acquisition of a spoken language but a severe or profound hearing loss has the greatest effect (Mogford 1993). Any loss above 80 dB means that the spoken language is acquired very slowly and is unlikely to reach the native adult level of a hearing person. In the presence of severe or profound deafness, no spoken language can be aurally processed; only visual information is available. This access is incomplete so that the acquisition process is certainly not as for a first language. If a sign language has been acquired as a first language, the acquisition of the spoken language will have been guided by knowledge of the first language (Morford & Mayberry 2000). The learning of the spoken language is therefore more comparable with the learning of a second language. The process is not totally comparable, however, since the deaf child has limited access to the spoken input. If a child becomes deaf around the age of three, then the child has already learned a great deal of the sound system, lexicon and grammar of the spoken language. That child then stands a better chance as an adult of being able to speak and speech-read and also of reaching a higher level in reading and writing (Mogford 1993; Strong & Prinz 2000).

The majority of deaf people are brought up by hearing parents (90–95%) who usually do not know a sign language before becoming a parent and who will learn it as a second language. Some hearing parents still choose to bring up their children with spoken language only. Others make every effort to learn the national sign language but the sign language input that these parents can offer their children is not comparable to that from a native signer. These parents are always second language learners and can be expected to have a smaller vocabulary and more limited grammar (Newport & Meier 1985; Galvan 1989 but see also Lindert in press). Many hearing parents learn a sign system such as Sign Supported Dutch (SSD). Such sign systems take the grammar of the spoken language and combine this with the lexical signs from the national sign language. Additional signs are used in such a system for grammatical forms not occurring in the sign language, for example a sign for plural. There is in fact a continuum between a sign system and a natural sign language whereby in the middle the grammar of the spoken language is only followed to some extent (Lucas & Valli 1992). With such input from their hearing parents many deaf people have learned a sign language later as a second language. This results in them having a varying competence in the national sign language and sometimes also being influenced by the sign system (Singleton 1989; Mayberry & Fisher 1989). The school setting is important for later language development for all children, but in the case of deaf children it is even more crucial. In the case of most deaf people, since they had hearing parents, language acquisition progressed slowly in the absence of native sign input at home and in the absence of full access to the spoken language (Musselman, Lindsay & Wilson 1988). Most deaf adults at this moment in time have not had the benefit of bilingual education, that is, an education where both the national sign language and the spoken language are used in school. Their education was based on an oral approach (spoken language only) or the use of a sign system. Bilingual education programs have recently been introduced or are currently being introduced — in some form or other — in some countries, for example in Denmark, Sweden and the Netherlands, in some federal states in Germany, and in some individual schools in Great Britain and the United States. There are different models for implementing the bilingual approach: the sign language can be used from the beginning as the first language and as the language of instruction, with the spoken language being introduced later and as a second language. Or both languages are used from the beginning with varied use of the sign language as the language of instruction (e.g. Johnson, Liddell & Erting 1989). Research has shown a relation between the level of sign language acquired and the ultimate success rate in the acquisition of the spoken language in various modalities like speaking and speech reading, writing and reading (e.g. Strong & Prinz 2000). It can therefore be expected that these children will emerge with a greater bilingual competence in both the sign language and spoken language than the previous generation.

We see that deaf adults are usually bilingual but their competence in both a sign language and a spoken language can be very variable due to a number of factors. The acquisition literature shows that there are considerable individual differences in the speed and style of language acquisition in hearing children (Bates, Dale & Thal 1995). It would seem likely that this kind of individual variation will also be at least as great in deaf people acquiring either a sign or a spoken language. With this variation in competence in both the sign language and the spoken language in deaf parents, it becomes even more important to describe the input offered to a deaf child when describing the acquisition process in deaf families.

1.2   Language input to deaf children in deaf families

Language input is of course a prerequisite for children to be able to acquire any language (Gallaway & Richards 1994; Snow & Ferguson 1977). Deaf children who are not exposed to a sign language will of course not acquire that language. Deaf native signers as parents can offer their children a full input in terms of grammar and lexicon and the children of such parents acquire the sign language as a first language. However, as described above, competence in the sign language in the deaf parents can vary. The parents' competence in a spoken language also varies. In addition, the spoken language is only available visually to deaf children; Dodd (1987) estimated that at most 30% of the information required to identify and reproduce sound is offered visually. If the input and learning situation are absent or inadequate, then a child cannot become highly proficient in either language or even in one language. It is an interesting question how much input needs to be offered for a child to acquire a language. De Houwer (1999) discusses the language background of hearing children exposed to two spoken languages and finds that not all children become actively bilingual. From this research it appears that amount of input is important but whether a child becomes actively bilingual is also related to the communicative necessity in the extended family. Deaf children in deaf families can vary too in this respect.

When two languages are used in a family, there are many ways in which these can be used. There can be a division between parents: one person, one language; or a division according to context, for example one language for talking about school and the other for home matters; or the languages can be used by the same person in the one and same context. This last situation is an example of language mixing that can be present at many different levels: changing from one language to the other between turns, between sentences in one turn and even within a sentence. Children can become bilingual with bilingual input of all these different types.

It is important to realize that there is a clear difference between language input in which two spoken languages are offered and input which consists of a sign language and a spoken language. The fact that the two languages are in two different modalities: that is, visual/manual on the one hand and aural/oral on the other, makes it possible to produce signs and words simultaneously. In spoken languages even where elements from different languages are produced within an utterance, the elements are sequential. In describing the input to deaf children, it is important to consider the languages used in the utterances and to analyse carefully how they are used.

Considering the way languages can be mixed in the input, it is also relevant to consider whether children are able to distinguish between the two languages. In the language production of bilingual children acquiring two spoken languages, there is evidence that children make a distinction between the two languages from early on in their lexicon at the one-word stage (e.g. Quay 1995) and that this continues in the acquisition of syntax (Genesee, Nicoladis & Paradis 1995; Meisel 1989). Since sign languages and spoken languages are in different modalities, it can be expected that children can also easily make a distinction between them. Petitto, Katerelos, Levy, Gauna, Tétreault and Ferraro (2001a) have studied bilingual hearing children learning Langue des Signes Québécoise and French and find parallel milestones in acquisition of these two languages. However, since there is a continuum between a sign language and a spoken language, analysis of simultaneously signed and spoken lexical elements is not in fact as straightforward as it seems. As stated above, it is important to carefully analyse the different variants on the continuum.

1.3 The aim of this study

Little attention has been paid to describing in detail the language input to young deaf children from their deaf parents. As discussed above, this input can vary considerably in terms of the structures offered in one language or the other (Singleton 1989), and how mixed the bilingual input can be. We then need to know what deaf children learn from this input.

In this chapter we will focus on the status of bilingualism in three prelingually deaf children in the Netherlands. The children are studied in the context of interaction with their deaf mothers. The input from the deaf mothers is described and related to the children's output in sign and speech. Both the quantity and the quality of the input are relevant in the two languages. The quantity in the input must be enough for acquisition to occur.

The situation of interaction with the mother is clearly favourable for the production of sign language, especially when the children begin to become aware that their mother is deaf and has only visual access to spoken language. In bilingual families children are sensitive to parental language choice from very early on (Grosjean 1982) but it takes some extra time to become aware of deafness and the special factors influencing sign language interaction. We must therefore reserve judgement on an absolute evaluation of these deaf children's abilities in Dutch since it is possible that they use more Dutch and Dutch of a more complex nature with monolingual Dutch conversation partners. Despite this restriction we are interested to see what the children do with the two languages in this situation as a possible indication of their emerging bilingualism.

2.   Research methodology

2.1 Subjects

The subjects of this study are three deaf children, Carla, and Laura and Mark, who are twins, and their mothers. Laura and Mark were filmed from age 0;11 up to age 8;0, and Carla from age 1;6 up to age 8;0 in a longitudinal study. For this study we will present data on 10 minutes of interaction when the children were aged 1;0, 1;6, 2;0, 2;6 and 3;0. Below follows a description of the children and their mothers.

Carla was diagnosed deaf at the age of 0;9 and at 1;1 showed no reaction in hearing tests. Carla's mother usually wears a hearing aid, with the help of which she can pick up some sounds; her degree of hearing loss is unknown. It is also unknown whether her hearing impairment was present from birth, although she suffered from no illness known to cause deafness in her youth. She is born deaf of hearing parents, with no known deaf relatives, and has used Dutch, SSD[2] and Sign Language of the Netherlands (SLN) since the age of 3;0 when she came into contact with other deaf children at the school for the deaf. The mother works at home, and at the time of the study was not very active in the deaf community since in the town where they live there is no club for the deaf. Carla's father is deaf (cause unknown) of hearing parents and he works outside the home. Carla has one deaf brother (hearing loss unknown), who is nearly two years older than Carla. The language used in the family is predominantly SLN and SSD; Carla has some contact with monolingual Dutch speakers in her extended family.

Laura was probably born deaf, and at 0;11 was diagnosed as having ≥80 dB hearing loss in her better ear. Over the years however it appeared that she showed only little reaction to the standard hearing tests, so her loss of hearing may be greater. Laura was 11 months old when she started participating in this study, and in the prelingual stage.

Mark was born with a hearing loss of ≥90 dB in his better ear. He also joined the study at age 0;11. Mark is Laura's twin brother.

Their mother has a hearing loss of ≥70 dB in the better ear, and usually wears a hearing aid, which enables her to pick up some sounds, for instance a passing motorcycle. However, she cannot hear spoken language. She was born deaf, and she has hearing parents and one deaf sister. She has used Dutch, SSD and SLN for most of her life. Before the children were born, she worked as a psychological assistant at the Christian Institute for the Deaf Effatha in Voorburg. She considers herself to be a member of the deaf community and has many contacts with other deaf people. The twins' hearing father has deaf parents[3] and is a native signer. He is an active member of the deaf community, and he has been working with deaf and hearing parents of deaf children, but he also develops sign language courses and is an interpreter. The twins have a hearing brother Jonas who is 14 months older. Jonas was still acquiring both SLN and Dutch during the research period (see Van den Bogaerde 2000 for details of his language acquisition).

The language situation of the twins at home is predominantly SLN, although both Sign Supported Dutch and Dutch are used in the family.

The three children Carla, Laura and Mark started going to pre-school at the Christian Institute for the Deaf Effatha in Voorburg when they were approximately two and a half years old. At the time the teachers in this school were using Sign Supported Dutch with the children (see Knoors 1992, 1994). The children were in a class of 5 to 7 children once or twice a week.

The three deaf children do not form a homogeneous group, even though the twins Laura and Mark of course share the same mother. Carla's parents were not very involved with the deaf community at the time of the filming, and this may have had its influence on the way they interact with their children.

2.2 Recording and transcription procedures

The mothers and children were filmed at home in a free play situation, with toys and books of their own choice. Each mother was filmed individually with one child by a hearing researcher who is fluent in SLN and Dutch. The researcher avoided interaction with the mother and child during the recording but it is possible that the presence of the hearing researcher could stimulate the use of spoken Dutch. The session of Mark and his mother at age 3;0 lasted approximately six minutes. All other sessions lasted about 30 minutes. Of all sessions except Mark's at age 3;0, 10 minutes of interaction were transcribed. Each transcript starts 5 minutes after the start of that particular session. Whenever the mother or the child is out of range of the camera, transcription is continued for another 10 seconds; transcription is then stopped until that person reappears on the screen.

All linguistic utterances of mother and child were transcribed in terms of glosses for signs and orthographic forms of words (there was no phonetic transcription). *Linguistic utterances* are those involving the use of a sign or word as a recognizable form. Utterances that were unintelligible or incomprehensible were excluded. Utterances that consisted only of a set phrase such as *yes* or *dunno* were not analysed. Neither were utterances that consisted only of a deictic gesture. This decision was taken since, although it is possible for a gesture to have the linguistic meaning of a pronoun in SLN, it is impossible to distinguish it from the non-linguistic pointing gesture when it occurs on its own. Contextual information (e.g. mother turns page) was noted as well as eye gaze direction. The transcription was carried out by the first author. Percentage of agreement with a second transcriber was higher than 79% for all signs and words (for details see Van den Bogaerde 2000).

2.3 Analysis

For this paper we will consider several aspects of the language production of the children in order to establish their level of bilingualism in the interaction with their mothers. It is essential to also describe the input to the children since without enough input in both the spoken and sign language no competence can be acquired by the children. Firstly we will consider the languages present in the input and what is produced by the children: are they offered and do they produce SLN, spoken Dutch or a mixed system? The use of phonation in the articulation of words is an interesting point here. Secondly we will look at the accessibility of the languages offered to the children since without visual access to SLN or spoken Dutch, the children cannot acquire either. We will then discuss lexical and structural aspects of the language production of the children in both languages, again in relation to the input they are offered. The techniques used for the analysis will be described briefly in each section.[4]

3. Language choice

It is possible to use a sign language and a spoken language in distinct contexts and to code-switch within one context, but in contrast to two spoken languages a sign language and a spoken language can be produced simultaneously in time. This is possible since they are produced in different modalities: visual-gestural for sign language, and aural-oral for spoken language. SLN is a sign language in which mouthed words, that is words articulated without phonation, often occur as an integral part of the sign language (see Boyes-Braem & Sutton-Spence 2001 on mouthing in several sign languages). They can have different functions, for example disambiguating or specifying a sign (Schermer 1990). In our opinion the use of mouthed words should therefore not be viewed as use of the spoken language alongside SLN. There is, however, a continuum between SLN and SSD, a relexified form of spoken Dutch. On this continuum phonation is often used as well as elements of Dutch grammar. It is impossible to draw a clear line on this continuum on the basis of the form, that is, use of Dutch grammar or phonation. We have chosen here to work on the basis of the semantics. The language in which the proposition is fully expressed determines whether the utterance is considered as SLN or Dutch/SSD.

1. Sign language of the Netherlands (SLN): Included here are all utterances in which the full proposition is expressed in signs. These utterances can be accompanied by mouthed words or words articulated with phonation that have the same semantic content but the words used must not express the full proposition for them to be included in this category.[5] An example is given in (1).

All examples are presented with a line *signed* in which the manual signs are written in capitals as glosses in English. The gloss indicated by INDEX represents a deictic gesture; the person, object or place pointed at is indicated in subscript. These indices are commonly viewed as pronouns. The line *spoken* indicates in italic lower case the Dutch words articulated with or without phonation. This line is followed by an English gloss of the *spoken* line. The whole utterance is then translated into an idiomatic English utterance.

(1) *signed:*   BOOK   FETCH $INDEX_{you}$
      spoken: *boek*   *pakken*
      English gloss: book   fetch
      translation: 'you fetch the book'

In this example 'book' and 'fetch' are both expressed in signs and words; '$INDEX_{you}$' is not expressed in words. The full proposition is therefore in signs and the utterance is categorised as an SLN utterance.

2. Dutch/SSD (NL): All utterances in which the full proposition is expressed in words, with or without phonation, (see example (2)) are considered to be NL.

(2) *spoken:*   *wat wil je drinken?*
      English gloss: what want you drink?
      translation: 'what do you want to drink?'

All utterances in which the full proposition is expressed in words with some accompanying signs are also classified as NL (example (3)).

(3) *signed:*   WHERE
    spoken: zoek   waar
    English gloss: search where
    Translation: 'where are you going to search?'

Some utterances were not analysable with regard to language choice since they expressed the same propositional content in both signs and words. No decision could therefore be taken as to whether they were SLN or Dutch/SSD. In most cases these were one sign/word utterances. For the analysis of language choice these utterances were placed in a separate category 'fully signed and fully spoken' and were excluded from further analysis.

Utterances in which the signs and words 'together' expressed the full proposition were categorised separately as a mixed system, which we call 'supplementary system' (ss).

3. Supplementary system (ss): Signs and words are produced simultaneously but have different semantic content and together form the proposition. See for an example (4).

(4) *signed:*   INDEX$_{shed}$ BICYCLE
    spoken: rood
    English gloss: red
    Translation: 'there is the red bicycle'

A separate sign ROOD 'red' does exist but is not used here. The spoken word *rood* 'red' adds to the meaning of the signed part of the utterance forming one proposition. Such an utterance cannot be considered SLN or NL and is therefore placed in this separate category.

Results

In Figure 1 we see the language choice of the mothers (a–c) and of the children (d–f) at the five age points. The proportions of SLN, NL and ss utterances were calculated as percentages of all linguistic utterances. Those utterances categorized as 'fully signed and fully spoken' are excluded. In the mothers we can see that this category represents a considerable amount in some cases; in the children there are very few but Carla has the most. The mothers offer mostly SLN with very few NL utterances. The mixed system (ss) is used slightly more than

NL. The children reflect the predominance of SLN in their language use. Only Carla clearly uses any NL utterances at all, in addition to a few mixed system utterances.

It is interesting to see that in their SLN utterances the mothers use many spoken words, whereas the children use hardly any. As mentioned above, the use of phonation is often considered an indication that on the continuum between a sign language and the sign supported system, a variant closer to the spoken language is being used (Boyes-Braem & Sutton Spence 2001; Lucas & Valli 1992). This is not always reliable however, particularly with children (Fortgens in preparation; Buré 2000). Also, there are researchers who do not agree with this view (Ebbinghaus & Hessmann 1996).

The mother of Carla uses her voice in both SLN utterances and NL utterances; the mother of Mark and Laura scarcely uses any phonation at all. Carla uses her voice almost always until the age of 2;6 and on average more so than Mark or Laura. She also produces the highest proportion of NL utterances.

In summary: all the children produce mainly SLN utterances. They all show a little evidence of producing some spoken words but only Carla regularly uses NL utterances or ss utterances with her mother. In terms of language choice Carla is the furthest in becoming bilingual. This is also apparent from her use of phonation. Apparently the spoken input is enough for the children to make a start with acquisition. It must be emphasised of course, as we mentioned above, that the context of interacting with their mother is conducive for the children to producing SLN rather than NL and cannot be seen as an absolute measure of the children's possibilities in Dutch.

4. Accessibility of the input and the output

Deaf children need to give visual attention to all language input in order to be able to access the linguistic information. This is true both for sign language and for spoken language. It is thus important to establish whether or not the children actually see the signs and words addressed to them. If they do not see a sign or word, actual input has not taken place.

In order to establish the accessibility of the linguistic input and output, we have coded all signs and words in all utterances produced by the mothers and the children with a plus (+) if they are visible to the conversational partner, and with a minus (−) if they are not.[6]

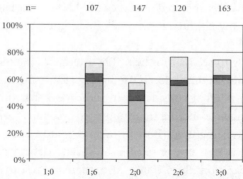

Figure 1a. Language choice of mother of Carla. No data avialable before age 1;6.

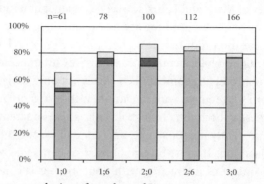

Figure 1b. Language choice of mother of Laura.

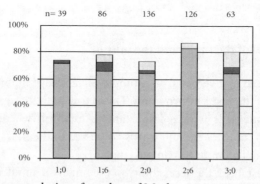

Figure 1c. Language choice of mother of Mark.

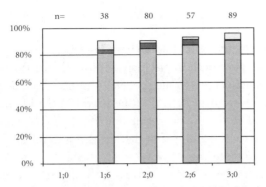

Figure 1d. Language choice of Carla. No data avialable before age 1;6.

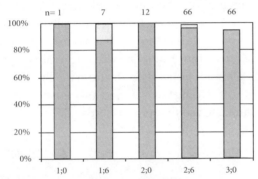

Figure 1e. Language choice of Laura.

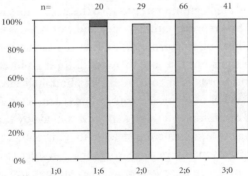

Figure 1f. Language choice of Mark. No analysable utterances produced at 1;0

Note: The category 'fully signed and fully spoken' where signs and words both make the full proposition is excluded. This is why at certain ages 100% is not reached.

Results

As can be seen from Figure 2 the children have 75–90% access to the sign input. Access to the spoken parts of the input increases with time up to 80%. Interestingly Carla has the least access to the spoken or mouthed words produced by her mother although we have seen that she produces the largest number of Dutch utterances. The figures do mean that the bilingual input from the mothers is available to the children but that the access to the Dutch words has increased from being quite low at age 1;6 to reasonably high at age 3;0.

The sign input has been easily accessible from the first recording and the children are clearly acquiring SLN. We saw above that Dutch was subordinate to SLN in terms of amount of input offered. In terms of accessibility we see again that Dutch is clearly subordinate to SLN, especially in the first years, but that it is available. It is probable that the Dutch input from the mothers is more accessible than the Dutch from monolingual Dutch speakers since hearing adults do not usually allow for visual attention from the children (e.g. Harris & Mohay 1997). Despite there being less NL input and its being less accessible the children are all beginning to acquire spoken words.

5. Lexical issues

We already know that the NL utterances produced by the children are very few but nevertheless they are beginning to produce them. In Table 1 we see when they produced their first representational signs and words. As is to be expected on account of their hearing impairment, the first representational words are produced later than signs but they are there in all three children by 1;6. The form of the signs and words is of course not yet phonologically correct. The children make the usual phonological errors in signs such as wrong movement or wrong location. For example the sign AMERICA is made by Mark at age 2;6 with a whole twisting body movement instead of moving both arms in front of the body in a circular movement. In their words they produce forms with final consonant deletion such as /pa/ for *bal*, which is a common process in hearing children but which persists in deaf children (Beers & Baker 1997).

Based on 10 minutes of interaction it is impossible to indicate the total sign or word vocabulary of the children. However we can indicate the relative number of different sign and word types they produced across all recordings. Types in words were defined using the common criteria, that is compounds and

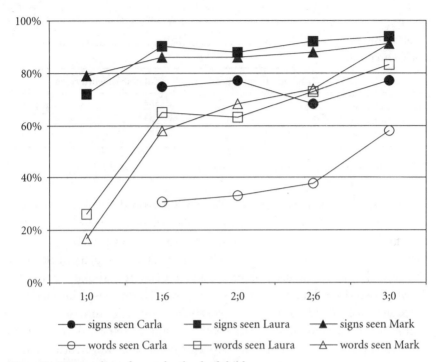

Figure 2. Signs and words seen by the deaf children.

Table 1. Age of the deaf children for first representational signs and words

	First representational sign at age	First representational word at age
Carla	<1;6*	<1;6*
Laura	0;10	1;6
Mark	0;10	1;6

*   No data available from before 1;6

fixed expressions were counted as one word; inflected and non-inflected forms count as one type. Types in signs were defined in a similar way — signs including bound morphemes were counted as the same type, for example verb inflections and classifiers. The sign and word counts were done in all linguistic utterances. It is possible to compare the number of sign and word types here since the manner of analysis reduced the differences in morphology between the languages.

In Table 2 we see the numbers of word and sign types in the input (mothers). It is interesting to note that the mothers offer a considerable variety of words to the children which is comparable to their variety in signs.

Table 2. Total number of sign and word types in the input of the deaf mothers, pooled over time

	Total no of sign types	Total no of word types
Mother of Carla*	206	205
Mother of Laura	239	204
Mother of Mark	201	167

* This count is based on 4 recordings, the others on 5

In Figure 3 we show the cumulative vocabulary of the signs and words of the children. The children show considerable variation in their signs and are reasonably comparable with one another. As expected they produce more signs than words and here we see that Carla has the greater vocabulary of the three. The growth in sign vocabulary occurs for all three children around age two. The growth in word vocabulary progresses very slowly. The increase which has been noted in hearing children around the vocabulary size of 50 words and with the beginning of combinations (Clark 1993) cannot be expected yet in these children and it is a question whether it occurs in the same way in deaf children learning a spoken language.

Lexical equivalence, that, is the use of words from two languages with the same meaning such as *tafel* and 'table' is often considered to be evidence for the separation of languages in the bilingual child (e.g. Petitto et al. 2001a; Quay 1995). Lexical equivalence clearly needs to be present in the input to facilitate this process. This was analysed for both the input and output in this study. Simultaneous combinations are not examples for lexical equivalence on their own but only when they occur alongside a separate single sign or word.[7] Since a large proportion of the vocabulary consisted of simultaneous combinations and relatively little use of separate single signs or words, there were few instances of lexical equivalents, neither in the input nor in the output. On the basis of this evidence we must conclude that the children are given little opportunity to separate the languages on the basis of the lexicon offered in this context. It needs still to be investigated whether a simultaneous combination in the input also leads to the acquisition of the spoken word on its own in these children or only to the acquisition of the simultaneous combination.

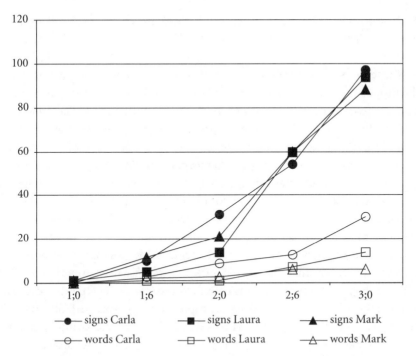

Figure 3. Cumulative vocabulary in sign and word types of the deaf children.

6. Structural aspects

The structure of the bilingual output gives an indication of how far the child is in the acquisition of each language. We will look at the following structural aspects for this analysis:

1. Mean Length of Utterance (MLU) of the different languages in input and output (in signs and words)
2. The verb system, in particular the numbers of utterances containing a verb, and the characteristics of the verb phrase such as arguments, verb position and inflection.

In those structural aspects in which the languages differ it is also possible to see to what extent the children are making a distinction between the two languages.

6.1 Mean Length of Utterance

We first looked at MLU as a global measure of the complexity of the children's language production. MLU can never exactly be compared across languages because they have different structures. If there are large differences in MLU, however, this does give an indication of a different level of development. We established the MLU of the SLN utterances (see Section 3 for the definition of SLN utterance), but in the calculation also included those utterances in which the proposition was expressed fully in both words and signs. As already mentioned, these utterances were mainly one sign/word utterances. The decision to include these utterances was taken in order not to artificially increase the MLU count by excluding a large number of one sign utterances. The MLU of the SLN utterances was counted in signs, not in morphemes. This choice was made since it is not clear in sign linguistic research what elements should be counted as separate morphemes (it is not clear, for instance, what the morphological status of classifiers might be). In the first two years of language acquisition in a sign language there is also very little evidence of morphology. The choice for a MLU count based on signs is therefore sufficient. Using our earlier examples in Section 3 we can see that the MLU of the SLN utterance in example (1) is 3. The MLU of the Dutch utterances was counted in words in the NL utterances and again in those utterances in which the proposition was expressed fully in words and signs. In example (3) the MLU is 2. The MLU of the ss utterances was counted separately and where a sign and word produced in the same utterance had the same meaning, they were only counted once. Thus the MLU of example (5) from one of the mothers is 6 – TAKE, WATER/*water*, IN_{book}/*erin, en, dan* and *alle* are each counted as one lexical item.

(5)   *signed:*   TAKE   WATER IN_{book}
      spoken: *en dan*   *alle water erin*
      English gloss: and then   all water   in there
      Translation: 'and then he puts all the water in there'

Results

We show the MLU of the mothers' input in Table 3 and of the children's output in Table 4. It must be remembered that the numbers of utterances in the NL and ss categories are relatively small (see Figure 1) and they must therefore be treated with caution.

In the input the MLU (signs) produced in SLN increased with time in each mother and was maximally 3.07. The MLU of the NL utterances also increased with time. The mothers were clearly using combinations of words frequently but these combinations were often not more than two words long. The MLU of the ss utterances was higher than the MLU for either the SLN or the NL

Table 3. MLU of SLN, NL and ss utterances in the input of the deaf mothers

	1;0	1;6	2;0	2;6	3;0
MLU SLN					
Mother of Carla	*	1.27	1.52	2.08	2.13
Mother of Laura	1.48	1.82	1.99	3.00	2.62
Mother of Mark	1.51	1.61	2.03	2.39	3.07
MLU NL					
Mother of Carla	*	1.19	1.38	1.54	1.56
Mother of Laura	1.25	1.47	1.53	1.82	1.87
Mother of Mark	1.38	1.53	1.35	1.49	1.66
MLU ss					
Mother of Carla	*	3.25	3.75	3.95	3.95
Mother of Laura	3.00	4.25	3.72	4.67	3.80
Mother of Mark	**	3.20	3.90	4.60	3.14

* No information before age 1;6 for Carla and her mother
** No ss utterances produced in this session

utterances. This can be partly explained by the fact that by definition ss utterances always must consist of at least 1 sign and 1 word with different meanings. The MLU count must be at least 2. Nevertheless it appears that the ss utterances are more complex than either the SLN or the NL utterances. This is an interesting fact and the more exact nature of the structure of these ss utterances will be explored in later analyses (see e.g. Van den Bogaerde & Baker in preparation).

The children (see Table 4) show an increase in MLU in their SLN utterances and they were making relatively frequent combinations of signs from the age of 2;6 onwards. Their Dutch utterances stay predominantly at the level of one word however. Again the MLU of the ss utterances is far greater; the explanation for this will be explored in another paper (see above).

6.2 The verb system

On the basis of the MLU we can already see that it is going to be difficult to compare properties of the verb systems of SLN and Dutch in the children since their Dutch utterances consisted predominantly of one word. We will look briefly at the input and the output — in the first instance with respect to the number of utterances that contained a verb. These are presented in terms of the number of utterances containing a SLN verb with or without a NL verb and those utterance containing a NL verb with or without a SLN verb. In Table 5 we

Table 4. MLU of SLN, NL and ss utterances in the output of the deaf children

	1;0	1;6	2;0	2;6	3;0
MLU SLN					
Carla	*	1.15	1.1	1.57	1.82
Laura	1.0	1.0	1.42	2.02	1.83
Mark	**	1.05	1.54	2.32	2.27
MLU NL					
Carla	*	1.0	1.0	1.0	1.0
Laura	**	**	**	1.0	1.4
Mark	**	1.0	1.0	1.0	**
MLU ss					
Carla	*	2.33	2.0	3.0	2.5
Laura	**	2.0	**	2.0	4.0
Mark	**	**	**	**	**

* No information before age 1;6 for Carla and her mother
** No ss utterances produced in this session

can see that the utterances from the mothers did not contain large numbers of verbs in either language (see for a comparison of noun-verb ratios Baker & Van den Bogaerde 2001). In general the percentages increase over time. The mothers produce more SLN verbs than NL verbs. Although the majority of signed utterances in the input had no verb, they were grammatical. A certain number of the NL utterances were ungrammatical due to the omission of the verb, for example as a result of omitting a copula. In those cases where the spoken input contained a verb, this was almost always in combination with a signed verb. The influence of SLN here is probable.

Table 5. Presence of signed and spoken verbs in the input of the deaf mothers in percentages; the numbers are given in brackets

	1;0	1;6	2;0	2;6	3;0
SLN verbs					
Mother of Carla	–	5 (5)	13 (15)	23 (27)	36 (46)
Mother of Laura	40 (23)	32 (22)	48 (42)	23 (25)	57 (91)
Mother of Mark	34 (13)	37 (30)	37 (50)	32 (39)	41 (26)
NL verbs					
Mother of Carla	–	7 (6)	15 (14)	23 (24)	28 (39)
Mother of Laura	47 (20)	34 (16)	43 (25)	17 (15)	42 (47)
Mother of Mark	33 (7)	30 (15)	31 (29)	21 (12)	31 (15)

In Table 6 we see that the children also show a general increase in the number of utterances with a SLN verb. Carla produces verbs from the age of 2;0 and the percentage increases from 4%, to 17% at the age of 3;0. She produces no NL verbs. Laura starts producing verbs from the age of 1;6; the percentages range from 20% to 55%. She produces only 2 NL verbs in total. Mark also produces SLN verbs from the age of 1;6 increasing from 17%, to 33%. He does not produce any NL verbs. The first SLN verbs produced by the children were clearly related to their activities: CRY, TAKE, PULL-APART, FLY. The two NL verbs were *praten* 'speak' and a particle verb *uit(doen)* '(take) off'; the phonology was of course not the adult form. Very few of their SLN utterances missing a verb were ungrammatical, whereas the NL utterances were. The two languages are clearly being produced at a different level with respect to syntactic complexity. The children have yet to show any evidence in this context of learning the verb system of Dutch.

Table 6. Presence of signed and spoken verbs in the output of the deaf children in percentages; the numbers are given in brackets

	1;0	1;6	2;0	2;6	3;0
SLN verbs					
Carla	*	0	4 (2)	9 (4)	17 (13)
Laura	0	55 (2)	44 (4)	20 (11)	52 (28)
Mark	0	17 (2)	14 (3)	25 (14)	33 (13)
NL verbs					
Carla	*	0	0	0	0
Laura	0	0	0	25 (1)	17 (1)
Mark	0	0	0	0	0

* No information available before 1;6

We cannot compare the structures of the two languages further in the output of the children since the amount of spoken output is so small, but it is interesting to note the following. The mothers showed relatively similar amounts of argument drop (subjects and objects) in their input compared to other studies on adult-adult signing (Bos 1993). In the spoken input argument drop was substantial and led to ungrammatical utterances, probably under the influence of the accompanying signs. The children also dropped arguments in their sign utterances, thus showing slightly less object drop than in the input. Their spoken output was too limited to analyse. The verb position in the input signing was as in adult-adult signing, that is, mostly final as in example (6).

(6)   (Mark's mother at age 3;0)
  signed: PAST SATURDAY CLOWN SCHOOL SEE
  spoken: zaterdag   clown   school   zien
  English gloss: Saturday   clown   school   see
  Translation: 'last Saturday we saw the clown at school'

In the spoken input 13% of the verbs were in an ungrammatical position, again probably under the influence of SLN. The signed output reflected the adult rules. Very few signed verbs were inflected in the input. Instead they appeared in the citation form and this is what the children also produced. The spoken input contained more uninflected verbs than finite forms, possibly under the influence of the accompanying SLN. In example (6) the Dutch verb *zien* should be inflected, have tense and be placed in second position. A paraphrase of the Dutch in example (6) would be *afgelopen zaterdag zagen wij de clown op school* ('last Saturday saw we the clown at school').

7.   Conclusions

We have shown here that the deaf children are receiving bilingual input from their deaf mothers — from one person (their mother) in one and the same situation. There is clearly input in SLN and this is dominant. The number of NL utterances as defined in this study is relatively small in the input and the utterances are also quite simple. The majority are grammatical but some utterances are ungrammatical. The question addressed at the beginning of this paper was whether the amount of input in the two languages is enough to lead to acquisition. Even though the context of the child in interaction with the mother is biased towards their production of SLN, there is evidence that the children are learning both languages. They are learning SLN and have made a start on syntax by the age of three years. The children's Dutch is clearly still very limited at the age of three years. They have acquired some vocabulary, but they are using spoken words above all in combination with signing. Their vocabulary is growing but has not shown any real spurt, though one might expect to see this when the first combinations appear. However there is not yet any real evidence of Dutch syntax; the children are still at the one-word stage. The phonology of the single words shows evidence of phonological processes such as final consonant deletion, which are also associated with the one-word stage.

For bilingual children, De Houwer (1999) stressed *amount* as important but also *communicative necessity*, in particular in the extended family or in contacts outside the family. The children in this study began to attend the pre-school from age two and a half where they were confronted with SSD from a hearing teacher as opposed to SLN. There was therefore some communicative necessity to use more Dutch words, but no clear emphasis on Dutch syntax. This may have been of influence in their slower development in Dutch alongside, of course, the fact that the Dutch input is only visually accessible.

As discussed in the first section of this chapter, there are various criteria for deciding if a person is bilingual or not. Most agree that the level of competence in a language is not a clear criterion, but rather daily use. The children clearly use both languages on a daily basis. However, if the presence of syntax were to be taken as a measure for the use of a language, then we would have to conclude that the children are not yet bilingual. But they are *on their way* towards becoming bilingual. From the limited Dutch input they are receiving in this situation, it would seem to be a difficult task for the child. Nevertheless it must be remembered that a considerable number of spoken components are being used in the SLN utterances, which may also be triggering the use of spoken words. Later observations that we made of the children outside this study confirm that they do become bilingual, although as we described above, their mother is not the only source of input for Dutch.[8]

We saw in the analysis of the language choice that both the mothers and children produced utterances which could neither be classified as Dutch/SSD or as SLN since the proposition was made up of both signs and words. This Supplementary System is possibly a third system in the sense indicated by Romaine (1995). She describes this as emerging in situations of intense language contact, which is the case here.

> In situations of intense language contact it is possible for a third language system to emerge, which shows properties not found in either of the input language. Thus, through the merger or convergence of two systems, a new one can be created. (Romaine 1995:4)

Both SLN and Dutch are used as systems in their own right but they can influence each other (Lucas & Valli 1992; Schermer 1990; Van den Bogaerde 2000). The utterances in this third system need to be analysed further to discover what properties they have (Van den Bogaerde & Baker in preparation).

In future work the data from the children in this study needs to be further analysed past the age of three years in order to chart their bilingual development. It is known from educational studies that bilingual development is crucial for the general development of deaf children in many aspects other than language. It is important to see that this development begins in the very earliest stages in these deaf families.

Notes

1. A child is considered 'deaf' when she or he has a hearing loss of more than 80 decibels in the better ear. This characterization follows the guidelines of the Dutch national report on Sign Language of the Netherlands *Meer dan een gebaar* (Baker et al. 1997:44). The term *pre-lingual* is used variably in the acquisition literature. Genesee (1988) considers primary language acquisition to take place during the first 5 years of life (1988:62). So a child who becomes deaf before the age of 5 would be considered to be pre-lingually deaf, because the first language acquisition period has not been completed yet. Others consider 3 years of age to be the threshold (see e.g. Mogford 1993).

2. Sign Supported Dutch is different from SLN in that SSD follows the grammar of spoken Dutch while using the lexicon of SLN. SLN has its own grammar. One clear difference is the order of constituents in main declarative clauses: SSD has the verb in second position following Dutch; SLN has the verb in final position.

3. The term used is CODA (Child of Deaf Adult).

4. For further details we refer the reader to the relevant sections of Van den Bogaerde (2000) although some aspects of analysis have been changed in this analysis.

5. Petitto et al. (2001a) in their study of bilingual hearing children learning a sign and a spoken language put utterances that consist of signs and words that are articulated with phonation in a separate 'mixed' category. This would seem to be related to the fact that they are studying hearing children for whom the phonation is distinctive. For deaf children this distinction is not relevant. Furthermore SLN signing adults frequently use both mouthed words and words articulated with phonation in their SLN production. Possibly this situation is different in Langue des Signes Québécoise.

6. Whether or not a sign or word is seen is dependent on the attention gaining strategies of the mothers and the attention giving behaviour of the children but this will not be described further here (see Van den Bogaerde 2000 for a detailed description).

7. See Van den Bogaerde 2000 for examples and detailed description.

8. The children were followed up to the age of 8 years at regular intervals, but this data has yet to be fully analysed.

Language emergence in a language-ready brain
Acquisition[*]

Judy Kegl

1. Introduction

1.1 First-language Acquisition

Numerous studies have addressed the independence of the first-language acquisition process from the tangible linguistic input to that process. Language is an extremely resilient human capacity that expresses itself fully even under adverse conditions such as limited cognitive capacities, non-native language models, or lack of access to auditory and/or visual modalities. However, there is a lower bound on what constitutes sufficient input to the first-language acquisition process and there are humans with language-ready brains who nonetheless can fail to acquire language.

This paper assumes a nativist position and argues that all human children are born with language-ready brains that are capable of creating language and recognizing language-relevant evidence in the environment. In the absence of language-relevant evidence, the language-ready brain fails to engage in the first-language acquisition process. However, this paper shows that language-relevant evidence need not be language. Chomsky (1986b) distinguished between two uses of the word *language* that will prove useful here. *I-Language* can be thought of as language competence, our innately specified internal language expectations that guide the language emergence process on a human-by-human basis. *E-Language* is the product of language use available in the environment external to the child. Chomsky has characterized it as the set of sentences produced by a population speaking a language. It is the evidence of the target language that acquirers strive to match.

While typically E-Language is the input to a child, input can fall far short of a full-fledged language target and still support the first-language acquisition process. In the context of this paper, E-Language takes on a broader meaning. While this meaning still subsumes the set of sentences produced by a population using a language, it also includes a broader set of language-relevant evidence that may fall short of the sentence or even of products of language production at all. E-Language includes any input that the child takes to be language-relevant evidence, even when that evidence is not language itself.

Several components of the language acquisition process are proposed:

1. sensitivity to prosody[1] and sequencing that leads acquirers to attend to language-relevant input;
2. awareness of one's ability to copy certain language-relevant stimuli and a tendency to attempt to copy such stimuli;
3. an innate set of language expectations that drive, direct and supplement the first-language acquisition process; and finally,
4. a drive to match the output of one's first-language acquisition process to already existing target languages available in the environment.

1.1.1   *Learning from native language user models*

The most highly studied cases in this field are those of typical first-language acquisition. Despite the fact that the child is born into a world awash with language, there is evidence that the child, to a certain extent, ignores aspects of that input in the first-language acquisition process. The input itself is inconsistent and noisy. Without some filter that allows the child to identify and attend to relevant language information and to ignore the noise, the input would be unusable. But the child does more than filter the input. The child comes to language acquisition with innate expectations of what language is and, to the extent that the input fails to meet those expectations, the child's brain fills in the missing infrastructure.

One thing the child expects is regularity. Although at first children seem to learn forms as wholes, they quickly begin to look for systematic, rule-governed aspects of the input they receive. Languages, however, tolerate much irregularity and are filled with exceptional and irregular forms. Often, once the language acquisition process has run its course, yielding forms like *goed* for *went* or *bringed* or *brang* for *brought*, the child adjusts the hypothesized grammar to meet the idiosyncrasies of the target language available in the environment, learning the exceptions. Nonetheless, cases of over-regularization show us that the child's engagement with language input is an active, creative, and analytical process that creates grammar anew on the basis of evidence from available input conditioned by the extent to which that input matches language expectations.

Despite the fact that input plays a somewhat tangential role in the acquisition of grammar, it serves as a target with which the child's emergent grammar is matched. Thus, while it is argued that each child creates human grammar anew from innately specified language expectations, the end product strives to match as closely as possible the viable language(s) available in the child's environment. This matching to target language(s) available in the environment serves to obscure the existing evidence for language as a direct product of the human brain. If the external language input to the child were to be perturbed, corrupted, or reduced and language acquisition were unaffected, such evidence would further support the argument that language is a product of the human brain.

1.1.2 *Creolization*

Bickerton (1981, 1984, 1992, among others) has used creolization to make one of the strongest cases for the nativist position. His argument is that non-optimal language input leads to creolization, the emergence of a new language in the context of pidgin input occurring between speakers of the superstrate language of a colonizer and non-mutually intelligible substrate languages spoken among relocated populations brought to work on plantations in those colonies. However, according to Bickerton, the creole is not the product of grammaticization of the superstrate/substrate pidgin. Rather the creole (language) is, as argued for first-language acquisition in general, the product of the human brain. He proposes that in cases where a first-language learner is not exposed to well-formed input (a full language), the learner defaults to an innate bioprogram for language as a grammar source. Reliance upon a bioprogram, as opposed to language diffusion from a widespread, shared source/target of language input, Bickerton argues, accounts for shared characteristics across the world's creoles.

Despite the fact that children may have primary contact with a pidgin as their external language input, the adult speakers of that pidgin have other languages in their repertoires and therefore children are exposed to at least fragments of the substrate languages at home. While Bickerton's bioprogram account precludes the role of substrates in determining the grammar of the creole, the presence of substrate languages in the environment has fueled numerous challenges to his position (Kegl & McWhorter 1997).

The first-language acquisition process is conditioned by which forms of input are taken to constitute the targets of acquisition. Pidgin input, albeit non-optimal, can be seen as a distinct target of the first-language acquisition process when it is the only input available to a child. In such a case, we expect the language expectations of the child to inform the first-language acquisition process, yielding a creole. However, the persistence of pidgins and trade jargons over generations also suggests that if there are full languages available and accessible for acquisition, they will be preferred. In such a case, the pidgin or trade jargon can remain outside the scope of the first-language acquisition process and remain only a bridge between mutually unintelligible languages. This suggests an innate ability on the part of individuals with language-ready brains to distinguish between those forms of E-language that are worthy of emulating and those that are not. This awareness is part of the language expectations of the language-ready brain. It could account for why, although language evidence can be drawn from non-optimal sources, at the end state of language acquisition the child does not attempt to match the output of the first-language acquisition process to non-optimal targets.

Thus, it is reasonable to assume that innate expectations could impact more heavily on the nature of the final product of language acquisition from pidgin input than on the acquisition of an acquirer's repertoire of full languages. Hence, under conditions of non-optimal input, language learners would surpass their models. A contemporary case in which there is no full language available in the language acquirer's environment would provide additional supporting evidence in favor of a nativist position. Such cases exist and have been reported. One is discussed in the next section.

1.1.3   Re-creolization

The original term *re-creolization* comes from Fischer (1978). Recognizing that only 6–10% of the Deaf population in the United States are Deaf children of Deaf parents, with an even smaller number having native ASL-signing Deaf parents, Fisher argued that ASL is unique in that it re-creolizes with each successive generation. Newport (1982) reiterated this point and argued that there are phonological regularities internal to ASL signs that can be re-analyzed as morphological by the re-creolizing child.

Singleton (1987, 1989) studied the case of Simon, a deaf child whose deaf parents were themselves late learners of American Sign Language (ASL). With no other signed language input save that of his parents' non-optimal signing of ASL, Simon was able to surpass the limited signing ability of his parents and demonstrate native-like capacity in ASL. Where his parents exhibited a pidgin-like, partial command of ASL, lacking consistent and productive use of inflectional and derivational morphology, syntactic agreement and other aspects of the complex structure of ASL, Simon exhibited mastery of these aspects of ASL grammar to a much greater degree. The case of Simon clearly demonstrates that young learners surpass their models, and therefore provides important support for the brain's contribution to language. Furthermore, because native ASL signers were not available to him, Simon's case eliminates the confounding situation caused by subsequent matching to the optimal ASL target as the child's grammar emerges.

However, while Simon surpassed his language models, the grammar he acquired was ASL. He did not create an independent signed creole as the result of exposure to non-optimal input. Thus, Simon's data do not support Bickerton's language bioprogram hypothesis in the strictest sense. Despite non-optimal input, evidence of a target language is available.

It can be argued that children of non-native signers are actually *re-creolizing to a language-specific target* (Kegl 1986). In other words, they are not creating a new language. They are reconstructing ASL from the evidence available in the fragments of ASL that they have been exposed to. First-language learners exposed to non-optimal input are able to reconstruct the grammar of ASL from sublexical morphological regularities within signs that have been learned as frozen wholes by their parents, although the internal regularities in these frozen signs are opaque to late learners.

Lexical items in ASL contain sufficient frozen remnants of verb morphology to allow a child acquirer to infer much of ASL morphosyntax. ASL has an extremely productive word formation component and most of the frozen lexicon involves complex forms involving nominalizations of sentential verbs embedded within other sentential verbs. Many of these verbs have associated object classifiers (Shepard-Kegl 1985) and exhibit spatial agreement (Padden 1980) and aspectual modulations (Klima & Bellugi 1979). Since late-learners (non-native signers) learn lexical items as frozen wholes, these forms remain unperturbed and intact.

1.1.4 *Language Emergence de novo*

Language emergence de novo refers to the acquisition of a first language by children in the absence of even fragments of a full language or languages in their input. Emergence de novo is a strong evidence for the poverty of the stimulus argument for innate language capacity. Language emergence de novo is a case of E-Language arising from non-E-Language and, as such, provides strong evidence for I-Language (or the innate expectations of what a language is).

While occurrence of such cases is rare, a case of language emergence de novo in Nicaragua has been being documented since 1986 (Kegl & Iwata 1989; Kegl, Senghas & Coppola 1999; Kegl 2000). Briefly, Nicaraguan Sign Language (Idioma de Señas de Nicaragua: ISN) came into being in the 1980s, after the end of the Nicaraguan Revolution in 1979. In contrast with the situation in the United States, where 6–10 percent of deaf children have deaf parents, there are virtually no deaf children in Nicaragua with deaf parents.[2] As a result, when language isolates came together in the early 1980s, there was no pre-existing signed language to contribute to their input, not even as a source of frozen lexical items. Nonetheless, a makeshift gestural contact communication arose among these students. The youngest of them took advantage of their critical period for language acquisition and used the non-optimal contact gesturing they were exposed to as input. In so doing, they brought into play their own innate expectations of what a language is. Where the input diverged from their expectations, their brains filled in the holes.

To date, we have documented 1433 deaf Nicaraguans. One hundred ninety two were verified as members of the initial cohort of contact gesturers brought together later than the age of 7 in the early 1980s. Approximately 30 were younger than the age of 7 when they entered school in the early 80s. Another 423 are, or were at first contact, language-less. Of these, 100 are currently in language intervention programs and are being followed longitudinally. By looking at the communication of members of these various subgroups of the Nicaraguan deaf population, we can get a sense of the precursors to and the developing forms of the signed language that has emerged over the past two decades.

1.2 The focus of this paper

In terms of input, we know that there can be too little. The gestures used among hearing people and among hearing families with a single deaf member are insufficient to support the first-language acquisition process. While there can never be too much, the input can fall far short of optimal (native language models) and still be sufficient to support successful first-language acquisition. In fact, the emergence of a full signed language in Nicaragua demonstrates that language can arise even when the input to young learners is not itself a language (not even one that is partially mastered).

At least two questions remain. What set of characteristics in the communication to which a child is exposed is sufficient to trigger the first-language acquisition process? To what extent does the input to a child (whether language or non-language input) condition the typological choices of the language that emerges?

This paper uses a morphophonological analysis and notational system presented in Shepard-Kegl (1985) to explore the sublexical structure of both productive and frozen signs in ASL. This analysis reveals sublexical regularities present in frozen ASL signs. Once the rich sublexical structure of ASL, a primary signed language, has been described, parallel grammatical properties in a verb construction in the newly emerged ISN are examined. A similar orchestration of discrete, recurring subunits systematically configured to construct the lexical units in hierarchically organized and constrained sequence patterns is found in both these languages.

Attention then turns to the input to the first-language acquisition process in ASL and ISN. If we look back two generations in each language, the basics of the re-creolization and concurrent natural language acquisition process for ASL can be seen to have remained the same, but the input situation for ISN differs drastically. Only two generations ago, ISN did not exist. We will consider the role of the gestural communication that existed when the first young signers came together in schools and began to acquire a language that did not yet exist.

1.3 Availability of the data

It is impossible in a limited space to present the data relevant to this paper in a form that does justice to both the raw data and its linguistic representation. The raw data are available as QuickTime videos on CD-ROM from the author. Data coded in SignStream®, a multimedia transcription and database format, are downloadable at http://schiller.dartmouth.edu/~signstr/repository.html.

2. Notation

In so far as it is feasible, a morphophonological analysis and notation system from Shepard-Kegl (1985) will be used as a means of presenting these data. This notation system is summarized in the next section.

2.1 The lexical and sublexical structure of ASL signs

Every sign in ASL has minimally four parts: a Movement (M), a Terminator (T), a locative marker (LOC), and an element that is coextensive with the

motion of the verb (THEME). A list of the kinds of morphemes that can fill
these positions in a sign appears in Table 1.

Table 1. Components of the ASL sign

	Physical Realization	Meaning
Movements:		
TO	movement to a location	movement to a goal
FROM	movement from a location	movement from a source
Ø	position at a location	to be at a location
Terminators:		
WARD	orientation toward a location	to be oriented toward a location or goal
IN	locating in a bounded space	to be in something
ON	locating on a surface	to be in contact with something
AT	pure location without orientation or contact	to be at some location
Locative Marker:		
LOC	a location in space, or lack of association with a location (Ø)	the reference point of movement or location
Theme:		
CL:B	flat hand	flat surface, vehicle
CL:G	index finger extended	long thin object, person
CL:S	closed fist	round solid object
CL:10	thumb extended from fist	liquid, watery or viscous
CL:R	index and middle finger crossed	twisted object
noun	concurrent with verb's movement	depends upon noun chosen
nominalization of a sentential verb	articulation reduced, restrained and often repeated	depends upon verb nominalized

A movement morpheme (TO, FROM, or Ø) forms the base of the sign. It is
conjoined with a Terminator that specifies the nature of the relation of the
beginning point of the movement for FROM; the end of a movement for TO in
terms of whether there is contact (ON), enclosure (IN), orientation toward
(WARD) or simple locating (AT). When the value of the Movement is Ø, this

indicates a basic locative verb. These locative base forms are also associated with Terminators indicating whether the locating involves contact, enclosure, orientation, or simple positioning. All of these base forms are associated with an abstract marker of location (LOC). The actual physical realization of location in sign space is determined by an agreement process in the morphology that associates a location value {i,j,k…n} to the LOC morpheme on the verb. This value can be set to Ø, meaning that the sign is not associated with a grammatically specified place (i.e., does not involve verb agreement). This is true of nouns. In fact, the process of nominalization entails embedding a verb form in a locative predicate unspecified for a location value (AT-LOC-Ø).

Inserting manual material into the Movement of the verb fills the theme slot and completes the basic sign. While the Movement of the verb can be articulated by movement from one or more of the major joints of the upper limbs, the configuration of the hand itself is still unspecified. This open channel is the theme slot. Both phonetically and semantically, the theme slot is filled by the entity that moves in a verb of motion or is located in a verb of location. In the basic sign, the theme slot is typically filled by one of a set of classifiers. These classifiers are realized by handshapes that are bound morphemes. They are usually comprised of a single phoneme (handshape) that identifies a set of referents sharing some physical or functional characteristic. Classifiers are represented as CL:x, where x equals the handshape used in the classifier. Some examples include the set of all long thin objects (CL:1^3), the set of all flat surfaces (CL:B), the set of all permeable objects (CL:5), the set of all rimmed objects (CL:C), the set of all round solid objects (CL:S), the set of twisted objects (CL:R), the set of liquid objects (CL:4), etc.

2.2 MOV-LOC Notation

We will use a basic schema to represent the internal composition of lexical items in ASL. The linear arrangement of morphemes is represented by a series of items linked by a dash; the closer conjoining of Movement and Terminator as the base form of the verb will be indicated by a plus sign. The coextensive realization of the theme and the base form of the verb will be represented by a triangle under the verb. This is a relation of dominance without linear precedence. Two distinct schemata reflect the different temporal unfolding in verbs involving sources (the FROM-type) versus goals (the TO-type). Locative verbs pattern like the TO-type class, without lexical movement.

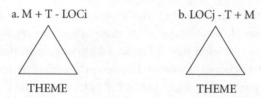

Figure 1. Basic Sign Schemata. M=Movement; T=Terminator; LOC=Location; *i, j, ...*
n=indices which associate LOCs to specific positions in the signing space.

The theme slot in ASL is not limited to classifiers. Other nominals may also occupy the theme position in the verb, including nouns as well as nominalizations of verbs. The embedding of nominalizations yields the possibility of multiple recursions of verbs within verbs all sharing a single theme slot in the matrix verb. Since ASL verbs have a rich inflectional morphology including person agreement for subject and object, number agreement, causative markers and reciprocal marking, as well as a rich variety of aspectual modulations, much evidence for ASL grammar can be locked into these nominalizations embedded within a single verb form. When such a verb is no longer productive and becomes part of the lexical inventory of ASL, its internal structure, while frozen, still retains evidence of the productive morphosyntactic system that gave rise to it.

3. Language

The lexicon is a repository of language evidence. However, first and second language learners access this repository in different ways. Second-language learners treat the lexicon as a source of linguistic gestalts to be borrowed. First-language learners treat lexical items as an additional source of linguistic evidence that may guide them in their creation of a grammar.

Sign internal recursion of the sort described above exists in all signed languages; however the depth of embedding might be correlated with language age. For example, a language like ASL includes a huge lexicon of frozen signs of varying internal complexity. Each time one of those frozen signs is productively embedded into the theme position of a verb we have the potential for eventually adding a new (more deeply embedded) frozen sign to the lexicon. The recursion discussed here is not necessarily productive, but it has the potential for being explored as relevant language-structure based evidence in the context of first-language acquisition.

Under this hypothesis, one might predict that an older language like ASL might show greater depth of sign-internal embedding than a younger language like ISN. This language-specific difference might be only superficial, and limited to non-productive aspects of the frozen lexicon. Productive insertion of nominals into the theme slot of a verb could remain a shallow process, where the actually embedding is only a single level deep in both languages. Nonetheless, each time a verb of this sort becomes frozen, the *sublexical evidence* for deeper and deeper recursion possibilities arises.

This non-productive, sublexical evidence could only be mined by the young learner's brain in the course of first-language acquisition. Once exploration of such frozen verbs is undertaken, the evidence in these lexical items could trigger a restructuring of the productive morphosyntax to allow productive multiple recursions within verbs. Such a reanalysis is especially feasible in those emergence contexts where a strong target language is unavailable. In cases like English or ASL (in an input-rich environment), where the target language is well-entrenched, sublexical regularities like latinate prefixation or sublexical verb internal recursion, could be kept in place (i.e., relegated to non-productive status) by the end-state acquisition process of matching to the available target language. While young children may make productive overgeneralizations concerning these forms when actively engaging in the first language acquisition process, they later learn that these are sporadic generalizations limited to a fixed set of frozen lexical items and are therefore just historical artifacts to be catalogued in the lexicon rather than subsumed under a set of productive word formation rules.

3.1 American Sign Language (sublexical morphology in frozen signs)

The concept behind re-creolization is that young signers are able to mine for grammatical evidence the frozen contents of ASL signs passed down to them as gestalts by their non-native language models. It is just a subcase of the analysis of E-Language evidence to inform I-Language development.

To make the argument that there is sufficient evidence of ASL grammar locked within a frozen sign to inform the first-language acquisition process of a child to yield a close approximation of ASL grammar, it is necessary to examine in depth the sublexical structure of some ASL signs. Consider two lexical verbs in ASL (ENCOURAGE and MEET) that have been borrowed as frozen signs into PSE (Pidgin Sign English)[4] or manually coded forms of English,[5] but which contain within them significant bits of evidence of ASL grammar. These are uninflected signs whose sublexical structure still preserves evidence of the morphophonological components of their derivational history.

While there are remnants of morphophonological processes recoverable from the sublexical structure of these signs, these regularities are no more a productive part of contemporary ASL grammar than Latinate prefix and root processes in words like con-vert, con-spire, con-flict are part of current English grammar. Nonetheless, children may well explore this level of recurrent systematicities in their quest to acquire English.

3.1.1   ENCOURAGE

Consider the frozen lexical sign ENCOURAGE. While frozen, a closer look at its internal structure reveals that it is built up from a series of embedded verbs: i.e., to ORIENT TOWARD a person$_i$ while continually PUSHING. The verb PUSHING is itself a lexicalized sign that is decompositional. It is built up from the verb MOVING-TO a LOCATION$_i$ while having one's hands (B:CL(2)-flat object) BE-ON a person (full body perspective = SBP (literally, Signer's Body Position). Each *while*-clause indicates another embedded nominalization. Furthermore, internal to this verb is evidence of spatial agreement, role prominence marking (indication of from whose perspective the action of the verb is viewed), iterative aspect via reduplication, theme classifiers (CL), embedding, a non-role prominent pronominal intimacy marker (called PBP (*Projected Body Pronoun*)), a causative marker (HCL:B(2); a classifier that indicates how something is handled (HCL), which in this case involved the use of two B-handhapes (flat hands)) as well as three productive locative/directional morphemes: WARD (orientation toward), TO (movement to a goal), and ON (contact).[6]

While the ASL verb ENCOURAGE does exhibit person agreement by orienting toward the position in space associated with the noun phrase serving as the syntactic object, this agreement is rarely realized when the verb is used in its frozen form. However, there is much evidence for other aspects of ASL grammar frozen within this lexical item.

Starting from the bottom of the representation, the classifier filling the lowest theme slot is itself complex. In addition to object classifiers that mark sets of referents sharing some physical or functional characteristic, there is also another set of classifier forms called *handling classifiers* (HCL; McDonald 1982).[7] They mark the involvement of some human (or personified) agent manipulating some object. The shape of the hands often indicates shape or functional characteristics of the affected object by how it is handled (by means of grasping a handle, holding the object (with pincers, with a curved hand, a flat

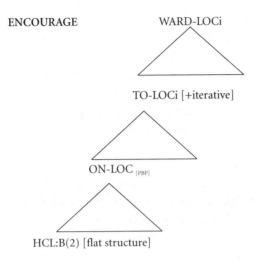

ENCOURAGE   WARD-LOCi

TO-LOCi [+iterative]

ON-LOC [PBP]

HCL:B(2) [flat structure]

Figure 2. The internal structure of the frozen sign ENCOURAGE, which is read as follows from top to bottom: (1) Orient toward person at location i; while (2) going forward repeatedly; while (3) being on a figurative body of person (PBP, Projected Body Pronoun); with (4) two flat surfaces (i.e., the palms of one's hands).

hand, and showing varying degrees of width or thickness). The handling classifier simultaneously registers the need to construe a causative agent in the sentence and the presence of the object of a transitive clause.

We can see that the signer's body (referred to as the Signer's Body Pronoun) takes on the agent role and has first person point of view on the action of the verb, even in the frozen form. The involvement of the signer's body in the sign marks the referent it is associated with as role prominent. Role prominence marking is a central marker of role shift, where the narrator takes on the role of another referent in the sentence. It is also frequently (but not obligatorily) associated with subject marking, which involves a less pronounced tilt of the signer's head toward the location associated with the subject of the verb (Bahan 1996). However, in both of these grammatical processes there is also a spatial association with the location of the noun phrase argument that bears the subject grammatical relation to the verb. This agreement is lost if the verb is frozen and therefore uninflected.

In the second to last embedding of ENCOURAGE, we see that the two flat hands contact (ON) an imaginary surface that is about the height and width of a human torso. This imaginary form is the Projected Body Pronoun (PBP) and is used when placing a greater degree of empathy on the object (e.g., viewing it as a whole person).

At the next level up, we see that the lower items comprising 'contacting a PBP with one's flat hands' are embedded within a motion verb GO-TO[forward], yielding PUSH. This entire form is then reduplicated. Reduplication is a morphological process of repetition for a grammatical purpose of the articulation (or part of the articulation) of a sign. In this case, the repetition marks iterative aspect yielding a form meaning 'repeatedly pushing.' This motion is also restrained, indicating a derivational process of nominalization that changes a noun to a verb.

At the upper level, this entire nominalization is embedded within a location verb of orientation. This matrix verb participates in actual syntactic agreement. Its subject is obligatorily anchored to the signer's body (body-anchored) and is therefore marked with role-prominence. It typically also exhibits head tilt in the direction of the subject NP as well as orientation toward and eye gaze to the location associated with the object NP.

However, when a verb is frozen and uninflected, it is as if it is embedded within a non-agreeing locative predicate, as in Figure 3.

$$\emptyset + \text{AT-LOC}_{\emptyset}$$

ENCOURAGE

Figure 3. The schema for a frozen verb basically removes any sentence relevant agreement from its form by embedding the verb in a basic AT predicate that is not spatially indexed.

In any multiply embedded ASL sign, material not in the matrix verb becomes nominalized and therefore opaque in terms of syntactic agreement even though remnants of agreement behavior may still be evident in embedded themes. ENCOURAGE, as a frozen sign, does not exhibit any of the syntactic agreement that it would show in ASL. Even when used in ASL all the material below the topmost orientation verb is syntactically opaque.

In summary, the sign ENCOURAGE contains within it evidence of numerous grammatical aspects of ASL:

1. role prominence markers and body-anchored verbs
2. projected body pronouns
3. handling classifiers/causative markers

4. morphological modulation/reduplication: iterative aspect
5. nominalization
6. combinatory properties of movement roots and terminators

3.1.2 *MEET*

Consider a second frozen lexical item, MEET, which involves two upright long thin objects (CL:1; persons) that move TO+ON each other [i,j/j,i] (reciprocal marking), while orienting TOWARD each other [i,j/j,i] (reciprocal marking). This verb offers evidence of cliticized object classifiers (CL#), reciprocal morphology, the classifier for long thin object, as well as the full expansion of the word formation rule for goals DIRECTIONAL (e.g., TO) + TERMINATION (e.g., ON) − LOCATION.

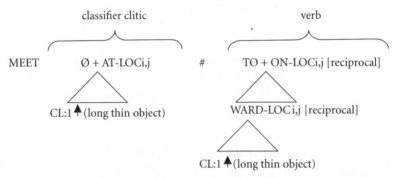

Figure 4. The internal structure of the frozen sign MEET, which is read as follows: To the left of the # is a classifier clitic. This form is read from top to bottom as (1a) be at location (i), with (2a) a long thin object (person) [non-dominant hand] and simultaneously (1b) be at location (j), with (2b) a long thin object (person) [dominant hand]. To the right of the # is the verb. This form is read from top to bottom as (1a) move into contact with location (i), with (2a) a long thin object (person) [dominant hand] and simultaneously (1b) move into contact with location (j), with (2b) a long thin object (person) [non-dominant hand].

In a productive sign, the item labeled *classifier clitic* above would correspond to the grammatical object of the sign MEET. Despite the fact that the noun phrase corresponding to the object of MEET would typically appear in postverbal position, its corresponding classifier clitic precedes and is cliticized to the verb. This grammatical ordering fact is frozen into the citation form of the lexical sign MEET that is often used by signers not fluent in ASL, late learners, or PSE signers.

The frozen sign MEET does not agree in space with its subject and object noun phrases in the sentence, but it is morphologically a reciprocal form (i.e., meet each other). The productive form of MEET, in contrast, is inflected for subject and object and spatially agrees with the noun phrases holding those grammatical relations in the sentence.[8] The productively used ASL sign MEET can be reciprocal or not. A native speaker of ASL would inflect the verb MEET differently in the contexts x meets y, y meets x, x and y meet each other, y meets each of many people, etc. The frozen lexical item, in contrast, freezes only the reciprocal form, and a late learner will use only a limited number of these options, typically only the citation form across all these contexts.

When the productive ASL sign MEET is marked as a reciprocal, there are simultaneously two classifier clitics (one at position i and the other at position j) and two verbs (one with a classifier (CL:1) moving toward the classifier clitic at position i and the other moving toward the classifier clitic at location j. The index finger realizing the theme of the classifier clitic (i) subsequently realizes the theme of the verb moving toward location (j); and the index finger realizing the theme of the classifier clitic (j) subsequently realizes the theme of the verb moving toward location (i). The two index fingers come to contact each other as they each move along the same path. The frozen sign MEET therefore does preserve evidence of the complex reciprocal verb form in ASL.

The verb MEET preserves grammatical information about:

1. reciprocal verb forms
2. object classifiers (long thin object, round solid object)
3. preverbal positioning of classifier clitics
4. morphological object agreement

3.1.3   Summary

The sublexical regularities identified in the two verbs above are echoed throughout the ASL lexicon as well as in productive aspects of the morpho-syntax of ASL. Like all primary signed languages, ASL exhibits a systematic patterning of form, basic form classes (noun, verb, adjective, adverbs, classifiers, etc.), systematic word formation rules, inflectional and derivational morphological processes, constraints on syntactic form, and syntactic rules to account for systematic permutations of the ordering of elements in a sentence. The recurring components of ASL grammar combine systematically to allow the expression of fine-grained distinctions in message and meaning, allowing users to communicate about anything, including information that contradicts or is not present in the shared knowledge of interlocutors.

A learner past the critical period for language acquisition and late second language learners view ENCOURAGE and MEET as unanalyzable wholes. Child learners, on the other hand, dissect these forms with their analytical language learning tools and mine them for evidence of the phonological, morphological, and syntactic characteristics of the language they are acquiring.

3.2 Nicaraguan Sign Language (sublexical morphology in productive signs)

The following example presents a sequence of three verbs produced by one of the native signers of ISN. These three verbs actually constitute a single grammatical construction referred to as a *verb sandwich* (Fischer & Janis 1990; Janis 1992). Verb sandwiches are common to both ASL and ISN. They tend to occur with verbs bearing complex morphological inflections. In such constructions, a simpler form of the verb (with fewer inflections) precedes a more complexly inflected form.

The translation of the verb sandwich presented below is: 'Each of many children in single file give the man an egg, and in return he gives each of them an Indian headdress.' The nouns *egg* and *Indian headdress* have been established in the prior discourse. In this verb construction, we find corresponding classifiers associated with these nouns (CL:babyC — narrow rimmed object and HCL:5 claw — handle a spherical object).

In this example, the signer produces a verb sandwich consisting of a serial verb of giving/receiving (already rather complex) followed by an even more complex reciprocal form of that same verb. Consider first the grammatical structure of the serial verb portion of the sandwich construction.

The serial verb has two conjuncts (V1 and V2). If we consider only the representation of the matrix verb (LOC3p[i,j,k]-AT+FROM+TO+AT-LOC3p[l]), each conjunct appears to have the same verb. However, there are many significant differences.

In the first conjunct syntactic subject agreement is with the givers (the children i,j,k), and in the second conjunct subject agreement is with the receiver (the man, l). Syntactic subject agreement is realized by a head tilt in the direction of the argument serving as subject. Similarly, syntactic object agreement is realized by eyegaze to the position associated with the referent serving as object. This differs across the two conjuncts as well. In the first conjunct, syntactic object agreement is with the man (l, the goal of giving) and, in the second conjunct, it is with the children (i-k, the source of the giving).

As in all of the primary signed languages studied to date, Nicaraguan Sign Language also has morphologically realized verb agreement in certain classes

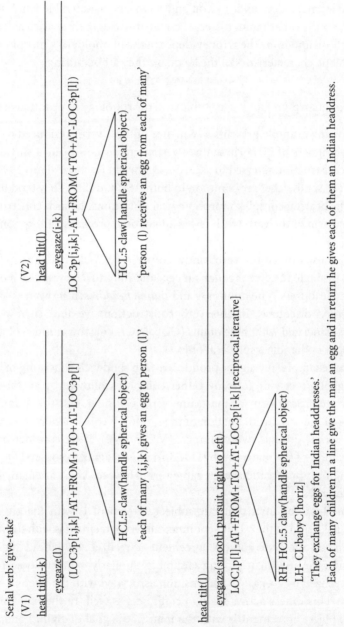

Figure 5. Complex verb sandwich construction consisting of a serial verb (GIVE/RECEIVE) followed by a reciprocal form of a verb for exchanging eggs for Indian headdresses.

of verbs. The verbs GIVE, TAKE, and RECEIVE fall into the class of morphologically agreeing verbs in ASL. GIVE moves between the giver (source) and the receiver (goal). In the canonical case, syntactic subject agreement (head tilt) is also associated with the giver. TAKE and RECEIVE are backwards agreeing verbs (see Fischer & Gough 1978; Brentari 1988; Meir 1998). Like other agreement verbs, backward verbs also move between the source and goal; however, syntactic subject agreement is associated with the receiver/taker (the goal).

When, as in the case of GIVE and RECEIVE, the verb has both morphological and syntactic agreement, morphological subject agreement can be reduced. This reduction phenomenon was first noted in Padden (1988) and further explored in Supalla (1997). Basically a verb like GIVE can drop its source marker and be realized as a goal-taking verb only.

However, the ISN serial verb example presented above, while reduced, still shows evidence of its fully elaborated morphological derivation. Shepard-Kegl (1985) showed that the word formation rules for FROM+TO verbs of this type in ASL involve more than simple compounding of a FROM verb (LOCi-AT+FROM) and a TO verb (TO+AT-LOCj). Consider the examples in V1 and V2 above. The subject is plural and the object is singular. Number agreement in ASL and in ISN is realized by mapping a verb stem into one of three templates: singular {Xi}, dual {Xi,Xj}, and plural {Xi,Xj,Xk}.

First, the goal component of the sign (TO+AT-LOC) is formed and inflected with singular agreement. Singular agreement involves mapping the verb stem into the singular template {Xw}, yielding TO+AT-LOCw. (Since i, j, and k in the above templates are simply variables, we will assign the singular template an alternate variable w to keep it distinct from the values assigned by the plural template.) Then the FROM morpheme is adjoined, followed by the Terminator (AT) and the Locative Marker (LOC). The entire resulting stem LOC-AT+FROM+TO-LOCw is then mapped into the plural template {XiXjXk}, yielding the discontinuous morphological form: iLOC-AT+FROM+TO-LOCw jLOC-AT+FROM+TO-LOCw kLOC-AT+FROM+TO-LOCw. The tripling of the singular object agreement (w) in both of these forms demonstrates that plural subject agreement is applied to the full FROM+TO stem. In contrast, a singular subject and plural goal would not yield a tripled subject value: wLOC-AT+FROM+TO+AT-LOCi TO+AT-LOCj TO+AT-LOCk. Schemata for these two contrasting verb forms appear in Figure 6 below.

In the serial verb above, both V1 and V2 show triple articulations. The first conjunct involves a handling classifier (HCL:5 claw) moving three times TO the location associated with the man. In the second conjunct, the same handling

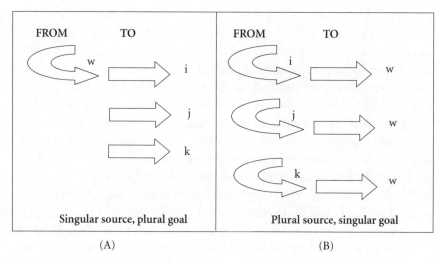

Figure 6. Schema illustrating plural agreement for source versus goal. Number agreement is applied to the goal component of the verb before the source is added on. The entire stem maps into the agreement skeleton (or binyan). Therefore, when the source is plural (as in (B)), the entire stem including the goal feeds into the plural agreement schema.

classifier moves three times from the location of the children in line. The linear arrangement of the children is actually established in a prior noun (CHILDREN-IN-LINE) and the arrangement established there is echoed in the GIVE/TAKE serial verb.

The handling classifier in both conjuncts matches the orientation of the role prominent subject in both verbs. This means that the subject of the second conjunct is not passive in the sense that the man 'was given' the eggs, but rather that he was an active receiver of the eggs. This is interpreted as two distinct verbs GIVE and RECEIVE, as opposed to one verb GIVE and its passive form WAS-GIVEN. This ISN serial verb construction has two active clauses that share a single argument (the man): 'each child gives to [a man] takes the eggs from the children.'

So, in each conjunct of the give/take serial verb we must take note of several factors: the direction of the head tilt, the direction of eyegaze, and the orientation of the handling classifier. Both conjuncts contain the same handling classifier filling the theme slot of the verb (HCL: 5 claw; handle a spherical/ovoid object); however, its orientation differs across the two conjuncts. In each conjunct head tilt is toward the subject, and the handling classifier is oriented toward the syntactic object of its matrix verb.

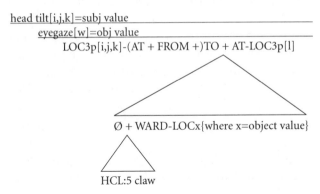

head tilt[i,j,k]=subj value
eyegaze[w]=obj value
LOC3p[i,j,k]-(AT + FROM +)TO + AT-LOC3p[l]

Ø + WARD-LOCx{where x=object value}

HCL:5 claw

Figure 7. Verb in Figure 6b with syntactic subject and object agreement indicated (as head tilt and eye gaze, respectively). The three iterations of the stem that result from plural number marking are not represented.

The serial verb, while complex in its own right, is simpler than the second, reciprocal verb in the ISN verb sandwich. We saw a reciprocal verb in the ASL sign MEET discussed previously. Basically, in a reciprocal inflection two articulations of a verb are signed simultaneously with the subject of the first serving as the object of the second and vice versa.

In contrast with the example MEET discussed earlier, the reciprocal verb in the second part of the ISN verb sandwich involves two distinct embedded themes (CL:babyC — thin/narrow rimmed object and HCL:5 claw — handle a spherical object). Because there is no contact involved in the verb, the two articulations of the verb can be fully articulated (moving along the complete path between subject and object). Thus, while the right hand articulates RECEIVE-A-SPHERICAL-OBJECT (LOC[i-k]-AT+FROM+TO+AT-LOCw with the theme HCL:5 claw) moving from the position of the children to the position of the signer, the left hand simultaneously articulates A-NARROW-CYLINDRICAL-OBJECT-GOES-TO-LOC[i-k] (LOCw-AT+FROM+TO+AT-LOC[i-k] with the theme CL:babyC). This pair of verbs is then marked for iterative aspect (repeatedly) by mapping it into the reduplication template {XiXiXi}. The entire simultaneous pair of verbs is repeated three times. The reciprocal verb with iterative inflection cannot also support the number agreement seen in the serial verb. Thus the two verbs participate in a verb sandwich to allow all the intended morphological operations to apply.

While the depth of recursion within the ISN verb may appear shallower than what is found in ASL, it should be noted that the handling classifier construction at the bottom of each verb (HCL:5 claw) is itself morphologically complex. The handling classifier involves a hand manipulating (contacting; ON) an imaginary object. The nature of the contact reflects the size and shape of the object, with only a finite set of handling configurations allowed, distinguishing this form from the wider range of possibilities possible in mime or gesture. Within a handling classifier is a productive derived nominal form called a Size and Shape Specifier.

ASL, ISN, and all the other signed languages described to date have a set of derived nominal forms called Size and Shape Specifiers (SASS; Klima & Bellugi 1979). These nominals are typically sculpted or traced in space by motion verbs whose one-handed or two-handed themes consist of object classifiers. For example, a rimmed object classifier (CL:C) moved LOCi-ON+FROM another rimmed object classifier (CL:C; in this case a classifier clitic: CL:C embedded in a locative verb, AT-LOCi) would form a SASS for cylindrical objects such as sewer pipes, tall glasses, tree trunks, etc. SASSs differ from classifiers in their ability to be modulated for detailed tracings of contour and length. In this respect, they straddle a point where the constrained elements of language can be modulated in an infinite variety of ways.

With the exception of the extended abilities for modification and the absence of any movement component, the handling classifier appears to incorporate the equivalent of a size and shape specifier in the way that motion/location predicates incorporate object classifiers. It simultaneously registers the presence of an agent as well, serving in ISN, as it does in ASL, as a causative marker.

3.3 Summary

Thus far we have seen evidence of the complex morphosyntax that can be found internal to signs borrowed from a full signed language or learned as frozen wholes by late learners. We have found a similarly complex morphosyntax to exist productively in a young signed language that emerged in the absence of contact with other signed languages. However, the sublexical complexity available to the ASL re-creolizer was not available to the first generation of ISN signers.

Over its history of barely a century and a half, ASL has packaged detailed evidence of its grammar into each sign that has become part of its frozen lexicon. By doing so it passes a partial blueprint of its grammar to each and every young child who encounters its vocabulary. Even those children not exposed to language models with native mastery of ASL grammar, can potentially unpack the evidence in these signs to arrive at a native grammar of ASL. In other words, children of non-native signing parents can recreolize to a language specific target: ASL.

Nicaraguan Sign Language, with a history of only two decades, presents us with important comparative evidence. ISN appears to exhibit sublexical structure of the same level of complexity as that seen in ASL, albeit perhaps shallower in depth of recursion. However, if we go back two generations, we find some important differences in the nature of the input available to young acquirers: ISN did not yet exist; there was no repository of pre-existing ISN signs; there was no Deaf community; there was no signed language available as input; there was no available source even of fragments of a signed language for children to unpack. There was only gesture.

4. Gesture

Both language and gesture are complex behaviors that humans are predisposed to use. Gesture is not language, but it usually coexists with language in a single individual.

4.1 Distinguishing gesture from signing

If we ask spoken language users what in their communication constitutes gesture and what constitutes language, they can, for the most part, fall back on modality differences to separate the two.[9] Signers, like speakers, gesture while they are using language (Emmorey 1999), and can also make this distinction, but cannot invoke modality as a simple differentiating factor because, for signers, both gestures and signing use the same modality.[10] A brief review of the literature on gesture provides a useful set of characteristics that distinguish sign language and gesture (Klima & Bellugi 1979; McNeill 1993; Morford 1996; Morford & Kegl 2000; Messing & Campbell 1999, in particular the preface; and Emmorey 1999) (Table 2).[11]

Based upon the characteristics above, gesturing and signing should be very easy to distinguish. Signing has rule governed sequences of morphologically complex signs whose interaction and configuration with respect to one another exhibit the systematic hierarchical interdependencies characteristic of the human languages with which we are familiar. It is possible in signing to detect

Table 2. Differences between language and gesture

Sign language	Gestures
Sublexical (phonological) structure	Holistic form
Lexical structure (parts of speech)	Do not belong to specific form classes (e.g., noun , verb, etc.)
Syntactic structure	Rarely occur in combination; successive gestures do not form a larger hierarchical structure
Standards of form and a community of users	Idiosyncratic with no agreed standards of form
Recognized successfully only by members of the community of users (a minority)	Recognizable by members of dominant (hearing/speaking) culture
The grammar of the signed language should allow discussion of specific information that can run counter to expectation and is independent of the present context	Utterances are context dependent and lend themselves to multiple interpretations in a given context

ungrammatical utterances and/or stylistically awkward sentences. However, only members of a community of signers are able to make such grammaticality judgments. Furthermore, there are signs that are only recognizable by other signers within the signing community. Finally, signed utterances are not context dependent for their interpretation. They can convey information counter to expectation and detached from the here and now.

Gesturing involves more amorphous, communicative behaviors that typically map a single action gesture to an entire event, with the gesturer serving as the agent of the action (Morford & Kegl 2000). While in gesture we may be able to distinguish communication about actions versus things, there is no distributional evidence for parts of speech such as noun, verb, adjective, etc. While some utterances may fail to be understood as intended by the interlocutors, the communication form does not lend itself to grammaticality judgments or stylistic preferences. Furthermore, if the gestures used are drawn by the isolate from the gestures of the wider cultural community, there is a greater likelihood that the gestures used will remain recognizable by individuals outside the small social sphere of the gesturer.

Gestures are dependent upon shared knowledge and context to be understood. Even then, gesture is inherently ambiguous. It is never possible to be sure that the interpretation assigned to a given gesture by its recipient is truly identical to the meaning intended by the gesturer.

4.2 Characteristics of gestural communication

To get a feel for the difference between the units of gestural communication and the highly decompositional and morphologically complex sign internal structure seen in ASL, ISN, and the other primary signed languages, we need to try to look at gesture with the same lens used to examine the internal structure of signed languages.

4.2.1 Gestures shared by a cultural group

Nicaraguans have a repertoire of gestures that are culturally shared. Some are local to a given family, others to a community, and still others to a region, the entire country, or even to the whole of Latin America. The gestures used by language isolates are not typically idiosyncratic to a single individual or family, but are drawn from gestures already in use or at least recognizable by the culture as a whole.

Consider the Nicaraguan (actually, wider Central American) gesture for 'eat/food',[12] a flat hand bending up and down in front of the mouth. This single gesture can be understood, depending upon the context, as any of a number of messages:

'That is food.'	'That is edible.'
'I want to eat.'	'Can I eat that?'
'Would you like to eat?'	'Is that edible?'
'Would you like some food?'	'You can eat that.'
'I have already eaten.'	'Eat that!'

4.2.2 The cooccurrence of gesture and language

For most Nicaraguans, gesture is a communicative system that coexists with a spoken language (Spanish, English, Miskitu, Mayangna, Ulwa, Garifuna, or combinations of these). Gestures can occur in isolation, or as gesticulations that accompany speech. Between hearing members of Nicaraguan culture, a gesture can supplement a language-based utterance or it can elicit an interpretation that is linguistic in nature, such as those listed above.

Hearing gesturers have a full language in their communicative repertoire. Some deaf gesturers have a signed language in their repertoire, but there are some deaf individuals for whom gesture is their sole mode of communication. These individuals are typically language isolates. For the language isolate exposed to the gestures of language users, the accompanying linguistic context (the language of the hearing gesturer/gesticulator) is inaccessible. Therefore, in all cases what is transmitted to the language isolate consists of single gestures in the context of whole events. A language isolate, reliant solely upon gesture, can produce a single gesture such as 'eat/food', but this does not imply that this gesture is able to convey any one of the specific linguistic messages listed above.

4.3 Gesturers influenced by exposure to a signed language after the critical period

Some language isolates can come into contact with a signed language at a point when they are already well beyond the critical period for language acquisition. While native acquisition of a signed language is no longer possible, effects of exposure to a signed language can often be seen. They react in special ways that suggest a sensitivity to language-relevant evidence persists even when the window for native language acquisition has already closed. Gesturers exposed to language late are drawn to its sequentiality and prosodic flow. They try to mimic that flow in a variety of ways, all of which converge on an expansion in the number of items produced in a single utterance. The changes we observe occur almost immediately, but are certainly strongly evident by two weeks of exposure.

4.3.1   *Repetition*
To an individual with single gestures labeling entire events, the flow of language and its prosody stand out as highly salient features. One of the more striking effects of language exposure is the attempt by former language isolates to adopt in their communication the prosody of the signers around them. For an individual who typically communicates with a single gesture for a whole event, adopting the intonational characteristics of the language around them requires a major restructuring of communication style. A major factor in this restructuring is the use of repetition.

We see a variety of adaptations: reiteration of a single gesture or stereotypic movement; stringing together of individual gestures; gestures accompanied by non-meaningful gestural movements; routinized gestural communication where a single event is acted out again and again; and sometimes just an expansion of the number of gestures produced in sequence.

4.3.2   *Lexicon*
As a result of contact, some formal signs can also be transmitted. Isolates post-contact may use a few signs interspersed with their gestures and may even produce somewhat more elaborate (albeit repetitious) sequences of signs and gestures, but in those sequences there is no evidence of a system of syntactic

organization or of productive awareness of sublexical structure.

Some signs are learned simply by exposure, but more are learned if explicitly taught. Acquisition at the lexical level can continue well past the critical period for language acquisition for most former isolates. However, for some, even lexical acquisition seems to be beyond their abilities.

4.3.3 *Grammar*

While isolates who contact language well beyond the critical period may become more and more effective gesturers and may acquire some sign vocabulary over time, even with extensive contact, native-like mastery of grammar eludes them. Our observations of over 100 individuals before and after contact over the past six years reveals that older isolates require explicit training in signs and signed language grammar to show any significant development of grammar. Furthermore, cognitive testing suggests that success at acquiring a language late is correlated with level of intelligence on the WAIS, WISC and a variety of other cognitive measures (Spitz & Kegl 1999). And, if such training is successful, the grammar learned is partial and fragile. Major changes in fluency take four to five years to appear. And, even then, fluency and basic grammar break down with increases in cognitive load, such as those brought on by distractions, divided attention, fatigue, or other factors.

All of these characteristics diverge from the resiliency and stability we would expect in an early acquired language. They suggest a very different brain organization for language learned after the critical period has passed.

4.4 Summary

For an individual who is already a language user, limited gestures can suffice to call up more sophisticated linguistic interpretations. For an individual without a language base, such gestures are just placeholders for communication. The receiver of the gesture (a language user) provides the interpretation, taking on the task of language encoding and relieving the language isolate of any demands to make explicit through grammar the participant roles and who does what to whom. Every time time a family member of a deaf isolate intervenes between a gesture and the need to be more linguistically implicit by using context to overinterpret limited gestures, that family member further deprives the language isolate from the need or the trigger to acquire a first language. Eventually, the gesturer is beyond the critical period and nothing will trigger the first-language acquisition process.

There are some behaviors on the part of late-learners suggesting that when an accessible language is encountered, it is still recognized as special and worthy of being emulated. Language isolates post critical period seem to retain a sensitivity to prosody and this may draw their attention to language relevant input. They also exhibit a mimicking response that could well bootstrap them into the first-language acquisition process. However, they lack the most essential component of the first-language acquisition process. Their language-ready brains have passed the critical period during which innate expectations act upon the raw materials and language evidence available in the input to drive the first-language acquisition process. Therefore, they cannot create a first language to match to a language-specific target available in the environment.

5.   Language-relevant non-language input

Of the 1433 deaf Nicaraguans documented to date, 423 are, or were when first contacted, language isolates. These individuals range in age from 2 to 80. Except for a few cases, where single isolated families had a large proportion of deaf members and family signed languages seem to have emerged (Kegl 2000), all of these isolates were languageless at first contact. Of the 423 languageless gesturers encountered, 100 (ages 4–37) are currently in or have been in language intervention programs and have been longitudinally followed over the past six years. Others who have remained isolates are tested at less regular intervals, if and when visits are possible.

The language isolates being studied now offer insights into the initial communication abilities of that first cohort of pupils who came together in the first deaf schools, in Managua in the late 1970s. Simple gesture is not viewed by the language-ready brain as language-relevant input. Therefore, the single gestures used to convey basic needs in the hearing home with a deaf child do not trigger the first-language acquisition process. Signed language input *is* viewed by the language-ready brain as relevant input and *does* lead to successful native language acquisition in young children.

Surprisingly, the communication that arises between the same deaf gesturers, once they come in contact with each other is *also* viewed by the language-ready brain as relevant input and *also* leads to successful native language acquisition in young children exposed to it. With no hearing parent or sibling to overinterpret single gestures, former isolates in contact begin to make multiple attempts at conveying information yielding sequences of gestures, repetition, and chunking of gesture groups. While not rule governed, the goal of transmission of information is evident and there are sequences and prosody that seem to be sufficient to draw the attention of learners both young and old to what is proposed here to be language-relevant, but non-language, input. The attention of young deaf children is spontaneously drawn to this input as a source of language-relevant evidence.

Attention to language-relevant input triggers the first-language acquisition process. Once the first-language acquisition process is set into motion the brain recruits available raw material and bits of language evidence to create language. Characteristics of the materials encountered can influence potential choices regarding the typological characteristics of the emergent language. The product of the language creation process is then matched to existing targets. In so far as the existing target falls short of language expectations, the target is ignored and the emergent language fills in the gaps.

Multiple emergent languages came into being simultaneously in the Nicaraguan deaf population as all the very young children engaged in the process of first-language acquisition. These emergent languages also participate in a matching process, converging in many respects on a final set of language options. The final product, having surpassed its input, takes its place as the target of acquisition. As with all languages, the end product of language emergence is actually a conglomeration of closely approximating languages, with language users each exhibiting their own idiolects. See Smith (1999) for arguments that a single communal language does not exist.

5.1 Gestural precursors to typological choices

While grammar is a product of the human brain (I-Language), its typological choices are affected by the evidence available in the environment (E-Language). This evidence is not just limited to language input. In the case where elaborated communication is taken to be language-relevant input, physical characteristics of gesture can condition certain typological choices that are made in the acquisition process. Several cases where gestural precursors of emergent language forms could be posited are enumerated below.

5.1.1 Null subjects
Gesturers use the whole body to act out actions, taking on the agent role. In elaborated gesture, while references to persons and things can occur, the agent is rarely referenced independently via pointing or a name sign. Children exposed

to elaborated gesture as the input to first-language acquisition, therefore, take this as evidence that they are learning a null subject language. From this, it can follow that in the emergent language subject pronouns will be optional. In fact, the 'avoid pronoun' (Chomsky 1986a) tendency is likely.

5.1.2   Role Prominence
Since gesturers use their bodies to act out the role of the agent or experiencer, that use of the body is likely to be reanalyzed in the emergent language as a marker of first person point of view and possibly as a marker of role prominence. As role prominence, in addition to reference, is frequently a property of subjects, the syntactic subject marker is likely to involve associating the signer's body with the referential index of the referent serving as the subject. In ISN (as in ASL) head tilt toward the spatial index of a given referent marks it as subject.

In addition, a full shift of the signer's body to the spatial index of another referent allows the signer to take on the role of another referent with first person point of view. This role shift allows for Point of View predicates (POV), which mark both direct speech and direct action predicates (see Lillo-Martin 1995; Lee, Neidle, MacLaughlin, Bahan & Kegl 1997 for discussion of direct speech and direct action in ASL). Once the role shift occurs, ISN signers consistently mark the shift from third to first person by signing a first person pronoun in the shifted position (i.e., 'I am now person x'). Distinguishing oneself from other in first person POV is not demanded in gesturing.

5.1.3   Causative markers
The use of whole body gestures also involves gestures that depict how one manipulates objects with one's hands like opening a jar, handling a cup, etc. By gesturers and gesturers in contact, handling gestures are used for both objects being handled and to show the movement of objects themselves.

When gestures are recruited as the raw material for language, handling gestures are frequently reanalyzed as handling classifiers serving as causative markers. Handling classifiers mark verbs as transitive and allow the construal of an agent in the clause, even when the subject is not marked with role prominence.

The emergence of object classifiers in ISN allows for gestures depicting the handling of objects to be restricted and reanalyzed as handling classifiers serving as causative markers (Kegl et al. 1999). The existence of handling classifiers as well as object classifiers allows for a grammatically signaled causative/inchoative distinction in ISN.

5.1.4   Spatial agreement

Spatial agreement is a hallmark of all signed languages. Noun phrases are associated with unique points in the signing space. Pronouns agree with these same index points to refer back to their antecedents. A subclass of agreeing verbs also move to, from, or are articulated at certain positions in space to signal those referents that hold specific grammatical relations with respect to them. The purpose of spatial agreement is linked referencing across phrases and/or stretches of discourse. This referencing is also constrained in specific ways by notions such as c-command, subjacency or a host of other syntactic constraints.

The problem is that many non-linguistic gestures can be translatory, moving between one location and another. While gesturers do not set up abstract referential indices in gestural space, if real persons or things are present in space, they can move gestures between them or toward them. These translatory gestures between real world objects have been elicited from home signers in experiments conducted by Coppola, Senghas, Newport and Supalla (1997) and have been given linguistic status in their analysis. This paper diverges from that position and considers these gestures to be non-linguistic.

Following Morford and Kegl (2000), these gestures are recognized as possible precursors of linguistic constructs yet to emerge. They can provide non-language evidence that may lead a child encountering them to create a grammar with spatial agreement. These gestures may even be recruited as the actual raw material for realizing a given translatory verb in the emergent language. Crucially, however, in the communication context where these translatory gestures occur, they are not verbs. A verb is a linguistic construct that is in configuration with its arguments in the context of a grammar.

Kegl, Morgan, Spitz and Kyle (1998) presented arguments that being translatory (i.e., simply moving between two points in space) cannot constitute verb status or verb agreement. In a related case study, a series of 60 video vignettes were presented to a language semi-isolate — someone who grew up as a language isolate, but has had very limited contact with ISN signers as an adult. Each vignette involves three people (two women and a man) sitting in a row facing the subject. The relative positions of these people change from clip to clip. Except for a few intransitive contexts (sleeping and jumping), many of the vignettes involve actions that relate sources and goals with a translatory action (i.e., hitting, pushing, giving, throwing, etc.). Many of the 83 action gestures produced moved between distinct points in space. In 78% of the responses to the video vignettes (46/60 responses), the action gestures moved or were located

correctly with respect to the relative positions (left versus right) of the individuals involved in the event. The remainder either lacked a translatory movement
where one was expected or reversed the direction of the movement.

This tendency to preserve left/right distinctions, however, doesn't mean
that the source and goal were unambiguously specified in these responses. The
diagram in Figure 8 illustrates the sets of situations that elicited identical
translatory gestures. In the upper part of the diagram, all left to right translatory
movements (labeled A) between any individuals share the same movement.
Similarly, in the lower part of the diagram, all right to left translatory movements (labeled B) also involve identical movements. In other words, identical
responses were given for the person in the middle giving to the person on the
left, for the person on the right giving to the person in the middle, and for the
person on the right giving to the person on the left. The subject sometimes
further specified gender by taking on the role of the woman in a man/woman
vignette, but was unable to use that strategy when there were two women.

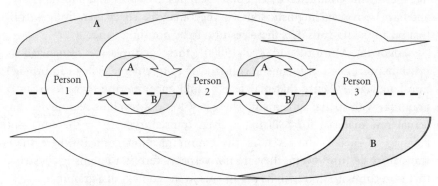

Figure 8. Relative directionality of translatory gestures. All relations marked as A are
signed the same, and all marked as B are also signed the same. No distinction is made
between referents 1,2, and 3. Only relative directionality tends to be preserved.

Senghas and Coppola (2001) refine the criterion for spatial agreement to
include not just use of space, but shared reference. Shared reference involves the
use of spatial locations that can be shown to share reference to a location in
space previously utilized to refer to or agree with the same referent in the
preceding discourse. The semi-isolate tends (78% of the time) in her gestures to
attend to real world spatial relations of left and right, but this spatial mapping
is too literal and is not sufficiently abstract to establish the kind of shared
referencing that is necessary for coreference and verb agreement within a

grammar. Furthermore, she was at best trying to establish shared reference with the positions of people in the video stimuli. She was not exhibiting shared linguistic reference across explicit phrases or discourse units. Nonetheless, the semi-isolate's gestural use of space could certainly lead a young child watching her communication to view her translatory gestures as evidence of a language that involves verb agreement with source and goal or even subject and object.

Gesturers will also recruit another individual as the goal of action gestures like 'throwing', actually expecting the other individual to gesture as if 'catching' the object thrown. The semi-isolate did this frequently during testing and actually chided the person next to her for not gesturally catching the imaginary ball that she threw. While there is no language that comes to mind that recruits a second person to complete ditransitive constructions, these non-linguistic translatory gestures can be taken as evidence of person and spatial agreement by first-language acquirers and the recruitment of an additional person may well favor the development of Projected Body Pronouns.

5.1.5   Auxiliaries

Many gestures, such as 'talking' (a single hand with the four fingers and thumb opposed opening and closing in front of the mouth) and 'look-at' (pulling down the lower lid with the tip of one's index finger) are not translatory. They are often followed in contact gesturing by a pointing gesture that moves from source to goal. These action gestures were recruited into the emergent language, but their articulation changed. The emergent sign TALK-TO/TELL blends the non-translatory gesture ('talk') and the translatory pointing gesture ('x to y') that followed it into a single sign that inflects for subject and object by moving from the source of the talking to the goal while closing the four fingers and thumb in a single gesture coupled with the translatory movement. The sign TALK is no longer anchored to the body (at the mouth) and the translatory pointing gesture ('x to y') no longer appears. The emergent sign LOOK-AT remains anchored to the body (at the lower lid), and is still followed by a sign that moves between the source and goal. The handshape in the second part of this sign is no longer an index finger. It is now a V-handshape that signals membership of this verb in the vision class.

As can be seen, in the emergent language some verbs (like GIVE) retain the translatory feature of their gestural precursors and link the endpoints to actual grammatically overt referential indices associated with subject and object. Others (like TALK) drop the body-anchored feature of their gestural precursors in favor of agreement with overt referential indices for subject and objects.

And, in some verbs it remains compounded with the verb but is modified as we saw with LOOK-AT.

The original gesture, which basically indicates a spatial relation 'from X to Y' with no additional verb content, did not disappear entirely. It appears to have been reanalyzed in ISN as a reduced verb, which is glossed as ^{i}TO^j. Its syntactic distribution is now very different. It appears in the reciprocal forms of verbs like SIGN-TO: NP^x NP^y xSIGN-TOy yTOx (literally, 'he signed to her, and she to him'). It also appears in sequences of agreeing verbs like NP^x ^{x}TELL^y ^{y}TO^z ^{z}TO^w ('Person[x] told person[y], and person[y] (told) person[z], and person[z] (told) person[w]'), almost like an across the board gapping construction.

But more importantly, the gesture 'y to z' seems to have been recruited into the emergent language and reanalyzed as an auxiliary. It is used regularly with body anchor verbs like WAVE, KNOW, LOVE, SIGN (e.g., sign ISN), etc. when the subject is not 1st person. In 'I waved to him' the verb WAVE simply orients toward the goal. But, in the form 'He waved to me', the auxiliary form appears in preverbal position before an uninflected verb and carries the agreement information: ^{i}TO^j WAVE ('he to me waves'). Notice that the auxiliary's syntactic distribution diverges from the post-action-gesture ordering seen in contact gesturing to preverbal position. The form of the gesture was recruited, but the syntax of ISN now dictates its ordering.

5.1.6   Serial verbs

Elaborated gestural communication is characterized by multiple hits on the same lexical conceptual structure (LCS) associated with an event. An LCS is the pre-linguistic representation of an event in terms of participant roles and relations/actions between them. A single LCS can involve many participant roles, but not all of those roles are instantiated in the linguistic encoding of any given event.

Without syntax, gesturers cannot use the hiererchical configuration of arguments and verb to express multiple roles. In fact, language isolates typically produce only an action gesture, using their bodies to articulate that gesture from the agent's perspective. Gesturers in contact have a valence of at most one gestured person or thing per action gesture.[13] Six language isolates referring to an event can be compared to the story of six blind men touching an elephant and from their point of contact providing very different descriptions. Each description is valid from that individual's vantagepoint, but no single description serves to capture the image of the elephant as a whole.

While shared context may allow a single-gesture utterance to call up an entire event and lead the interlocutor to infer an intended meaning from context, no single utterance produced by the gesturer captures the full information intended to be conveyed. Like the six blind men, deaf gesturers in contact can be expected to contribute variety to the range of possible gestures that can relate the same event. In addition, a member of this contact community can be expected to have seen many different gestures picking out the same event, even if they typically produce only one. Under experimental conditions, when we probe for more and more information on a single event stimulus, gesturers can respond with more and more distinct single hits on the same LCS. It is a simple step from there to a single gesturer in contact recruiting more than one gestural option to further clarify an event or using multiple gestures in a single utterance to assure understanding.

Once deaf gesturers in contact begin to elaborate their communication to indicate who does what to whom, they string together a series of action gestures (action chains), adding an action for each additional participant role referred to, with the consequence of substantial redundancy.

Action chains are reanalyzed in the emergent language as serial verbs. What starts as a sequence of 'push get-pushed' in elaborated gesture can be taken as evidence for serial verb constructions in the emergent language. In a serial verb construction, X PUSH Y GET-PUSHED, two conjuncts of a single complex verb share a common argument. Y is the object of conjunct 1 and the subject of conjunct 2. Syntactic evidence for the reanalysis in the emergent grammar is spatial agreement with Y on the object of PUSH and topicalization of the Y referent to the beginning of the entire sequence: Y, X PUSH GET-PUSHED, showing that the two verbs are conjuncts of a single serial verb construction. (See Kegl et al. 1999 for more detail). In addition, the conjuncts of a serial verb show parallel agreement morphology, as seen in Figure 5.

5.1.7   Reduplication for aspect marking on verbs

What in isolated gesturers or gesturers in contact is non-linguistically relevant gesture repetition gets reanalyzed in ISN as a set of morphological modulations of verbs to indicate various types of aspect marking: continual, iterative, etc.. As was seen in the example produced by the native ISN signer and discussed in 2.2 (Figure 5) above, these morphological modulations are also mirrored on both conjuncts in a serial verb construction. The extensive use of non-linguistically relevant repetition that characterizes gesturers in contact is dropped in the emergent language.

5.1.8   Nonmanual markers for questions

The gesture of wrinkling one's nose is recognized throughout Central American countries as meaning 'What's up?' It was carried into the gestural contact communication as well, where instead of occurring as just a facial expression, it would co-occur with a gesture of shrugging the shoulders while extending the hands with fingers spread and palms upward. In emergent ISN, the wrinkled nose facial expression was reanalyzed as a grammatical marker of *wh*-questions.

5.1.9   Topic marking

In contact gesturing, ordering is difficult to determine because in many cases there is so much repetition that almost any order appears. There is a tendency, if signing more than a single gesture, to use a patient-action ordering and to leave the agent unexpressed, since the gesturer takes on the role of the agent. Systematic permutations in ordering only become evident in the emergent language. One of the most consistent permutations of ordering involves the appearance of topics at the beginning of the sentence, both moved and base-generated. As noted earlier, serial verb constructions frequently establish an argument in the second conjunct as the topic of the entire serial verb construction.

Gesturers in contact rarely produce more than a single overt argument associated with any action gesture, whereas native ISN signers frequently produce multiple argument verbs. Interestingly, late-learners brought into contact with full forms of ISN rather than just other gesturers in contact, skip the single-valence verb stage in their acquisition. Instead, they produce multiple argument verbs but with one of the arguments in a topic position, leaving the verb with only a single overt argument in configuration with it. Topics are marked with a raising of the eyebrows in ISN. Nonmanual markings such as this are not evident in isolated gesture and contact gesturing. ISN signers transcribing the gestures of language isolates and late-learners in contact identify the lack of facial expression as the single most discriminating feature contrasting the output of gesturers and signers.

5.1.10   Summary

Gestural precursors such as the candidates enumerated above suggest that input plays a significant role in determining the typological features of the final language that a child settles upon. However, while the environment may affect some of the language choices made by a child while acquiring a first language, we have already seen evidence that I-Language is playing an even more influential role. For example, while the ISN auxiliary bears a strong resemblance to the translatory 'x to y' pointing gesture, we see it become restricted in its distribution once reanalyzed and restructured to become a true auxiliary. It now appears pre-verbally in a position within INFL (syntactic inflection), which doesn't follow in any predictable way from the consistent occurrence of its gestural precursor after the action gesture.

The next two sections of the paper address language features that are not attributable to E-Language-based evidence. Section 5.2 discusses emergent language features not present in the input. Section 5.3 addresses strong candidates in contact gesturing and more widely used Nicaraguan gestures for gestural precursors of emergent language constructs that were not recruited during the first-language acquisition process that led to the emergence of ISN.

5.2 Emergent language characteristics not evident in the input

Four features of emergent language are not evident in the non-linguistic gestural input to it. These include the spreading of nonmanual facial expressions over syntactic domains; multiple arguments associated with a single verb; three distinct morphological classes of verbs: plain, person agreeing, and locative agreeing; and a rich set of object classifiers. All of these emergent grammatical constructs have been noted in all primary signed languages studied to date and may well be candidates for modality specific implicational language universals. In the emergence of ISN, they came into existence abruptly. Their existence appears to be driven by innate language expectations rather than existing regularities in the gestural input.

5.2.1 *Nonmanual grammatical facial expressions over syntactic domains*
We saw earlier that the wrinkled-nose facial gesture for 'What's up?' was recruited into ISN and reanalyzed as a *wh*-facial expression. That facial expression is no longer restricted to occurring alone or in combination with a single gesture. In ISN it can spread over the entire sentence. The same is true of the yes/no question face, and the face that marks negation. Despite lack of any such distributional evidence in the contact gesturing of late-learners, ISN signers spread facial expressions over linguistically relevant domains (c-command domains). There is no evidence for c-command in gesture. The *wh*-facial expression can also co-occur with a sentence final *wh*-word; or, in some signers, appear as a quick nose wrinkle at the location of the complementizer position where the *wh*-feature is generated. Nonmanual flashes of this sort are a characteristic of ISN that has not been previously reported in other signed languages.

5.2.2 Multiple arguments associated with a single verb

Gestured utterances tend to be a single unit in length. Gesturers act out events, using their whole bodies in a single gesture, with no separate gestures for the participant roles involved in the event (agent, patient, theme, goal, etc.). Gesturers in contact provide some name signs (define) and pointing gestures in their utterances, but rarely produce more than a single argument for any action gesture. When more than a single participant role is mentioned, there is generally a repetition of an action gesture or a new action gesture for each additional role. This yields chains of action gestures that are later reanalyzed in ISN as serial verbs. But ISN is not limited to producing verb chains or serial verbs to refer to more than a single participant role. ISN has a syntax and therefore can use the configuration of noun phrases relative to a verb (the functional architecture of its clauses) to differentiate multiple arguments holding distinct grammatical relations with respect to a single verb. The syntax of ISN is not evident in its gestural precursors.

5.2.3 Three distinct morphological classes of verbs: Plain, agreeing, locative

We have seen translatory and non-translatory gestures that can be recruited and reanalyzed as spatially agreeing verbs. This suggests that once translatory gestures are reanalyzed as having grammatical agreement, this grammatical mechanism can generalize to include more verbs (like TALK-TO/TELL and LOOK-AT) that select for two arguments. At this point in language emergence we see grammar driving communication, with the systematic use of movement between points in space to mark grammatical relations.

But, once spatial agreement emerges and splits into classes of person agreeing and locative agreeing verb classes, not all action gestures are reanalyzed as spatially agreeing verbs. For example semantic classes of cognition, perception, and emotion verbs remain non-translatory and linked to the signer's body (i.e., body-anchored), even though these verbs take multiple arguments. It is striking that while such classes are not evident in the gestural precursors to signed languages, all documented signed languages to date exhibit these three morphological classes of morphological verb agreement types: agreeing, locative, plain.

Interestingly, the verbs that fall into the classes of plain verbs, person agreeing verbs, or locative agreeing verbs in the emergent sign language are not isomorphic with the gestural characteristics of their precursors. They fall into universally instantiated semantic classes like psychological verbs of cognition, perception, and emotion (plain verbs); verbs of transference of possession or causation (person agreeing verbs) or verbs of displacement (locative agreeing verbs). Membership in a particular morphological class is driven by semantics and not by a gesture that may have been recruited to articulate the verb.

5.2.4   Object classifiers

If there is a typological universal that holds across the world's signed languages, it is the invariable presence of object classifiers. If there is one thing most striking about gesture vs. signing in Nicaragua, it is the noticeable absence of object classifiers in the gestures of deaf isolates. Gesturing is done with the whole body exclusively.

The contact communication between the first cohort of gesturers to come together in schools in Managua[14] in the late seventies/early eighties also lacked object classifiers. On the other hand, the gestural precursors to Size and Shape Specifiers (SASSs) and handling classifiers were plentiful. In fact, gestures involving handling had a broader use in the contact communication (Kegl et al. 1999; Senghas 1995) than in the emergent language, ISN. In the contact communication, gestures involving the manipulating of objects can refer both to events where an explicit agent is involved and to cases where the object moves on its own. In ISN, handling becomes restricted to those instances where an agent actually handles an object, leaving the cases where an object moves on its own to be specified by the use of an object classifier. The emergence of object classifiers allows the emergence of a causative/inchoative distinction and the grammaticization of handling classifiers serving as causative markers.

5.2.5   Recursion

A fifth emergent language characteristic not present in the input is recursion. An extremely productive process of nominalization allows multiple embeddings of nominalized verbs within verbs. And the emergence of syntactic categories also allows for recursion of clauses within other clauses and phrases within other phrases.

5.3   Typological characteristics divergent from the input

Several gestural precursors to linguistic constructs have been suggested in this paper as well as in Morford and Kegl (2000). These *precursors* are, under this analysis, aspects of human behavior available in a child's environment that may be mistaken by the child as offering evidence relevant to the first-language acquisition process. The actual recruitment of these gestural precursors into the emergent language is conditioned by the innate language expectations of the child.

Recruitment of language precursors is also conditioned by constraints placed on the acquisition process by the modality through which language evidence is accessed and through which language is expressed.

It has been argued elsewhere that universals of language and creole characteristics have been determined on the basis of evidence provided by the study of language in the auditory and vocal modalities (Kegl et al. 1999; Kegl & McWhorter 1997). As we bring signed languages to bear as evidence for universal language characteristics, we find that implicational universals sensitive to modality become more and more plausible.

While spoken languages can be isolating (averaging one morpheme per lexical item), primary signed languages have thus far demonstrated a strong preference for agglutinative morphology (many morphemes in a single lexical item). There is processing evidence that lends a possible explanation for this preference. The human/mammalian auditory system is able to discriminate rapid temporal changes between sounds in sequence within a small temporal window (e.g., less than 45 msec), whereas similarly rapid sequences of visual material will be fused and therefore non-discriminable (Poizner & Tallal 1987).

The occlusion of the speech articulators precludes the complex visual spatial analysis that would allow discrimination in speech of a more simultaneous layering of sublexical morphological information within a word. Spatial discrimination in a visual gestural signed language, presenting language data in a larger, visually unoccluded form allows for more information to be displayed and processed in the same temporal space in time but in spatially distinct packages of information. Rather than temporally spacing the production of many isolated morphemes in linear order, signed languages opt for multitiered and simultaneous constellations of spatially discriminable linguistic units.

It follows from this that universal language options favored in a spoken language may not have a similar weighting in a signed language, and vice versa. Thus, we would expect that certain apparent candidates for language-like precursors in the gestural contact communication that young deaf children are drawn to focus on might be rejected because they are not favored as highly by languages in the visual gestural modality. Below we will consider two potential candidates for linguistic recruitment in contact gesturing that have failed to be recruited in the emergent signed language in Nicaragua.

5.3.1   *A noun classifier system*
In contact gesturing, a common new feature is the compounding of a gesture for a thing followed by another gesture that further classifies it. The examples

considered in this section are strongly suggestive of what we would expect to see in a language with a noun classifier system. In fact, they appear to be the most grammar-like constructions to be found in the early contact gesture system in Nicaragua. However, these apparent noun+classifier forms do not always survive the shift from gesture to language. Instead, ISN develops a rich verbal classifier system — a grammar where object classifiers are incorporated into the theme slots of verbs. All primary signed languages documented to date seem to favor verbal classifier systems over noun classifier systems, yet both are typologically plausible in spoken languages.

While gesturers might use the gesture for 'eat/food' for any food or act of eating, gesturers in contact can begin to link two action gestures to make further distinctions. Often foods are characterized by the way they are prepared and compounded with the gesture 'eat/food'. The overall schema for combination is *fruit-prep+eat/food*, where fruit preparation can be how it is cut, squeezed, cleaned, or held for eating. For example, 'rub-on-shirt+eat/food' = apple; 'slice-off-top-with-machete+eat/food' = pineapple; 'slice-vertically-front-and-back+eat/food' = avocado; 'slice-horizontally-along-long-surface+eat/food' = papaya, 'squeeze+eat/food' = orange; etc. (see Morford and Kegl (2000)).

Another set of compounds are a characteristic of an animal (scratching, biting, two long teeth + long ears) or a characteristic means of killing the animal for food (e.g., stab to the neck) followed by a gesture for 'small animal' (an L handshape with the fingertips pointing downward). The overall schema is *characteristic + small-animal*: 'scratch + small-animal' = cat; 'bite + small-animal' = dog; 'two-teeth + long-ears + small-animal' = rabbit; 'stab-to-neck + small-animal' = pig.

The examples above appear in deaf gesturers once they come into contact, but are not yet using language. Such forms appear to be strong precursors of a noun classifier system in the emergent language and if we found them in the context of a full-fledged grammar, there is no doubt they would be analyzed as such. Yet, while compounding does indeed exist in the emergent language, noun classification never became a strong feature of ISN.

In ISN, signs for fruits and vegetables dropped the 'eat/food' component and in some cases developed alternate signs of their own. For example, the sign PINEAPPLE, which became two curved hands with palms facing each other tapping three times, first at the wrists and then the finger tips then moving upward tapping at the wrist again (sculpting in space the ovoid shape of the pineapple and then its cluster of leaves at the top). Perhaps, surprisingly, the compounded animal gestures have been replaced by a variety of signs that no longer involve the 'small-animal' gesture. Thus, a very robust candidate for a noun classification system in ISN fell away when the language emerged.

There were no object classifiers in the initial contact gesturing. The closest thing to an object classifier was the 'small-animal' gesture mentioned above. In some early narratives from the first generation of ISN signers, a few signers used the 'small-animal' gesture in ways that appeared like a classifier filling the theme slot of locative verbs, as in CHICKEN++, Ø+AT-LOC[distributed]i 'There were many chickens scattered around the barnyard'. While we see it sporadically in location verbs of some ISN signers, the SMALL-ANIMAL form is limited in occurrence and never occurs in motion verbs. The SMALL-ANIMAL form has grammaticized instead into a height marker (i.e., 'it was about so high') that moves upward to indicate the relative height of an animal.

Despite the emergence of an extremely robust system of object classifiers that productively fill the theme slot in most ISN verbs, the likely gestural candidate for membership in this class, (CL:L (small animal)), failed to be grammaticized as such. In fact, a later borrowing into ISN of the CL:bentV classifier for SMALL-ANIMAL (possibly from ASL) into ISN also ended up being restricted to indicating postural relations of located animals, but never occupying the theme slot of verbs of motion. Characteristics of the gesture system did in this case have an influence on the emergent language, but not the one we might have expected. The restricted nature of the 'small-animal' gesture (possibly as a classifier of nouns and not verbs) ended up placing restrictions on the range of uses that even a borrowed classifier with the same semantic function could serve.

Morford (1996) has pointed out that homesigners often master in a later-learned sign language those grammatical constructions that seemed to be prefigured in their homesign systems. In this case, it looks like constraints may be able to carry over from homesign (or in this case contact gesturing) as well.

In the early contact gesturing among older vocational students in another school in Managua, there was another set of compound forms that involved a shape compounded with a following action. For example, 'rectangle + turn knob' = television, 'large rectangle + rest head on chin and watch' = movie, 'rectangle + turn knob + dance' = radio, etc. The gesture for *rectangle* is a tracing in space of a rectangle with two index fingers mirroring each other's movements. The first conjunct in these forms are size and shape specifiers (SASSs), which are common in all signed languages. In ASL, for example, a similar SASS combines with a following adjective to form a productive class of nouns: SMALL-RECTANGLE + WHITE = *envelope*; SMALL-RECTANGLE + RED = *brick*, RECTANGLE + ELECTRIC-SPARK[reciprocal] = *microwave oven*, etc (Klima & Bellugi 1979).

While ISN, has indeed developed a rich system of SASSs, the possible precursors of SASS-based forms above have fallen by the wayside. It is possible that the failure of these forms to thrive is tied to the part of speech of the second conjunct. The ISN and ASL forms cited above differ in this regard, with the ISN SASSs followed by action gestures expected to be recruited as verbs, and the ASL forms followed by adjectives. In ISN, there are a parallel set of compound nouns involving classifiers + adjectives that have developed and thrived: HCL: openO(handle small ovoid object) + RED = *tomato*, HCL:1 + th (handle small object) + RED = *bean*, CL:F(flat round object) + RED = *bus token*, etc. The last ASL example above for *microwave oven* would seem to be an exception, but it is also the case that this form seems to be dropping out of ASL as well. Nonetheless, this particular recruitment failure doesn't seem attributable to modality.

5.3.2   *Lip-pointing as a means of deixis*

Another robust feature of Central American gesture that carried over into contact gesturing as well is lip-pointing. Hearing Nicaraguans and many other Latin American cultures consider pointing with the index finger to be rude. Instead the lips are used to point to people and things. These deictic gestures seem the most likely candidates for pronouns and locative adverbs in the emergent signed language. However, ISN did not recruit lip-pointing as a grammatical device. Instead, despite the cultural taboos against pointing, a system of pointing with the index finger arose to assume this role. Today, ISN uses indexing as grammatical determiners, adverbs, and pronouns, all of which are distinguishable via their syntactic distribution. The only place where we see the possible vestige of a lip pointing gesture is in the ISN relative clause, where the relative pronoun involves pointing with the index finger concurrent with a pulling downward of the lower lip typically on the side ipsilateral with the dominant hand. We sometimes see this lip gesture also mirrored on the domain noun in situ in the relative clause (Stickney & Kegl 2002).

Lip-pointing, however, did not disappear. In fact, its use has expanded. In non-deaf Nicaraguan culture lip-pointing is fairly simple in its use. It is used to point to people and things that are present in the environment. The most complex combination of gestures might be a lip point to someone or something followed by a nose wrinkle to ask someone, 'What's up with that/that person?' ISN signers have expanded the use of lip-pointing in gesture.

In ISN, lip-pointing is used as a covert communication device. Signers lip point when they don't want to be *overseen* talking about others in their midst or at times when their hands are otherwise occupied. Lip-pointing combined with lexical facial expressions typical of certain signs has actually developed into a *secret code* used among fluent signers.

Most verbs and many adjectives in ISN have distinct accompanying facial expressions. By using lip-pointing in conjunction with one of these characteristic facial expressions to point pronominally, and moving the lips from an orientation towards one point in space to an orientation towards another as a form of verb agreement, most ISN signers can converse quite well regarding shared knowledge of individuals and things present in their shared environment. The expanded use of lip-pointing has taken a gestural correlate of language and expanded it to serve as a secret/covert code dependent upon language for its interpretation, much like whistle languages or drum languages that have been reported in other cultures. With lip-pointing and facial expression alone, an ISN signer can convey a message like, 'Look at the two of them over there. That one's dress looks hideous on her. What do you think they are talking about? It can't be good. Why don't you go over and see what's up.' A study of lip-pointing and its expanded use appears in Vega, Kegl and Ellis (2000).

Rather than be reanalyzed as part of ISN grammar, lip-pointing has remained in the gestural repertoire of ISN signers. It has been expanded as a gestural secret code that can piggyback on language devices like lexical facial expressions, spatial agreement, and indexing for pronominal and adverbial use to convey information covertly, or at least unobtrusively, between ISN signers.

5.4 Summary

The input to the first-language acquisition process, while ideally involving rich exposure to a full-fledged target language in the child's social environment, need not be a language at all. Humans seem to be predisposed to attend to certain kinds of sounds/gestures (specifically those with prosody and flow) to focus them in on those stimuli (E-Language) that would be most likely to richly support language acquisition and get them to their community's shared target language as easily as possible. But, as the Nicaraguan case demonstrates, while arriving at the existing target language may be most socially advantageous, the first-language acquisition process once engaged seems able to arrive at a viable end-state human language (albeit, a language with a single native user) with very little need for external evidence. Once the first-language acquisition process begins, the language-relevant material in the external environment may function as little more than a repository of raw materials for language output.

6. Conclusion

Gesture and language are distinct systems of human communication. These two systems can coexist within the same individual with little interference, even when they share the same modality. Signs and gestures are easily discriminated by fluent interlocutors in the communication of signed language users. While hearing users of spoken languages can often distinguish gesture from language on the basis of modality alone, there are also vocal gestures that cooccur with spoken language. Interlocutors have no problems distinguishing vocal gestures from spoken language components.

It is rare for an individual without an acquired aphasia or language deprivation to grow up with only one of these communication systems (gesture or language) in their repertoire. Both hearing acquirers of spoken languages and Deaf acquirers of signed languages develop coexisting language and gesture systems. Both systems are core human behaviors — each with its own purpose. Gesture is not proto-language. It remains in the human repertoire as a distinct, non-language communication system.

However, gesture can develop in the absence of language when an individual born with a language-ready brain is born unable to access the language of their home environment. In the case of an auditory language like English, profound deafness can block access to primary language input. Since gesture is not language, exposure to gesture alone will not trigger a child to engage in the first-language acquisition process. It will simply result in learned gesturing, relying upon any innate expectations humans may have that are specific to gesture development.

Prosody and sequencing are characteristics of language that appear to draw the attention of children and even of late-learners to language-relevant material. Single gestures calling up whole shared events, such as those used with and by deaf gesturers in hearing families, are not sequenced into prosodic units. Although shared experience allows a single gesture to serve as a placeholder for language, language isolates are neither challenged by syntactically encoded input nor required to produce grammatically conditioned output. Therefore, it is no surprise that individuals in these environments fail to engage in the first-language acquisition process.

Let us conclude by constructing a possible scenario for how a signed language might be born. The initial premise is that human children are born with language-ready brains.

When deaf language isolates come together, the conditions for communication change. The number of interlocutors increases and the range of topics about which to communicate expands. There are no longer language users in the mix who are able to respond to single gestures and fill in the details. Therefore, it takes greater effort and more explicit detail to convey information.

Despite lacking a formal language, gesturers in contact may share similar conceptual representations of events. Different gesturers may take different perspectives on the same event and in so doing share alternate gestural strategies with their interlocutors. Or a gesturer may try two or more attempts at event encoding to convey information. The likelihood of multiple attempts is increased, since limits on shared knowledge result in reciprocal message sending and verification of understanding. Whatever strategies work get included in the available tools for communication. As use continues, specific gestural strategies become conventionalized. Communication, while not syntactically rule-governed, becomes more sequenced, and groups of gestures aimed at conveying a single event are chunked into groups. This contact gesturing has sequencing and prosody.

While falling far short of being a full language, the features of this more elaborated gesturing may resemble language sufficiently for a child to treat it as language rather than gesture. Its prosody and sequencing are enough to draw the attention of the language-ready child and trigger the first-language acquisition process. With gestures as candidate input to the language acquisition process, the creative first-language acquisition process in which all children engage begins to create language. Expectations fill in the gaps. As the language takes shape, it is checked against plausible language target(s) in the environment. Where the input meets the language expectations of the child, an attempt at matching occurs; where it does not, the language learner's product takes precedence.

The bridge from gesture to language is built when a child with a language-ready brain is exposed to communication that moves beyond the demands of a simple call system. In a call system a single vocalization or gesture can serve as a placeholder or mnemonic for an entire message. When deaf gesturers come into contact and begin to communicate in the absence of language users who can do language for them and in the absence of a large body of shared experience that can contextualize minimal gestures, communication demands increase. The solutions to increased demands generally involve repetition, multiple attempts at conveying a single idea, and feedback when a message is not understood or misunderstood. As haphazard as the solutions may be, they are sufficient to trigger the child exposed to them into first-language acquisition mode. From that point, given sufficient interaction to maintain the process, language takes care of itself.

Notes

* 1. Kegl's work was supported in part by National Science Foundation Grants #SBR-9996330 #SBR-9996297 to the University of Southern Maine. I am indebted to the Nicaraguan Deaf community for their participation in this research as both subjects and as collaborators in the transcription and analysis of the data. Special thanks go to The Nicaraguan National Association of the Deaf (ANSNIC), the Nicaraguan Ministry of Education (Ministerio de Educación; MED), and the Foundation for Children and their Families (Fondo Nicaragüense de la Niñez, FONIF, formerly INSSBI). These data are owned jointly by NSLP, Inc. and ANSNIC.

I am also grateful for input from colleagues in conjunction with presentations of related work at the Annual Meeting of the American Association for the Advancement of Science (AAAS) in San Francisco, The National Endowment for the Humanities invited conference 'Unified Theory of Language Acquisition' in Tulsa, and the mini-colloquium 'The Emergence of New Languages' at the symposium 'Explaining Humans' in San Diego. Finally, I thank three reviewers for useful comments and suggested revisions on this paper.

1. See Mehler et al. (1988) and Jusczyk (1997) for evidence of the role of prosody in spoken language acquisition.

2. Since 1986, we have identified two actual cases of deaf children with deaf parents, and one deaf child with a deaf grandmother. In all three cases, the (grand)parents had only limited gestures. The only child who became fluent in ISN did so from exposure to other deaf ISN signers at school. Another child raised by a hearing mother and deaf father was hard of hearing. His communication with his father was richer than would be expected for an isolate, but he also had significant exposure to Spanish. The deaf grandchild was raised by a hearing relative with only limited contact with her grandmother.

3. Symbols 1, I, B, etc. refer to labels for these handshapes taken from the handshapes used for numerals and letters of the ASL manual alphabet.

4. Pidgin Sign English (PSE) is a form of contact communication in which ASL remains the lexifier language, but grammar is influenced to varying degrees by the grammar of English. For example, SVO ordering will be more strongly favored, figure may precede rather than obligatorily follow ground, locative relations may be expressed by independent prepositions rather than incorporated in to the verb, and some adverbials typically realized in ASL as a single sign (e.g., FLY[+reduplication for durative aspect]) are realized as phrases comprised

of a sequence of isolated words (e.g., *fly for a long time*). For a more detailed discussion of PSE see Reilly and McIntire (1980) and Woodward (1973).

5. Manually coded forms of English are artificial codes for realizing English on the hands. English word order is strictly followed. Many lexical items are borrowed from ASL, some are invented, and others are borrowed from ASL but modified by incorporating letters that correspond to the first letter of the corresponding English word. For example, the same ASL sign that would be used to mean 'group', 'family', 'team', and 'class', would be initialized with the fingerspelled letters *G, F, T,* and *C* in Manually Coded English (MCE). ASL signs borrowed into MCE are uninflected. Verbs no longer agree with their subject and objects, nor do they mark aspect morphologically. Instead, a set of invented endings for -ed, -ing, etc. are suffixed to them. For more information on Manually Coded English see Wilbur (1979, 1989).

6. For more discussion of Signer's Body Position and Projected Body Position see Shepard-Kegl (1985).

7. See Kegl (1985) for an argument that these handling classifiers are causative markers in ASL.

8. It should be noted that ASL allows both null subjects and objects. Therefore the antecedent that a given verb agrees with may be overtly realized elsewhere in the preceding discourse.

9. There are some exceptions. For example, spoken languages do have a number of gestural vocalizations as well.

10. There are also in signed languages various mouth gestures that, while silent, could also be seen as vocal gestures. These are often used for onomatopoeia: pth (e.g., associated with bills emerging from an ATM machine); thup (e.g., associated with a pile of objects disappearing suddenly, as in food that has been scarfed up; etc.)

11. It should be noted here that we are distinguishing gesture alone from the sequences of gestures a language-user might use to communicate without speaking. The latter are driven by knowledge of language and do not reflect characteristics of gesture alone.

12. Use of words in lower case in quotes (e.g., 'eat/food') throughout this paper indicates conventionalized gestures as opposed to signs.

13. Occasionally contact gesturers will take on the role of agent with their bodies and point to one other participant in the event, but not with any regularity.

14. We are referring here to that first group of gesturers brought out of isolation into contact in the context of schools.

The development of complex sentences in British Sign Language*

Gary Morgan and Bencie Woll

1. Introduction

In current research on the acquisition of grammar, one area of exploration has focused on questions concerning the conceptual representation of events and how they come to be mapped onto semantic and grammatical structures (Pinker 1989, 1994; Valian 1991; Tomasello 1992; Theakston, Lieven, Pine & Rowland 2001). The most systematic work in this area has looked at children's acquisition of verbs and argument structures and when children can be said to have at their disposal an abstract set of verb frames. We have been studying aspects of BSL grammar development and the complex mapping between conceptual and grammatical relations. In this chapter we describe young children's early development of linguistic devices including verb agreement in sign space and non-manual markers used to express perspective shift. The main part of the chapter will deal with how these devices are combined and recruited in older children's complex sentences.

The chapter is organised as follows: The first section reviews current work on the mapping between conceptual and linguistic representations, in particular verbs and argument structures in language acquisition; Within this framework we describe aspects of signed languages which employ spatial grammar, as well as non-manual morphology; following this we discuss data on the early use of spatial grammar, non-manual morphology and the mapping of verb agreement relations during the first stages of American Sign Language (ASL) and British Sign Language (BSL) grammar development. This leads to a description of a study of 30 children aged between 3;2 and 12;0 and their different performances in comprehension and production tests of simple and complex sentences. In the final section we discuss the development of abstract patterns for mapping specific conceptual categories onto BSL verb structures.

2.   The mapping problem in language acquisition

A major theme in current language acquisition research centres on the 'mapping problem' (Chiat 2000; Pinker 1989). How do children learn to map conceptual representations of events they understand, recognise and think about, such as 'cause', 'transfer' and 'affect' onto the specific morphosyntactic devices available in their language (Gleitman 1990)? Different psycholinguistic models have focused on different parts of this mapping. Levelt (1989, 1992) and Levelt, Roelofs and Meyer (1999) concentrated on the retrieval and production of linguistic forms from the conceptualiser to the formulator. Jackendoff (1997) and Pinker (1989) have focused on the form of the conceptual representation itself as it reaches the linguistic system and the role of semantic representation in mapping conceptual categories onto linguistic forms (especially verb argument structures).

In our work on the development of BSL we have focused on the interaction between conceptual categorisation, semantic representation and argument structure. Verbs act as the semantic core of a sentence. Conceptual categories and the verbs which encode them involve participants, which carry thematic roles, such as agent, theme, source, goal, patient and experiencer. Constituents combine with the main verb in the form of arguments. With nouns, mostly single concepts are mapped onto names for single objects, whereas the mapping of eventive concepts onto verbs is more varied across languages. Verbs label actions that are often relational, short-lived and carried out by different actors (Tomasello 1992).

Children are faced with the tasks of learning which concepts may be mapped onto which verbs, as well as selecting which arguments are needed and how the arguments combine with the verb. Verbs, however, can take different argument structures e.g. transitive frames obligatorily take objects e.g. *Sue broke the chair* while intransitive frames have no object e.g. *The chair broke.* In English much meaning is derived from the order in which the constituents appear in a sentence. In other languages word endings and inflections can also relate events and arguments.

The child's strategy in developing meaning to form mappings appears to involve generalizations. The stage in development at which argument structures are acquired is the subject of intense debate. Children developing spoken language between ages 2;6 and 4;0 are reported to produce the different verb argument structures of their language with very few errors (Pinker 1989). Evidence for the child's acquisition of a rule comes from data where children occasionally apply systematic argument structures from the adult language to verbs whose meanings and structures do not fit that pattern e.g. *Daddy go me round* (from Bowerman 1982). In one approach to the problem the early correct mapping of concepts onto verbs and their argument structures is explained by theories of *bootstrapping*, where knowledge of semantic or syntactic structure enables the child to break into the relationship between concept and linguistic form (e.g. Gropen, Pinker, Holander & Goldberg 1991; Fisher, Hall, Rakowitz & Gleitman 1994). The semantic bootstrapping approach assumes that the child is endowed with abstract grammatical knowledge such as subject, object, transitive and intransitive verb frames. The child links previously entertained conceptual representations to new verbs in order to assign them appropriate semantic representations.

Another, more conservative, view maintains children's knowledge of verb semantics and argument structure initially develops around individual verbs (Tomasello 1992; Allen 1996) and individual lexical frames (Lieven, Pine & Baldwin 1997). Children do more general learning, based on specific experiences, rather than possessing abstract categories from the start of grammar development. Some time later in development, once several verbs and lexical frames have been learned, the child may begin to apply a productive word formation rule, deriving specific meanings from the use of an abstract verb frame such as intransitive and transitive.

Whatever the theoretical perspective taken, the task for the child is far from straightforward, in part due to the differences in how languages licence different mappings. Across languages the link between form and meaning is mapped out in different ways. In (1)–(3) we compare the surface realisation of verb agreement in English and BSL. In (1) the meaning of *ask* includes two thematic roles, the agent and the patient. These thematic roles are mapped onto the verb's argument structure. Word order and morphological agreement provide the intended interpretation.

(1)   The girl asks the boy

The same meaning in BSL requires a different linguistic mapping. In all signed languages studied so far, morphological agreement is realised by the movement of the verb sign between locations in front of the signer (in sign space). These locations have been previously set up by the signer identifying a noun phrase (NP) with an area of sign space, through a pointing sign (IX). The indexed locations subsequently function as the subject (the agent) and object (the patient) of the proposition. This is shown in an English gloss in (2). The movement of the sign between locations in sign space is shown in Figure 1.[1]

(2)   ___>< __ down & left   __down & right ____down & left
      GIRL$_j$ IX$_j$ BOY$_k$ IX$_k$ $_j$ASK$_k$

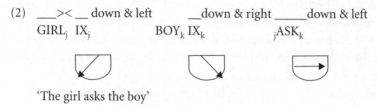

      'The girl asks the boy'

Figure 1. 'The girl asks the boy.'

Another option in BSL for expressing the same meaning is through a perspective shift as in (3). The signer still uses locations in sign space but now a perspective shift marker (#) carried on the face, head or upper body indicates that the verb's meaning is from the perspective of the subject (agent). The movement of the sign between locations acting as syntactic indexes now involves the position of the signer's own body and a third person location in front of the signer. Eyegaze as well as the sign's movement toward this third person location indicates the argument structure. This is shown in Figure 2.

(3)   __>< __right   __ØØ ____right
      BOY$_j$ IX$_j$ GIRL$_k$ # $_k$ASK$_j$

      'The girl asks the boy'

In (3) the signer chooses to articulate a shifted first person perspective; there is no point into sign space (IX) associated with the agent. As in (2), the signer looks at and inflects the verb towards the indexed location of the object of the sentence (on this occasion in front and to her right) but she uses her own body position as the syntactic index of the sentence subject. The perspective shift

Figure 2. 'The girl asks the boy.'

marker is an eye close (ØØ) and a movement of the upper body and head from a referentially neutral to the active referential position of shifted first person. The perspective shift is in alignment with the previous spatial locations assigned to subject and object. This referential option is very frequent in signed languages (Morgan 1998, 1999; Janzen, O'Dea & Shaffer 2001). In contrast it has been described as a marked referential option in some spoken languages (Engberg-Pedersen 1995).

As examples (1)–(3) show, the specific forms available across languages for concept mapping may differ for the same event. BSL uses devices in a spatial grammar, simultaneously combined with linguistic markers carried on the face, head and body. Subjects and objects are assigned spatial locations in sign space. The verb is inflected between locations to express intended meaning. The markers of perspective shift are essential in order to interpret the sentence.

Returning to our interest in the mapping problem, conceptual categories map onto BSL verb semantics and are articulated through radically different grammatical structures to those available in spoken languages. Across different spoken languages representations of events in cognition are also mapped onto words for actions, processes and mental states. The linguistic devices available to speakers to express aspects of events vary across languages. English verbs of motion conflate information about movement and manner of movement ('slither', 'bounce', 'tip-toe' etc) while in Spanish, similar verbs typically conflate movement and path information e.g. *salir* meaning 'to go out', *bajar* meaning 'to go down' and *subir* meaning 'to go up' (Talmy 1985), which in English translation require a verb and a spatial preposition.

In acquiring the correct linguistic subcategorisation for verbs and argument structures in BSL, children must work out how the sets of manual and non-manual devices are integrated. The use of correct argument structures has been reported in children acquiring spoken languages before age 4;0. They achieve this very quickly, although there are some mappings which take longer to master. The structures which appear later in children's language are of interest in our investigation of later BSL grammar. For example, the semantic alternation mapped through the passive voice appears later (Harris 1976), although only in certain syntactic contexts (Pinker, Lebeaux & Frost 1987; Sudhalter & Braine 1985), and not in all languages (e.g. Allen 1996; Pye 1994). This suggests that the pattern of acquisition is related to specific cues in the language being acquired. Equally the use of some constructions e.g. the inalienable possessive (*he washed himself on the foot*) is also a late development (e.g. Carpentier 1969) related to the difficulty of matching concept and linguistic structure.

Before children use full adult forms, they express concepts with the devices available to them in their still developing grammars, as in the *Daddy go me round* example previously mentioned. Through development, children learn more accurate meanings for an increasing number of verbs, forming links between more complex conceptual categories and corresponding language specific linguistic structures. Children's errors in using verbs and argument structures may occur for a number of reasons: they may have semantic misrepresentations for some verbs; or they may have not noticed semantic constraints on certain verbs; or they may have been influenced by discourse pressures in the act of speaking (Pinker 1989).

In our study of BSL development we have compared different types of events and how children encode them in their unfolding grammars with different verbs and argument structure patterns, including the intransitive, transitive, 3-place predicates and passive type structures. We have looked in-depth at a complex sentence type in BSL in which an agent affects a body-part of a patient. This is realised by means of a double-verb structure (termed AB verb here) and two perspective shifts realised by the non-manual markers described previously. Before describing the development of the AB verb in BSL, we review developmental data from children acquiring ASL and BSL, focusing on two main features of signed languages that are involved in the AB verb structure. This background is necessary to unpick the different aspects of grammar involved in the complex sentences we describe later.

3.   BSL development and modality specific language forms

BSL and other signed languages exploit two linguistic devices, which contrast with all spoken languages. We have mentioned both of these previously in examples (2) and (3). The first is linguistically organised sign space. The second feature is the use of non-manual morphology to articulate parts of the linguistic message. In this section we describe one use of sign space for marking person agreement with different verbs. The non-manual features addressed are those used for marking perspective shift.

3.1 Sign Space and verb agreement morphology

There are three basic classes of verbs in BSL depending on what information they carry: plain verbs — which can be modified morphologically to show manner, aspect and the class of direct object; spatial verbs — which can be modified to show manner, aspect and location; and agreement verbs — which can be modified to show manner, aspect, person, number, and class of direct object (Sutton-Spence & Woll 1999).

Plain verbs (e.g. KNOW, THINK, FEEL, BELIEVE, WANT and LIKE) do not move in sign space between locations. Signers use points to themselves and others or to arbitrary syntactic locations assigned to non-present referents to express different relations e.g. IX_3 $LIKE_3$ TEA 'he/she/it likes tea'. Spatial verbs agree with locations, and allow agreement with a wider range of spatial points around the signer's body (e.g. GO-TO, BRING/CARRY, COME-FROM).

Agreement verbs (e.g. ASK, GIVE or EXPLAIN) mark person agreement either through movement between indexed locations in sign space or between the signer and shifted reference points in the context of shifted first person perspective. Verb agreement morphology in BSL operates under semantic restrictions: it is used only with transitive verbs with eventive meaning. The stative transitive verb LIKE cannot be moved between locations j and k in sign space e.g. $*_j LIKE_k$ 'he likes her'.

What marks the use of verbs in transitive frames is that the signer's own body is normally associated with the agentive role in the event being described (see also Kegl 1990; McDonnell 1996 and Padden 1981). The consistent syntactic pattern in the BSL sentence therefore, is that subjects are less overtly marked than objects. When a participant is physically present, the verb is moved between either the signer's own body location and the present partici-pant (e.g. 'you asked me/I asked you') or between an abstract third person indexed location and the present participant (e.g. '3rd person asked you/you asked 3rd person').

Plain verbs can appear in intransitive and transitive syntactic frames e.g. BOY DRINK 'the boy drank' and BOY LIKE TEA 'The boy likes tea'. Agree-ment verbs take part in transitive patterns e.g. BOY_j $_j PUSH_k$ $GIRL_j$ 'the boy pushed the girl', including those with 3-place predicates e.g. BOY$_j$ PRESENT$_k$ $_j$GIVE-PRESENT$_k$ GIRL$_l$ 'The boy gave a present to the girl', and there has been some work claiming a passive construction exists in ASL e.g. BOY$_j$ GOT-HIT$_j$ 'The boy got hit' (Kegl 1990; Janzen et al. 2001).

Research on spoken language acquisition shows that children begin using argument structures at the same age that they are producing multi-word utterances. This is also reported in languages where morphology is quite complex (Bloom 1970; Hirsh-Pasek & Golinkoff 1996; MacWhinney 1985; Slobin 1982). As described earlier there is disagreement on the age at which children can be said to have acquired abstract categories such as intransitive and transitive verb frames.

Research in signing children (mainly on ASL) has shown that young children use sign inflections somewhat later than data reported for spoken language acquisition. This is despite the fact that sign languages have rich morphological systems, suggesting children would begin using inflections relatively earlier compared with the acquisition of languages with fewer morphological markers of person agreement e.g. English. Meier (1981, 1982 and this volume), and Newport and Meier (1985) and Meier (this volume) demonstrated that children initially use word order without inflections. They mark grammatical relations in a sequential way. Thus sign space is not used at the earliest stage of grammatical development. The first uses of sign inflections to indicate arguments begin with reference to present participants. Meier found that children begin to use agreement morphology at about 2;0–2;6, many verbs remain uninflected up till 3;6, and for more complex morphology, acquisition continues beyond 5 years. Thus verb agreement is a later development in sign languages than in spoken languages. There exists the possibility that this pattern of acquisition stems from an added cognitive burden; the surface manifestation of agreement involves a spatial element not present in spoken language morphology.

During development of sign space grammar there are examples of child errors resembling those reported for spoken language acquisition, such as errors of omission (uninflected citation forms) of second and third person arguments. Although less common, errors of commission are also reported (Fischer 1973, Casey 2000), such as overgeneralizing agreement to verbs that do not govern agreement e.g. with plain verbs EAT, DRINK, SLEEP in ASL.

In a longitudinal study of BSL development in a child aged from 1;10 to 3;2 (Morgan, Barrière & Woll 2001a), grammatical use of sign space was initially absent in multi-sign utterances. Between the ages of 1;10 to 2;1, although two and three nouns were being combined, almost all verbs were produced in single sign utterances. From a total of 60 verb tokens recorded during this period, there was one combination of a verb with another sign: PUSH ME (1;10,19). As in previous studies of ASL, all the verbs appeared in citation form i.e. there was no use of sign space for grammatical purposes. Descriptions of actions included verbs classified as intransitive in the adult language: FLY, CRY, SLEEP and JUMP. Transitive verbs included BITE, CLOSE, EAT and THROW. All verbs were produced without an overt subject or object. At this early age the child used himself as the subject, in keeping with the BSL preference for the signer taking the subject location. In the adult language, the inflection of verbs from the signer's own location is normally accompanied by overt subject and object NPs and perspective markers, although verbs can be used without NPs if subject and object can be retrieved from surrounding discourse.

At 2;1 there was one attempt to provide information about the object of an event through the combination of a verb and a holistic (whole-body) gesture. When describing a boy biting a girl, the child signed BITE in the citation form, followed by a depiction of the bitten girl's reaction (a shudder of the body and a startled facial expression). Through this combination the child went some way in mapping out the concept of cause and affect through quasi argument structure. Although the child is using the correct subject, marked through the own body option, the obligatory non-manual marker of shifted perspective and the morphological inflection of the verb sign in sign space are absent.

From 2;2–3;2 the child's use of sign space increased in complexity. Meier states that this is the time period for the first uses of sign space in ASL. At this age the BSL signing child began to introduce verbs into multi-sign combinations. The first uses of sign space with verb inflections were for simple agreement relations without expressed objects. The first object and action concepts to be mapped out through verb inflections in sign space involved visual perception, object transfer and causality. These inflections occurred with only a small number of verbs:

LOOK-AROUND, BOY GIVES-FOOD, BOY PUSH-OUT, LOOK-AT-ME (all at 2;9,21)

Although sign space inflections began to be used at this age, the majority of transitive verbs continued to be produced as citation forms e.g. MAN KICK, DUCK BITE, ICE-CREAM POUR, MUMMY BREAK or in single sign utterances: BREAK, SCRATCH, CUT, SEE. Some intransitives already in the child's lexicon appeared with subject NPs e.g. DRIVE MUMMY, BOY CRY, BIRD FALL; however new verbs entering his vocabulary were signed in one-sign utterances e.g. DRAW, VOMIT, WEE-WEE, SLEEP, BUMP-OWN-HEAD, CYCLE, WAKE-UP. We could see no evidence in the production data of the child's use of frames for the newly acquired transitive or intransitive verbs at this age. Supporting previous literature on young children's use of sign space in ASL, we did not see extensive use of verb agreement morphology, or productive use of transitive and intransitives verb categorisation before 3 years (Meier 1981, 1982; Newport & Meier 1985). There was a consistent preference for producing verb utterances from the perspective of the signer. In comparison with the acquisition of verb morphology, verb agreement and verb categorisation in spoken language, signing children take longer to master these particular linguistic devices. Before using sign space, children express concepts through sequential ordering of signs and points, as well as some combinations of verb signs and holistic gestures (e.g. BITE *get-bitten* at 2;1).

The studies described so far show that, as in the acquisition of spoken languages, children developing signed languages begin with a bias towards simple conceptual-linguistic mappings in their first verbs. Single arguments are used with verbs before two argument structures. Children start with a preference for expressing the subject or agent of the sentence using their own body and objects are left unexpressed. More complex morphology, takes longer to master, related to conceptual and linguistic complexity. During signed language development children may over-generalise verb agreement patterns but this is not seen until the child has a productive rule for use of the verb frame. We need to stress that what we have described up to now is based on sign production data. The *bootstrapping* approaches have proposed that children use existing linguistic knowledge in order to assign correct representations for new verbs that they are hearing i.e. comprehension data.

More complex sentence structures involve the incorporation of verb inflections towards locations for non-present referents in sign space and the use of markers of perspective shift. Compared with the verb agreement data reviewed there is relatively less known about this aspect of children's signing and most data come from the study of ASL. We now turn to the second set of linguistic devices used in complex sentences.

3.2 The acquisition of non-manual features

Specific markers on adult signers' faces serve not only affective functions, as they do in spoken language discourse, but also constitute a part of the grammar.

Sets of non-manual markers signal structures such as negation, interrogation, topicalisation, conditional clauses, and relative clauses. The markers can occur with a single sign or as a scope marker occurring across several signs. Two sets of distinctions are illustrated in the following examples:

a. declarative and interrogative distinction
JOHN LIKE ICECREAM
'John likes ice-cream'

_____brow raise
JOHN LIKE ICECREAM
'Does John like ice-cream?'

b. assertion and negation distinction
_____head nod
JOHN EAT MEAT
'John definitely eats meat'

_____headshake
JOHN EAT MEAT
'John doesn't eat meat'

Acquisition studies have shown that children between the ages of 2;3 and 3;6 acquire the manual and non-manual components of ASL as separate morphemes. Grammatical non-manual markers appear subsequently as bound morphology. The 'hands before faces' order is attested across different grammatical contexts (Anderson & Reilly 1998a). In children's first negations and questions the non-manual markers are either omitted or appear randomly as gestural markers surrounding the signs so that NO, DON'T-WANT or *wh*-question signs are produced without the accompanying head shake and upper face markers, contrasting with the adult language where both channels are combined. When non-manual morphemes first appear, errors are common (see Reilly & Anderson this volume).

A different set of non-manual features is involved in the sentence types analysed in this chapter, where perspective shifts are needed. Perspective shift involves the signer distancing herself as a protagonist from the agentive role in the sentence. It is achieved by marking the shift with a head and/or body movement from a neutral to a referentially active position. The head and eye-gaze move towards a location assigned to the shifted first person. If the verb is transitive, the eye-gaze will be directed towards the end point of the inflection, that is, the object's syntactic position in sign space. Formationally these markers resemble what has been termed 'role-play' (e.g. Loew 1984) but this term is more appropriate for talking about how a character is represented in signed discourse (e.g. the slow movements of an old woman character in a narrative). In contrast, the complexity of this structure when marking perspective shift *within* the sentence is highlighted by its prolonged development in first language acquisition and its indicator of a signer's non-nativeness in second language acquisition (Morgan, Smith, Tsimpli & Woll 2002).

The development of non-manual morphology for marking conditional and relative clauses continues for a protracted period (5–7 years). Reilly and Anderson suggest the 'hands before faces' strategy is comparable with general acquisition strategies, for example the use by some children of lexical items, such as *yesterday* or *last night* to encode past time, before acquiring the past tense marker *-ed* (Brown 1973). Acquisition of non-manual morphology, as with verb agreement, progresses in a gradual analytic manner.

To summarise this section, children developing BSL grammar need to learn the correct mappings between conceptual categories and linguistic forms (including verb inflections in sign space and non-manual features). Children must find and exploit generalised patterns in the combination of verb frames and meanings. The use of general transitive and intransitive verb frames is not seen across the lexicon until after 3 years (Morgan et al. 2001a; Newport & Meier 1985), with younger children using sign order to express syntactic relations and omitting non-manual features in the development of verb inflection.

We now turn to the main emphasis of this chapter, the development of complex sentences. We focus on children's use of verb frames in an elicitation task where children had to describe events which require verb constructions of differing complexity. In this study (Morgan, Herman & Woll 2001b) we have previously argued that children between 3 and 6 years use generalised knowledge of verb frames in order to describe events. The specific linguistic structures investigated in this study revolved around the use of both verb inflections in sign space and non-manual markers of perspective shift. Before presenting the child data, some linguistic background will be described.

4.   AB verb constructions

The events that elicit AB verbs are depictions of actions performed by an individual on a specified body part of another individual. Examples can be translated into English as 'the boy taps the girl on the shoulder', 'the girl combs the boy's hair' or 'the boy puts a hat on the snowman's head'. Although these examples are syntactically different from each other in English, they map onto a single BSL structure, which we have termed an AB verb. Semantic information is expressed across both the manual and non-manual channels. The AB verb stem is modified in order to carry the extra semantic information of the affected patient and specifies the affected body-part in its inflection.

These 2-participant events require the signer to locate two referents in sign-space through spatial indexing, but the main verb is inflected from two shifting perspectives. The first perspective specifies an agent and action pair e.g. 'boy taps', 'girl combs', 'boy puts a hat'; the second specifies the action, the experiencer, and the body-part affected e.g. 'tap girl's shoulder', 'comb boy's hair', 'put hat on snowman's head'. An example is given in (4).

(4) $\underline{\qquad >< \qquad}$ $\quad >> \quad$ $\emptyset\emptyset$ $<<$ $\underline{\qquad\qquad}$
 $\text{GIRL}_j \; \text{BOY}_k \text{PERSON-LEFT}_k \; _j\text{HIT}_k$ $\qquad _j\text{GET-HIT-IN-FACE}_k$

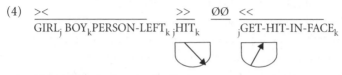

'the girl hit the boy in the face'

In (4) there are no index points; instead the signer uses a proform for 'person' at the same time as she signs BOY. The person proform is located on the left side of sign space. The signer inflects the verb HIT between the syntactic location of the subject and that of the object. The affected body-part can also be specified through a lexical sign such as FACE, HEAD or SHOULDER after the verb sign HIT, POUR-WATER, or TAP, although adult native BSL signers use an incorporated body part in the verb stem rather than a separate lexical sign. This two-part verb construction has been described previously in other signed languages to encode perspective shifts (e.g. ASL — Bellugi, Lillo-Martin, O'Grady & van Hoek 1990a; Kegl 1990; Metzger 1995; Swedish Sign Language — Ahlgren & Bergman 1994; Danish Sign Language — Enberg-Pedersen 1995; Italian Sign Language — Pizzuto, Giuranna & Gambino 1990).

The non-manual marker of perspective shift in this construction is produced twice, in contrast to the normal agreement verb pattern where the perspective marker only indicates the subject's point of view. The three arguments encoded by the AB verb cannot be mapped through a single verb, and in the AB construction, the extra argument of the affected body part is mapped onto the B-part of the verb. The use of AB verb constructions involves an exchange of reference locations in sign-space and therefore brings a number of specific requirements to processing. Children find the AB verb construction difficult to produce, which we argue is related to how the event's meaning is mapped onto the construction's semantic categorisation.

We have adopted Kegl's (1990) analysis of ASL passives and AB verbs in terms of 'control hierarchy' shifts. We see the interface between the semantic and argument structure as the source of its complexity. In Kegl (1990) the referent that is co-indexed with the signer's own body is said to be highest in a semantic focus hierarchy but when the signer shifts to show the affected body part, this leads to a shift in the hierarchy. The verb specifies an active meaning in the A-part e.g. 'he paints her'. The presence of an agent in this first part of the construction is a typical transitive verb inflection. In the second part of the construction the agent is still understood to be carrying out the action but with much weaker focus compared with the now promoted patient. The movement of the B-verb is associated with the agent, even though it has been demoted in the control hierarchy, whereas the patient is in a prominent focus position, as the main perspective. The B-part of the verb moves from a location previously associated with the agent towards the signer's own body.

Mapping of the AB verb requires the signer to use the verb's movement in two ways in order to describe two perspectives within the same situation. Importantly the agreement relations do not change although the perspective does. Thus the AB verb represents a marked structure compared to the more typical agent perspective verbs in BSL.

4.1 Children's use of AB verbs

In studies of sign language acquisition where AB verbs were elicited, young children produce interesting morphological innovations, similar to those made by children acquiring spoken languages with complex verb morphology. In Bellugi et al. (1990a), children acquiring ASL were asked to describe a picture showing a boy painting a girl's face. One child (younger than 5;0) signed PAINT-FACE on both sides of her own face to encode the shift between two perspectives. This is ungrammatical in adult ASL.

In studies of BSL acquisition we first became interested in this construction because of a set of regular errors in the use of this form in children before 6 years (Morgan 1996, 1998). Before this age children produced fragmented utterances where only one part of the AB verb is produced. The error is shown in (5) from a child aged 5;6 and (6) from a child aged 5;7. The children signed the B-part of the AB verb with direct object agreement, but without the A-part of the verb. This use of an inflection onto the signer's own body without previous mention of an external agent would in adult signing be interpreted as a reflexive i.e. 'the boy painted himself'. The obligatory non-manual markers were also absent.

(5) ＿ØØ ＿＿＿＿＿＿＿＿＿＿＿＿＿＿＿＿＿＿＿neutral
GIRL_j PAINT-FACE_j BOY_k PAINT-FACE_k

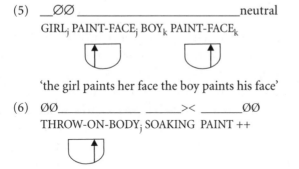

'the girl paints her face the boy paints his face'

(6) ØØ＿＿＿＿＿＿＿ ＿＿＿＿>< ＿＿＿＿ØØ
THROW-ON-BODY_j SOAKING PAINT ++

'throws water on herself, soaking wet then paints and paints'

These two examples revealed that the children, by using the B-part of the construction, were attempting to encode the perspective shift. Aspects of the event got encoded but they had not yet mastered the full linguistic realisation of the conceptual structure. Part of the difficulty involved the child's combination of both the manual and non-manual channels. The children were using the eye-close marker but because eye-gaze was neutral or at the addressee (><)and the A part of the verb was missing, reference is ambiguous. Puzzled by this error we investigated this type of event description in a larger group. In Morgan et al. (2001b) we analysed comprehension and production data from 30 native signing children. Subjects were split into 3 age groups, made up of ten children each: 3;0–5;11, 6;0–8;11 and 9;0–12;0. As control data, 12 adult deaf native signers carried out the same tests. We investigated both comprehension and production of these sentence types.

In the sentence comprehension task each child watched a series of short signed sentences on video and was asked to select the corresponding picture from a choice of four alternatives in front of them. The sentences we focus on here are the two sentences with an AB verb. The children were asked to describe 40 pictures in the sentence production task.

P1) shows an adult handing a book to a child
P2) depicts two children playing in the bath; an older boy washes a younger boy's face.

The first sentence (P1) requires a 3-place predicate structure with a transitive verb inflection. The second event (P2) requires an AB verb. Based on the semantic complexity of the perspective shift encoded by the AB verb it was expected that children would perform better on the P1 sentence than the P2.

5.   Results

In the comprehension of the AB verb the 12 adult signer controls all selected the correct target picture from four alternatives. In production they all produced AB verbs with accompanying non-manual markers of perspective shift. This confirmed that these events are mapped consistently onto AB verbs in the adult grammar. The adults marked the contrast between perspectives by an eye-gaze movement along the horizontal plane (e.g. right to left), and an eye close at the moment of shift. The eye close marks the perspective shift while the eye gaze direction coupled with the verb inflection indicates the argument structure. The non manual markers are produced in agreement with the inflections of the verb in sign space.

Four of the youngest children correctly identified the AB verb's meaning in the comprehension test, contrasting with their failure to use the AB verb correctly in the production test. Success in the comprehension task increased with age across the groups. This is shown for both sentences in Table 1.

Table 1. AB verb correct comprehension scores for two sentences

Age group	N	Sentence 1 POUR-WATER-ON-HEAD	Sentence 2 HIT-FACE
3;2–5;11	10	40%	40%
6;0–8;11	10	60%	80%
9;0–12;0	10	90%	90%

When comparing their correct comprehension with their errorful productions, there was an asynchrony, suggesting that there are more demands made in mapping from the conceptual system to the linguistic, than in the other direction. As the figures in Table 2 show, although the children were able to conceptualise the event, mapping it onto BSL linguistic devices was beyond the youngest children. The specific production error identified in previous studies (Morgan 1996, 1998) was confirmed in this age group with the majority of the youngest children (9/10) using only the B-part of the AB verb construction in a transitive verb frame (indicated as sole B-part).

Table 2. AB verb correct production scores and patterns of sentence production types

Age group	N	Sole A-part	Sole B-part	A-part with separate lexical item	Full AB verb
3;2–5;11	10	10%	90%	0%	0%
6;0–8;11	10	10%	40%	10%	40%
9;0–12;0	10	10%	10%	10%	70%

An example is shown in (7) from a child aged (3;6):

(7) _____neutral

WASH-FACE$_j$

'washes face'

Interestingly the one child who did not use the B-part of the AB verb was the youngest child in the sample (3;2). He correctly produced the P1 sentence, but in the P2 task he produced only the A-part of the verb as in (8),

(8) $_j$WASH

'washes'

Although the verb was inflected towards an object location, the subject and affected body part were both under-specified. This should be viewed in the context of the earlier mention of an attempt to describe a perspective shift by means of combining an uninflected verb with a holistic gesture, from the study of a child aged 2;1 (Morgan et al. 2001a). We do not know if the children in this study also used these sign/holistic gesture combinations but the error in (8) is somewhat more advanced, as the verb is inflected. The use of the B-part of the verb on its own by the other children is again more advanced, as more parts of the event are mapped out in the B-part inflection than in the A-part. We therefore are proposing a continuum from use of the sign/holistic gesture, to use of the A-part of the verb on its own, and then to the use of the B-part.

The bias towards producing the B-part of the AB verb inflection in the P2 sentence also appeared in the slightly older children (ages 6;0–8;11), but in a smaller percentage. Although 40% (4/10) correctly produced the AB verb inflection there was a marked absence of non-manual markers of perspective shift, as in (9).

(9) _____neutral

ⱼWASHₖ   ⱼGET-FACE-WASHEDₖ

'he washes him on the face'

What we see is that the manual part of the construction is being mastered before the non-manual features. However these same markers, carried on the non-manual articulators, are used correctly in other sentence types. One child who produced the B-part of the AB verb was questioned by the tester who had interpreted the child's utterance as a reflexive, 'he washes himself on the face'. The child indicated that she definitely did not intend this meaning, but was still unable to modify her response. This reluctance to modify an incorrect response after probing by the adult, coupled with data from the comprehension test where the AB verb was identified significantly earlier than in the production task, suggests that the developmental problem lies not in understanding the event but in getting the complete conceptual-linguistic mapping.

The AB verb does not appear suddenly in the children's linguistic repertoire. There were other attempts at encoding the event in the 6–8;11 age group. One child attempted to encode the location of the affected body part by mapping out the face location through the A-part of the verb followed by the separate lexical sign FACE, rather than through an incorporated locative, as in (10). This sequential ordering of thematic roles is successful although un-adult-like and ungrammatical.

(10)   ⱼWASHₖ   FACE

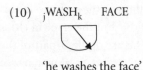

'he washes the face'

In group 3 (ages 9;0–12;0), 70% (7/10) of children correctly produced AB verbs. While the AB verb was used, the use of non-manual markers still appeared un-adult-like. Eye-closes to mark the perspective shift were absent in some children's productions. In others, the subtle changes in head and eye-gaze orientation observed in adult productions were only partially seen. For example, the AB verb was produced correctly but non-manual features appeared only on the B-part of the verb.

The gradual acquisition of the AB verb's manual and non-manual morphology, with one child in the oldest age group still producing the B-part of the verb, is strong evidence for the complexity of the mapping of this structure in BSL. Later aspects of BSL grammar involve combining different devices in this mapping process. In the 6;0–8;11 age group the children use inflections to locations in sign space to map out the argument structure, with the eye-gaze feature the last to develop. This is particularly interesting as we have seen that in studies of early signing (Morgan et al. 2001a) children are capable of using holistic gestures to characterise features of a referent. However, this appears to have no linguistic structure and when these features begin to be incorporated into the linguistic system they are incorrectly produced.

6. Discussion

The findings of the complex sentence experiment suggest that the 3-place-predicate structure which encodes a single perspective e.g. MOTHER GIVE-BOOK CHILD appears in children's signing before the AB verb, as was predicted. The consistent error in using the B-part of the AB verb in children confirms that the mapping problem is solved to some extent by children over-generalising what they already know about the BSL verb. Before 3 years old there is little evidence for productive knowledge of how sign space is used with different verb frames. Development of verbs and argument structures is gradual and learned separately for individual verbs. While children as young as 3 years old correctly comprehend AB verbs, the appropriate AB verb argument combinations are a late development in the same children's production.

In the first stage of development of the AB verb there are occasional examples of use of the A-part of the verb. Some of the children produce a serial ordering of thematic relations, a similar finding to those reported by Meier (1982) and Newport and Meier (1985). In producing the construction in this way, processing demands are presumably reduced, although we do not have an empirical model of sign production with which to explain why sequential ordering is preferred to the combination of manual and non-manual features.[2]

Following this there is a systematic pattern of argument omission in production. Children attempt to map the three thematic roles contained in the event (agent, patient and affected body part) onto a transitive verb frame. This strategy allows the core event of agent demotion to be expressed rather than distributing the full event structure across both parts of the AB verb. We have argued that at this age (around 3;6) and not before, children's errors suggest they are applying productive knowledge of verb frames and argument structure.

At the same time children are showing that they can decode the AB verb correctly. It is possible that the comprehension task provides the opportunity for the child to use alternative but related linguistic representations of the event in order to arrive at the target response. For example, the sentence with the AB verb may be represented as two predicates. This would allow the child to interpret the linguistic message without processing the complex AB verb argument structure. If there were different demands in sign comprehension, children would be able to make the link between form and meaning through more than one route. An empirical model of sign processing will need to reflect developmental data such as these.

In the beginning of the chapter we attempted to articulate issues around the mapping problem in language acquisition. Much of children's use of verbs and argument structures is related to their development of semantic categorisations for conceptual knowledge. Our limited data from one child up to 3 years points to a gradual unfolding of verb semantics and argument structures (Tomasello 1992; Allen 1996), although we cannot say whether the bootstrapping strategies proposed by Pinker et al. (1991) or Fisher et al. (1994) are available.[3] Our work at the level of complex sentences in BSL and the development of the AB verb has been guided by what Kegl (1990) and Janzen, et al. (2001) term the encoding of a semantic re-alignment. When choosing the AB verb to describe the experimental stimuli in BSL, there is a required shift from agent to patient's perspective, with the hierarchical pattern of agents represented on the signer's own body needing to be temporarily modified. The consistent preference for using the B-part of the verb construction suggests that before children have mapped this shift onto the AB verb, they use a strategy of representing only one perspective, as the AB verb comes from a verb class that marks grammatical relations in this way. Thus they map the specific conceptual representation of the agent affecting the patient's body part onto the B-part of the AB verb. In this way they preserve the consistency of showing salient referents on their own body, but in doing so produce ungrammatical structures.

The gradual development of the AB verb points to a continuum from the early use of sign/holistic gestures, to the use of the sole A-part of the verb and then the B-part generalisation. If we are correct in making this proposal, we hope to highlight the creative nature of BSL acquisition. In mapping different events, children have to combine sets of manual and non-manual features. It has been shown in other domains of signed language grammar that children have difficulty in combining these two channels, which prolongs acquisition. During this process children analyse the construction piecemeal, producing parts of the AB verb and/or parts of the non-manual morphology.

In our case study of early BSL development (Morgan, et al., 2001a) we found no evidence for the child's exploitation of an abstract set of verb frames before 3;2. The child appeared to build argument structure afresh with each new verb and these verbs were uniquely tied to their communicative function. At the age at which our study of AB verb development begins (by 3;6) we see more evidence for the use of rules. The developmental patterns observed in BSL acquisition therefore support current notions that the mapping between conceptualisation and linguistic form is solved to some extent by the child looking for general abstract patterns.

Notes

* Aspects of this chapter were presented at the VIIIth International Congress for the Study of Child Language, July 1999, Donostia, The Basque Country and the Child Language Seminar, University of Hertfordshire, UK, July 2001. We are grateful to Rosalind Herman and Isabelle Barrière. We thank the children and adults who gave up their time to participate in the studies reported. We are also indebted to Sallie Holmes for collecting the data on the BSL assessment project (Herman, Holmes and Woll, 1999) as well as to Graham Welton and Sami Salo for help in coding and transcription.

1. Signed sentences that appear in the text follow standard notation conventions. Signs are represented by UPPER-CASE English glosses. Non-linguistic gestures are represented by lower-case *italicised* English glosses. When a sign is inflected morphologically and more than one English word is required, this is shown by hyphenated glosses e.g. YOU-PUSH-ME. When no hyphenation occurs it is because the signs were produced as citation forms e.g. YOU PUSH ME. Repetition of signs is marked by '+'. 'IX' is a pointing sign and subscripts indicate arguments. Semi circles represent the sign space with the flat edge nearest to the signer's perspective. Arrows indicate the direction of the agreement verb's movement. Above the glosses, eye-gaze markers such as closes (ØØ), direction (left/right or neutral space) and gaze towards the addressee (><) are indicated by a vertical line across the affected segment.

2. A sign production model is a necessary next step in describing how the mapping problem in language acquisition applies to signing children. One piece of this puzzle comes from research into working memory for signs which has suggested that the sign phonological loop may be structurally different than in spoken language (Wilson & Emmorey 1997).

3. One way of assessing 'bootstrapping' theories with signing children would be to carry out similar experimental studies on their comprehension and attribution of meaning to nonsense signs in different contexts. Lillo-Martin (1988) has carried out nonsense sign studies but focused on morphological productivity.

Afterword

A view from research
on spoken language development

Elena V. M. Lieven

1. Introduction[1]

I will concentrate here on questions of how research on the acquisition of a sign language as a first language could be informed by recent research on the development of spoken first languages and vice versa. In what follows, I will largely confine myself to language development in typical populations, i.e. language development in children learning one (or two) languages in an environment to which they have full access. Most of the articles in this book deal with children learning a sign language in these circumstances. However, as pointed out in the Introduction and in Marschark (this volume) and as is apparent from many of the other chapters, this is very different from the circumstances in which most children learn sign language. Unless children grow up in families with at least one highly skilled (and preferably first-language signer) they will be exposed to sign language late and, quite probably, to a non-native version. Of course this can raise extremely interesting research questions, of which the question of the status of home sign (Goldin-Meadow & Mylander 1990) and the invention of a sign system (Kegl this volume) are potentially of great importance. But, clearly, comparisons between later learners of a sign language and children learning a spoken language as their first language in a speaking-hearing environment will be much more problematic. It also means that many of the questions I raise will have to await the time when a far larger proportion of deaf children, or the hearing children of signing parents, grow up with a sign language as their naturally acquired first language.

2.   Laying the foundations for language

Thanks to the pioneering studies of the late Peter Juszcyk and his colleagues, we know a considerable amount about developing speech perception in the first 18 months of life. Hearing babies in hearing-speaking environments gradually become increasingly sensitive to, and discriminating of, the distinctions made in the ambient language. Towards the end of the first year of life, they can identify words that they have heard when they are embedded in spoken texts (Juszcyk 1997b) and identify underlying distributional patterns (Saffran, Aslin & Newport 1996; Gomez & Gerken 1999; Marcus, Vijayan, Bandi Rao & Vishton 1999).

It would be difficult to repeat this range of experiments on babies learning sign languages since very large numbers of participants are required (babies are notoriously problematic to test!). But there may be some specific questions that arise from the differences in modality which would be interesting to explore. Major developments in speed of processing and connecting sounds to meaning take place between 0;9 and 1;10 (Fernald, Pinto, Swingley, Weinberg & McRoberts 1998). Fernald et al. show that the time course for turning to look at a named object changes between 0;9 and 1;10. At 0;9 months babies do not turn to the named object until a few milliseconds after the word has ended, at 1;3 they turn at the end of the word. By 1;10 they are turning as soon as they hear the discriminating vowel (for instance the 'a' in 'baby' contrasted with the 'a' in 'ball'). Since deaf mothers with children of this age seem to train their children to attend initially to the signed utterance and then look for the referent (Kyle & Ackerman 1990), this might mean that speed to process within-sign, co-articulation develops somewhat later. However attention to how the child processes these signs and where 'processing compression' occurs in development could be both interesting and important for understanding the problems that later signers may have in becoming fluent.

There is also potential here for exploring the role of morphology in situating the sign. For instance, between 1;0 and 2;0, children become increasingly sensitive to the mappings between the structure of what they hear and what they see as shown in preferential looking tasks (Hirsch-Pasek & Golinkoff 1996) and it might be possible to adapt this methodology to explore the early sensitivities of children learning a sign language to the relationships between sign-meaning mappings.

3.   The language environment

3.1 Dyadic interaction

Marschark (this volume) puts great emphasis on dyadic interaction for the acquisition of sign language and this accords with a similar emphasis by many researchers of spoken child language. However there are real issues about the kind of environment that is required for language to develop normally. One does not have to be a nativist, with a tendency to minimise the role of ambient speech to triggering or to the provision of exemplars, to recognise that many children the world over may grow up in much less dyadic environments than those we usually study (Lieven 1994). It remains an open question whether all these children are actually getting a considerable amount of one-on-one interaction, but in private contexts usually unobserved by the researcher, and that this provides the basis of their language learning (de Leon 2000). The alternative is that some children's language learning is based more on observational skills and polyadic interaction. We know almost nothing about whether or how a child might learn a language through observation and this is potentially highly relevant to children who may be learning a sign language in nursery or school settings.

3.2 Attention to the ambient language

Even when children are not being directly addressed, the assumption has been that they must be paying attention to the meaning of what is going on if the ambient speech is to play a role in their language learning. However the role of visual attention is different for signers and speakers. Sign language learners must attend to the signer to get linguistic information and have to learn to shift visual attention from the signer to the objects referred to in the environment (Harris 2000). They may learn to pay attention to cues in the visual peripherary but the attentional structure and organisation of gaze is likely to differ considerably from that of overhearing spoken language. (Harris & Mohay 1997). The fact that in a signing environment, sign-meaning mappings involve visual attention to both signal and referent may make this more accessible to study than is the relationship between what the child hears and how s/he understands its reference.

3.3 How much language do children need to see/hear?

There is also the question of how much language children need to hear or have directed to them to ensure fluent native acquisition. We do not have estimates of this for children in signing environments. Certainly children in the spoken language environments usually studied are hearing very large numbers of utterances. In the 'dense databases' collected in our Leipzig and Manchester labs, where we record for 5 hours per week over a year, we have collected between 8,000 and 13,000 adult utterances to each child in 20 hours of recording per month. Corpora of this size contain a considerable degree of latent structure that is recoverable by a variety of computational analyses. Thus Redington and Chater (1997) performed a cluster analysis on words in child directed speech (CDS) on the CHILDES database and showed that the words clustered into categories very close to the semantic and syntactic categories of English grammar. In the Brent and Siskind study (2001) words which occurred alone in adult CDS were successfully used to segment the same corpus. And Elman's work (e.g.1990) shows that under certain circumstances, often with artificial languages, machines can 'deal with' distance dependencies such as agreement and recursion. Of course whether these studies are at all similar to the ways in which the child analyses what s/he hears is the subject of much debate. However there also needs to be much more discussion of how reductions in the size of an input corpus or the relative diversity of the utterance structures in it might affect recoverability of underlying patterns and it is here that comparative studies of children learning sign language might be very informative.

Clearly these are also important issues for those deaf children who are not being raised in a native sign language environment but who are placed early in sign language settings such as dedicated nurseries. However, the study of differing aspects of the environment and how they relate to the children's sign language development is not only of major practical importance but also has the potential to inform the debate about the precise roles of the language environment in all children's language learning.

4. Language typology and the crosslinguistic study of language acquisition

That sign languages *are* languages should no longer be in any doubt, though the chapters by Meier and Kegl show that there is still contention about the relationship between non-linguistic gesturing and the linguistic status of aspects of sign languages. However, I think there are real issues about what kind of languages sign languages are, typologically speaking. While it has always been recognised that they differ extensively from the languages of the Indo-European, hearing-speaking communities in which they have mainly been studied, comparisons made have usually been with those languages, and with the spoken language development of children learning those languages. But if Hoiting and Slobin (this volume) are right and sign languages are really more like poly-synthetic languages, with serial verbs (as Kegl's analysis also shows), then comparisons with children learning English, French or Spanish will only get us so far. Comparisons should also be made with children learning languages with similarly complex morphology, such as languages with polycomponential utterances (Fortescue & Olson 1992; Allen 1996). Unfortunately we know nothing like as much about how children learn these languages as we do about how children learn English.

There are many difficulties in comparing languages with complex morphology like sign languages to isolating languages like English, of which I shall raise two. First there is the question of measuring MLU. The less advanced learners are, the more reasonable it probably is to compare MLUs of speaking and signing children (e.g. as in Schick, this volume) but comparisons beyond this point are going to run into trouble, as they do in comparisons between children learning very typologically different spoken languages. Languages with null subjects, high degrees of permissible ellipsis and/or high levels of portmanteau morphology present great difficulties in the measurement of MLU and I suspect this is true for sign languages as well. In part this might account for the low MLU of 3.07 signs for the Child Directed Speech in van den Bogaerde and Baker's findings (this volume). If a language has a great deal of complex morphology then the difference between a MLU counted in words or signs and one counted in morphemes will be much greater than it will be for English or Dutch.

A second example of the problems of crosslinguistic comparisons concerns lexical categories. Sign languages have highly productive systems for creating denominal verbs and deverbal nouns — although describing it like this pre-judges the issue of whether sign-meaning correspondences are stored as separate noun and verb categories or whether these come into being as the speaker places the sign in a syntactic context. Thus signs can mean LION/ROAR or EAT/FOOD depending on their contexts and the morphology attached to them. Croft (2001) argues that while the communicative acts of reference and predication are universal and correlated with the categories of noun and verb, languages can differ considerably in where the boundaries between these categories are placed. Following on from this, comparisons of the relative proportions of nouns and verbs acquired by children learning different languages will be very problematic. In this context, the emphasis that most sign language researchers place on the importance of the morphology which situates the meaning of a sign in an utterance makes a great deal of sense.

In considering this problem of crosslinguistic comparisons, I found Hoiting and Slobin's (this volume) identification of 'meaning cores' and their associated morphology helped clarify many aspects of how sign languages work. It also has the potential to form the basis of wider crosslinguistic comparisons both between spoken languages and between signed and spoken languages. Hoiting and Slobin's chapter also demonstrates clearly that decisions about how to transcribe are central to these comparisons and, more generally, to the kinds of research questions that can be asked. This is apparent throughout this volume as we encounter a range of different transcription systems.

5.   Early utterances: Productivity, sampling and the adult models

A number of authors in this volume suggest that aspects of morphology and syntax come in 'late' in the L-1 acquisition of sign language. Thus Meier states that children do not show mastery of the manual signs for Subject and Object agreement in ASL until about 3;0. Morgan and Woll report similar findings for BSL and Pizzuto's evidence also suggests that the inflection of inflectable nouns and verbs for children learning LIS is a relatively late development. It is, however, difficult to assess the significance of this lateness without careful consideration of whether and how productivity is being measured. Thus the presence of a form in the language of a child obviously does not mean that the child is productively able to use that form. Equally if a form is absent, this may not be significant if it is not present in the input — the child will not learn it if it is not there.

5.1 Productivity

Many markers of syntactic relations are often first used in very limited ways by children. Thus an agreement marker may be restricted to a small number of verbs or to a particular person (e.g. 3rd person: Rubino & Pine 1998) or children may treat one verb or group of verbs differently from another (de

Villiers 1985; Tomasello 1992; Pine, Lieven & Rowland 1998). In these cases it can be difficult to decide whether the child is operating with a syntax of limited scope, mainly generated by particular lexical items, or whether, despite the restricted nature of the child's productions, these are the product of a more general and abstract grammar. The most extreme version of this latter view would be that the abstractness of the grammar is there from the beginning and the child 'simply' has to work out how it translates into the language s/he is hearing. In this view, the limited nature of production arises from (a) performance limitations (b) the nature of conversations between adults and small children (e.g. what they want to talk about) (c) different rates of learning the forms of the language and (d) the limitations of sampling. The last two points are related since, in many cases, there are very high correlations between the order of emergence of particular markers in the child's speech and their frequency of use in the adult speech to them (Theakston et al. n.d., Rowland & Pine 2000). Since the adults are certainly operating with a full grammar, it is possible that a skewed order of emergence could arise from sampling.

5.2 The limitations of sampling

In the dense data base studies that I and my colleagues are currently undertaking in Leipzig and Manchester, we are collecting an estimated 7–10% of what the children say and hear and a further set of studies is underway which is collecting even denser data. By contrast, we estimate that the sampling intervals typical of most studies (about 1 hour every 3 weeks) sample roughly 1–2% of everything the child hears. Much denser data may help us to work out the extent to which the seemingly limited productivity that has been observed in early child language is an outcome of limited sampling. It may be that this will differ for different aspects of language and/or for different languages. Thus Behrens (2001) in a study of the development of plural marking in German, shows that a much denser level of sampling will pick up overgeneralisation errors that remain largely unattested in less rich data. On the other hand, a pilot study of an English child using dense data shows the same form of highly lexically-specific nature of children's early multiword speech that has been frequently observed in other studies (Braine 1976; Tomasello 1992; Lieven, Pine & Baldwin 1997).

5.3 The distribution of forms in the input

In assessing the implications of the presence or absence of forms in the child's language, it is obviously very important to analyse the language that they see or hear. Pizzuto, van den Bogaerde and Baker, and Schick (all in this volume) raise this issue. Pizzuto's data shows that the inflection of inflectable nouns and verbs in LIS is late relative to studies of inflectional acquisition in some spoken languages and that children use substantial numbers of uninflectable nouns. However she also points out that this is true for the adults who are interacting with the child (and amounts to 33% of their nouns and verbs). Van den Bogaerde and Baker also find very little inflection of optionally inflectable verbs in the SLN utterances of adults to their children which may well account for the relatively late development of optional inflection in the children's language.

The contexts of adult-child interaction mean that much of the language that children actually hear is fairly repetitive in terms of content, structure and vocabulary. This may both assist children in learning the language and it may also in part account for patterns of development that we see. Thus in a study of 12 English-speaking mothers and their children, we have shown that the adult speech is quite lexically specific (45% of the mothers' utterances started with just one of 17 words and 52 lexically-specific phrases accounted for 50% of the mothers' utterances (Cameron-Faulkner, Lieven & Tomasello n.d.). We suggest that this may in part account for the very lexically specific nature of English-speaking children's early multiword speech that I mentioned earlier. In addition, despite the fact that the adults involved are speaking English, a proto-typical SVO language, utterances in SVO word order are in the minority. The children hear relatively larger number of copulas, questions and imperatives. The implication from the child's point of view is that SVO word order may be initially less salient than other, more easily accessible and surface, aspects of the language and this will be reflected in the types of productivity that the children show in their utterances.

A similar point is made by Schick (this volume), who is interested in two-year-old children's use of word order to mark grammatical relations in ASL. She finds that children produce very few explicit agent arguments and many more explicit theme arguments. However these do not show a consistent word order across verbs. Although there may be positional tendencies for some verbs, there are also sometimes inconsistencies for particular verbs. She points out that although ASL is described as SVO, features such as topicalisation, null arguments and verb repetition mean that the child is likely to hear large numbers of utterances in non-SVO word order. She cites work by Aksu-Koç and Slobin (1985) showing that Turkish children use a wide variety of word orders early on but these are almost always pragmatically appropriate and reflect the patterns of word order in what they hear.

Of course children will reflect what they see/hear in their ambient language but it is the level at which this is analysed that can be revealing. Adults are generating their language from the full adult system, however that is described in different linguistic paradigms. However what children take in may be a much more limited version of this based on the specific characteristics of the language sample they are receiving. If, in turn, this forms the basis of their language, this may be more concrete and less fully productive than that of the adults with whom they are interacting. Clearly there will be important ways in which children's utterances differ from those of the adults around them. There are plenty of examples of this throughout this book, in our own data and that of others. But equally clearly we need to know much more about the distributional characteristics of the child's input, at the structural level but also at the lexical and morphological levels, before we can begin to identify these differences and focus on their significance.

5.4 Experimental approaches to identifying productivity

Consistent and reasonably conservative definitions of productivity, together with denser sampling and accurate descriptions of the input, will allow us to get a clearer picture of the order in which language development occurs for both speaking and signing children. However there is no doubt that corpus approaches to these issues need to be complemented by experimental approaches where one can control what the child hears or sees and in what contexts.

Thus a number of experiments complement corpus studies of English-speaking children's productivity with word order (see Tomasello 2000 for an overview). These studies also indicate that the ability of children to use English word order productively in their utterances develops over the period from 2;0–5;0 depending on the complexity of the task. There have been claims in the literature for much earlier evidence for the grasp of word order in comprehension studies (Hirsh-Pasek and Golinkoff 1996; Naigles 1990). However here too, children show development which indicates that it is unlikely that the whole system is present at the outset. These matters are currently under intense dispute (see the discussion between Fisher in press and Tomasello & Abbot-Smith 2002) and this short paper is not the place to try to sort them out in any further detail. Of course experimental methodologies require very good design and, in particular, controls, if we are to be able to conclude anything from them. In addition, the design of experiments on productivity for young sign language learners would require considerable ingenuity. However I feel fairly sure that such experiments will become important in working out what it sign language learners know about the nuts and bolts of their language at different points in development.

6.   More complex language

Sign languages allow many possibilities for coarticulation. However it is interesting to note how many authors in this book find that these opportunities are not utilised by children until relatively late in development. Thus Karnopp in her discussion of the development of phonology in LIBRAS reports that the facial expressions which are cooarticulated with handshapes, movements and palm orientations are the last to appear. The chapters by Morgan and Woll and Reilly and Anderson agree with this. In addition, according to Pizzuto, the coarticulation possibilities in LIS that depend on the use of two hands are also a late development. Where it is possible, children seem to use manual lexical equivalents to the face or head movements of the adult language to mark negation, *wh*-questions and refusal (Reilly & Anderson, this volume). The equivalent of this in spoken languages seems to be the ways in which stress and intonation interact with syntactic structure in the marking of information structure (topic, focus, anaphora). This raises the interesting possibility that "producing an empirical model of sign production to account for why sequential production seems easier than parallel" as Morgan and Woll call for, might be a research area which could inform language development theory in general. There is little work either on the development of stress and intonation or, indeed, on how these factors work in adult languages. It may well be that it is easier to study the separate contributions of face, head, fingers, hand location, movement and orientation than it is to try to separate out the factors contributing to stress and intonation in speech because of the different way in which these latter are packaged into the speech signal.

Once children do start using these coarticulation devices, there are interesting questions about the precise temporal relations between them and how this relates to the syntactic structure of the utterance. Children have problems with this in terms of coordinating the complex perspective shifts that require repetition of a verb with changes in person marking, together with a perspective shift marked on the face (Morgan & Woll this volume). Morgan and Woll suggest that children build up this structure piece by piece in development. Kegl reports that, in emergent ISN, some signers use the face markers for negation, yes/no questions and *wh*-questions in ways that reflect linguistic dependencies. However, as noted above, Reilly and Anderson (this volume) demonstrate that this is a relatively late development in ASL, with children initially preferring the lexical versions of these structures. Morgan, Barrière and Woll (2001a) suggests that when children do start to use the facial markers for these syntactic operations in BSL, this might be a developmental phenomenon, with younger children producing the facial sign at the beginning of the utterance, or much less specifically tied to the syntax, while later on they produced it at the right point in the utterance. Thus it might be possible to follow the development of children's understanding of more abstract syntactic structure by tracking the temporal relationship between the facial markers of these operations and the structure of the utterances with which they are coarticulated.

7.   Bilingualism and second language learning

Petitto, Kateleros, Levy, Gauna, Téteault and Ferraro (2001) have shown for the early developmental stages that under the right conditions it is perfectly possible for children to grow up fully bilingual in a sign language and a spoken language. Because the modalities are different it is much easier to get a clear view of whether and how much mixing is occurring between the two languages. Immature phonology makes it hard to do this in the case of a child learning two spoken languages simultaneously. Clearly if children are getting good exposure to both languages, the fact that they may have very different structures (e.g. one pro-drop and the other not, one polysynthetic and the other isolating) will not matter any more than it does to a child learning two very different spoken languages. As Petitto, et al. (2001) show, these children exhibit all the classic abilities of bilingual language learners to keep their languages basically separate. However most children are unfortunately not in this situation. If they are deaf, they will be lucky to be immersed in a sign language and an important issue for their general development is whether and how they become bilingual in both signed and spoken language.

Mouthing or voicing is part of the repertory of many sign languages and signing speakers and in this volume the chapters by Pizzuto and by van den

Bogaerde & Baker both report extensive amounts of it in the adult input. This is made more complex by the fact that as well as sign languages proper, there are often signed versions of the ambient spoken language which together with finger spelling will form a variable part of each deaf signer's repertoire. These versions are, in principle, much closer in structure to the spoken language, though Pizzuto reports that signing children and adults tend to follow the structure of the sign language when mouthing or voicing. That is, a related oral word is voiced at the same time as the sign. Thus, to the extent that word order and inflectional sequences differ between the signed and the spoken languages the oral components of their utterances will be more or less ungrammatical in terms of the ambient spoken language. This does not seem to be a problem for sign language learning. More attention may need to be paid, however, to the effects of this on the attempts to teach deaf children a spoken language in either its spoken or written form, which is clearly important for their general development, as van den Bogaerde and Baker point out.

8.   Additional issues

I have not done justice to the question of the phonology of sign languages and how children develop it (Karnopp this volume). I am sure there are important parallels and differences between the phonological development of children learning spoken languages and those learning sign languages that would make for interesting comparisons. This may, in part, have to wait for more work comparing the phonology of different sign languages.

Secondly, there is the fascinating question of the diachronic history of sign languages, both their emergence and the ways that they have changed over time (Kegl this volume). Most sign languages are relatively young and I would have thought that, as such, they provide a testing ground for some of the more contested positions in theories of language emergence and change. This would be a major enterprise since it would require information on the similarities and differences between different sign languages and different sign language communities speaking the same language. Meier (this volume) makes some interesting points on this question. He shows that sign languages are similar to spoken languages in that degrees of verbal agreement across languages are correlated with flexibility of word order. On the other hand, sign languages are very similar to each other in their agreeing characteristics, which is not the case for spoken languages. Meier suggests that this is due to the difference in the time depth of spoken as opposed to sign languages. Related to this, Kegl points to the invariable presence of object classifiers in sign languages and discusses the way in which, while these are recruited from gesture, they lose their iconic status as soon as they enter the linguistic system. To examine how these languages are changing under the influence of more signers, more contact between signers, and the development of writing systems (Miller & Weinert 1998), we would also need sociolinguistic studies of interaction between signers. This would need to include information about what signers bring to these situations in terms of their previous attempts to communicate, using what they know of spoken language, of the various signing systems around them, and what they have developed in gestural communication with others. We also would need to know the range of individual differences among native signing adults and children. Differences between speakers and groups of speakers can be one of the factors in language change (Croft 2000).

Finally, it is clear that individual differences between speakers are extensive (Pizzuto this volume) but it is unclear whether they are, in fact, greater than individual differences between children learning spoken languages. I have argued that, since it is possible for a child to learn any of the world's languages, systematic individual differences between how children tackle different aspects of the language they are learning can be used to gain insights into the range of skills that must be brought to language learning (Lieven 1997). This approach should apply equally well to the study of differences between children learning sign languages.

9. Summary and conclusion

I have very much enjoyed my engagement with this book and have found it extremely thought provoking. I have learned a great deal about sign languages and the ways in which children learn them, but the chapters have also clarified for me a number of issues in relation to spoken language development. Let me briefly summarise the main points I have raised:

1. The nature of crosslinguistic comparisons and where sign languages fit in typologically.
2. The ways in which children learn to segment the language around them.
3. The development of utterance-meaning connections and how this relates to early interaction and the structuring of attention.
4. Issues in defining and measuring types of productivity.

5. The importance of an accurate account of the language to which particular children are actually exposed and the level at which this is analysed.
6. The question of whether the medium and structure of sign languages would make certain issues more accessible to research than is the case in spoken languages.

In the current situation of many deaf children, the questions I am asking may seem less urgent than the large numbers of practical and applied issues that have to be solved if these children are to have much greater access to a sign language than is often currently the case. However there is an intimate relationship between understanding the fundamentals and successful practical applications. And I also think there is real potential for using the learning of a sign language to illuminate a number of issues in the study of language development which are difficult to study in spoken languages because of the parameters of producing sound in time.

Note

1. Thanks to the Editors of this volume and to Kirsten Abbot-Smith, Heike Behrens, Nancy Budwig, Pat Devine, Holger Diessel and Angelika Wittek for very helpful comments.

Conclusions and directions
for future research

Bencie Woll and Gary Morgan

1. Introduction

The collection of papers in this volume presents the state of the art in sign language acquisition. Although the field is relatively new and small, research in this area has already made an important contribution to a wide range of mainstream research areas. Early speculations on the course of sign language acquisition hypothesised that the course of early language development would be significantly different from that of spoken language: it would be rapid and easy to acquire, since it appears to be gesture-like; it would be robustly resistant to deficient input, since most deaf children do not have parents who are fluent signers; and would be less likely to show critical period effects, since many deaf children learn to sign only after they have started school. The studies reported here and elsewhere have provided more complex answers. The basic similarity of the course of acquisition of signed and spoken language is strikingly similar, from early pre-linguistic behaviours, and child-adjusted behaviour of adults, through universal developmental milestones, to age-of-acquisition effects.

2. Sign language and the brain

Advances in neuroscience using functional imaging techniques with Deaf and hearing signers have enabled consideration of a number of issues relating to the localisation of language in the brain and neural plasticity. Sign languages are left-lateralised like spoken languages (and unlike gesture) (Poizner, Klima & Bellugi 1987; Ronnberg, Soderfeldt & Risberg 2000; Petitto, Zatorre, Gauna, Nikelski, Dostie & Evans 2001b). Although no acquisition studies have been carried out to date, functional imaging studies have indicated that differences exist between adults who are hearing native signers and deaf native signers

(Soderfeldt, Ronnberg & Risberg 1994; MacSweeney, Woll, Campbell, McGuire, Calvert, David, Williams & Brammer in press). These studies indicate that children's exposure to sign language during the early years can result in the reassignment to sign language processing of areas normally considered to have a specialist auditory processing function — but only in those born deaf. Such studies also raise further questions: why is language (spoken and signed) localised to the left hemisphere? To what extent are the critical periods for native-like acquisition of signed and spoken languages identical? How should models of language and the brain deal with processing of sound and processing of visual-spatial information in terms of their being systems on the edge of language?

The recent revival of interest in the evolution of human language has also begun to look at signed language as providing possible clues to the origins of language. It should be stressed that the sign languages found in the world today (including new sign languages such as Nicaraguan Sign Language) cannot directly provide evidence, since they are the products of what Kegl calls in this volume the "language-ready brain". On the other hand, they have served to draw attention to the interface between gesture (and other non-linguistic forms of communication) and language, in relation to the development of children's communicative systems.

3.   Psycholinguistic research

Of course, the opening up of the field has highlighted how much more we still need to learn about sign language acquisition. There have been relatively few experimental psycholinguistic studies, except for those concerned with Theory of Mind in deaf children (Russell, Hosie, Gray, Scott, Hunter, Banks & Macaulay 1998; Courtin & Melot 1998; de Villiers & de Villiers 2000; Peterson & Siegal 2000; Jackson 2001; Remmel, Bettger & Weinberg 2002). These have illuminated the complex interaction between language acquisition and cognition. The development of Theory of Mind has been reported to be delayed in deaf children, and this has been linked both to linguistic factors (for example, the relatively late development of such linguistic structures as role shift) and social factors (the limited conversational interactions which most deaf children experience in comparison to hearing children).

Psychological and psycholinguistic studies of deaf native signing adults have identified enhanced abilities in comparison with hearing non-signers, including, extended reverse digit span; improved perception in the periphery of vision; eyewitness event recall, memory for complex visual patterns, etc (Neville 1991; Emmorey, Kosslyn & Bellugi 1993, reviewed in Siple 1997a). Comparable studies with deaf children have revealed similar findings (Bellugi, O'Grady, Lillo-Martin, O'Grady, van Hoek & Corina 1990b, reviewed in Siple 1997a).

4. Issues of bilingualism in language acquisition

Bilingual approaches to the education of deaf children are relatively new. Before linguistic research on sign languages in the 1970s, deaf children were regarded as monolingual, with greater or lesser mastery of spoken/written language. Even those systems which used signed versions of spoken language (for example Signed English, the Paget-Gorman Sign System, the Rochester Method) or keyword signing (signs for content words accompanying speech, e.g. Makaton (Peter & Barnes 1982) were explicitly monolingual. Interestingly, early research on the sociolinguistics of sign languages adopted a diglossic model, viewing sign language and spoken language as existing at opposite ends of a continuum, with Signed English occupying a middle position (Deuchar 1984). The recognition of the Deaf community as an essentially bilingual community, and the moves towards explicitly bilingual education (Pickersgill & Gregory 1998) have not yet been accompanied by studies of signed and spoken language learning in childhood within such a framework. For example, there have been no longitudinal studies of native or non-native sign language acquisition by deaf children in hearing families, exposed to different language environments.

It is theoretically possible that differences between deaf and hearing children acquiring sign language will be apparent throughout language acquisition, particularly when we consider that the two learning situations are in fact quite different.

Hearing children in Deaf families are almost always in a full bilingual bicultural environment (Singleton & Tittle 2000). As well as access to sign language, they can also access spoken language (via family members, pre-school programmes, television). Thus exposure to a second language takes place from a very early stage and is concurrent with exposure to sign language. Interestingly, some early research on hearing children in Deaf families ignored this factor, focusing solely on spoken language skills and reporting these children to be at risk of language delay. However, in the majority of cases where hearing children are exposed to spoken and sign languages, few instances of delayed spoken language are found (Schiff-Myers 1988).

Deaf children from Deaf families are more likely to be monolingual, at least until they start school. Even where there is exposure to spoken language in the home, speech perception is difficult and spoken communication that is not directed at them is generally inaccessible. Development of spoken language by deaf children therefore frequently occurs after acquisition of a sign language, or sequentially.

The literature on bilingual language acquisition is ambiguous on the degree to which bilinguals and monolinguals may be compared, and on the relative language skills of simultaneous versus sequential bilinguals. In a study of bilingual narrative development (BSL and English) in hearing children in deaf families, Morgan (2000) reported such interference to occur. However, no longitudinal studies of receptive language development are available, specifically exploring interference effects over time.

Several studies (Jones & Quigley 2002; Siedlecki & Bonvillian 1993a) have compared hearing children in deaf families with hearing and deaf peers on grammatical and phonological measures and both report no difference between groups.

A different question relates to whether bilingualism in two spoken languages is the same as bilingualism where the languages use different modalities. To date many of these issues have not been addressed in the literature, and cannot therefore be satisfactorily answered.

There have still been relatively few studies of the differences between deaf and hearing native signers, either in terms of end-state sign language abilities, or differences in the course of development (Gallaway & Woll 1994). Most importantly, in view of the non-optimal language-learning environment experienced by the majority of deaf children (those with hearing parents), little is known about the minimum input requirements for sign language acquisition in deaf and hearing children.

5.   The Deaf community and research

As with research on the acquisition of other minority languages, the importance of deaf researchers and native signers in the research effort cannot be over-emphasised. Without the embedding of sign language research in the deaf community and an understanding of the relationship between the deaf community and sign language, insights will inevitably be limited. This is particularly important in view of the history of psychological research on deaf children as examples of *language-less* subjects (cf. Furth 1991), where researchers' ignorance of sign language has resulted in mistaken assumptions about the relationship between language and cognition. The distinctive characteristics of the sociolinguistic context in which children acquire a sign language shape our understanding of that acquisition process.

6. Research methodology

Most language acquisition research to date has been on ASL, although this volume represents the first to provided data across a relatively wide range of languages. Although many findings are relevant to other sign languages such as BSL, individual sign languages are distinct from each other and merit research in their own right. From the perspective of linguists and language specialists, there remains a need for further information about the normal sequence and process of development of sign languages other than ASL. There is a need for more comparative sign language acquisition studies and more studies of bilingual acquisition, including those of children acquiring more than one sign language as first languages, and of deaf children acquiring a spoken language in early childhood as a second L1. The contemplation of such studies also highlights the need for tools with which to assess sign language development, since almost no standardised measures have been published for assessing the development of any sign languages, including ASL (see Haug 2002 for a comprehensive review).

Common to almost all research in sign language acquisition is the problem of small numbers of subjects, many studies relying on single cases or small groups. This is in part because of the intensive nature of this type of research, but also because the population of children in deaf signing families is itself a small one — only 10% of deaf children have deaf parents. We therefore need to be particularly cautious about interpreting findings taken from small-scale studies.

Of the available research, there are few longitudinal studies of sign language acquisition. These are particularly important in allowing researchers to link early behaviour with later results, to trace through developmental patterns and consider individual differences (e.g. Harris, Clibbens, Chasin & Tibbitts 1989).

7. Transcription and coding of data

One of the major issues for sign language researchers is how to describe languages for which there are no conventional transcription systems and which have no written form. There have been numerous attempts to introduce notation systems such as HamNoSys (Prillwitz, Leven, Zienert, Hanke & Henning 1989), and Stokoe Notation (Stokoe, Casterline & Croneberg 1976) and an orthography for signed languages (Signwriting 'Sutton 1999') which have to date met with only limited acceptance. The notation systems are generally satisfactory for the representation of citation forms of signs as used by adults, but not for e.g. phonetic features of child signing (Takkinen 2002) or for connected discourse. It is now possible to provide transcription in the form of moving video images linked with notation (e.g. SignStream — Neidle, MacLaughlin, Bahan, Lee & Kegl 1997) and this is likely to be increasingly used in the future. The Berkeley Transcription System (Slobin, Hoiting, Anthony, Biederman, Kuntze, Lindert, Pyers, Thumann & Weinberg 2002), which is CHILDES compatible, should also help with developments in child language research.

8.   Lexical development

As mentioned in the introduction, there is one question that appears to be unsettled concerning the age at which children exposed to a signed language produce their first signs, some studies reporting this to occur significantly earlier than hearing children typically pronounce their first words.

Several explanations have been put forward for this reported sign advantage. One suggestion is the differing maturation rates of the motor system for hand movements when compared with that of the speech apparatus. Bonvillian and colleagues (Bonvillian, Orlansky & Folven 1990) argue that the appearance of first signs before completion of the sensori-motor period and the development of symbolic play challenges the cognitive basis of early language acquisition. They propose that evidence from sign language acquisition raises questions about the legitimacy of sensori-motor tasks and symbolic play as precursors to language development, as has been argued on the basis of spoken language acquisition.

Arguments against the sign advantage rest on the linguistic status of these early forms. Volterra (1983) and Petitto (1988) have noted the close relationship which exists between gestures and signs. Gestures and signs occur within the same modality and often share many formational parameters. It is often difficult to tell if early gestures are in fact primitive signs. For example, sign languages contain a lot of index pointing used for grammatical purposes; however such points occur frequently among the early gestures of both deaf and hearing children.

An alternative explanation for the sign advantage has been attributed to the iconicity of signs compared to spoken words. However, early child sign vocabulary is not related to iconicity.

Other studies have reported that early signs and gestures occur at the same time, and that signs are not preceded by gestures but rather that the use of gestures increases as sign language vocabulary increases. The definition of what constitutes a sign as opposed to a gesture thus needs closer consideration. Hand movements made by a 5 month old child in a speaking family are unlikely to be given much attention, although vocalisations may attract more interest. The same movements may be interpreted very differently by a signing family. The relationship between early gestures and first signs is an area in need of further research, particularly in view of the recent marketing of books and videos targeted at parents of hearing children, with the aim of teaching them 'sign language' before they develop spoken language: *Sign with your Baby* (Garcia 1999); *Baby signs: how to talk to your baby before your baby can talk* (Acredolo & Goodwyn 2000). Both of these books claim that children can learn signs before they can learn words, and that teaching them signs will lead to measurable differences in behaviour and cognition:

> Research in the USA reports that, by being taught signs, hearing babies can understand and express language long before they are physically able to speak. Parents who have used Garcia's methods for signing with hearing babies as young as seven or eight months claim that it can help communication, verbal language development and dramatically reduce frustration... even a few simple signs like 'more', 'eat', and 'milk' can make a big difference in empowering and meeting the needs of babies. (from the publisher's catalogue).

These claims have not been supported in published studies. A study by Goodwyn, Acredolo and Brown (Goodwyn et al. 2000) reports that training of 11 month old infants in symbolic gestures resulted in a spoken language development advantage on standardised tests at 36 months, compared to infants receiving no gesture training, but a control group receiving enhanced spoken language input were comparable to the gesture training group. Crucially, this study does not distinguish signs from gestures: "parents of those in the *sign* training group modelled symbolic *gestures* and encouraged their infants to use them" (Goodwyn et al. 2000:81, our italics). While training in symbolic gestures may be an enjoyable experience for both infant and parent (parents often spontaneously train infants to produce gestures such as *bye-bye* and *blowing a kiss*), claims that learning a signed language is easier than learning a spoken language are unsupported by acquisition studies.

9.   Studies of developmentally atypical signers

Greater understanding of sign language acquisition has begun to make it possible to explore atypical sign language development. This is of importance for several reasons: firstly, there has been an assumption in deaf education that sign language acquisition is impervious to age-of-acquisition effects and that therefore deaf children can be introduced to a sign language in mid-childhood if they have failed to make progress in spoken language. Studies by Mayberry (1993) and Kegl (this volume) indicate that this is not true and that such an approach leads to *semilingualism* with no complete L1 acquired. Studies of the negative effect of late L1 exposure have begun to influence educational practice towards early introduction of sign language. Secondly, normal progress in sign language acquisition is a good predictor of a positive outcome in relation to spoken language acquisition following cochlear implantation, and thus can be used as a screening measure. Finally, an understanding of sign language acquisition has begun to permit exploration of atypical acquisition, in deaf children with developmental disorders (e.g. autism (Poizner et al. 1987), Down syndrome (Woll & Grove 1996) and also in hearing children (for example those with Landau-Kleffner syndrome: Sieratzki, Calvert, Brammer, Campbell, David & Woll 2001).

As an example, Woll and Grove (1996) explored the language deficits of hearing twins with Down syndrome who had deaf parents. Signing is often used with children with Down syndrome because it is considered easier to access, recall and produce than spoken language. Indeed, these children often make more progress with signs than with speech; however why this should be so remains unclear. One explanation is related to modality, signs succeeding because they bypass a weak auditory-vocal processing system. An alternative explanation is that there is a deficit in the underlying linguistic system.

The study of hearing twins with deaf parents who are bilingual in English and BSL presents a unique opportunity to explore the issue. The authors argue that if the advantage conveyed by sign is related to modality, these twins should demonstrate age appropriate BSL development. If difficulties are caused by an underlying linguistic deficit, this should be evidenced by problems with BSL grammar as well as English grammar. Errors made by the twins indicated specific areas of difficulty related to complexity of BSL morphology, and difficulties handling three-dimensional representations of space for linguistic (as opposed to gestural) use. Woll and Grove conclude that children with Down syndrome find BSL no easier than English, therefore providing support for the existence of an underlying linguistic difficulty common to language in general.

Herman (2002) reports on assessments of children with apparent language disorders. One was the hearing child of deaf parents, with English and behavioural problems, both of which were affecting his school work. It was unclear whether his difficulties in English were due to his having BSL as a first language and English as a (weaker) second language, or if he had a language learning disorder. His pattern of errors, particularly highlighted through assessment of comprehension, was felt to be more indicative of a language disorder than a straightforward language delay.

In BSL, he showed good vocabulary skills but inconsistent knowledge of basic negatives, number and distribution, and handling classifiers, failing simpler items and passing more complex ones. His ability to understand syntactic and morphological contrasts was extremely limited. The assessment results highlighted difficulties in both BSL and English. The errors noted could be partly explained by limited exposure to good language models; however, the presence of anomalous patterns (compared with normal development), the more severe difficulties with comprehension of grammar, and the relative intactness of vocabulary and expressive language all pointed to a language disorder.

Further research on disorders of language development — both those that are cross-modal, and those which occur in spoken but not signed language, or vice versa, will help our understanding of the relationship of language and modality, as well as opening new possibilities for remediation.

10. Looking to the future

Linguists and psycholinguists have begun to introduce research on sign language into the wider study of language. This can be seen in the integration of material on sign language acquisition in textbooks (for example, in Fromkin and Rodman's *An Introduction to Language* (1993)) other than references to the teaching of ASL to primates.

Sign language acquisition research permits exploration of modality-specific features of language acquisition, such as the role of the face in expressing affect and grammatical information, and the linguistic manipulation of spatial information. This in turn illuminates the relationship between modality and the acquisition of spoken language, particularly important in the context of the controversy around the role of auditory processing disorders in developmental language impairments. The full contribution of sign language research to the field of child language is still to come.

Glossary

Abbreviations

ASL: American SL
BSL: British SL
LIBRAS: Brazilian SL
ISN: Nicaraguan SL
LSQ: Québécoise SL
LIS: Italian SL
SLN/NGT: Dutch SL

Terminology

Cherology
An older term for the study of sign phonology

Classifiers/pro-forms
A class of handshapes which function to categorise nouns in verbs of motion

Directional verbs/Agreement verbs
A class of verbs which indicate subject and object arguments through movement in sign space

Finger spelling/manual alphabet
Configurations of the hands (and sometimes the arms) which are used to represent the alphabet of a particular written language

Handshape
Form of the hand

Homesign
Creation of systematic gestures by deaf children and hearing family members to communicate basic needs in the absence of a sign language

Iconic/non-iconic signs/visual motivation
The relationship between the form of a sign and its meaning

Index (abbreviated IX)
Pointing serving a variety of linguistic functions

Loci
Locations serving linguistic functions

Manually Coded English (MCE)/Signing Exact English 2 (SEE2)/Sign Supported English, French etc.
The manual representation of the morphology of a spoken/written language

Mouthing/oral component
Mouth actions derived from spoken language

Name signs
Signs for a person or place

Orientation
How the hand is positioned relative to the body

Perspective shift
Sentence marker of shifted first person

Plain verbs/body-anchored verbs
A class of verbs which do not move between locations in sign space

Role shift/Role play
Discourse marker of reported sign

Sim-Com
Speaking and signing at the same time

Sign space
Area within which signers produce the linguistic message

Simultaneous signs
Sentences where each hand simultaneously refers to different constituents of the sentence

Size and Shape Specifiers (SASS's)
Signs which describe the outline, thickness or other attribute of an object

Spatial verb
A class of verbs representing directing movement

Subordinate hand/non-dominant hand
The hand which is systematically used less in signing

Topographic space
A description of a real or imagined spatial layout (e.g. a room) in sign space

Verb sandwiches
Construction involving two verbs with the same meaning which carry different inflections

Bibliography

Aarons, D. 1994. *Aspects of the syntax of American Sign Language*. Doctoral Dissertation, Boston University, Boston, MA.

Abrahamsen, A., Cavallo, M. M. and McCluer, J. A. 1985. "Is the sign advantage a robust phenomenon? From gesture to language in two modalities." *Merrill-Palmer Quarterly* 31: 177–209.

Acredolo, L. P. and Goodwyn, S. W. 2000. *Baby signs: how to talk to your baby before your baby can talk*. Chicago: Ingram International.

Ahlgren, I. and Bergman, B. 1994. "Reference in narratives." In *Fifth International Symposium on Sign Language Research*, I. Ahlgren, B. Bergman and M. Brennan (eds), 29–36. Durham: International Sign Language Association.

Ajello, R., Mazzoni, L. and Nicolai, F. 1997. "Gesti linguistici: la labializzazione in LIS." *Quaderni della sezione di glottologia e linguistica. University of Chieti* G. D'Annunzio, Vol. 9: 5–45.

Ajello, R., Mazzoni, L. and Nicolai, F. 2001. "Linguistic Gestures: Mouthing in Italian Sign Language". In *The hands are the head of the mouth: The mouth as articulator in sign languages*, P. Boyes-Braem and R. Sutton-Spence (eds), 231–246. Hamburg: Signum Verlag.

Akamatsu, C. T., Musselman, C. and Zweibel, A. 2000. "Nature vs. nurture in the development of cognition in deaf people." In *Development in context: The deaf child in the family and at school*, P. Spencer, C. Erting and M. Marschark (eds), 255–274. Mahwah, NJ: Lawrence Erlbaum Associates.

Aksu-Koç, A. A. and Slobin, D. I. 1985. "The acquisition of Turkish." In *The crosslinguistic study of language acquisition, Vol. 1*, D. I. Slobin (ed), 839–878. Hillsdale, NJ: Lawrence Erlbaum Associates.

Allen, S. E. M. 1996. *Aspects of argument structure acquisition in Inuktitut*. Amsterdam: John Benjamins.

Allen, S. E. M. 2000. "A discourse-pragmatic explanation for argument representation in child Inuktitut." *Linguistics* 38: 483–521.

Anderson, D. E. and Reilly, J. S. 1998a. "The puzzle of negation: How children move from the communicative to grammatical negation in ASL." *Applied Psycholinguistics* 18: 411–429.

Anderson, D. E. and Reilly, J. S. 1998b. "Pah! The acquisition of adverbials in ASL." *Sign Language and Linguistics* 1: 117–142.

Anderson, D. E. and Reilly, J. S. 2002. "The MacArthur Communicative Development Inventory for American Sign Language: The normative data." *Journal of Deaf Studies and Deaf Education* 7: 83–106.

Anderson, J. and Ewen, C. 1987. *Principles of dependency phonology*. Cambridge: Cambridge University Press.

Anthony, M. 2002. *Examining the relationship between classifiers and literacy in deaf children.* Doctoral dissertation, University of California, Berkeley.

Appel, R. and Muysken, P. 1987. *Language contact and bilingualism.* London: Edward Arnold.

Arends, J., Muyksen, P. and Smith, N. 1995. *Pidgins and creoles: An introduction.* Amsterdam: John Benjamins.

Armstrong, D. F., Stokoe, W. C. and Wilcox, S. E. 1994. "Signs of the origins of syntax." *Current Anthropology* 35 (4): 349–368

Armstrong, D. F., Stokoe, W. C. and Wilcox, S. E. 1995. *Gesture and the nature of language.* New York: Cambridge University Press.

Aronoff, M., Meir, I. and Sandler, W. 2000. "Universal and particular aspects of sign language morphology." Unpublished manuscript, State University of New York at Stony Brook.

Bahan, B. 1996. *Non-manual realization of agreement in American Sign Language.* Doctoral dissertation, Boston University.

Baker, A. E., Hendriks, A. C., Knoors, H., van de Lem, G. J., Levelt, W. J. M., Schadee, M. E. and Wesemann, J. B. 1997. *Méér dan een gebaar.* Report of the Committee of Sign Language of the Netherlands. The Hague: SDU.

Baker A. E. and Van den Bogaerde, B. 2001. "Nouns and verbs in the early lexicon of children learning a sign language". Paper presented at the conference on Early Lexical Acquisition, Lyon, December 2001.

Baker, A. E. and Woll, B. 1999. "Methods and procedure in sign language acquisition studies." University of Amsterdam and City University of London. ⟨http://www.sign-lang.uni-hamburg.de/intersign/workshop4/Baker/Baker.html

Baker, C. 1977. "Regulators and turn-taking in American Sign Language discourse." In *On the other hand: New perspectives on American Sign Language,* L. Friedman (ed), 215–236. New York: Academic Press.

Baker, C. and Cokely, D. 1980. *American Sign Language: a teacher's resource text on grammar and culture.* Silver Spring, Maryland: T. J. Publishers.

Baker, C. and Padden, C. 1978. "Focusing on the nonmanual components of American Sign Language." In *Understanding language through sign language research,* P. Siple (ed), 27–57. New York: Academic Press.

Baker-Shenk, C. 1983. *A microanalysis of the non-manual components of questions in American Sign Language.* Doctoral Dissertation, University of California, Berkeley.

Baker-Shenk, C. and Cokely, D. 1980. *American Sign Language: A Teacher's Resource Text on Grammar and Culture.* Washington, DC: Clerc Books.

Bates, E. 1979. *The emergence of symbols: Cognition and communication in infancy.* New York: Academic Press.

Bates E., Dale, P. S. and Thal, D. 1995 "Individual differences and their implications for theories of language development." In *The handbook of child language,* P. Fletcher and B. MacWhinney (eds), 96–151. Oxford: Blackwell.

Bates, E. and MacWhinney, B. 1982. "Functionalist approaches to grammar." In *Language acquisition: The state of the art,* E. Wanner and L. R. Gleitman (eds), 173–218. New York: Cambridge University Press.

Bates, E., Thal, D., Whitesell, K., Fenson, L. and Oakes, L. 1989. "Integrating language and gesture in infancy." *Developmental Psychology* 25: 1004–1019.

Battison, R. 1978. *Lexical borrowing in American Sign Language.* Silver Spring, MD: Linstok Press.

Beers, M. and Baker, A. E. 1997. *De fonologische ontwikkeling van dove kinderen in de leeftijd van 4 tot 10 jaar.* [The phonological development of deaf children aged 4–10 years]. Onderzoeksrapport voor de Overbeek Stichting. [Research Report].

Behrens, H. 2001. "Learning multiple regularities: Evidence from overgeneralization errors in the German plural." In *Proceedings of the 26th Annual Boston University Conference on Language Development*, A. H.-J. Do, L. Domínguez and A. Johansen (eds), Somervill, MA: Cascadilla Press.

Bellugi, U. and Klima, E. S. 1982. "The acquisition of three morphological systems in American Sign Language." *Papers and Reports on Child Language Development* 21: 1–35.

Bellugi, U., Lillo-Martin, D., O'Grady, L. and van Hoek, K. 1990a. "The development of spatialized syntactic mechanisms in American Sign Language." In *Sign Language Research 8*, W. H. Edmonson and F. Karlson (eds), 16–25. Hamburg: Signum Verlag.

Bellugi, U., O'Grady, L., Lillo-Martin, D., O'Grady, M., van Hoek, K. and Corina, D. 1990b. "Enhancement of spatial cognition in deaf children." In *From gesture to language in hearing and deaf children*, V. Volterra and C. Erting (eds.), 278–298. New York: Springer Verlag.

Berko, J. 1958. "The child's learning of English morphology." *Word* 14: 150–177.

Beronesi, S., Massoni, P. and Ossella, M. T. 1991. *L'italiano segnato esatto nell'educazione bimodale del bambino sordo.* Rome: Omega.

Bickerton, D. 1981. *Roots of Language.* Ann Arbor, MI: Karoma.

Bickerton, D. 1984. "The language bioprogram hypothesis." *Behavioral and Brain Sciences* 7: 173–221.

Bickerton, D. 1992. "The creole key to the black box language." In *Thirty Years of Linguistic Evolution*, M. Pütz (ed), 97–108. Amsterdam: John Benjamins.

Bjerkan, B., Martinsen, H., Schjølberg, S. and von Tetzchner, S. 1983. "Communicative development and adult reactions." Paper presented at the 2nd International Conference on Social Psychology and Language, Bristol England, July, 1983.

Blees, M., Crasborn, O., van der Hulst, H., van der Kooij, E. 1996. *SignPhon: a database tool for phonological analysis of sign languages. Manual, version 0.1.* Leiden: Holland Institute of Generative Linguistics.

Bloom, L. 1970. *Language development: Form and function in developing grammars.* Cambridge, MA: MIT Press.

Bloom, L. 1991. *Language development from two to three.* New York, NY: Cambridge University Press.

Bonvillian, J. D., Orlansky, M. D. and Folven, R. J. 1990. "Early sign language acquisition: Implications for theories of language acquisition." In *From gesture to language in hearing and deaf children*, V. Volterra and C. Erting (Eds.), 219–232. New York: Springer Verlag.

Bonvillian, J. D. and Folven, R. 1993. "Sign language acquisition: Developmental aspects." In *Psychological perspectives on deafness*, M. Marschark and M. D. Clark (eds), 229–265. Hillsdale N. Y.: Lawrence Erlbaum Associates.

Bonvillian, J.D. and Siedlecki, T. 1996. "Young children's acquisition of the location aspect of American Sign Language signs: Parental report findings."*Journal of Communication Disorders* 29: 13–35.

Bonvillian, J.D. and Siedlecki, T. 1997. "Young children's acquisition of the handshape aspect of American Sign Language signs: Parental report findings." *Applied Psycholinguistics* 18: 17–39.

Bonvillian, J.D., Richards, H.C. and Dooley, T.T. 1997. "Early sign language acquisition and the development of hand preference in young children." *Brain and Language* 58: 1–22.

Bos, H. 1993. "Agreement and prodrop in Sign Language of the Netherlands." In *Linguistics in the Netherlands,* F. Drijkoningen and H. Hengeveld (eds), 37–47. Amsterdam: John Benjamins.

Bowerman, M. 1982. "Evaluating competing linguistic models with language acquisition data: implications of developmental errors with causative verbs." *Quaderni di Semantica* 3: 5–66.

Boyes-Braem, P. 1990. "Acquisition of the handshape in American Sign Language: A preliminary analysis." In *From gesture to language in hearing and deaf children,* V. Volterra and C.J. Erting (eds), 107–127. Berlin: Springer Verlag.

Boyes-Braem, P. and Sutton-Spence, R. 2000. "The mouth as articulator in sign languages." Paper presented at the 7th International Congress on Theoretical Issues in Sign Language Research, Amsterdam, The Netherlands, July 23–27, 2000.

Boyes-Braem, P. and Sutton-Spence, R. (eds.). 2001. *The hands are the head of the mouth: The mouth as articulator in sign languages.* Hamburg: Signum Verlag.

Braine, M.D.S. 1976. *Children's first word combinations.* With Commentary by Melissa Bowerman. *Monographs of the Society for Research in Child Development* 41.

Brennan, M. 1992. "The visual world of BSL: An introduction." In *Dictionary of British Sign Language/English,* D. Brien (ed), 1–133. London: Faber and Faber.

Brennan, M. 2001. "Encoding and capturing productive morphology." *Sign Language and Linguistics* 4, 47–62.

Brent, M.R. and Siskind, J.M. 2001. "The role of exposure to isolated words in early vocabulary development." *Cognition.* 81(2): 33–44

Brentari, D. 1988. "Backward Verbs in ASL: Agreement Re-opened." *Proceedings of the 24th Meeting of the Chicago Linguistic Society* 2: 16–27.

Brentari, D. 1995. "Sign language phonology." In: *The Handbook of Phonological Theory,* J. Goldsmith (ed), 615–639. Cambridge, MA: Blackwell.

Brentari, D., van der Hulst, H., van der Kooij, E. and Sandler, W. n.d. "One over All and All over One." Manuscript.

Brown, R. 1973. *A first language.* Cambridge, MA.: Harvard University Press.

Bruner, J. 1975. "The ontogenesis of speech acts." *Journal of Child Language* 2: 1–19.

Buré, M. 2000. *Gebarentaal voor Nederlands: over leesstrategieën van dove kinderen met de Nederlandse gebarentaal als onderwijstaal.* [Sign language for Dutch: on reading strategies of deaf children who have Sign Language of the Netherlands as their language of instruction]. MA thesis, University of Amsterdam.

Butcher, C. and Goldin-Meadow, S. 2000. "Gesture and the transition from one- to two-word speech: when hand and mouth come together." In *Language and gesture,* D. McNeill (ed.), 235–257. Cambridge: Cambridge University Press.

Calderon, R. and Greenberg, M. 1997. "The effectiveness of early intervention for deaf children and children with hearing loss." In *The effectiveness of early intervention*, M. J. Guralnik (ed), 455–482. Baltimore: Paul H. Brookes.

Calderon, R. and Low, S. 1998. "Early social-emotional, language, and academic development in children with hearing loss." *American Annals of the Deaf* 143: 225–234.

Calderon, R. and Naidu, S. 2000. "Further support for the benefits of early identification and intervention for children with hearing loss." *Volta Review* 100 (5): 53–84.

Cameron-Faulkner, T., Lieven, E. V. M. and Tomasello, M. submitted "A construction based analysis of child directed speech."

Campos, J., Barret, K. C., Lamb, M. E., Goldsmith, H. H. and Stenberg, C. 1983. "Socioemotional development." In *Infancy and development: psychobiology* [P. Mussen (ed.) *Handbook of Child Psychology, Vol. II*], M. Haith and J. Campos (eds), 783–915. New York: Wiley Press.

Capirci, O., Montanari, S. and Volterra, V. 1998. "Gestures, signs, and words in early language development." In *The Nature and Functions of Gesture in Children's Communication*, J. M. Iverson and S. Goldin-Meadow (eds), 45–60. San Francisco, CA: Jossey-Bass.

Carney, A. E. and Moeller, M. P. 1988. "Treatment efficacy: Hearing loss in children." *Journal of Speech, Language, and Hearing Research* 41: S61.

Caron, R. F., Caron, A. and Myers, R. S. 1982. "Abstraction of invariant face expressions in infancy." *Child Development* 53: 1008–1015.

Carpentier, C. 1969. *Etude grammaticale du langage des enfants de 3, 4 et 5 ans*. Travail de fins d'études, Institut de Psychologie, Université de Liège.

Caselli, M. C. 1983. "Communication to language: deaf children's and hearing children's development compared." *Sign Language Studies* 39: 113–144.

Caselli, M. C. and Volterra, V. 1990. "From communication to language in hearing and deaf children." In *From gesture to language in hearing and deaf children*, V. Volterra and C. J. Erting (eds), 263–277. Berlin: Springer Verlag.

Caselli, M. C., Maragna, S., Pagliari Rampelli, L. and Volterra, V. 1994. *Linguaggio e Sordità*. Firenze: La Nuova Italia.

Casey, S. 2000. "Relationships between gestures and signed languages: Indicating participants in actions." Paper presented at the 7th International Conference on Theoretical Issues in Sign Language Research, Amsterdam, The Netherlands.

Casey, S. in press. "Indicating participants in actions: From prelinguistic gestures to signed languages." *Proceedings of the annual meeting of the Berkeley Linguistics Society, vol. 27*. Berkeley, CA: Berkeley Linguistics Society.

Chamberlain, C., Morford, J. and Mayberry, R. (eds) 2000. *Language acquisition by eye*. Mahwah, NJ: Lawrence Erlbaum Associates.

Chen, D. 1999. "Investigation of word order acquisition in early ASL." In: *Cranberry Linguistics*, D. Braz, K. Hiramatsu and Y. Kudo (eds), 12–16. [University of Connecticut Working Papers in Linguistics, 10].

Chiat, S. 1981. "Context-specificity and generalisations in the acquisition of pronominal distinctions." *Journal of Child Language* 8: 75–91

Chiat, S. 1982. "If I were you and you were me: The acquisition of pronouns in a pronoun reversing child." *Journal of Child Language* 9: 359–379.

Chiat, S. 2000. *Understanding children with language problems.* Cambridge: Cambridge University Press.

Chomsky, N. 1986a. *Barriers.* Cambridge, MA: The MIT Press.

Chomsky, N. 1986b. *Knowledge of language: Its nature, origin, and use.* New York: Praeger.

Clark, E. V. 1993. *The lexicon in acquisition.* Cambridge: Cambridge University Press.

Cole, E. and Paterson, M. 1984. "Assessment and treatment of phonologic disorders in the hearing-impaired." In *Speech disorders in children*, J. Castello (ed), 93–127. San Diego, CA: College Hill Press.

Coppola, M. V., Senghas, A., Newport, E. and Supalla, T. 1997. "Emergence of grammar: Evidence from family-based sign systems in Nicaragua." Paper presented at the Annual Meeting of the Boston University Conference on Language Development, October 1997.

Corina, D. P. 1999. "Neural disorders of language and movement: evidence from American Sign Language." In *Gesture, speech, and sign*, L. S. Messing and R. Campbell (eds), 27–42. Oxford: Oxford University Press.

Corina, D. P., Poizner, H., Bellugi, U., Feinberg, T., Dowd, D. and O'Grady, L. 1992. "Disassociation between linguistic and non-linguistic gestural systems: A case for compositionality." *Brain & Language* 43: 414–447.

Cormier, K. 1998. "How does modality contribute to linguistic diversity?" Unpublished paper, University of Texas at Austin.

Cormier, K. 2002. *Grammaticization of indexic signs: How American Sign Language expresses numerosity.* Doctoral dissertation, University of Texas at Austin.

Cormier, K., Wechsler, S. and Meier, R. P. 1998. "Locus agreement in American Sign Language." In *Lexical and constructional aspects of linguistic explanation*, G. Webelhuth, J.-P. Koenig and A. Kathol (eds), 215–229. Stanford: CSLI Press.

Coulter, G. R. 1980. *American Sign Language typology.* Doctoral Dissertation, University of California, San Diego.

Coulter, G. R. and Anderson, S. R. 1993. "Introduction." In *Current Issues in ASL Phonology, Phonetics and Phonology, Vol. 3*, G. R. Coulter (ed), 1–17. New York: Academic Press.

Courtin, C. and Melot, A-M.1998. "Development of theories of mind in deaf children." In *Psychological perspectives on deafness*, M. Marschark and M. D. Clark (Eds.), 79–102. Mahwah NJ: Lawrence Erlbaum Associates.

Crasborn, O. and van der Kooij, E. 1997. "Relative orientation in sign language phonology." In *Linguistics in the Netherlands*, J. Coerts and H. Hoop (eds), 37–48. Amsterdam: John Benjamins.

Croft, W. 2000. *Language change: an evolutionary approach.* London: Longman.

Croft, W. 2001. *Radical construction grammar: syntactic theory in typological perspective.* Oxford: Oxford University Press.

Crystal, D. 1987. *The Cambridge Encyclopedia of Language.* Cambridge: Cambridge University Press.

De Houwer, A. 1999. "A macro-level approach to input in bilingual acquisition." Paper presented at the Second International Symposium on Bilingualism, April 1999, Newcastle, United Kingdom

De Leon, L. 2000. "The Emergent Participant: Interactive Patterns in the Socialization of Tzotzil (Mayan) Infants." *Journal of Linguistic Anthropology* 8 (2): 131–161.

De Quadros, R. M. 1999. *Phrase structure of Brazilian Sign Language*. Doctoral dissertation, Pontifícia Universidade Católica do Rio Grande do Sul.

De Quadros, R. M., Lillo-Martin, D. and Chen, D. 2000. "A little change goes a long way: Capturing differences between Brazilian Sign Language and American Sign Language." Paper presented at the 7th International Conference on Theoretical Issues in Sign Language Research, Amsterdam, The Netherlands.

de Villiers, J. 1985. "Learning how to use verbs: Lexical coding and the influence of the input." *Journal of Child Language* 12: 587–595.

de Villiers, J. G. and de Villiers, P. A. 2000. "Linguistic determinism and the understanding of false beliefs." In *Children's reasoning and the mind*, P. Mitchell and K. J. Riggs (Eds.), 191–228. Hove: Psychology Press/Taylor & Francis.

DeCasper, A. J. and Spence, M. J. 1986. "Prenatal maternal speech influences newborns' perception of speech sounds." *Infant Behavior and Development* 9: 133–150.

Dodd, B. 1987. "The acquisition of lip-reading skills in normally hearing children." In *Hearing by eye: the psychology of lip-reading*, B. Dodd and R. Campbell (eds), 163–175. Hillsdale, N. J.: Lawrence Erlbaum Associates

Drasgow, E. 1998. "American Sign Language as a pathway to linguistic competence." *Exceptional Children* 64: 329–342.

Deuchar, M. 1984. *British Sign Language*. London: Routledge & Kegan Paul.

Ebbinghaus, H. and Hessmann, J. 1996. "Signs and words: Accounting for spoken language elements in German Sign Language." In *International Review of Sign Linguistics, vol. 1*, W. H. Edmondson and R. B. Wilbur (eds), 23–56, Mahwah, N. J.: Lawrence Erlbaum Associates

Ekman, P. 1972. "Universal and cultural differences in facial expressions of emotion." In *Nebraska symposium on motivation 1971*, J. K. Cole (ed), 207–283. Lincoln, NE: University of Nebraska Press.

Ekman, P. 1979. "About brows: Emotional and conversational signals." In *Human ethology*, M. von Cranach, K. Foppa, W. Lepenies and D. Ploog (eds), 169–248. London: Cambridge University Press.

Ekman, P. and Friesen, W. 1978. *Facial action coding system*. Palo Alto, CA: Consulting Psychologists Press.

Elman, J. 1990. "Finding structure in time." *Cognitive Science* 14: 179–211.

Emmorey, K. 1999. "Do signers gesture?" In *Gesture, Speech and Sign*, L. S. Messing and R. Campbell (eds), 133–159. New York: Oxford University Press.

Emmorey, K. 2000. "Classifier construction in sign languages." Paper presented at the 7th International Congress on Theoretical Issues in Sign Language Research, Workshop on "Sign Language Typology", Amsterdam, The Netherlands, July 23–27, 2000.

Emmorey, K. 2001. *Language, cognition, and the brain: Insights from sign language research*. Mahwah, NJ: Lawrence Erlbaum Associates.

Emmorey, K. (ed.) in press. *Perspectives on classifier constructions in sign languages*. Mahwah, NJ: Lawrence Erlbaum Associates.

Emmorey, K., Bellugi, U., Friederici, A. and Horn, P. 1995. "Effects of age of acquisition on grammatical sensitivity: Evidence from on-line and off-line tasks." *Applied Psycholinguistics* 16: 1–23.

Emmorey, K., Kosslyn, S.M. and Bellugi, U. 1993. "Visual imagery and visual-spatial language: enhanced imagery abilities in deaf and hearing ASL signers." *Cognition* 46: 139–181.

Emmorey, K. and Lane, H. (eds.) 2000. *The signs of language revisited: an anthology to honor Ursula Bellugi and Edward Klima.* Mahwah, NJ: Lawrence Erlbaum Associates.

Emmorey, K. and Reilly, J.S. 1995. "Theoretical issues relating language, gesture, and space: An overview." In *Language, gesture, and space*, K. Emmorey and J.S. Reilly (eds), 1–16. Hillsdale, NJ: Lawrence Erlbaum Associates.

Engberg-Pedersen, E. 1993. *Space in Danish Sign Language: The semantics and morphosyntax of the use of space in a visual language.* Hamburg: Signum Verlag.

Engberg-Pedersen, E. 1995. "Point of view expressed through shifters." In *Language, Gesture and Space*, K. Emmorey and J. Reilly (eds), 133–154. Hillsdale, NJ: Lawrence Erlbaum Associates.

Erting, C. 1988. "Acquiring linguistic and social identity: Interactions of deaf children with a hearing teacher and a deaf adult." In *Language learning and deafness*, M. Strong (ed), 192–219. Springfield, IL: Charles C. Thomas.

Erting, C., Prezioso, C. and Hynes, M. 1990. "The interactional context of deaf mother-infant interaction." In *From gesture to language in hearing and deaf children*, V. Volterra and C. Erting (eds), 97–106. Heidelberg: Springer Verlag.

Ewen, C. 1995. "Dependency Relations in Phonology." In: *The Handbook of Phonological Theory*, J. Goldsmith (ed.), 570–585. Cambridge, Massachussets: Blackwell.

Facchini, M. 1985. "An historical reconstruction of events leading to the congress of Milan in 1880." In *SLR '83. Proceedings of the 3rd International Symposium on Sign Language Research*, W. Stokoe and V. Volterra (eds), 356–362. Rome/SilverSpring: CNR/Linstok Press.

Fernald, A., Taeschner, T., Dunn, J., Papoušek, M., de Boysson-Bardies, B. and Fukui, I. 1989. "A cross-language study of prosodic modifications in mothers' and fathers' speech to preverbal infants." *Journal of Child Language* 16: 477–501.

Fernald, A., Pinto, J.P., Swingley, D., Weinberg, A. and McRoberts, G.W. 1998. "Rapid gains in speed of verbal processing by infants in the 2nd year." *Psychological Science* 9: 228–231.

Fischer, S.D. 1973. "Verb inflections in American Sign Language and their acquisition by the deaf child." Unpublished paper presented at the winter meeting, Linguistic Society of America.

Fischer, S.D. 1975. "Influences on word order change in ASL." In *Word order and word order change*, C. Li (ed), 1–25. Austin, TX: University of Texas Press.

Fischer, S.D. 1978. "Sign languages and creoles." In *Understanding language through sign language research*, P. Siple (ed.), 309–331. New York: Academic Press.

Fischer, S.D. 1996. "The role of agreement and auxiliaries in sign language." *Lingua* 98: 103–119.

Fischer, S.D. and Gough, B. 1978. "Verbs in American Sign Language." *Sign Language Studies* 18: 17–48.

Fischer, S.D. and Janis, W. 1990. "Verb sandwiches in American Sign Language." In *Current trends in European sign language research: Proceedings of the 3rd European Congress on*

Sign Language Research, S. Prillwitz and T. Vollhaber (eds), 279–293. Hamburg: Signum Verlag.

Fisher, C. in press. "The role of abstract knowledge in language acquisition: A reply to Tomasello." *Cognition*.

Fisher, C., Hall, D., Rakowitz, S. and Gleitman, L. 1994. "When it is better to receive than to give: syntactic and conceptual constraints on vocabulary growth." *Lingua* 92: 333–375.

Folven, R. J. and Bonvillian, J. D. 1987. "The onset of referential signing in children." Paper presented at biennial meetings of the Society for Research in Child Development, Baltimore MD, April 1987.

Fontana, S. and Fabbretti, D. 2000. "Classificazione e analisi delle forme labiali della LIS in storie elicitate." In *Viaggio nella città invisibile — Atti del 2° Convegno Nazionale sulla Lingua Italiana dei Segni*, C. Bagnara, G. Chiappini, M. P. Conte and M. Ott (eds), 103–111. Tirrenia (Pisa): Edizioni del Cerro.

Fortescue, M and Lennert Olsen, L. 1992. "The acquisition of West Greenlandic." In *The Crosslinguistic Study of Language Acquisition, Volume 3*, D. I. Slobin (ed), Hillsdale, NJ: Lawrence Erlbaum Associates.

Fortgens, C. in preparation. *Het scheiden van twee talen: de taalproductie van dove kinderen in een tweetalig programma*. [The separation of two languages: the language production of deaf children in a bilingual programme.] Doctoral Dissertation, University of Amsterdam.

Franchi, M. L. 1987. "Componenti non manuali." In *La Lingua Italiana dei Segni — La Comunicazione Visivo-Gestuale dei Sordi*, V. Volterra (ed), 159–178. Bologna: Il Mulino.

Fromkin, V. and Rodman, R. 1993. *An introduction to language, 5th edition*. Fort Worth TX: Harcourt Brace.

Furth, H. G. 1991. "Thinking without language: a perspective and review of research with deaf people." In *Constructivist perspectives on developmental psychopathology and atypical development*, D. P. Keating and H. Rosen (eds), 203–227. Hillsdale NJ: Lawrence Erlbaum Associates.

Gallaway, C. and Richards, B. J. (eds.). 1994. *Input and interaction in language acquisition*. Cambridge: Cambridge University Press.

Gallaway, C. and Woll, B. 1994. "Interaction and childhood deafness." In *Input and interaction in language acquisition*, C. Gallaway and B. J. Richards (eds), 197–218. Cambridge: Cambridge University Press.

Galvan, D. B. 1989. "A sensitive period for the acquisition of complex morphology: evidence from American Sign Language." *Papers and Reports on Child Language Development* 28: 107–114.

Garcia, J. 1999. *Sign with your baby*. Stratton Kehl Publications.

Genesee, F. 1988. "Bilingual Language Development in preschool children." In *Language Development in Exceptional Circumstances*, D. Bishop and K. Mogford (eds), 62–80. Edinburgh: Churchill Livingstone.

Genesee, F., Nicoladis, E. and Paradis, J. 1995. "Language differentiation in early bilingual development." *Journal of Child Language* 22: 611–631.

Gleitman, L. 1990. "The structural sources of verb meanings." *Language Acquisition* 1: 3–55.

Goldin-Meadow, S., Butcher, C., Mylander, C. and Dodge, M. 1994. "Nouns and verbs in a self-styled gesture system: What's in a name?" *Cognitive Psychology* 27: 259–319.

Goldin-Meadow, S. and Feldman, H. 1977. "The development of language-like communication without a language model." *Science* 197: 401–403.

Goldin-Meadow, S. and Mylander, C. 1984. "Gestural communication in deaf children: The effects and noneffects of parental input on early language development." *Society for Research in Child Development Monographs Serial No. 207*: 49.

Goldin-Meadow, S. and Mylander, C. 1990. "Beyond the input given: The child's role in the acquisition of language." *Language* 66: 323–355.

Gomez, R.L and Gerken, L. 1999. "Artificial grammar learning by 1-year-olds leads to specific and abstract knowledge." *Cognition* 70 (2): 109–135.

Goodwyn, S.W., Acredolo, L.P. and Brown, C.A. 2000. "Impact of symbolic gesturing on early language development." *Journal of Nonverbal Behavior* 24: 81–103.

Goswami, U. 1998. *Cognition in children*. Hove: Psychology Press.

Greenberg, M.T., Calderon, R. and Kusché, C. 1984. "Early intervention using simultaneous communication with deaf infants: The effect on communication development." *Child Development* 55: 607–616.

Gregory, S. 1995. *Deaf children and their families*. Cambridge: Cambridge University Press.

Gregory, S. and Barlow, S. 1989. "Interaction between deaf babies and their deaf and hearing mothers." In *Language development and sign language. Monograph 1*, B. Woll (ed), 23–35. Bristol, UK: International Sign Language Association.

Gregory, S. and Hindley, P. 1996. "Communication strategies for deaf children." *Journal of Child Psychology and Psychiatry* 37: 895–905.

Gropen, J., Pinker, S., Hollander, M. and Goldberg, R. 1991. "Affectedness and direct objects: the role of lexical semantics in the acquisition of verb argument structure." *Cognition* 41: 153–195.

Grosjean, F. 1982. *Life with two languages*. Cambridge, Mass.: Harvard University Press.

Grosjean, F. 1992. "The bilingual and bicultural person in the hearing and deaf world." *Sign Language Studies* 77: 307–320.

Grove, N. and Walker, M. 1990. "The Makaton Vocabulary: using signs and graphic symbols to develop interpersonal communication." *Augmentative and Alternative Communication* 6: 15–28

Harris, M. 1976. "The influence of reversibility and truncation on the interpretation of the passive voice by young children." *British Journal of Psychology* 30: 419–428.

Harris, M. 1992. *Language experience and early language development: From input to uptake*. Hove: Lawrence Erlbaum Associates.

Harris, M. 2000. "Social interaction and early language development in deaf children." *Deafness and Education International* 2: 1–11

Harris, M., Clibbens, J., Chasin, J. and Tibbitts, R. 1989. "The social context of early sign language development." *First Language* 9: 81–97.

Harris, M. and Mohay, H. 1997. "Learning how to see signs: A comparison of attentional behaviour in eighteen month old deaf children with deaf and hearing mothers." *Journal of Deaf Studies and Deaf Education* 2: 95–103.

Hart, T.R. and Risley, B. 1995. *Meaningful differences in the everyday experience of young American children*. Baltimore: Paul H. Brookes.

Haug, T. 1999. "Review of sign language testing and assessment tools." Paper presented at the International Workshop on Sign Language Acquisition, European Science Foundation Network — Project "Intersign: Sign Linguistics and Data Exchange". London, September 4–6, 1999. http://www.signlang-assessment.info/eng.html

Haug, T. in press. "Review of sign language tests and assessment tools." *Sign Language and Linguistics.*

Herman, R. C. 1998. "The need for an assessment of British Sign Language development." *Deafness and Education* 22 (3): 3–8.

Herman, R. C., Holmes, S. and Woll, S. C. 1999. *Assessing BSL Development.* Coleford: Finest Book Services.

Herman, R. C. 2002. *The development of an assessment of British Sign Language development.* Doctoral dissertation, City University, London.

Hiatt, S, Campos, J. and Emde, R. 1979. "Facial patterning and infant emotional expression: happiness, surprise and fear." *Child Development* 50: 1020–35.

Hickok, G., Bellugi, U. and Klima, E. S. 1996a. "The neurobiology of sign language and its implications for the neural basis of language." *Nature* 381: 699–702.

Hickok, G., Bellugi, U. and Klima, E. S. 1998. "The neural organization of language: evidence from sign language aphasia." *Trends in Cognitive Sciences* 2: 129–136.

Hickok, G., Say, K., Bellugi, U. and Klima, E. S. 1996b. "The basis of hemispheric asymmetry for language and spatial cognition: clues from focal brain damage in two deaf native signers." *Aphasiology* 10: 577–591.

Hirsh-Pasek, K. and Golinkoff, R. M. 1996. *The origins of grammar: Evidence from early language comprehension.* Cambridge, MA: MIT press.

Hoffmeister, R. J. 1978a. "Word order in the acquisition of ASL." Paper presented at the Boston University Child Language Conference, Boston, MA.

Hoffmeister, R. J. 1978b. *The development of demonstrative pronouns, locatives, and personal pronouns in the acquisition of American Sign Language by deaf children of deaf parents.* Doctoral dissertation, University of Minnesota.

Holzrichter, A. and Meier, R. P. 2000. "Child-directed signing in American Sign Language." In *Language acquisition by eye,* C. Chamberlain, J. P. Morford and R. I. Mayberry (eds), 25–40. Mahwah, NJ: Lawrence Erlbaum Associates.

Jackendoff, R. 1997. *The architecture of the language faculty.* Cambridge, MA: MIT Press.

Jackson, A. L. 2001. "Language facility and theory of mind development in deaf children." *Journal of Deaf Studies and Deaf Education* 6: 161–176.

Jamieson, J. R. 1994. "Instructional discourse strategies: Differences between hearing and deaf mothers of deaf children." *First Language* 14: 153–171.

Janis, W. D. 1992. *Morphosyntax of the ASL Verb Phrase.* Doctoral Dissertation, State University of New York at Buffalo.

Janis, W. D. 1995. "A crosslinguistic perspective on ASL verb agreement." In *Language, gesture, and space,* K. Emmorey and J. Reilly (eds), 195–223. Hillsdale, NJ: Erlbaum.

Janzen, T., O'Dea, B. and Shaffer, B. 2001. "The construal of events: Passives in American Sign Language." *Sign Language Studies* 1 (3): 281–310.

Johnson, R. E., Liddell, S. K. and Erting, C. J. 1989. *Unlocking the curriculum: Principles for achieving access in deaf education.* Gallaudet Research Institute Working Paper 89:3.

Jones, B. W. and Quigley, S. P. 2002. "A study of complementation in the language of deaf and hearing students." *American Annals of the Deaf* 124: 23–29.

Jusczyk, P. W. 1997a. *The discovery of spoken language.* Cambridge, MA: The MIT Press.

Jusczyk, P.W. 1997b. "Finding and remembering words: Some beginnings by English-learning infants." *Current Directions in Psychological Science* 6: 170–174.

Kantor, R. 1982a. *Communicative interactions in American Sign Language between deaf mothers and their children: A psycholinguistic analysis.* Doctoral Dissertation, Boston University.

Kantor, R. 1982b. "Communication interaction: Mother modification and child acquisition of American Sign Language." *Sign Language Studies* 36: 233–282.

Karnopp, L.B. 1994. *Aquisição do parâmetro configuração de mão na Língua Brasileira de Sinais (LIBRAS): estudo sobre quatro crianças surdas, filhas de pais surdos.* Dissertação de Mestrado, PUC, Porto Alegre.

Karnopp, L.B. 1997. "Aquisição fonológica nas línguas de sinais." *Letras de Hoje* 32 (4): 147–162.

Karnopp, L.B. 1999a. "Pro-Gestos database." Manuscript.

Karnopp, L.B. 1999b. *Aquisição fonológica na Língua Brasileira de Sinais: estudo longitudinal de uma crianca surda.* Porto Alegre, PUCRS: Tese de Doutorado, 1999.

Keenan, E.L. 1976. "Towards a universal definition of *subject of.*" In *Subject and topic*, C.N. Li (ed), 303–333. New York: Academic Press.

Kegl, J.A. 1985. "Causative marking and the construal of agency in American Sign Language." In *CLS 21, Part 2: Papers from the Parasession on Causatives and Agentivity*, I.W. Eilfort, P.D. Kroeber and K.L. Peterson (eds), 120–137. Chicago, Illinois: Chicago Linguistic Society.

Kegl, J.A. 1986. "The role of sub-lexical structure in recreolization." Paper presented at the 18th Annual Stanford Child Language Research Forum, Stanford University. April 6, 1986.

Kegl, J.A 1990. "Predicate argument structure and verb class organisation in the ASL lexicon." In *Sign language research: theoretical issues*, C. Lucas (ed.), 149–175. Washington DC: Gallaudet University Press.

Kegl, J.A. 2000. "Is it soup yet? Or, When is it Language?" In *Proceedings of the Child Language Seminar 1999*, I. Barrière, G. Morgan, S. Chiat and B. Woll (eds), 97–114. City University, London.

Kegl, J. and Iwata, G. 1989. "Lenguaje de Signos Nicaragüense: A Pidgin Sheds Light on the Creole? ASL." In *Proceedings of the Fourth Meetings of the Pacific Linguistics Conference*, R. Carlson, S. DeLancey, S. Gildea, D. Payne and A. Saxena (eds), 266–294. Eugene, Oregon: Department of Linguistics, University of Oregon.

Kegl, J. and McWhorter, J. 1997. "Perspectives on an emerging language." *Proceedings of the 28th Annual Child Language Research Forum*, E. Clark (ed), 15–38. Stanford: CSLI publications.

Kegl, J., Morgan, G., Spitz, R. and Kyle, J. 1998. "Attribution of verb agreement, argument structure, and case marking to older Nicaraguan homesigners is unwarranted." Paper presented at the Annual Meeting of the Boston University Conference on Language Development.

Kegl, J., Senghas, A. and Coppola, M. 1999. "Creation through contact: Sign language emergence and sign language change in Nicaragua." In *Language contact and language change: The intersection of language acquisition, Creole genesis, and diachronic syntax*, M. DeGraff (ed.), 179–237. Cambridge, MA: MIT Press.

Kegl, J. and Stickney, H. 2002. "Description of Relative Clauses in Nicaraguan Sign Language (ISN)." Poster presented at the Annual Meeting of the Linguistic Society of America, San Francisco.

Klima, E. S. and Bellugi, U. 1979. *The signs of language*. Cambridge, MA: Harvard University Press.

Klinnert, M, Campos, J., Sorce, J., Emde, R., and Svejda, M. 1983. "Emotions as behaviour regulators: social referencing in infancy." In *Emotions: Theory, research, and experience, vol. 2*, R. Plutchnik and H. Kellerman (eds), 57–86. New York: Academic Press.

Knoors, H. 1992. *Exploratie van de gebarenruimte*. [Exploration of signing space]. Doctoral Dissertation, Koninklijke Ammanstichting Rotterdam. Delft: Eburon.

Knoors, H. 1994. "School Sign Language of the Netherlands: the language of Dutch non-native signing deaf children." *Perspectives on sign language usage, Volume 2. Papers from the Fifth International Symposium on Sign Language Research*, I. Ahlgren, B. Bergman and M. Brennan (eds), 333–344, Durham: ISLA.

Koester, L. S. 1994. "Early interactions and the socioemotional development of deaf infants." *Early Development and Parenting* 3: 51–60.

Koester, L. S., Brooks, L. and Traci, M. A. 2000. "Tactile contact by deaf and hearing mothers during face-to-face interactions with their infants." *Journal of Deaf Studies and Deaf Education* 5: 127–139.

Kyle, J. and Ackerman, J. 1990. "Signing for infants: Deaf mothers using BSL in the early stages of development." In *International Studies on Sign Language and Communication of the Deaf 10*, W. H. Edmondson and F. Karlsson (eds), 200–211. Hamburg: Signum Verlag.

Lane, H., Pillard, R. and French, M. 2000. "Origins of the American Deaf world: Assimilating and differentiating societies and their relation to genetic patterning." In *The signs of language revisited: an anthology to honor Ursula Bellugi and Edward Klima*, K. Emmorey and H. Lane (eds), 50–77. Mahwah, NJ: Lawrence Erlbaum Associates.

Launer, P. B. 1982. *'A' plane 'is not' to fly: Acquiring the distinction between related nouns and verbs in American Sign Language*. Doctoral Dissertation, City University of New York.

Lederberg, A. R. and Everhart, V. S. 1998. "Communication between deaf children and their hearing mothers: The role of language, gesture, and vocalizations." *Journal of Speech, Language, and Hearing Research* 41: 887–899.

Lee, R. G., Neidle, C., MacLaughlin, D., Bahan, B., and Kegl, J. 1997. "Role Shift in ASL: A syntactic look at direct speech." In *Syntactic structure and discourse function: An examination of two constructions in ASL*, C. Neidle, D. MacLaughlin and R. G. Lee (eds.), 24–45. Boston, MA: Boston University. [American Sign Language Linguistic Research Project Report 4].

Lenneberg, E. 1967. *Biological foundations of language*. New York: John Wiley & Sons.

Levelt, W. J. M. 1989. *Speaking from intention to articulation*. Cambridge, MA: MIT press.

Levelt, W. J. M. 1992. "Accessing words in speech production: stages, processes and representations." *Cognition* 42 (1–3): 1–22.

Levelt, W. J. M., Roelofs, A. and Meyer, A. S. 1999. "A theory of lexical access in speech production." *Behavioural and Brain Sciences* 22: 1–75.

Liben, L. S. 1978. "Developmental perspectives on experiential deficiencies of deaf children." In *Deaf children: Developmental perspectives*, L. Liben (ed), 195–215. New York: Academic Press.

Liddell, S. 1977. *An investigation into the syntactic structure of American Sign Language.* Doctoral Dissertation. University of California, San Diego.

Liddell, S. 1978. "An introduction to relative clauses in ASL." In *Understanding language through sign language research*, P. Siple (ed), 59–90. New York, NY: Academic Press.

Liddell, S. 1980. *American Sign Language syntax.* The Hague: Mouton.

Liddell, S. 1986. "Head thrust in ASL conditional marking." *Sign Language Studies* 52: 243–262.

Liddell, S. 1990. "Four functions of a locus: re-examining the structure of space in ASL." In *Sign Language Research: Theoretical Issues*, C. Lucas (ed), 176–198. Washington, DC: Gallaudet University Press.

Liddell, S. 1995. "Real, surrogate and token space: grammatical consequences in ASL." In *Language, Gesture and Space*, K. Emmorey and J. S. Reilly (eds), 19–41. Hillsdale, NJ: Erlbaum Associates.

Liddell, S. 1998. "Grounded blends, gestures, and conceptual shifts." *Cognitive Linguistics* 9: 283–314.

Liddell, S. 2000. "Indicating verbs and pronouns: pointing away from agreement." In *The signs of language revisited*, K. Emmorey and H. Lane (eds), 303–320. Mahwah, NJ: Erlbaum.

Liddell, S. and Metzger, M. 1998. "Gesture in sign language discourse." *Journal of Pragmatics* 30: 657–697.

Lieven, E. 1994. "Crosslinguistic and crosscultural aspects of language addressed to children." In *Input and interaction in language acquisition*, C. Gallaway and B. J. Richards (eds), 56–73. Cambridge: Cambridge University Press.

Lieven, E. 1997. "Variation in a cross-linguistic context." In *The cross-linguistic study of language acquisition, Volume 5* , D. I. Slobin (ed), 199–263. Mahwah, NJ: Lawrence Erlbaum Associates.

Lieven, E., Pine, J. and Baldwin, G. 1997. "Lexically-based learning and the development of grammar in early multi-word speech." *Journal of Child Language* 24 (1): 187–219.

Lillo-Martin, D. C. 1988. "Children's new sign creations." In *Language learning and deafness*, M. Strong (ed), 162–183. Cambridge: Cambridge University Press.

Lillo-Martin, D. C. 1991. *Universal grammar and American Sign Language.* Dordrecht: Kluwer.

Lillo-Martin, D. C. 2000. "Early and late in language acquisition: Aspects of the syntax and acquisition of Wh-questions in American Sign Language." In *The signs of language revisited: an anthology to honor Ursula Bellugi and Edward Klima*, K. Emmorey and H. Lane (eds), 355–401. Mahwah, NJ: Lawrence Erlbaum Associates.

Lillo-Martin, D. C. in press. "Where are all the modality effects?" In *Modality and structure in signed and spoken languages*, R. P. Meier, K. Cormier and D. Quinto-Pozos (eds). Cambridge: Cambridge University Press.

Lillo-Martin, D. C. and Klima, E. S. 1990. "Pointing out differences: ASL pronouns in syntactic theory." In *Theoretical Issues in Sign Language Research. Vol. 1: Linguistics,* S. D. Fischer and P. Siple (eds), 191–210. Chicago: University of Chicago Press.

Lindert, R. B. 2001. *Hearing families with deaf children: Linguistic and communicative aspects of American Sign Language development.* Doctoral dissertation, University of California, Berkeley.

Lindert, R. B. in press. "American Sign Language classifiers: can hearing mothers learn to use them effectively?" In *Crosslinguistic perspectives in sign language research*, A. E. Baker, B. van den Bogaerde and O. Crasborn (eds). Hamburg: Signum.

Loew, R. 1984. *Roles and reference in American Sign Language: A developmental perspective.* Doctoral dissertation, University of Minnesota.

Lucas, C. and Valli, C. 1992. *Language contact in the American deaf community.* San Diego: Academic Press.

Luetke-Stahlman, B. 1993. "Research-based language intervention strategies adapted for deaf and hard of hearing children." *American Annals of the Deaf* 138: 404–410.

MacSweeney, M., Woll, B., Campbell, R., McGuire, P. K., Calvert, G. A., David, A. S., Williams, S. C. R. and Brammer, M. J. in press. "Neural systems underlying British Sign Language sentence comprehension." *Brain.*

MacTurk, R. H., Meadow-Orlans, K. P., Koester, L. S. and Spencer, P. E. 1993. "Social support, motivation, language, and interaction. A longitudinal study of mothers and deaf infants." *American Annals of the Deaf* 138: 19–25.

MacWhinney, B. 1975. "Rules, Rote, and Analogy in Morphological Formations by Hungarian Children." *Journal of Child Language* 2 (1): 65–77.

MacWhinney, B. 1985. "Hungarian language acquisition as an exemplification of a general model of grammatical development." In *The crosslinguistic study of language acquisition, vol. 2,* D. I. Slobin (ed), 1069–1156. Hillsdale, NJ: Lawrence Erlbaum Associates.

MacWhinney, B. 2000. *The CHILDES project: Tools for analyzing talk.* Third Edition. Mahwah, NJ: Lawrence Erlbaum Associates.

Maestas y Moores, J. 1980. "Early linguistic environment: Interactions of deaf parents with their infants." *Sign Language Studies* 26: 1–13.

Mallory, B. L., Zingle, H. W. and Schein J. D. 1993. "Intergenerational Communication Modes in Deaf-Parented Families." *Sign Language Studies* 78: 73–92.

Marcus, G., Vijayan, S., Bandi Rao, S. and Vishton, P. 1999. "Rule-learning by seven-month-olds." *Science* 283: 77–80.

Marentette, P. F. 1995. *It's in her hands: A case study of the emergence of phonology in American Sign Language.* Doctoral Dissertation, McGill University, Montreal.

Marschark, M. 1993. *Psychological perspectives on deafness.* New York: Oxford University Press.

Marschark, M. 1994. "Gesture and sign." *Applied Psycholinguistics* 15: 209–236.

Marschark, M. and Everhart, V. S. 1997. "Relations of language and cognition: What do deaf children tell us?" In *Relations of language and thought: The view from sign language and deaf children,* M. Marschark, P. Siple, D. Lillo-Martin, R. Campbell and V. S. Everhart (eds), 3–23. New York: Oxford University Press.

Marschark, M., Lang, H. G. and Albertini, J. A. 2002. *Educating deaf students: From research to practice.* New York: Oxford University Press.

Marschark, M. and Lukomski, J. 2001. "Understanding language and learning in deaf children." In *Cognition, context, and deafness,* M. D. Clark, M. Marschark and M. Karchmer (eds), 71–86. Washington, DC: Gallaudet University Press.

Marschark, M., Siple, P., Lillo-Martin, D., Campbell, R. and Everhart, V. 1997. *Relations of language and thought: The view from sign language and deaf children*. New York: Oxford University Press.

Masataka, N. 2000. "The role of modality and input in the earliest stage of language acquisition: Studies of Japanese Sign Language." In *Language acquisition by eye*, C. Chamberlain, J.P. Morford and R.I. Mayberry (eds), 3–24. Mahwah, NJ: Lawrence Erlbaum Associates.

Mathur, G. and Rathmann, C. 2001. "Why not GIVE-US: an articulatory constraint in signed languages." In *Signed languages: Discoveries from international research*, V. Dively, M. Metzger, S. Taub and A.M. Baer (eds), 1–26. Washington, DC: Gallaudet University Press.

Mayberry, R.I. 1993. "First-language acquisition after childhood differs from second-language acquisition: the case of American Sign Language." *Journal of Speech and Hearing Research* 36: 1258–1270.

Mayberry, R.I. and Eichen, E.B. 1991. "The long-lasting advantage of learning sign language in childhood: Another look at the critical period for language acquisition." *Journal of Memory and Language* 30: 486–512.

Mayberry, R.I. and Fischer, S.D. 1989 "Looking through phonological shape to lexical meaning: The bottleneck of non-native sign language processing." *Memory & Cognition* 17(6): 740–754.

McBurney, S.L. in press. "Pronominal reference in signed and spoken language: Are grammatical categories modality-dependent?" In *Modality and structure in signed and spoken languages*, R.P. Meier, K. Cormier and D. Quinto-Pozos (eds). Cambridge: Cambridge University Press.

McDonald, B. 1982. *Aspects of the American Sign Language Predicate System*. Doctoral dissertation, University of Buffalo, Buffalo, New York.

McDonnell, P. 1996. *Verb categories in Irish Sign Language*. Doctoral Dissertation, University of Dublin.

McIntire, M. 1977. "The acquisition of American Sign Language hand configurations." *Sign Language Studies* 16: 247–266.

McIntire, M. (ed.). 1994. *The acquisition of American Sign Language by deaf children*. Silver Spring, MD: Linstok Press.

McNeill, D. 1992. *Hand and mind: What gesture reveals about thought*. Chicago: University of Chicago Press.

McNeill, D. 1993. "The circle from gesture to sign." In *Psychological Perspectives on Deafness*, M. Marschark and M.D. Clark (eds), 153–183. Hillsdale, NJ: Lawrence Erlbaum Associates.

McNeill, D. (ed.). 2000. *Language and Gesture*. Cambridge, UK: Cambridge University Press.

Meadow-Orlans, K.P. and Spencer, P.E. 1996. "Maternal sensitivity and visual attentiveness of children who are deaf." *Early Development and Parenting* 5: 213–223.

Mehler, J., Jusczyk, P.W., Lambertz, N., Bertoncini, J. and Amiel-Tison, C. 1988. "A precursor of language acquisition in young infants." *Cognition* 29: 144–178.

Meier, R.P. 1981. "Icons and morphemes: Models of the acquisition of verb agreement in ASL." *Papers and Reports on Child Language Development* 20: 92–99.

Meier, R.P. 1982. *Icons, analogues and morphemes: the acquisition of verb agreement in American Sign Language*. Doctoral Dissertation, University of California, San Diego.

Meier, R.P. 1983. "Mother does it right: verb agreement in American Sign Language motherese." Unpublished manuscript, University of Illinois at Urbana-Champaign.

Meier, R.P. 1984. "Sign as creole." *Behavioral and Brain Sciences* 7: 201–202.

Meier, R.P. 1987. "Elicited imitation of verb agreement in American Sign Language: Iconically or morphologically determined?" *Journal of Memory and Language* 26: 362–376.

Meier, R.P. 1990. "Person deixis in American Sign Language." In *Theoretical issues in sign language research. Vol. 1: Linguistics*, S.D. Fischer and P. Siple (eds), 175–190. Chicago: University of Chicago Press.

Meier, R.P. 1991. "Language acquisition by deaf children." *American Scientist* 79: 60–70.

Meier, R.P. 2000. "Diminishing diversity of signed languages." *Science* 288: 1965.

Meier, R.P. 2001. "Review of *Second Language Acquisition and the Critical Period Hypothesis*, by David Birdsong (Erlbaum, 1999)." *Journal of Child Language* 28: 222–228.

Meier, R.P. and Newport, E.L. 1990. "Out of the hands of babes: On a possible sign advantage in language acquisition." *Language* 66 (1): 1–23.

Meier, R.P. and Willerman, R. 1995. "Prelinguistic gesture in deaf and hearing infants." In *Language, gesture, and space*, K. Emmorey and J.S. Reilly (eds), 391–409. Hillsdale, NJ: Lawrence Erlbaum Associates.

Meir, I. 1998. "Syntactic-semantic interaction in Israeli Sign Language verbs: the case of backwards verbs." *Sign Language and Linguistics* 1: 3–33.

Meir, I. 2000. "Modality and grammaticalization: The emergence of a case system in Israeli Sign Language." Paper presented at the 7th International Conference on Theoretical Issues in Sign Language Research, Amsterdam, The Netherlands.

Meisel, J. 1989 "Early differentiation of languages in bilingual children." In *Bilingualism across the lifespan*, K. Hyltenstam and L. Obler (eds), 13–40. Cambridge: Cambridge University Press.

Messing, L.S. and Campbell, R. 1999 (eds.). *Gesture, Speech and Sign*. New York: Oxford University Press.

Metzger, M. 1995. "Constructed dialogue and constructed action in American Sign Language." In *Sociolinguistics in Deaf Communities*, C. Lucas (ed), 225–271. Washington DC: Gallaudet University Press.

Metz-Lutz, M.N., de Saint Martin, A., Monpiou, S., Massa, R., Hirsch, E. and Marescaux, C. 1999. "Early disassociation of verbal and nonverbal gestural ability in an epileptic deaf child." *Annals of Neurology* 46: 929–932.

Miller, C. 1994a. "A note on notation." *SignPost* 7 (3): 191–202.

Miller, C. 1994b. "Simultaneous constructions and complex signs in Quebec Sign Language." In *Perspectives on sign language structure — Papers from the Fifth International Symposium on Sign Language Research*, I. Ahlgren, B. Bergman and M. Brennan (eds), 131–147. Durham, UK: International Sign Linguistics Association and Deaf Studies Research Unit, Vol. 1.

Miller, J. and Weinert, R. 1998. *Spontaneous spoken language*. Oxford: Clarendon Press.

Mogford, K. 1993 "Oral language acquisition in the prelingually deaf." In *Language Development in Exceptional Circumstances*, D. Bishop and K. Mogford (eds), 110–131. Edinburgh: Churchill Livingstone.

Mohay, H., Milton, L., Hindmarsh, G. and Ganley, K. (1998). "Deaf mothers as communication models for hearing families with deaf children." In *Issues unresolved: New perspectives on language and deafness*, A. Weisel (ed), 76–87. Washington DC: Gallaudet University Press.

Moody, B. 1983. *La langue des signes, vol. 1: Histoire et grammaire*. Paris: Ellipses.

Morford, J.P. 1996. "Insights to language from the study of gesture: a review of gestural communication of non-signing deaf people." *Language and Communication* 16: 165–178.

Morford, J.P. and Kegl, J. 2000. "Gestural precursors of linguistic constructs: How input shapes the form of language." In *Language and Gesture*, D. McNeill (ed), 358–387. Cambridge: Cambridge University Press.

Morford, J.P. and Mayberry R.I. 2000 "A reexamination of *early exposure* and its implications for language acquisition by eye." In *Language Acquisition by Eye*, C. Chamberlain, J.P. Morford and R.I. Mayberry (eds), 111–127. Mahwah, N.J.: Lawrence Erlbaum Associates.

Morford, J.P. n.d. "Accessibility and availability in language development of deaf children." Unpublished manuscript.

Morgan, G. 1996. "The development of narrative in British Sign Language." In *Issues in Normal and Disordered Child Language: from Phonology to Narrative*, C. Schelletter, C. Letts and M. Garman (eds), 159–176. Reading: FECS Press.

Morgan, G. 1998. *The development of discourse cohesion in British Sign Language*. Doctoral Dissertation, University of Bristol.

Morgan, G. 1999. "Event packaging in British Sign Language discourse." In *Story Telling and Conversation: Discourse in Deaf Communities*, E. Winston (ed), 27–58. Washington, DC: Gallaudet University Press.

Morgan, G. 2000. "Discourse Cohesion in Sign and Speech." *International Journal of Bilingualism* 4 (3): 279–300.

Morgan, G., Barrière, I. and Woll, B. 2001a. "The emergence of lexical categories in British Sign Language." Paper presented at the Child Language Seminar, University of Hertfordshire, July, 2001.

Morgan, G., Herman, R. and Woll, B. 2001b. "The development of perspective shifting in British Sign Language." In *Research on Child Language Acquisition: Proceedings of the 8th Conference of the International Association for the Study of Child Language*, M. Almgren, A. Barreña, M. Ezeizabarrena, I. Idiazabal and B. MacWhinney (eds), 1421–1428. Somerville, MA: Cascadilla Press.

Morgan, G., Smith, I., Tsimpli, I. and Woll, B. 2002. "Language against the odds: the learning of BSL by a polyglot savant." *Journal of Linguistics* 38 (1): 1–41.

Mühlhäusler, P. 1986. *Pidgin & creole linguistics*. Oxford: Blackwell.

Musselman, C.R. and Churchill, A. 1991. "Conversational control in mother-child dyads." *American Annals of the Deaf* 136: 99–117.

Musselman, C. R., Lindsay, P. H. and Wilson, A. K. 1988 "The effect of mothers' communication mode on language development in preschool deaf children." *Applied Psycholinguistics* 9 (2): 185–204.

Naigles, L. 1990. "Children use syntax to learn verb meanings." *Journal of Child Language* 17: 357–374.

Neidle, C., Kegl, J., MacLaughlin, D., Bahan, B. and Lee, R. 2000. *The syntax of American Sign Language: Functional categories and hierarchial structure.* Cambridge, MA: The MIT Press.

Neidle, C., MacLaughlin, D., Bahan, B., Lee, R. G. and Kegl, J. 1997. *The SignStream™ Project (Rep. No. 5).* Boston: Boston University.

Nelson, C. A. 1987. "The recognition of facial expressions in the first two years of life: Mechanisms of development." *Child Development* 58: 890–909.

Nelson, K. E., Loncke, F. and Camarata, S. 1993. "Implications of research on deaf and hearing children's language learning." In *Psychological perspectives on deafness,* M. Marschark and M. D. Clark (eds), 123–152. Hillsdale, NJ: Lawrence Erlbaum Associates.

Neville, H. J. 1991. "Whence the specialization of the language hemisphere?" In *Modularity and the motor theory of speech perception,* I. G. Mattingly and M. Studdert-Kennedy (Eds.), 269–294. Hillsdale NJ: Lawrence Erlbaum Associates.

Neville, H. and Lawson, D. 1987. "Attention to central and peripheral visual space in a movement detection task: An event-related potential and behavioral study. I. Normal hearing adults." *Brain Research* 405: 253–267.

Neville, H., Kutas, M. and Schmidt, A. 1982. "Event-related potential studies of cerebral specialization during reading. II. Studies of congentially deaf adults." *Brain and Language* 16: 316–337.

Newport, E. L. 1982. "Task specificity in language learning? Evidence from speech perception and American Sign Language." In *Language Acquisition: The state of the art,* E. Wanner and L. Gleitman (eds), 450–486. New York: Cambridge University Press.

Newport, E. L. 1990a. "Constraints on learning and their role in language acquisition: Studies of the acquisition of American Sign Language." *Language Sciences* 10 (1): 147–172.

Newport, E. L. 1990b. "Maturational constraints on language learning." *Cognitive Science* 14: 11–28.

Newport, E. L. and Meier, R. P. 1985. "The acquisition of American Sign Language." In *The crosslinguistic study of language acquisition, Vol. 1,* D. I. Slobin (ed), 881–938. Hillsdale, NJ: Lawrence Erlbaum Associates.

Newport, E. L. and Supalla, T. 2000. "Sign language research at the Millennium." In *The Signs of Language Revisited.* K. Emmorey and H. Lane (eds). 103–114. Mohwah, NJ: Lawrence Erlbaum Associates.

O'Grady, W. 1997. *Syntactic development.* Chicago: The University of Chicago Press.

Ochs, E. 1979. "Transcription as theory." In *Developmental pragmatics,* E. Ochs and B. B. Schieffelin (eds), 43–72. New York: Academic Press.

Olguin, R. and Tomasello, M. 1993. "Twenty-five-month-old children do not have a grammatical category of Verb." *Cognitive Development* 8: 245–272.

Oller, D. K. and Eilers, R. E. 1988. "The role of audition in infant babbling." *Child Development* 59: 441–449.

Oller, D.K., Eilers, R.E., Bull, D.H. and Carney, A.E. 1985. "Prespeech vocalizations of a deaf infant: A comparison with normal metaphonological development." *Journal of Speech and Hearing Research* 28: 47–63.

Orlansky, M.D. and Bonvillian, J.D. 1984. "The role of iconicity in early sign language acquisition." *Journal of Speech and Hearing Disorders* 49: 287–292.

Orlansky, M.D. and Bonvillian, J.D. 1985. "Sign language acquisition: Language development in children of deaf parents and implications for other populations." *Merrill-Palmer Quarterly* 31: 127–143.

Ossella, T., Ardito, B., Bianchi, P.M., Gentile, S., Luchenti, S., Tieri, L., Caselli, M.C., Pizzuto, E., Bosi, R. and Cafasso, R. 1994. "Lo sviluppo dei processi di simbolizzazione nei bambini sordi, strategie di comunicazione verbale e non verbale e ripercussioni sulle modalità in ambito familiare e sociale." Research Report 92/02/P/283, Rome: Institute of Psychology, CNR & Pediatric Hospital Bambino Gesù.

Paatsch, L.E., Blamey, P.J. and Sarant, J.Z. 2001. "The effects of articulation training on the production of trained and untrained phonemes in conversations and formal tests." *Journal of Deaf Studies and Deaf Education* 6: 32–42.

Padden, C.A. 1981. "Some arguments for syntactic patterning in ASL." *Sign Language Studies* 32: 239–259.

Padden, C.A. 1983. *Interaction of morphology and syntax in American Sign Language.* Doctoral dissertation, University of California, San Diego.

Padden, C.A. 1988. *Interaction of morphology and Syntax in American Sign Language.* New York: Garland Publishers.

Padden, C.A. 1990. "The relationship between space and grammar in ASL verb morphology." In *Sign Language Research: Theoretical Issues,* C. Lucas (ed), 118–132. Washington, DC: Gallaudet University Press.

Padden, C.A. 1998. "The ASL lexicon." *Sign Languages and Linguistics* 1: 39–60.

Peter, M. and Barnes, R. 1982. *Signs, Symbols and Schools.* London: National Council for Special Education.

Peters, A.M. 1985. "Language segmentation: Operating principles for the perception and analysis of language." In *The crosslinguistic study of language acquisition, Vol. 1,* D.I. Slobin (ed), 1029–1067. Hillsdale, NJ: Lawrence Erlbaum Associates

Peterson, C.C. and Siegal, M. 2000. "Insights into theory of mind from deafness and autism." *Mind & Language* 15: 123–145.

Petitto, L.A. 1987. "On the autonomy of language and gesture: Evidence from the acquisition of personal pronouns in American Sign Language." *Cognition* 27: 1–52.

Petitto, L.A. 1988. "*Language* in the prelinguistic child." In *The development of language and language researchers: Essays in honor of Roger Brown,* F.S. Kessel (ed), 187–221. Hillsdale, NJ: Erlbaum.

Petitto, L.A. 2000. "The acquisition of natural sign languages: lessons in the nature of human language and its biological foundations." In *Language acquisition by eye,* C. Chamberlain, J. Morford and R. Mayberry (eds), 41–50. Mahwah, NJ: Lawrence Erlbaum Associates.

Petitto, L.A., Katerelos, M., Levy, B.G., Gauna, K., Tétrault, K. and Ferraro V. 2001a. "Bilingual signed and spoken language acquisition from birth: Implications for the mechanisms underlying early bilingual language acquisition." *Journal of Child Language* 28: 453–496.

Petitto, L.A. and Marntette, P.F. 1991. "Babbling in the manual mode: Evidence for the ontogeny of language." *Science* 251: 1493–1496.

Petitto, L.A. and Seidenberg, M. 1979. "On the evidence for linguistic abilities in signing apes." *Brain and Language* 8: 162–183.

Petitto, L.A., Zatorre, R.J., Gauna, K., Nikelski, E.J., Dostie, D. and Evans, A.C. 2001b. "Speech-like cerebral activity in profoundly deaf people processing signed languages: implications for the neural basis of human language." *Proceedings of the National Academy of Science* 97: 13961–13966.

Pickersgill, M. and Gregory, S. 1998. *Sign bilingualism: a model*. Middlesex, UK: Adept Press.

Pietrandrea, P. 1995. *Analisi semiotica dei dizionari della Lingua Italiana dei Segni*. Undergraduate Dissertation, University of Rome "La Sapienza".

Pietrandrea, P. 1997. "I dizionari della LIS: analisi quantitative e qualitative." In *LIS — Studi, esperienze e ricerche sulla Lingua dei Segni in Italia*, M.C. Caselli and S. Corazza (eds), 255–259. Pisa: Edizioni del Cerro.

Pine, J., Lieven, E. and Rowland, G. 1998. "Comparing different models of the development of the English verb category." *Linguistics* 36: 4–40.

Pinker, S. 1989. *Learnability and cognition: the acquisition of argument structure*. Cambridge: Cambridge University Press.

Pinker, S. 1994. "How could a child use verb syntax to learn verb semantics?" *Lingua* 92: 377–410.

Pinker, S., Lebeaux, D.S. and Frost, L.A. 1987. "Productivity and constraints in the acquisition of the passive." *Cognition* 26: 195–267.

Pizzuto, E. 1986. "The verb system of Italian Sign Language." In *Signs of Life*, B.T. Tervoort (ed), 17–31. Amsterdam: University of Amsterdam.

Pizzuto, E. 1987. "Aspetti morfosintattici." In *La Lingua Italiana dei Segni — La Comunicazione Visivo-Gestuale dei Sordi*, V. Volterra (ed), 179–209. Bologna: Il Mulino.

Pizzuto, E., Ardito, B., Caselli, M.C. and Corazza, S. 1999. "The development of Italian Sign Language (LIS) in deaf preschoolers: data from lexical and sentence elicitation tasks." Paper presented at the 7th International Congress of the International Association for the Study of Child Language, San Sebastian, Spain, 12–16 July,1999.

Pizzuto, E., Ardito, B., Caselli, M.C. and Corazza, S. 2000a. "La LIS dai 4 ai 6 anni: nuovi dati su bambini sordi figli di genitori sordi." In *Viaggio nella città invisibile — Atti del 2° Convegno Nazionale sulla Lingua dei Segni, Genova, 25–27 settembre 1998*, C. Bagnara, G. Chiappini, M.P. Conte, M. Ott (eds), 365–376. Pisa: Edizioni del Cerro.

Pizzuto, E., Ardito, B., Caselli, M.C. and Volterra, V. 2001. "Cognition and language in Italian deaf preschoolers of deaf and hearing families." In *Context, Cognition and Deafness*, M.D. Clark, M. Marschark and M. Karchmer (eds), 49–70. Washington, DC: Gallaudet University Press.

Pizzuto, E. and Caselli, M.C. 1992. "The acquisition of Italian morphology: Implications for models of language development." *Journal of Child Language* 19: 491–557.

Pizzuto, E. and Caselli, M.C. 1994. "The acquisition of Italian verb morphology in a crosslinguistic perspective." In *Other Children, Other Languages*, Y. Levy (ed), 137–187. Hillsdale, NJ: Lawrence Erlbaum Associates.

Pizzuto, E., Caselli, M. C., Ardito, B., Ossella, M. T., Albertoni, A., Santarelli, B. and Cafasso, R. 1998. "Assessing cognitive, relational and language abilities in preschool Italian deaf children." In *Issues Unresolved: New Perspectives on Language and Deaf Education*, A. Wiesel (ed), 41–52. Washington, DC: Gallaudet University Press.

Pizzuto, E., Caselli, M. C. and Volterra, V. 2000b. "Language, Cognition and Deafness." *Seminars in Hearing* 21 (4): 343–358.

Pizzuto, E. and Corazza, S. 1996. "Noun morphology in Italian Sign Language (LIS)." *Lingua* 98: 169–196.

Pizzuto, E. and Corazza, S. 2000. "Segni senza parole: osservazioni sui 'classificatori' della LIS." In *Viaggio nella città invisibile — Atti del 2° Convegno Nazionale sulla Lingua dei Segni, Genova, 25–27 settembre 1998*, C. Bagnara, G. Chiappini, M. P. Conte and M. Ott (eds), 50–59. Pisa: Edizioni del Cerro.

Pizzuto, E., Giuranna, E. and Gambino, G. 1990. "Manual and nonmanual morphology in Italian Sign Language: grammatical constraints and discourse structure." In *Sign Language Research: Theoretical Issues*, C. Lucas (ed), 83–102. Washington, DC: Gallaudet University Press.

Pizzuto, E. and Pietrandrea, P. 2001. "The notation of signed texts: open questions and indications for further research." *Sign Language and Linguistics* 4, 29–45.

Pizzuto, E. and Volterra, V. in press. "La Lingua dei Segni Italiana (LIS)." In *La Linguistica Italiana alle soglie del 2000*, C. Lavinio (ed.). Rome: Bulzoni.

Pizzuto, E., Wilcox, S., Hanke, T., Janzen, T., Kegl, J. A., Shepard-Kegl, J. 2000c. "Cross-linguistic investigations of signed languages: can similarities and differences be detected without appropriate tools for representing and analyzing signed texts?" Workshop presented at the 7th International Congress on Theoretical Issues in Sign Language Research. Amsterdam, The Netherlands, July 23–27, 2000.

Poizner, H., Klima, E. S. and Bellugi, U. 1987. *What the hands reveal about the brain*. Cambridge, MA: MIT Press.

Poizner, H. and Tallal, P. 1987. "Temporal processing in deaf signers." *Brain and Language* 30: 52–62.

Polich, L. G. 1998. *Social agency and deaf communities: a Nicaraguan case study*. Doctoral dissertation, University of Texas at Austin.

Polich, L. G. 2000. "The Search for Proto-NSL: Looking for the roots of the Nicaraguan deaf community." In *Bilingualism and identity in Deaf communities*, M. Metzger (ed), 255–305. Washington, DC: Gallaudet University Press.

Poulin, C. and Miller, C. 1995. "On narrative discourse and point of view in Quebec Sign Language." In *Language, Gesture, and Space*, K. Emmorey and J. Reilly (eds), 117–131. Hillsdale, NJ: Lawrence Erlbaum Associates.

Pressman, L. J., Pipp-Siegel, S., Yoshinaga-Itano, C. and Deas, A. 1999. "Maternal sensitivity predicts language gained in preschool children who are deaf and hard of hearing." *Journal of Deaf Studies and Deaf Education* 4: 294–304.

Prillwitz, S. Leven, R., Zienerth, H., Hanke, T. and Henning, J. 1989. "HamNoSys, Version 2.0. Hamburg Notation System for Sign Languages. An Introductory Guide." *International Studies on Sign Language and the Communication of the Deaf, Volume 5*. Hamburg: Signum Press.

Prinz, P. and Prinz, E. 1981. "Acquisition of ASL and spoken English by a hearing child of a deaf mother and hearing father: Phase II, early combinatorial patterns." *Sign Language Studies* 30: 78–88.

Provine, K., Reilly, J., and Anderson, D. 1993. "Language development in deaf children: The CDI for ASL." Poster presented at the American Speech and Hearing Association, Los Angeles, CA, November 1993.

Pye, C. and Quixtan Poz, P. 1988. "Precocious passives and antipassives in Quiche Mayan." *Papers and Reports on Child Language Development* 27: 71–80.

Quay, S. 1995. "The bilingual lexicon: implications for studies of language choice." *Journal of Child Language* 22: 369–387.

Quittner, A. L., Smith, L. B., Osberger, M. J., Mitchell, T. V. and Katz, D. B. 1994. "The impact of audition on the development of visual attention." *Psychological Science* 5: 347–353.

Rathmann, C. 2000. "Does the presence of person agreement marker predict word order in signed languages?" Paper presented at the 7th International Conference on Theoretical Issues in Sign Language Research, Amsterdam, The Netherlands.

Rathmann, C. and Mathur, G. in press. "Is verb agreement the same cross-modally?" In *Modality and structure in signed and spoken languages*, R. P. Meier, K. Cormier and D. Quinto-Pozos (eds). Cambridge: Cambridge University Press.

Rea, C. A., Bonvillian, J. D. and Richards, H. C. 1988. "Mother-infant interactive behaviors: Impact of maternal deafness." *American Annals of the Deaf* 133: 317–324.

Redington, M. and Chater, N. 1997. "Probabilistic and distributional approaches to language acquisition." *Trends in Cognitive Science* 1 (7): 273–281.

Reilly, J. S. 1983. "What are conditionals for?" In *Papers and Reports on Child Language Development* 22: 1–8.

Reilly, J. S. 2000. "Bringing affective expression into the service of language: acquiring perspective marking in narratives." In *The Signs of Language Revisited — An Anthology to Honor Ursula Bellugi and Edward Klima*, K. Emmmorey and H. Lane (eds), 415–433. Mahwah, NJ: Lawrence Erlbaum Associates.

Reilly, J. S. and Bellugi, U. 1996. "Competition on the face: Affect and language in ASL motherese." *Journal of Child Language* 23: 219–236.

Reilly, J. S. and McIntire, M. L. 1980. "ASL and Pidgin Sign English: What's the difference?" *Sign Language Studies* 27: 151–192.

Reilly, J. S. and McIntire, M. L. 1991. "WHERE SHOE: The acquisition of wh-questions in ASL." *Papers and Reports in Child Language Development* 30: 104–111.

Reilly, J. S., McIntire, M. L. and Bellugi, U. 1990a. "The acquisition of conditionals in American Sign Language: Grammaticized facial expressions." *Applied Psycholinguistics* 11 (4): 369–392.

Reilly, J.S, McIntire, M. L. and Bellugi, U. 1990b. "Faces: The relationship between language and affect." In *From gesture to language in hearing and deaf children*, V. Volterra and C. J. Erting (eds), 128–141. Berlin: Springer-Verlag.

Reilly, J. S., McIntire, M. L. and Bellugi, U. 1991. "BABYFACE: A new perspective on universals in language acquisition." In *Theoretical issues in sign language research: Psycholinguistics*, P. Siple (ed.), 9–24. Chicago, IL: University of Chicago Press.

Reilly, J. S., McIntire, M. L. and Seago, H. 1992. "Affective prosody in American Sign Language." *Sign Language Studies* 75: 113–128.

Remmel, E., Bettger, J.G. and Weinberg, A. 2002. "Theory of mind development in deaf children." In *Context, cognition and deafness*, M.D. Clark and M. Marschark (Eds.), 113–134. Washington DC: Gallaudet University Press.

Ritter-Brinton, K. and Stewart, D. 1992. "Hearing parents and deaf children: Some perspectives on sign communication and service delivery." *American Annals of the Deaf* 137: 85–91.

Romaine, S. 1988. *Pidgin and creole languages*. London: Longman.

Romaine, S. 1995. *Bilingualism*. Oxford: Basil Blackwell.

Ronnberg, J., Søderfeldt, B. and Risberg, J. 2000. "The cognitive neuroscience of signed language." *Acta Psychologica* 105: 237–254.

Rossini, P., Reilly, J., Fabbretti, D. and Volterra, V. 2000. "Aspetti non manuali nelle narrazioni LIS." In *Viaggio nella città invisibile — Atti del 2° Convegno Nazionale sulla Lingua dei Segni, Genova, 25–27 settembre 1998*, C. Bagnara, G. Chiappini, M.P. Conte and M. Ott (eds), 112–119. Pisa: Edizioni del Cerro.

Rowland, C.F. and Pine, M.J. 2000. "Subject-auxiliary inversion errors and wh-question acquisition: what children do know?." *Journal of Child Language* 27: 157–181.

Rubino, R. and Pine, J. 1998. "Subject-verb agreement in Brazilian Portugese: What low error rates hide." *Journal of Child Language* 25: 35–60.

Russell, P.A., Hosie, J.A., Gray, C.D., Scott, C., Hunter, N., Banks, J.S. and Macaulay, M.C. 1998. "The development of theory of mind in deaf children." *Journal of Child Psychology & Psychiatry & Allied Disciplines* 39: 903–910.

Russo, T. 1999. *Immagini e Metafore nelle Lingue Parlate e Segnate. Modelli Semiotici e Applicazioni alla LIS (Lingua Italiana dei Segni)*. Doctoral Dissertation, Universities of Palermo, Calabria and Rome "La Sapienza".

Russo, T., Giuranna, R. and Pizzuto, E. 2001. "Italian Sign Language (LIS) poetry: iconic properties and structural regularities." *Sign Language Studies* 2 (1): 84–112.

Saffran, J., Aslin, R. and Newport, E. 1996. "Statistical learning by 8-month-old infants." *Science* 274: 1926–1926.

Sandler, W. 1989. *Phonological representation of the sign: linearity and nonlinearity in American Sign Language*. Dordrecht: Foris.

Sandler, W. 1990. "Temporal aspects and ASL phonology." In: *Theoretical issues in sign language research, vol. 1: Linguistics.*, S. Fischer and P. Siple (eds), 7–35. Chicago: University of Chicago Press.

Sandler, W. 1995. "One phonology or two? Sign language and phonological theory." *Glot International* 1 (3): 3–8.

Schembri, A. 1999. " Rethinking 'classifiers' in signed languages." Unpublished Manuscript, University of Sydney.

Schermer, T.M. 1990. *In search of a language. Influences from spoken Dutch on Sign Language of the Netherlands*. Doctoral Dissertation, University of Amsterdam, Delft: Eburon Publishers.

Schiff-Myers, N. 1988. "Hearing children of deaf parents." In *Language development in exceptional circumstances*, D.V. Bishop and K. Mogford (Eds.), 47–61. London: Livingstone.

Schlesinger, H.S. and Meadow, K.P. 1972. *Sound and sign: Childhood deafness and mental health*. Berkeley, CA: University of California Press.

Schley, S. 1991. "Infant discrimination of gestural classes: Precursors of ASL acquisition." *Sign Language Studies* 72: 77–296.

Seal, B.C. 1998. *Best practices in educational interpreting*. Boston: Allyn and Bacon.

Senghas, A. 1995. *Children's contribution to the birth of Nicaraguan Sign Language*. Doctoral dissertation, Massachusetts Institute of Technology.

Senghas, A. 2000. "The development of early spatial morphology in Nicaraguan Sign Language." In *The proceedings of the Boston University Conference on Language Development, vol. 24*, S.C. Howell, S.A. Fish and T. Keith-Lucas (eds), 696–707. Boston: Cascadilla Press.

Senghas, A. and Coppola, M. 2001. "Children creating language: How Nicaraguan Sign Language acquired a spatial grammar." *Psychological Science* 12 (4): 323–328.

Senghas, A., Coppola, M., Newport, E.L. and Supalla, T. 1997. "Argument structure in Nicaraguan Sign Language: The emergence of grammatical devices." In *The proceedings of the Boston University Conference on Language Development, vol. 21*, E. Hughes, M. Hughes and A. Greenhill (eds), 550–561. Boston: Cascadilla Press.

Serry, T. and Blamey, P. 1999. "A 4-year investigation into phonetic inventory development in young cochlear implant users." *Journal of Speech, Language, and Hearing Research* 42: 141–154.

Shepard-Kegl, J. 1985. *Locative Relations in American Sign Language Word Formation, Syntax, and Discourse*. MIT Working Papers in Linguistics, Cambridge, MA.

Siedlecki, T. and Bonvillian, J. 1993a. "Location, handshape and movement: Young children's acquisition of the formational aspects of American Sign Language." *Sign Language Studies* 78: 31–51.

Siedlecki, T. and Bonvillian, J. 1993b. "Phonological deletion revisited: Errors in young children's two-handed signs." *Sign Language Studies* 80: 223–242.

Siedlecki, T. and Bonvillian, J. 1997. "Young children's acquisition of the handshape aspect of American Sign Language signs: Parental report findings." *Applied Psycholinguistics* 18: 17–39.

Sieratzki, J.S., Calvert, G.A., Brammer, M.J., Campbell, R., David, A.S. and Woll, B. 2001. "Accessibility of spoken, written, and sign language in Landau-Kleffner syndrome: a linguistic and functional MRI study." *Epileptic Disorders* 3: 79–89.

Singleton, J.L. 1987. *When learners surpass their models: The Acquisition of American Sign Language from impoverished input*. Master's thesis, University of Illinois, Urbana-Champaign.

Singleton, J.L. 1989. *Restructuring of language from impoverished input: Evidence for Linguistic Compensation*. Doctoral Dissertation, University of Illinois, Urbana.

Singleton, J.L., Goldin-Meadow, S. and McNeill, D. 1995. "The cataclysmic break between gesticulation and sign: Evidence against a unified continuum of gestural communication." In *Language, gesture, and space*, K. Emmorey and J.S. Reilly (eds), 287–312. Hillsdale, NJ: Lawrence Erlbaum Associates.

Singleton, J.L. and Newport, E.L. in press. "When learners surpass their models: The acquisition of American Sign Language from inconsistent input." *Cognitive Psychology*.

Singleton, J.L. and Tittle, M.D. 2000. "Deaf parents and their hearing children." *Journal of Deaf Studies and Deaf Education* 5: 221–236.

Siple, P. 1997a. "Modules and the Informational Encapsulation of Language." In *Relations of Language and Thought: the view from sign language and deaf children*, M. Marschark, P. Siple, D. Lillo-Martin, R. Campbell and V.S. Everhart, 163–171. Oxford: Oxford University Press.

Siple, P. 1997b. "Universals, generalizability, and the acquisition of signed language." In *Relations of language and thought: The view from sign language and deaf children*, Marschark, M., Siple, P., Lillo-Martin, D. and Everhart, V., 24–61. New York: Oxford University Press.

Slobin, D.I. 1982. "Universal and particular in the acquisition of language." In *Language acquisition: The state of the art*, E. Wanner and L.R. Gleitman (eds), 128–170. New York: Cambridge University Press.

Slobin, D.I. 1985. "Why study acquisition crosslinguistically?" In *The crosslinguistic study of language acquisition*, Vol. 2, D.I. Slobin (ed), 3–22. Hillsdale, NJ: Lawrence Erlbaum Associates.

Slobin, D.I. (ed.) 1985. *The crosslinguistic study of language acquisition, Vols. 1&2*: Hillsdale, NJ: Lawrence Erlbaum Associates.

Slobin, D.I., Hoiting, N., Anthony, M., Biederman, Y., Kuntze, M., Lindert, R., Pyers, J., Thumann, H. and Veinberg, A. 2001. "Sign language transcription at the level of meaning components: the Berkeley Transcription System (BTS)." *Sign Language and Linguistics* 4, 63–96.

Slobin, D.I., Hoiting, N., Kuntze, M., Lindert, R., Weinberg, A., Pyers, J., Anthony, M., Biederman, Y. and Thumann, H. in press. "A cognitive/functional perspective on the acquisition of *classifiers*." In *Perspectives on classifier constructions in sign languages*, K. Emmorey (ed). Mahwah, NJ: Lawrence Erlbaum Associates.

Smith, N.V. 1999. *Chomsky, ideas and ideals*. Cambridge: Cambridge University Press.

Smith, W. 1990. "Evidence for auxiliaries in Taiwanese Sign Language." In *Theoretical issues in sign language research. Vol. 1: Linguistics*, S.D. Fischer and P. Siple (eds), 211–228. Chicago: University of Chicago Press.

Snow, C.E. and Ferguson, C.A. (eds.). 1977. *Talking to children: Language input and sensory acquisition*. Cambridge, MA: Cambridge University Press.

Søderfeldt, B., Ronnberg, J. and Risberg, J. 1994. "Regional cerebral blood flow during sign language reception: Deaf and hearing subjects with deaf parents compared." *Sign Language Studies* 84: 199–207.

Spencer, P.E. 1993a. "Communication behaviours of infants with hearing loss and their hearing mothers." *Journal of Speech and Hearing Research* 36: 311–321.

Spencer, P.E. 1993b. "The expressive communication of hearing mothers and deaf infants." *American Annals of the Deaf* 138: 275–283.

Spencer, P.E. 2000. "Looking without listening: Is audition a prerequisite for normal development of visual attention during infancy?" *Journal of Deaf Studies and Deaf Education* 5: 291–302.

Spencer, P.E. 2002. "Language development of children with cochlear implants." In *Cochlear implants in children: Ethics and choices*, J. Christiansen and I. Leigh (eds), 222–249. Washington, DC: Gallaudet University Press.

Spencer, P. E., Bodner-Johnson, B. A. and Gutfreund, M. K. 1992. "Interacting with infants with a hearing loss: What can we learn from mothers who are deaf?" *Journal of Early Intervention* 16: 64–78.

Spencer, P. E. and Hafer, J. C. 1998. "Play as 'window' and 'room': Assessing and supporting the cognitive and linguistic development of deaf infants and young children." In *Psychological perspectives on deafness. Volume 2*, M. Marschark and M. D. Clark, (eds), 131–152. Mahwah, NJ: Lawrence Erlbaum Associates.

Spitz, R. and Kegl, J. 1999. "Cognitive Consequences for Critical Periods of Language Acquisition." Grand Rounds, Maine Medical Center, Dana Center. Portland, ME. (manuscript in preparation)

Stack, K. 1999. *Innovation by a child acquiring Signing Exact English II*. Doctoral dissertation, University of California, Los Angeles.

Stenberg, C. R. and Campos, J. J. 1990. "The development of anger expressions in infancy." In *Psychological and biological approaches to emotion*, N. Stein, B. Leventhal and T. Trabasso (eds), 247–282. Hillsdale, NJ: Lawrence Erlbaum Associates.

Stoel-Gammon, C. and Otomo, K. 1986. "Babbling development of hearing-impaired and normally hearing subjects." *Journal of Speech and Hearing Disorders* 51: 33–41.

Stokoe, W. C. 1960. *Sign language structure*. Studies in Linguistics Occasional Papers 8. Buffalo, NY: University of Buffalo Press.

Stokoe, W. C., Casterline, D.C and Croneberg, C. G. 1965. *A dictionary of American Sign Language on linguistic principles, 1st edition*. Washington, DC: Gallaudet College Press.

Stokoe, W. C., Casterline, D. C. and Croneberg, C. G. 1976. *A Dictionary of American Sign Language on Linguistic Principles, 2nd edition*. Silver Spring, MD: Linstok Press.

Stokoe, W. C. and Marschark, M. 1999. "Signs, gestures, and signs." In *Gesture, speech, and sign*, L. Messing and R. Campbell (eds), 161–182. Oxford: Oxford University Press.

Strong, M. and Prinz, P. M. 2000. "Is American Sign Language skill related to English Literacy?" In *Language acquisition by eye*, C. D. Chamberlain, J. Morford and R. Mayberry (eds), 131–141. Mahwah, NJ: Lawrence Erlbaum Associates.

Sudhalter, V. and Braine, M. D. S. 1985. "How does comprehension of passives develop? A comparison of actional and experiential verbs." *Journal of Child Language* 12: 455–470.

Supalla, S. J. 1991. "Manually Coded English: The modality question in signed language development." In *Theoretical issues in sign language research. Volume 2: Psychology*, P. Siple and S. D. Fischer (eds), 85–109 Chicago: University of Chicago Press.

Supalla, S. J. and McKee, C. in press. "The role of Manually Coded English in language development of deaf children." In *Modality and structure in signed and spoken languages*, R. P. Meier, K. Cormier and D. Quinto-Pozos (eds). Cambridge: Cambridge University Press.

Supalla, S. J., Singleton, J., Wix, T. and Maller, S. 1998. "The development and psychometric properties of the American Sign Language Assessment." Unpublished Manuscript, University of Arizona, Tucson.

Supalla, T. 1990. "Serial verbs of motion in ASL." In *Theoretical issues in sign language research. Vol. 1*, S. D. Fischer and P. Siple (eds), 127–152. Chicago: The University of Chicago Press.

Supalla, T. n.d. "An implicational hierarchy in verb agreement in American Sign Language." Unpublished manuscript, University of Rochester.

Supalla, T. and Webb, R. 1995. "The grammar of International Sign: A new look at pidgin languages." In *Language, gesture, and space*, K. Emmorey and J. Reilly (eds), 333–352. Hillsdale, NJ: Lawrence Erlbaum Associates.

Sutton, V. 1999. "SignWriting: On the occasion of its 25th anniversary November 1999." *Sign Language and Linguistics* 2: 271–281.

Sutton-Spence, R. and Woll, B. 1999. *The linguistics of British Sign Language: an introduction.* Cambridge: Cambridge University Press.

Swisher, V. M. 1992. "The role of parents in developing visual turn taking in their young deaf children." *American Annals of the Deaf* 137: 92–100.

Swisher, V. M. 1993. "Perceptual and cognitive aspects of recognition of signs in peripheral vision." In *Psychological Perspectives on Deafness*, M. Marschark and M. D. Clark (eds), 209–228. Hillsdale, NJ: Lawrence Erlbaum Associates.

Takkinen, R. in press. "HamNoSys (Hamburg Notation System for Sign Languages) as a tool for transcribing basic forms and the signing of children." *Sign Language and Linguistics*.

Talmy, L. 1985. "Lexicalization patterns: Semantic structure in lexical form." In *Language typology and semantic description. Vol. 3: Grammatical categories and the lexicon*, T. Shopen (ed), 36–149. Cambridge: Cambridge University Press.

Taub, S. 2001. *Language from the body: Iconicity and metaphor in American sign language.* Cambridge: Cambridge University Press.

Tervoort, B. 1953. *Structurele Analyse van Visueel Taalgebruik binnen een Groep Dove Kinderen. [Structural analysis of visual language use within a group of deaf children.] Deel 1.* Amsterdam: North-Holland Publishing Company.

Tervoort, B. 1958. "Acoustical and visual communication systems." *The Volta Review* 60: 374–380

Tervoort, B. 1959. "Language development in young deaf children." *Proceedings of the 39th Convention of the American Instructors of the Deaf*, eds??, 120–124. Colorado Springs: National Association of the Deaf.

Theakston, A., Lieven, E., Pine, J. and Rowland, C. 2001. "The role of performance limitations in the acquisition of verb argument structure." *Journal of Child Language* 28: 127–152.

Theakston, A., Lieven, E., Pine, J. and Rowland, C. n.d. "Semantic generality, input frequency and the acquisition of syntax." Ms submitted for publication.

Tobey, E., Geers, A. and Brenner, C. 1994. "Speech production results: Speech feature acquisition." *The Volta Review* 96: 109–129.

Tomasello, M. 1992. *First verbs: a case study of early grammatical development.* Cambridge: Cambridge University Press.

Tomasello, M. 2000. "Do young children operate with adult syntactic categories?" *Cognition* 74, 209–253.

Tomasello, M. and Abbot-Smith, K. 2002. "A Tale of two theories: Response to Fisher." *Cognition* 83, 207–214.

Traugott, E., ter Meulen, A., Reilly, J. and Ferguson, C. (eds.). 1986. *On Conditionals.* Cambridge: Cambridge University Press.

Tye-Murray, N. and Kirk, K. I. 1993. "Vowel and diphthong production by young users of cochlear implants and the relationship between the Phonetic Level Evaluation and spontaneous speech." *Journal of Speech and Hearing Research* 36: 448–502.

Valian, V. 1991. "Syntactic subjects in the early speech of American and Italian children." *Cognition* 40: 21–81.

Valli, C. and Lucas, C. 1992. *Linguistics of American Sign Language: An introduction.* Washington, DC: Gallaudet University Press.

Van den Bogaerde, B. 2000. *Input and interaction in deaf families.* Doctoral Dissertation, University of Amsterdam. Utrecht: LOT.

Van den Bogaerde, B. and Baker A. E. in press. "Code-mixing in mother-child interaction in deaf families?" *Sign Language and Linguistics, Special issue on Acquisition.*

Van der Hulst, H. 1993. "Units in the analysis of signs." *Phonology* 10: 209–241.

Van der Hulst, H. 1995a. "Dependency relations in the phonological representation of signs." In: *Sign Language Research 1994*, H. Bos and T. Schermer (eds), 11–38. Munich, Hamburg: Signum Press.

Van der Hulst, H. 1995b. "Acquisitional evidence for the phonological composition of handshapes." In: *Proceedings of GALA*, C. W. F. Koster and F. Wijnen (eds), 22–33.

Van der Hulst, H. 1996. "On the other hand." *Lingua* 98: 121–43.

Van der Kooij, E. 1997. "Contact: A phonological or a phonetic feature of signs?" In: *Linguistics in the Netherlands*, J. Coerts and H. Hoop (eds), 109–122. Amsterdam: John Benjamins.

Vega, I., Kegl, J. and Ellis, E. 2000. "Lip pointing in Idioma de Señas de Nicaragua (Nicaraguan Sign Language)." Paper presented at the 7th International Conference on Theoretical Issues in Sign Language Research, Amsterdam, July 27, 2000.

Volterra, V. 1983. "Gestures, signs and words at two years." In *Language in Sign*, J. G. Kyle and B. Woll (Eds.), 109–115. London: Croom Helm.

Volterra, V. (ed.) 1987. *La Lingua Italiana dei Segni — La Comunicazione Visivo-Gestuale dei Sordi.* Bologna: Il Mulino.

Volterra, V. and Iverson, J. 1995. "When do modality factors affect the course of language acquisition?" In *Language, gesture, and space*, K. Emmorey and J. S. Reilly (eds), 371–390. Hillsdale, NJ: Lawrence Erlbaum Associates.

Von Tetzchner, S. 1984. "First signs acquired by a Norwegian deaf child with hearing parents." *Sign Language Studies* 44: 226–257.

Wallace, V., Menn, L. and Yoshinaga-Itano, C. 2000. "Is babble the gateway to speech for all children? A longitudinal study of children who are deaf or hard of hearing." *Volta Review* 100 (5): 121–148.

Waxman, R. P. and Spencer, P. E. 1997. "What mothers do to support infant visual attention: Sensitivities to age and hearing status." *Journal of Deaf Studies and Deaf Education* 2: 104–114.

West, L. 1960. *The sign language: An analysis.* Ann Arbor, MI: U. M. I.

Whitehurst, G. J. and Valdez-Menchaca, M. C. 1988. "What is the role of reinforcement in early language acquisition?" *Child Development* 59: 430–440.

Wilbur, R. B. 1979. *American Sign Language and Sign Systems.* Baltimore: University Park Press.

Wilbur, R. B. 1989. "Manual Language Codes." In *International Encyclopaedia of Communications, Vol. 4*, 69–71. Oxford: Oxford University Press.

Wilbur, R. B. 1994. "Foregrounding structures in American Sign Language." *Journal of Pragmatics* 22: 647–672.

Wilbur, R. B. 1997. "A prosodic/pragmatic explanation for word order variation in ASL with typological implications." In *Lexical and Syntactic Constructions and the Construction of Meaning*, M. Verspoor, K. D. Lee and E. Sweetser (eds), 89–104. Amsterdam: John Benjamins.

Wilson, M. and Emmorey, K. 1997. "A visuospatial 'phonological loop' in working memory: Evidence from American Sign Language." *Memory and Cognition* 25 (3): 313–320.

Woll, B. and Grove, N. C. 1996. "On language deficits and modality in children with Down Syndrome: a case study of hearing DS twins with Deaf parents." *Journal of Deaf Studies and Deaf Education* 1: 271–278.

Woodward, J. 1973. "Some characteristics of Pidgin Sign English." *Sign Language Studies* 3: 39–64.

Yoshinaga-Itano, C. 2000. "Development of audition and speech: Implications for early intervention with infants who are deaf or hard of hearing." *Volta Review* 100 (5): 213–234.

Yoshinaga-Itano, C. and Stredler-Brown, A. 1992. "Learning to communicate: Babies with hearing impairments make their needs known." *Volta Review* 95: 107–129.

Young, A. M. 1997. "Conceptualizing parents' sign language use in bilingual early intervention." *Journal of Deaf Studies and Deaf Education* 2: 264–276.

Zeshan, U. 2000. *Sign language in Indo-Pakistan: A description of a signed language*. Amsterdam: John Benjamins.

Index